ABOUT THE AU

Born in Dorking, Surrey, in 1943, Jenny Steele Scolding started her working life in the BBC Overseas Service at Bush House. She went on to travel and work all over the world, including 20 years as a film and television researcher in Ottawa, New York and London, working for the Canadian Film Institute at Expo 67, the Canadian Broadcasting Corporation, BBC television, MGM and Channel 4. While in New Delhi she broadcast for All-India Radio, and in northern Nigeria she worked for two years as an English teacher. She moved to Cornwall in 1986 and represented SKEUSOW, the Cornish Film & Television Association, at conferences and festivals in Wales and Brittany. For several years she taught English to overseas students in Cornwall.

In 2000 she was awarded a writer's residency at Fundación Valparaíso in Mojácar, Spain, and in 2006 her monologues – *The Red Channel: Tales of Migration* – were performed in London at the Southwark Playhouse and at the Arcola's studio theatre. She has written *A Guide to Cornish Fish* and two children's books, *Percy Pengelly and the Wibble-Wobble* and *Percy Pengelly and Tumbili the Monkey*.

Jenny lives in Cadgwith on the Lizard Peninsula with her husband Bill, a graphic designer. Her children, Gwen and Jake, live nearby with their families.

VAGABOND GIRL

JENNY STEELE SCOLDING

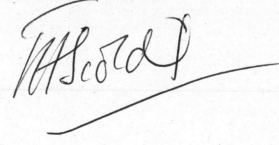

Set in 11/14pt Minion Pro

First published in 2020 by
Serpentine Design
3 Coastguard Houses, Cadgwith
Helston, Cornwall TR12 7JZ

www.serpentine-design.com

ISBN: 978-0-9572851-5-6

In loving memory of my parents,
Marion and Tim Steele,
who raised me with the confidence to be wild.

For my husband, Bill,
with whom I have continued the journey
and for my children, Gwen and Jake,
and my grandchildren Leo and Amelie,
that they may know me, warts and all.

To move, to breathe, to fly, to float,
To gain all while you give,
To roam the roads of lands remote,
To travel is to live.

Hans Christian Andersen

Good girls go to heaven.
Bad girls go everywhere.

Attributed to Mae West

These memoirs are based on detailed diaries and
correspondence written at the time. However, experiences
and memories are subjective and others may have a different
take on the events and relationships described.

In order to respect privacy, a few names have been changed
and some people and events have been omitted.
I hope that those who are described in full will indulge their
inclusion. For good or ill, they made me what I am today.

THANKS
to my brother, Phil, for reading a draft of this book
and giving me reminders and suggestions;
to Bob Burns and Dawn Wright from the
School of Oriental and African Studies;
and above all, to Bill – husband, editor, designer and best friend
– for his patience and dedication in producing this book.

CONTENTS

PREFACE

The year is 2011. My husband, Bill, and I are in Paris when we stumble on a restaurant in the Jewish quarter. The place is packed and we settle down to flatbreads stuffed with falafel and salad. Spread across the entire wall facing me is a photograph of a huge, modern tourist resort, buildings stacked skywards like Lego. I stare at it. There is something vaguely familiar about it – and yet it can't be. I must be wrong. 'Where's that?' I ask the waiter, pointing to the photograph. 'Eilat,' he says proudly, and I well up. I hesitate. 'I was there in 1964,' I say, but he's already moved on. I am old, and he's too young to remember my desert paradise, the place where it all began.

The world has changed since then. As I hitchhiked to India or braved the roads in Africa, my parents had little idea of my whereabouts – my sporadic letters would take at least a month to arrive. For me, there has never been anything to match the heady freedom of rough travel, of never knowing where you'll wash up or what lies ahead. Without preconceptions, without knowing the rules, you are on your toes, sharp, living in the moment and for the moment.

In 2007, aged 64 – and four years prior to that interlude in Paris, I went backpacking round China by myself for ten weeks. I didn't hitchhike, but I travelled 'hard sleeper' on the trains, and on one or two old-fashioned country buses. Without admitting it to myself, I wanted to test whether I could still do it, but China, with its perfect modern infrastructure, was no challenge. Most of the time I stayed in youth hostels (yes, they still let me in), accommodation which I booked ahead online. As the young people arrived I was aghast at the paraphernalia they brought with them – laptops, expensive cameras, mobile phones, MP3 players – and I realised they had no concept of what it meant to be cut off and isolated.

Tourism in multiple guises had taken over worldwide. Everyone was plugged into a surfeit of information, advice and reviews. Adventure and risk had become controlled. Travellers were signing up for guided tours to places deemed off-the beaten-track, often indulging in extreme sports to get that hit of adrenalin. Homestays were on offer as part of the tour, rather than arising from spontaneous hospitality. The plus side was that previously impoverished communities were thriving on jobs provided by tourism.

Despite these changes, I continued to harbour a missionary zeal for travel. For me, the excitement lay in personal exchanges which provided an insight into this complicated world. I have learnt more from talking to people and staying in their homes than from newspapers or television. The Chinese who befriended me on trains and shared their food, the Cuban veteran who'd fought in Angola, the Sri Lankan fishermen who made me welcome and the Tibetan monks in Lhasa – such grass-roots encounters have always given me hope and immense faith in human nature.

However, as I write this, the world is in lockdown as Covid-19 spreads across the globe; planes are grounded, all travel has ceased, and every nation is affected. Will humankind reinvent itself, start afresh? Will people ever travel again in my lifetime? If they do, I doubt it will be the same as before – the frequency, the freedom, the exhilaration. Perhaps exploration will be confined to virtual travel, without the sounds and smells, without the warm tactile encounters with people.

It's possible that the world that moulded me has gone forever.

Cadgwith, Cornwall, April 2020

PROLOGUE

I ALWAYS WANTED TO TRAVEL. I can still picture myself as a small child, lying on my stomach on the floor of my grandfather's study, leafing through an ancient encyclopaedia. I would stare mesmerised by photographs of foreign lands and people who looked extraordinary and exciting. I painted endless pictures of Africans with babies on their backs and Indians in saris standing beneath palm trees – and a lot of gypsies. As I got older, I longed for the freedom of those who wandered and I devoured books about their lives. My heroes were hobos, explorers and seafarers. I may have dreamt of exotic places, of deserts and jungles, but I was surrounded by post-war austerity.

In 1941, on summer evenings, as my newly-wed parents relaxed in the garden of their little cottage in Capel, Surrey, they would hear a steady humming, a drone which increased to a roar, as wave upon wave of British bombers headed south across the Channel to the continent. My father, 33 at the outbreak of war and just too old to be called up, had been evacuated with his firm to the Surrey countryside, while my mother remained in London, braving the air raids and the blitz. I was born in March 1943, the week 27 merchant ships were sunk in the Atlantic by German U-boats. I was a war baby.

I was two-and-a-half when we moved to the large red-brick house in Dorking – a four-bedroomed Victorian dwelling with a sprawling garden – and three years after that my little brother, Philip, was born. From my bedroom window I could look across the rooftops of the town towards Ranmore and watch the small train chuffing along the valley to Guildford.

My parents may have managed to acquire a big house, but in those early days it was sparsely furnished. Philip and I had fold-up metal beds which had been sold off by the army after the war, together with thin flock mattresses and rough grey blankets. Walls were whitewashed with distemper, and a chenille table cloth served as a carpet in the morning room. Mother made most of our clothes: trousers for Philip out of Dad's old cricket whites; little winter coats out of old jackets. Many of our toys were passed down from friends and family and given a lick of paint; others were home-made. Heating was provided by coal fires and when we emerged from our beds on winter mornings there would be Jack Frost patterns on the inside of the window panes. Until I was 11 post-war rationing was in place and we had to take coupons with us when we went shopping.

Despite this austerity, I look back on a golden childhood. We were surrounded by my mother's family – my grandparents lived in the same road, my aunts, uncles and cousins nearby – and our house was always overflowing with visitors and friends. We were particularly close to the Hunka family across the road. With their boys – Martin and Nick – Philip and I enjoyed the freedom of the countryside, where we climbed trees and made camps. Unsophisticated and self-inspired, our play was of its time, and we would disappear for hours without supervision.

The first time I set eyes on a television was on 2 June, 1953. Some friends of my parents invited a group of us to watch the Coronation of Queen Elizabeth II and we crowded into their sitting room, squinting at the panoply unfolding on a miniscule screen. At home, we relied on entertainment provided via a sturdy Bakelite radio, or 'wireless', and music from a small wind-up gramophone.

Although my mother was a typical 1950s housewife, she was also an artist. At 17 she had attended Goldsmiths for a while, and when we were children she took up painting again, studying at Epsom School of Art and at the Heatherly School of Fine Art in London. One of the founding members of the Dorking Group of Artists, she ended up teaching adult education classes for Surrey County Council. My father also painted,

Above: my parents get engaged, 21 December 1940.
Top right: Mum at Alliance Assurance, Eltham.
Right: Dad and colleagues working in the wartime
blackout, at Alliance Assurance, Ockley.

Below: my parents' home in Capel, Dad cleaning his
Home Guard rifle. **Below right:** me at nine months.

Above: '*Clovelly*', *my childhood home in Dorking, Surrey.* ***Above right:*** *me, aged three, 1946.*
Below: *me (on left, aged 12) at St Andrew's Convent, Leatherhead; girl guide patrol leader, aged 13.*

Left: Philip, aged 11. ***Below:*** *with the family in Looe, aged 17, 1960.*

but was particularly talented with pen-and-ink drawings. He wrote poetry and, with others, my parents started up the Miscellany, a group of writers who met monthly. Many of my parents' friends were artists and as children we would accompany them on picnics and sit and paint alongside the adults.

For over a decade, from 1946 until the early 60s, we went on regular holidays to the Cornish fishing village of Polperro. A Hillman Minx bought by Dad in 1935, our car had running boards, a crank start, and a hole in the rusty floor at the back, through which Philip and I could glimpse the road passing beneath. Leaving Dorking far behind and after a journey of about 13 hours, and usually a puncture or two, we would arrive at Polperro in time for high tea. Our hosts, with their strong Cornish accents, seemed exotic and foreign and unlike anyone I had ever met at home.

During those halcyon Cornish days we would watch the boats unloading fish in the harbour, walk the coast path above the jagged rocks and wild seas, or descend through fields of sweet-smelling hay to the beaches and rocky coves. In autumn we rose at dawn to pick field mushrooms and in November, we witnessed great storms and listened to the soulful chime of the bell-buoy warning of danger. We took home sea thrift and planted it in our garden to remind us of Polperro, and Philip and I, following advice for little people in *The Enid Blyton Holiday Book,* carried our own small piece of Cornwall back to Dorking: wide strips of seaweed to be hung from our bedroom windows for predicting the weather.

When my brother Philip was 13, he won a scholarship to Felsted, the independent boarding school in Essex where my father had been. Despite the age gap between us, I missed him and I worried how he would fare so far from home. My schooling had been different. We weren't Roman Catholics, but my mother, influenced by her own convent education, had wanted the same for me; from the age of five I was taught almost exclusively by nuns. My most formative years were spent at St Andrew's Convent, Leatherhead, where we had excellent teachers. I was immersed in Catholic ritual and I loved it: the incense and the reliquaries; the statues and holy pictures where daggers protruded from exposed hearts; the halos, blasts of light, and drops of blood. I revelled in the poetic focus on the Virgin, the prayers and the hymns.

Although surrounded by Catholicism during the week, at home I was very much Church of England and I went to church regularly until I was 20. I was a member of the church youth club, church hand-bell ringers, and eventually became a Sunday school teacher. Religion was never imposed on me, but neither was Christianity questioned. It was just there, an accepted part of everyday life.

My parents were liberal for the era. From the age of 16 I would arrive home from dances and parties at one or two in the morning, bringing home young people for coffee long after Mum and Dad had retired to bed. I partied and danced away my teenage years with an uncountable number of boyfriends. I was in love with being in love and I loved them all. There was kissing and cuddling and a bit of very innocent groping, but it would have been unthinkable to have had sex with anyone.

Aged 17, I went to Ewell County Technical College to do a secretarial course. I had nine GCE O-Levels, but I wanted to leave school. Nobody persuaded me to stay on and do A-levels. From amongst all my friends at school and home, only two girls went to university and about half a dozen boys. Most people just left school and got a job. At Tech we were groomed to be personal secretaries, a role more akin to today's PAs. Besides shorthand and typing we studied law, economics, commerce and book-keeping. To give us a rhythmic touch, we learned to type to music – 30 girls bashing out an exercise in unison, usually to a classical piece, and varying our speeds as if a conductor were in the room. We were schooled in the art of keeping our future bosses happy: 'Remember how he takes his coffee; how he likes his desk arranged; his wife's favourite flowers.'

I passed my exams and worked briefly in the tiny office of a factory that exported railway tracks, serving a niche market where non-standard gauges were still in use. Orders would land on my desk from far-flung places with unpronounceable names, and I would revel in the connection between my dusty little office and those lands where our tracks would be laid across jungles and deserts. I had only been at the railway factory a couple of months, however, when I landed a job in an environment that was to feed all my dreams and obsessions. Life was about to kick off.

CHAPTER ONE

ON MY WAY

Working for Auntie

THE CZECHS AND SLOVAKS WERE FIGHTING in the corridor. As I walked to my office a missile whizzed past my head, followed by a stream of abuse. No sooner was I seated at my desk than Jo Kalina entered the room. A cuddly bear of a man, he proceeded to dictate a script to me with tears pouring down his face. I was 18. It was the first day of my first proper job and nothing at secretarial college had prepared me for the mayhem which surrounded me.

When I walked through the grandiose portals of the BBC External Services at Bush House, I was told to report to the Czech Section and had assumed I was on my way to Accounts. Instead I was ushered into the office of Gregory Macdonald, Head of the BBC Central European Service, who sat me down and explained that I had to sign the Official Secrets Act. 'You will undoubtedly be put on a list denying you entry to any Eastern Bloc country,' he warned. I knew little of politics, but earlier that year whilst on holiday in Austria, I had felt a shiver of fear when the Berlin Wall went up, creating a tangible boundary between democracy and communism. Mac, as he was known, had been involved with Polish broadcasts during the war and had been head of the Polish Service. Now he was the much-loved father figure of the entire Central European Service, looking after an array of extraordinary personalities: Czechs, Slovaks, Finns, White Russians, Poles and Hungarians. Avuncular and pipe-smoking, he was remarkably warm and informal, keeping tabs on us all and, despite his elevated position, remaining entirely approachable.

I was to become accustomed to displays of emotion. Most of the people I worked for were exiles from countries invaded by the Soviet

Union, broadcasters who found transmissions to their homeland incredibly upsetting. Many were intellectuals who had held important posts and taken part in political unrest and revolution against the incoming regime. They were a volatile lot, expressing anger, joy and sadness in equal measure. Above all, they were fun. The work was boring, typing scripts and records of the programmes broadcast, but my colleagues embraced me, included me as part of their extraordinary family in exile.

Those I fell in love with were the Hungarians. The Hungarian Section was run by a smooth individual called Feri Rentoul. Good-looking, immaculately turned-out and the epitome of cool, he had smouldering dark eyes and a keep-off-the-grass attraction. The other Hungarians exuded warmth and craziness in equal measure, but Mr Rentoul made me self-conscious and nervous and was aware that he did so. The most famous contributor I dealt with was journalist and author George Mikes. His popular post-war book *How to be an Alien* had poked gentle fun at the English: *Continental people have sex lives; the English have hot water bottles.* He was a charming, unassuming individual who made a fuss of me, but there were numerous others who came and went – intellectual, charismatic, eccentric characters who were well known in Hungary.

My favourites were Miklós Ember and Tomás Szalay. A decade older than I was, Ember had left Hungary in 1956, the year of the uprising against the Soviet Union. Conventionally handsome and dapper, he wore blazers with gold buttons, pressed flannels and a signet ring. To me, he was the height of sophistication, a view enhanced by the fact that he was going out with a glamorous woman in the BBC French Section, who wore a lot of gold costume jewellery. I was in awe of him and tried to sound intellectual in his presence, an endeavour which undoubtedly failed miserably. A decade later he was to morph into the well-known Radio 4 producer Michael Ember, who created *Start the Week* and *In the Psychiatrist's Chair.* He went everywhere with Tomás Szalay, an attractive young married man, who was more approachable and down to earth.

My best friend, Pat, worked as a secretary for the Hungarians after I left, and so my connection with my idols remained. I was utterly in love with Ember and Szalay, particularly Szalay, and they both knew it. To them I must have seemed a naïve little girl, but they humoured me by being flirtatious and genuinely friendly. 'You look pretty today,' they'd say, or 'What a beautiful dress! You made it yourself?' All their flattery was noted in my journal of the day. 'When Ember dictates a script to me,' Pat confided, 'I get in such a tizz that my fingers slip down between the typewriter keys.' We would frequently meet the two men for lunch or coffee in the canteen and sometimes join them in the studio during broadcasts to Hungary.

For a few months I worked for another Hungarian, György Tarján, the Assistant Head of the Central European Service. It was whilst working for Mr Tarján that I was reminded how broadcasting to the Eastern Bloc could be dangerous. I inadvertently opened an envelope, marked confidential, that contained a political poison pen letter addressed to him. I was terrified at having seen it. I apologised for my mistake and passed it on to my boss, anticipating repercussions, but he took it without comment and never mentioned it. During this time our broadcasts were often jammed. If I had worked on an English language script I would be eager to hear it go out, but no sooner had I tuned in than the rhythmic pulse of the jamming intervened, rendering hours of hard work redundant.

For someone who had always wanted to travel, working in Bush House with about 40 nationalities was like arriving in heaven. When the canteen was crowded, I found myself sitting next to Africans or Arabs, Vietnamese or Malaysians. I well remember a Christmas Eve at the BBC Club in Aldwych, the only time I spent drinking with the entire Central European Service. In my diary I listed those who had bestowed Christmas kisses upon me during the afternoon, a childish record of strange foreign names which included nearly everybody, including the elusive Mr Rentoul. I went dancing back to Bush House in their company, holding the hand of my favourite, Tomás Szalay. That evening, as I left Bush House to go to Waterloo Station, I was chased along Aldwych by a man in a bowler hat and pinstriped suit brandishing a sprig of mistletoe. It had been an unforgettable London Christmas Eve where I was suddenly aware that I had become a woman and that, what's more, I was the centre of attention.

BBC secretaries were sent off regularly on training courses. There was no commercial radio in Britain at the time and the tutors played us recordings of overseas commercial broadcasts to illustrate how crass the competition was; we fell about laughing at the speed of the presentation. 'They're not concerned with quality,' we were told. 'For them, time means money.' We were always instilled with the feeling that we were part of a large BBC family which would look after us. Self-improvement was encouraged and BBC staff, from cleaner to studio manager, could study anything in their spare time at the BBC's expense. I continued with German and French and later, when I fell in love with a Moroccan, I had a stab at Arabic, all paid for by Auntie.

For the first nine months at the BBC I was commuting to London from my parents' home in Dorking. After one Saturday shift at Bush House I arrived at Victoria station to find myself struggling through massive crowds of newly-arrived West Indians. I was flabbergasted. The only black people I had ever seen, apart from the few at Bush House, were two African girl guides who had attended an international jamboree and visited Dorking in the 1950s. In the early 60s black people in London were few and far between, and rarely seen in the West End or around Aldwych where I worked.

I had been desperate to continue working for my beloved Hungarians, but it had been a temporary post. Instead, I went off to BBC English by Radio and Television, where I worked for English language experts and philologists in a poky little office in Queen's House at the top of Kingsway. My colleagues were kind, but after the volatile Hungarians, Czechs and Poles, they seemed stuffy. I continued to whizz down the road to Bush House at every opportunity, but back in my office I despaired of the endless scripts about phonetics and English grammar. One day on my way to Bush House I encountered a small crowd at the bottom of Kingsway. A group of young men were entering Associated Rediffusion, later known as Television House. I accosted one of the onlookers, a bowler-hatted gent. 'What's all the fuss about?' I enquired. 'Who are those people?' 'I'm told,' he replied, 'that one of them is known as a Rolling Stone.'

A reprieve from my regular work came in the form of *Walter and Connie,* the BBC's first English by Television series which ended up being immensely successful in 73 countries. These initial episodes were made by Augusta Film Productions and were shot at St John's Wood studios during the long hot summer of 1962. I logged shots for the cameraman, watched the rushes, and went on location on a river boat down the Thames. The actors and crew included me in everything, and the props man, just back from filming *Lawrence of Arabia* in Jordan, took a shine to me. It was my first grown-up summer. I wore a white linen dress and jacket which accentuated my tan and made me feel attractive, and lunchtime drinks followed by mountains of strawberries seemed like sophisticated fare. At the end of the filming Ted Beaumont, the production manager, offered me a job, but I declined. I was already hankering after working overseas.

For two consecutive years I helped run the English by Radio summer schools at Westfield College, University of London. The students were selected from those who listened to our broadcasts: the skipper of a Danish fishing trawler; a blind Spaniard, who was allocated to my care; a Dutch priest… I helped with everyday organisation, took the students on tours of London and attended their English language lectures. The first year I fell for Hamid, a handsome young Moroccan whose father had sold his *djellaba* to pay for his son's schooling. Hamid opened my eyes to another culture and to large-scale poverty, a subject that had never previously crossed my radar. A year or so later I learned from BBC broadcaster René Cutforth, that Hamid had been jailed in Morocco for subversive politics. The second year I met Georg, a young German who worked for Lufthansa and who invited me to spend Christmas with his family near Aachen. As we walked through the snowy forest on Xmas

First job, at Bush House, in 1961.

*Brian McDermott and Anne Lawson in the BBC English by TV series, 'Walter and Connie'. **Below:** at St John's Wood studios with Anne Lawson, 1962.*

Above: *Gispert Crespo, WS Allen (philologist) and Hamid Chriouitta, English by Radio summer school, 1962.*
Below: *summer school 1963 (front row – Jennifer Houghton, my boss René Quinault and me, aged 20).*

With Andy Irwin, 1962.

With Manfred and Georg Reimer, Germany, Xmas 1963.

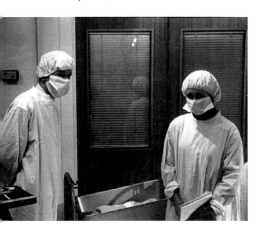

*As a production secretary for BBC TV Enterprises Production Unit 1963, filming the birth of a baby **(left)** with sound recordist Bruce White and **(above)**, holding notebook, on the left of the picture.*

C*ameraman Jimmy Court films my image transmitted by laser beam.*

With Bruce White in Cornwall.

day, his father described smuggling Jewish children across the nearby border into Belgium, during the war.

Back in the boring old office in Queen's House, I was now working with my friend Jan who had been a secretary in the Czech Section at Bush House. Apart from discussing sex, of which neither of us had any experience, and how to use tampons, which was still not the norm, we also had long talks about politics and religion. It was the height of the Cold War and the nuclear threat was uppermost in everyone's minds. Two years previously at Ewell Tech we had been given a civil defence lecture about what to do in a nuclear attack: set aside a bucket as a lavatory; whitewash all windows; stock up with water and tins of food! In 1962 nuclear testing was taking place on a huge scale and there was also a fear of spies (a year later double agent Kim Philby defected to the Soviets). The Cuban Missile Crisis brought everything to a head and, for a week, we were terrified, talking of nothing else.

In September 1963 I moved back to Bush House to work as a production secretary for BBC Television Enterprises, a unit which made or adapted BBC films for sale overseas. My new boss was producer Duncan Griffin-Beale, a kindly, old-fashioned man who looked as if he had stepped off the cover of a 1950s knitting pattern. A few days after my arrival, when Duncan and I were on location filming car racing at Oulton Park, we went on an early morning recce of the race track. We were ambling along the edge of the circuit with the cameraman, noting good spots for filming later in the day, when a racing car came hurtling towards us on a practice run. We ran for our lives, scrambling up the bank just in time. When we watched the rushes we discovered the cameraman had caught this escapade on film; it was pure Mack Sennett.

Although I still had to type scripts, I now organised all aspects of location shooting, as well as keeping track of shots and continuity. One film I worked on highlighted a moment of historic innovation: it was entitled *LASER*. We visited laboratories where lasers were being developed and filmed the glass tubes down which the laser beams were travelling; unsurprisingly, the cameraman suffered headaches for several days afterwards. The next experiment they shot showed images of me being transmitted down a laser beam onto a television monitor.

I loved the film crew. Cameramen Jimmy Court, Gene Carr and Keith Hopper, who went on to film early episodes of *Dr. Who*, used cameras encased in huge blimps to mask extraneous sound and which rendered the equipment heavy and unwieldy. I was also fond of the sound recordists: John with his dry sense of humour, and Bruce with whom I ended up having a long-term serious love affair. In the cutting rooms at that time, 26 episodes of *The Great War* were being edited, and I excelled myself by dropping the core out of a giant reel of 35mm film. It was an absolute disaster. Ron, the kindly editor, stood in a sea of tangled film, chuckling. 'Don't worry, love,' he said. 'You'll only ever do that once.'

A home away from home

By the time I arrived at Television Enterprises I had left home and was living in Earls Court. With my BBC friend Pat, a childhood friend Amanda, and a couple of other girls, I rented accommodation at Lexham Gardens in a run-down Victorian three-storey house. The landlord, a genial Pole, had given our flat a cheap facelift; the rooms with their thin fitted carpets and streamlined furniture seemed the height of modernity. There were four girls living above us, four young men in the flat below, and in the basement a crazy Irishman called Charles, who was slightly older than we were. Charles was unemployed, but his flatmate worked as a chauffeur and drove his boss's Rolls. Charles found it amusing to arrive at the dole queue in the Rolls, driven by his friend in his smart coat, peaked cap and white gloves. It was my first time away from parental guidance and I went crazy, partying every night and turning up sluggishly at work after only three or four hours' sleep. Earl's Court was known as Kangaroo Valley and the gatherings I attended in the neighbourhood's dank subterranean flats were largely peopled by young Australians. Informal and less staid, they were different from anyone

I had previously encountered. And, for the first time, I encountered a smattering of black people: *There were negroes at the party last night!* I exclaimed in my diary.

None of us could really afford to live independently. When my parents visited and opened the fridge they were horrified. 'You haven't got any food!' exclaimed my mother. She opened the kitchen cupboards which were almost empty. 'You'll be ill,' she warned. I ignored her – and became ill. To supplement my income, I worked as a waitress in the evenings at a restaurant called the Sri Lanka. I would finish my day at the BBC, change into my sari, and start work all over again. The manager employed me because, with my long black hair, I looked Asian, or maybe it was because he had designs on me which became evident when he backed me up against the wall in the store room. His amorous advances were brought to an abrupt halt by the arrival of a salesman peddling wooden elephants. At the back of the restaurant, the small, greasy kitchen contained enormous vats of curry stirred by an obese cook, stripped to the waist and pouring with sweat. Beads of perspiration would slide off his wet flab into the curry. By contrast, front of house, in a room with red fitted carpets and flocked wall paper, diners sat at candlelit tables with starched white cloths and napkins. I was not a good waitress. I found my sari difficult to manage, the end draped over my arm frequently trailing food across the table as I served diners. Once, when lighting a candle, I came within a hair's breadth of setting a man's moustache on fire and he leapt to his feet in horror. Despite my inadequacies the staff were kind and, more importantly, they fed me.

I didn't tell my parents about this second job until one weekend, when visiting home, I took my sari with me, intending to wash and dry it secretly. On arrival I dumped my belongings in the hallway and settled down for a pre-dinner drink. 'What's that weird smell?' wondered Mother. 'It's coming from your bags,' said Dad. 'What on earth have you got in there?' Reluctantly I produced my sari, stained with grease and spotted with curry. 'You'll wear yourself out,' warned Mum, unaware that the alternative to working all night was partying all night.

For several months I was in love with a young man called Andy who drove one of Brook Bond's famous little red vans around London delivering tea. He and his friends smoked what they termed *reefers*, but were so clandestine that I can only assume they felt unable to rely on my discretion. With Andy I used to visit a club in Wardour Street, a place that subsequently featured in the press because of a shoot-out. However, I was still very naïve; all I remember was dancing to my favourite song, *Island of Dreams* by the Springfields. We also frequented The Rising Sun on the Fulham Road, an old-fashioned pub full of extraordinary characters, where people played the piano and everyone sang. 'Watch out for her,' warned Andy, nodding in the direction of an elderly woman looking arty in a black cloak. 'She's pretending to fit in, but she's a coppers' nark.'

Towards the end of my time at Television Enterprises I worked with Harry Lowe shot-listing a test match series being revamped for overseas sales. As every cricket match looked identical to me, I found the whole job a nightmare. However, the work was in west London and about this time I started hanging out at Television Centre where I had quite a few friends. On the 22 November, 1963, I was propping up the bar in the Television Centre Club, when the evening current affairs programme was interrupted with a newsflash. President John F Kennedy had been assassinated. A year later I would come across newspaper cuttings of JFK pinned to the mud walls of peasant houses in Iran.

A proposal

When I began dating Bruce, the BBC sound recordist, it didn't take me long to discover that we shared a love of Cornwall. Raised on an inland Cornish farm, his experience of the county was very different from my own. He introduced me to the clay country around Par, the tin mines and the moors. We steeped our days in the romance of Tristan and Iseult, visiting Castle Dore, where King Mark was said to have held court, and the nearby church at Golant which boasted mythical links to the lovers.

In Tregaminion Chapel of Ease, near Daphne du Maurier's Menabilly estate, we knelt hand in hand at the altar and prayed, before climbing the creaking steps to the belfry where we rang the single bell and listened as the sound flew across the fields, across the tiny harbour of Polkerris and echoed out to sea. I was in love with life, in love with Bruce and always, above all, immersed in the magic of Cornwall.

Short, small-featured, with straight blonde hair, Bruce had a larger-than-life personality. He was 19, I was 20, and we were soul mates. In London, after work at the BBC, we would wander the alleys of the East End down by the docks, stumbling on backstreet pubs where we were welcomed with surprise and where there was often someone playing the piano and people singing old music hall songs. We walked miles along the Embankment, watching the river barges or sitting on steps which led down to the water, discussing politics, poetry or the latest films. Occasionally, on a summer evening, we would sit in the park and join the throngs, young and old, who listened to brass bands: bandsmen like toy soldiers with braid and shiny buttons, entertaining us from the ornate bandstands of yesteryear. We saw all the new films, many of which were destined to become classics: The Beatles in *A Hard Day's Night;* Kubrick's *Dr Strangelove.* We sat transfixed by the new, widescreen Cinerama screenings: *It's a Mad Mad Mad Mad World* and *How the West Was Won.* And it was Bruce who introduced me to sex.

It was months before I sanctioned the dreaded act. I wasn't prudish, but in addition to lingering religious inhibitions, like everyone else I was terrified of getting pregnant. At school the only nod towards sex education had been the biology of the rabbit. I knew vaguely about contraceptives but they were only available from behind the counter and I had never actually seen any. Bruce, patient and persistent, finally turned up with a packet of condoms. I regarded them with suspicion. 'How do you know it won't burst?' I asked. 'I'll show you,' he said, pulling a condom over a tap. I watched as the rubber swelled until it was a giant water-filled balloon nestling in the wash basin. 'There you are,' he said. 'It didn't burst or leak, did it?' I was finally convinced.

Several months later when I was at home in Dorking, in the course of a telephone conversation Bruce suggested we should get married. Although I thought I was in love with him, I desperately wanted to travel and was far from sure about long-term commitment. The following day the proposal was confirmed in a letter: *I want to marry you,* he wrote. *I am absolutely serious. Please say Yes.* We had sometimes shared romantic dreams about marriage, children, and a cosy rural idyll, but when these turned into a concrete offer, I declined. Jumping on my bike, I raced for miles along the country lanes, the wind in my hair, mulling over what had happened. I was euphoric that someone had paid me such an honour; it seemed like a milestone on the road to adulthood.

Around that time one of my BBC girlfriends had gone off to work in Israel. *Why don't you come and join me?* she wrote. *It's easy to get work on a kibbutz.* Kibbutzim were communes, she explained, places where you could do farm work. I had hardly any money, but this was an arrangement that seemed feasible and more interesting than grape-picking in France, which is what most people did. I shot off to be interviewed by Hechalutz B'Anglia, the kibbutz office in London, and they confirmed that I was eligible to work in Israel. They would send my details to the Tel Aviv office which would allocate a placement for me.

Now, for the first time in ages, I thought of Trampie. I had met him when, aged 17, I had cycled from Dorking to Plymouth with a school friend. As we had inched our way across Dorset and Devon, we kept bumping into the same young man. 'He's like a tramp,' I said, succumbing to my usual fixation with vagabonds, and so we dubbed him Trampie. Twenty-five, tall, with a large nose and brilliant blue eyes, he ambled along in shabby glory carrying a beaten-up rucksack containing a small suitcase: 'In case I need to stay somewhere respectable,' he explained. He had taken each youth hostel by storm, thrilling his teenage audience with tales of adventure on the road. A far cry from the their usual fresh-faced clientele, he was unpopular with the wardens, and when his Tom Lehrer songs found their way onto the hostel's record player, *The Old Dope Peddler* was more than they could tolerate. He was sent packing.

We were to bump into him again in a small museum, where he donned a tribal mask and chased me round the room with a spear. Never had I met anyone so naughty, so irreverent and so free. He told me about the countries he had visited, how it was possible to survive on odd jobs and roam at will, and I had mentally added him to my list of wandering heroes. Now, three years later, when considering Israel, Trampie niggled away at my consciousness. I knew I would follow in his footsteps. .

The last few months of my relationship with Bruce were upsetting. He didn't want me to leave. He told me he was seriously ill, but then he would go out partying, leaving me totally confused about his condition. My diary records turmoil and tears, as well as guilt that I should even consider deserting a sick man. Secretly I contacted Harry Edwards, the famous spiritual healer, whose reply simply indicated he would pray for Bruce. Eventually I found the situation so harrowing that I could no longer cope. I decided to escape, telling myself that distance would give me a better perspective on the degree of my love for him, and that I could return if his illness got worse.

Two years later, when I arrived home from my travels, Bruce was very much alive and kicking. We revisited Cornwall together, but we had changed and so had Cornwall. Polperro, the beloved fishing village of my childhood, was packed with tourists and commercialised. As for Bruce and me, we were no longer the innocent children who had knelt in Tregaminion Chapel. Cornwall remained magical and stunningly beautiful, but although it still tugged at my heart-strings, it had been reduced to a single glittering fragment in my mosaic of the wider world.

CHAPTER TWO

HALLELUJAH, I'M A BUM

A journey to the Promised Land

IS THAT MAN PEEING? I thought. Glancing surreptitiously towards the open side of the ornate metal boutique on the pavement, I confirmed my suspicions. I had never been to Paris, and *le pissoir* had certainly never featured in school French lessons. What with that, my inappropriately large suitcase and unwanted attention from lecherous strangers, Paris was proving a bit of a strain.

That morning I had boarded the boat train in London, said a tearful farewell to Bruce, and I was on my way to Israel with a one-way ticket and £20 in my pocket – about £300 in today's money. I am not Jewish. All I knew about Israel was that it was warm, foreign and I could work there. It was 1964, holidays to warmer climes were only just taking off, and my notions of travel were romantic rather than practical. The previous year Cliff Richard's film *Summer Holiday* had been a big hit; a load of youngsters crossing Europe on a double-decker bus had seemed crazily exciting and had fuelled my wanderlust.

The suitcase I was dragging round Paris was filled with fashionable trappings which would fast prove redundant: nylon baby-doll pyjamas; a lilac girdle which extended from waist to thigh with embroidered roses just above the suspenders; a silk-lined dress and spiky hair rollers. I had no suntan lotion, no hat, no guide books, but I did have a money belt, about an inch wide and made of stiff leather.

It was dark as I made my way to the Gare de Lyon for my train to Marseille. North African men swarmed around the wagons-lits; I was a lone woman caught up in a tide of flirtatious males with moustaches. Having located my sleeping compartment, I was relieved to find it occupied by a Japanese family. I retreated to my couchette, shed a tear or two for Bruce, and sank into a deep sleep.

A few hours later I drew back the curtains and beheld the blinding magic of a Mediterranean morning. Marseille shimmered in a heat haze, its sun-bleached buildings pale, with paint peeling off the shutters. Alleyways feathered with palm fronds squeezed between tall houses. Pink and purple bougainvillea trailed papery garlands across sills and grills, courtyards and walls. Pavement cafes and stalls were unfurling their awnings ready for the heat of the day.

My first task was to locate the Turkish Maritime Lines and pick up my boat ticket for Israel. Raised with the mantra 'If in doubt, ask a policeman', I accosted a gendarme. I was impressed with the attention he paid me, by the fact he escorted me all the way to the shipping office, but less so when I realised his interest extended beyond the call of duty. It took me a while to get shot of him and I wrote an outraged postcard home: *Can you imagine an English bobby behaving like that?* A young French fisherman had a gentler approach. He bought me a sandwich and we sat on the harbour wall, dangling our legs above the water and chatting.

Eventually, in the oppressive heat of the afternoon, I struggled along the docks, dragging the infernal suitcase in my wake, and boarded *SS Adana*, a Turkish ship bound for Istanbul via Haifa. I located my cabin, shared with an Israeli woman and, early that evening, as the ship slipped its mooring, I watched the rose-tinted French coast receding in the distance, until the world turned pink and scarlet, ruby red, and was drowned by the setting sun.

There were 12 nationalities on my first voyage into the unknown. Jo and Diana were English girls with whom I was to become friends. Alain, a handsome young Frenchman, permitted me to practise my French, thrown in with a kiss or two, and there was Chaim, the manic dancer and guitar player, with whom I cavorted nightly on the top deck beneath the fairy lights and stars. Part-Israeli, part-South American, he taught us Hebrew, enlightened us regarding Jewish ritual – including the fact that men from certain sects made ablutions seven times after sexual intercourse – and invited us to visit his home in Ashkelon. However, it was Anmun who fascinated me. He had been in the Israeli army but I found it impossible to imagine him in any kind of military role. Gentle and enigmatic, his great love was the desert. He fixed me with his beautiful dark eyes and talked quietly of the sand and the heat, the colours and the shadows. 'I love the silence,' he said. 'At night I look up at the stars and for that moment I am alone, just me and the desert.'

I danced my way across the Mediterranean, thrilling to new experiences: Middle Eastern food, including my first-ever olives and figs; dolphins and flying fish; enticing islands, their secrets held hostage by the sea; foreign ports with colourful houses stacked up to the sky. These were sultry days where we lay on the deck in the hot sun until the stormy seas around Crete hurled spray onto our scorched skin.

As we neared Israel, a group of Moroccan Jews with skull caps, flowing robes and long beards, celebrated their imminent arrival in the Promised Land. Lighting candles, they poured libations of wine, and embarked on ritual wailing and prayers. Other Jewish passengers joined in, until everyone was leaning over the railing, eyes riveted on the distant smudge that was landfall. A flotilla of small boats came out to meet us, whereupon everyone burst into song. As *SS Adana* drew into the port of Haifa I was caught up in the rapture of the welcome. I had arrived.

Once we had docked, four of us jumped into a taxi bound for Tel Aviv. 'Wait!' shouted Chaim, opening the door. 'Take these. I'll follow,' and he dumped an assortment of his belongings on top of us: a key-cutting machine, a typewriter, a guitar, a tambourine and a bundle of South American mats. In Tel Aviv we stood on the pavement like itinerant peddlers, surrounded by his possessions. I popped into a shop to buy a drink and tried in vain to extricate Israeli currency from my stiff, narrow money belt. The shopkeeper shook his head in exasperation and produced a hook with which he extracted the bank notes! As I emerged, Chaim arrived. 'It's Yom Kippur,' he announced unexpectedly, 'the Day of Atonement. Everything will be shut for two days.' I had assumed that on arrival I would contact the kibbutz office and be allocated a place of work. Not so. Come nightfall, with nowhere to stay and insufficient funds for a hotel, the warm sand on the beach seemed a comfortable prospect. It was late by the time Chaim set off for home and the rest of us settled down in our sleeping bags.

I awoke in brilliant sunshine to find a man standing over me brandishing a spike. In the dark we had inadvertently camped beneath a rubbish bin and were inhibiting his litter-picking. Behind him, the beach was packed with middle-aged people, jumping about, arms flailing, greeting the day with exercise routines. A portly man was standing in the sea, scrubbing his back with a long-handled brush. The spike-bearer stabbed some nearby rubbish and deposited it in a bin above my head. Beside me, my companions stirred, reluctantly coming to life, before sitting bolt upright in astonishment as they beheld the mass workout in progress.

'Oh my God, my bag's gone,' I wailed, as I struggled out of my sleeping bag. 'So's mine, so's mine,' came the multiple echo. We had stuffed our money at the bottom of our sleeping sacks, beneath our feet, but had used small bags and other belongings as pillows. Thieves had taken the lot. I had lost not one passport but two! In those days, if onward travel to an Arab country was likely, the Foreign Office issued two passports so that one could be kept blank, without evidence of travel to Israel. They were meant to be separated, one hidden, but mine were still tied together with a rubber band. I had been in Israel just 24 hours and to all intents and purposes I was stateless, a situation which didn't faze me in the slightest. I would contact the police and the British Consul all in good time; after Yom Kippur.

Kibbutz Dovrat

Kibbutz Dovrat was a fertile haven scraped out of hostile terrain. A backdrop of hills surrounded us, sharpened by sunlight, smudged by shadow or veiled by dust, according to the time of day. A cornucopia of

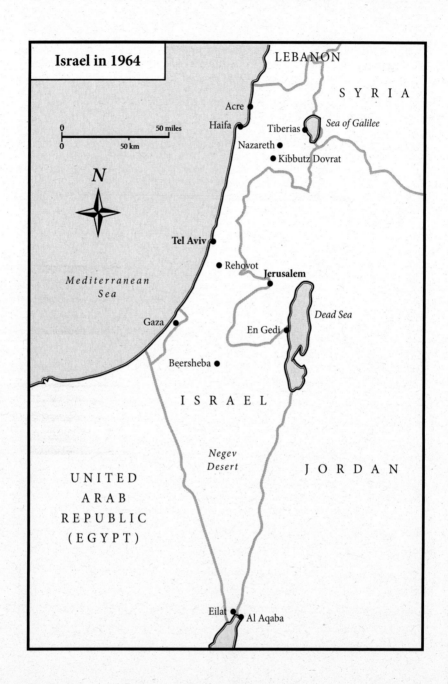

Israel in 1964

LEBANON

SYRIA

Acre

Haifa

Tiberias   *Sea of Galilee*

Nazareth

Kibbutz Dovrat

0   50 miles
0   50 km

N

Tel Aviv

Rehovot

Jerusalem

*Mediterranean
Sea*

Dead Sea

Gaza

En Gedi

Beersheba

ISRAEL

*Negev
Desert*

JORDAN

UNITED
ARAB
REPUBLIC
(EGYPT)

Eilat   Al Aqaba

apples and quince, oranges and grapefruit, melons and grapes, spilled across the valley. There were fields of cotton and corn as well as livestock. A self-sufficient community of over 300 souls, one could not but admire the dedication and perseverance that had created such an idyll.

The kibbutz had its own school. There was separate accommodation for single people, married couples, children, students, and workers such as myself, as well as the *ulpan*, where newly-arrived Jewish immigrants were immersed in Israeli culture and language. Facilities included a laundry, a kitchen and a large dining hall which also served as a space for lectures and film screenings. The buildings were modern, surrounded by lawns and flowers, and there was a swimming pool where you could float on your back gazing up at the Galilean hills. In front of the pool a large memorial commemorated those who had fallen in the War of Independence.

I shared a room with two girls. We were issued with khaki shirts, shorts which resembled big bloomers, boots and floppy hats. At 4.30am there was a wake-up call and at 5am sharp the tractors and trailers departed for the *matayim*, the orchards. Latecomers and stragglers were not tolerated. Figures would emerge sleepily from the dormitories and, still dressing, stumble through the eucalyptus trees, before racing after the tractors. It was a rude awakening, running faster and faster until the final leap of faith, when you were hauled aboard the trailer by those who had been more punctual. After breaks for breakfast and lunch, the working day finished at 4.30 in the afternoon.

For me, working in the orchards proved a nightmare. Allergic to the apple spray, and possibly the dust and grass, I would scale the ladder, reach the top of the tree, and within a few minutes I would be sneezing so much that I could barely retain my perch. What's more, my co-worker, a young Spaniard called Rafael, found it amusing to pelt me with rotten apples. As the day progressed and the sun became hotter our work was almost unbearable. Sweaty, scratched by twigs and, in my case, with streaming itchy eyes, we would seek brief respite in the shade and quench our thirst. At the end of the day, however, the evidence of our labour was rewarding: cartloads of perfect apples, fit for Adam and Eve.

Because of the allergy I was transferred to other duties and for a while I was employed in the laundry where, supervised by a solid German matron called Tova, I had to iron clothes for the entire kibbutz. 'This is not good enough,' she would bark, slinging back garments that retained even the tiniest of creases. 'But they're for wearing in the fields,' I protested. 'So?' she retorted angrily. 'Everything must be perfect.' Tova believed that laundry attained perfection through a regimented approach. To iron a shirt you began with the collar, moved on to cuffs, then the sleeves; next came the back and, finally, the two sides in front. How astonished she would have been to learn that half a century later her reprehensible laundry worker would still iron shirts according to her regime. Having to cater for the whole community was hard work. So much ironing gave me blisters and later, as a kitchen worker, my hands became raw and itchy from the sheer volume of washing up. Some of the pots I scoured were so enormous I could almost have climbed inside.

My brief interlude picking grapes was the best. Working my way slowly along the garlands of vines I could absorb the beauty of the surrounding hills. One day I was jolted from my peace by thudding hooves and an Arab on a large white steed reined in nearby. I was working alone and I was aware he should not have been on kibbutz land; I was nervous for him as well as for myself. I broke off a large bunch of grapes and walked towards him, arm outstretched. He took them and shouting '*Todo rabat*,' thank you, cantered away up the track which led over the hills to Nazareth.

Apart from the hard work, I lived in a buzz of excitement. Spending time with so many nationalities was stimulating, my multilingual efforts rewarding. My big pals were Eli and Joseph, two young Moroccan Jews who had just arrived on the *ulpan* and who, speaking French, would endeavour to teach me Hebrew. In the workplace I had a chance to practise my French and German with a smattering of Hebrew thrown in. I found the names of my companions romantic: Joshua who played the guitar; Benjamin who discussed theology; Jehuda who loved poetry;

Mordecai who introduced me to Israeli food – unfamiliar tastes such as hummus, yoghurt and falafel which were then unavailable in Britain. Our youthful world resonated with song: we sang as we worked; we accompanied Joshua's guitar playing; and Susan, my English friend from Morecombe, performed solos in the candlelight. Dancing round in circles in the traditional Jewish way, we belted out *Hava Negila*, the evocation of joy and happiness which reverberates throughout the Jewish world.

One of the people I liked most was Peter, an Italian Australian. Arriving in Israel fresh from matador training in Spain, he was also known as Don Pedro. Determined to keep his cape work up to scratch, he could be seen daily on the lawn, haughty yet graceful, sweeping the cape from side to side to avoid the imaginary charge of *el toro*.

The *kibbutzniks* were suspicious of him. It wasn't his bullfighting that worried them; it was when he dropped his Spanish persona and behaved like an Arab. He had lived for a while with some Bedouin and frequently extolled their virtues. When working in the fields he wore his Arabic clothes: 'So much more comfortable in this heat,' he insisted. The kibbutz had armed guards to deal with any potential Arab threat and, on one occasion, they rushed into the fields to challenge him. With his dark hair and moustache, his sunburnt Italian skin, and a habit of squatting on his haunches, the confusion was understandable. I hung on Peter's every word. Despite his eccentricities, he never struck me as a poser, but quietly spoken and genuine. 'I nearly became a Trappist monk,' he told me one day when we were discussing religion. It didn't surprise me.

Until a year before I had been a pillar of the church and it was a strange feeling to be living in the Holy Land. With Peter and one or two others I hitchhiked to the Sea of Galilee, where I stood in awe on the sites of supposed miracles. I wandered the ruins of Capernaum, running my fingers over ancient oil presses and mill stones. As I struggled up the Mount of the Beatitudes, my childhood Bible picture book leapt to life: a shepherd boy played a pipe while his sister danced; men in Arab robes reclined in the shade of their tents. I stood on the sacred spot where

Christ had delivered his sermon – blessed are the poor, the meek, those who hunger – and watched the River Jordan snaking its way into the distance far below. It was an unforgettable pilgrimage, the culmination of years of childhood piety, but it was also the swansong of my faith.

At night I would sometimes wander alone along the cart track that led to the orchard. Beneath a Christmas card sky, the dark Biblical hills rose before me, sleeping shepherd boys bivouacked in their embrace. Drowned by the sawing cacophony of cicadas, muted snatches of conversation drifted through the sultry evening from the kibbutz; muffled footsteps, laughter and distant music. The lights of Nazareth, a halo in the distance, reminded me of my ever-growing doubts about religion. I was beginning to find other things disturbing as well. I was emerging from my cocoon.

The Melting Pot

Out of reach, yet just visible on the hill across the valley, Nazareth seemed tantalising. 'Let's go there,' said Diana. 'It's not far on the bus.' Nazareth Iliit, the modern Jewish part of town, was situated on a hill and entirely separate from the old Arab quarter where we got off the bus. No sooner had we arrived than we were set upon by barefoot urchins. Tugging at our clothes they dragged us into shops heaped with oriental temptation: tall brass coffee jugs; pendant earrings heavy with turquoise; embroidery, silver, slippers and skull caps. A small boy sidled up to us in the dim musky interior, hissing to attract our attention. 'You want man?' he enquired. 'You want boy?'

Eventually, emerging into the white-walled radiance outside, we were sucked into an aromatic whirlpool of oil and spice, tropical fruit, manure and rotting rubbish. A woman sat in the gutter breastfeeding her baby. Dusty chickens, claws knotted together with string, lay in feathery heaps, while tethered goats awaited their death sentence. Overwhelmed by brilliant colours, unfamiliar sounds and smells, I was seduced for the first time by that exotic veil which is drawn across the face of poverty.

On SS Adana *Marseille to Haifa, 1964:* **(left)** *dressed for dinner;* **(right)** *Chaim, on air guitar, behind Diana.*
Below *at Kibbutz Dovrat, 1964:* **(left)** *Peter Sidoti ('Pedro') in Arab dress; practising his matador cape moves;*
(right) *outside the foreign worker hostel – me in back row, second on left; Susan sitting on top step.*

Above: *Eli (on left) working in the kibbutz 'matayim'; with Ike in Acre: meeting up with Chaim in Jerusalem.*
Below: *donkey rides and Arab hospitality in Nazareth.*

As we stood taking stock, a big-bellied Arab approached, top-heavy on a dainty donkey. A porter, his job was to transport goods around Nazareth, but catching sight of us he homed in on an unexpected opportunity. 'Come,' he said. 'I am a good guide, very good.' We declined. 'Donkey ride,' he insisted. 'See Nazareth on donkey.' Reluctantly we succumbed to his declaration of international friendship and, taking it in turns to ride, we negotiated a labyrinth of alleyways until, mounting the hillside, we could see the old village spread out before us. At this point our guide encountered a friend leading a large ass. 'For you,' he exclaimed, grinning at Diana.

The countryside shimmered and we squinted in the relentless glare. In the shade of a thorn tree an elder with skin like crackled parchment surveyed his goats through hooded eyes. We mounted our steeds and had just begun picking our way downhill, when Diana's male donkey, lured by the enticing call of a female, bolted into the abyss below. Braying with lust it careered downhill, Diana clinging on for dear life and the animal's owner in hot pursuit. With the errant donkey finally captured, our hosts led us through a door to a courtyard where we sat on low stools as they plied us with small glasses of sweet grainy coffee. It was my first taste of Arabic hospitality and a fitting conclusion to my visit to Nazareth.

We had been warned by Israelis against mixing with Arabs and on the kibbutz they were unhappy about our visits to Nazareth. Perhaps there were resonances of earlier times, when Bedouin had raided farms and sabotaged irrigation systems, or maybe it was the proximity to intermittent fighting on the Syrian border. Time and again they reminded us that Israel had its back to the sea and was surrounded by Arab countries which were hostile.

It was 1964 and the heyday of the kibbutz movement. Their farms were well established; their Utopian communities, originally based on socialism and Zionism, had proved successful, resulting in an arrogance and confidence which were exclusive. Those of us providing cheap labour were interlopers whose presence was a threat to the bubble of secrecy in which they operated, and any links we forged with local Arabs only accentuated this threat. Most *kibbutzniks* of our age barely spoke to us and it was no coincidence that I spent much of my time with recent immigrants, the friendly Jewish Moroccans .

The structure of Israeli society was complex. At the top of the pecking order were the *sabras*, those who had been born in Israel. Then came the Ashkenazi, Jews of European origin, who considered themselves a cut above the rest. In those days the Mizrahi, or Middle Eastern Jews, were disparaged as culturally inferior; they may have been Jewish but they spoke Arabic and looked like the enemy. Finally there were the non-Jewish Arabs, Palestinians who lived in Israel and were Israeli citizens. I met Arabs who were Christian, Arabs who were Muslim, Arabs who were Jewish; Jews who spoke Arabic, Arabs who spoke Hebrew, and European Jews – some of whom had numbers tattoed on their arms from the concentration camps – who only spoke Yiddish. I found it impossible to differentiate between political, ethnic, historical and religious allegiances. Israel was a melting pot where I became involved with people of every persuasion. As for those aloof kibbutzniks, I was to discover that urban Israelis referred to them as country hicks and that they were the butt of numerous jokes.

Kibbutz Dovrat had the reputation of being exceptionally strict. There were rules that seemed to be there just for the sake of it: the closure of the swimming pool at times when it would have been most convenient to swim; regulations about ironing and kitchen work which seemed impractical. Children lived apart, attending school and eating and sleeping in separate quarters. They visited their parents once a week, usually for Sabbath, and even then they didn't stay over. Everyone on the kibbutz, including children, was kept on constant alert with daily drilling and firearms practice. Despite this there were social events to which foreign workers were invited: a party by the swimming pool with music and dancing; a visit to a kibbutz family's home. Kibbutznik Abe and his wife, middle-aged London cockneys, took me under their wing, as did Ike who was to open my eyes in other ways.

Ike took me to Acre where we explored the ancient city with its Ottoman and Crusader connections. It was there, in the old fort, that it first occurred to me that history books might be politically slanted or inaccurate. I learned that under the British Mandate in Palestine the fort had been a high security prison where hundreds of Arabs had been executed. However, the museum I was visiting with Ike focused on the Jewish underground rather than Arabs. I knew absolutely nothing about the British in Palestine. The guide spoke in English for my benefit, pointedly directing the information at me: 'Here, six young Jewish men were hung by the British,' he said. 'They were fighting in self-defence and for freedom but, for the British, this was treason.' The only British person in the group, I was startled and acutely embarrassed. We were shown photographs of the boys who had died, the cells where they had languished, the ropes on which they had been hung. I felt like a Nazi. Why hadn't I been taught about the British in Palestine?

A week or two later, on a trip to Jerusalem, I was to learn more. As I approached the city I saw battered tanks and jeeps left rusting as a permanent memorial to the War of Independence. I visited Jerusalem's celebrated King David Hotel, once British HQ, which had been blown sky-high by the Zionist Irgun only 18 years before. I walked in the no-man's land between Israel and Jordan, between the new and ancient parts of a divided Jerusalem; because it was a danger zone, poor people were allowed to live there free amidst ruins pock-marked by bullets. From a disused minaret on the summit of Mount Zion, I looked down on Golgotha, the Holy Sepulchre, the Mount of Olives, the mosques, domes and rooftops of ancient Jerusalem. At that time they were in Jordan, but three years later, in 1967, they would be assimilated into the State of Israel during a six-day war, when Israel increased its territory threefold, annexing land which belonged to Egypt, Jordan and Syria. The Israel I knew would never exist again.

My next foray was to Haifa where I had to sort out my replacement passport with the British Consul. I had also discovered that in Haifa I could sell my blood and that a single pint would fetch nearly four times my weekly wage on the kibbutz. I was nervous. I had never given blood before, but making a quick buck was tempting. The clinic proved hygienic and efficient and I anticipated repeating the performance a few weeks later. Then came the unexpected downside: I had to sell the blood to the relatives of those who needed it. I was horrified. I opened the door to be besieged by a line of down-at-heel supplicants. An old lady tugged at my sleeve. She needed four pints and had already purchased three. She began to haggle, weeping, wailing and dabbing her eyes. I reduced the price, gave her the receipt to show she had paid for blood, and off she went to claim her full quota.

Around this time I met Izat. A well-educated Arab, a lawyer and fervent Christian, he was proud of living in Nazareth. 'The Annunciation took place here,' he told me, as we wandered the streets together, 'and over there is the room where the holy family lived.' At the edge of the village he pointed to a flat rock where Christ had dined with his disciples. He spoke with certainty, as if there were no historical doubt about exactly when and where these events occurred. He was a kind, hospitable young man and I enjoyed his company, but the Nazareth I saw before me with its noise, smells and busy streets was pretty much as it would have been in the time of Christ. It was basic and real, a place where angels and miracles seemed like fairy tales. My visits to the holy sites had only served to put things in a historical rather than spiritual perspective, creating a void where once childhood beliefs had existed.

The Desert

The Negev was my first desert. I had not anticipated the extraordinary rock formations, burnished gold and tinged rose red, or the kaleidoscope of ochre and heliotrope that moved with the changing light across the land. For the first time I thrilled to the silhouette of an Arab leading camels across the skyline against the setting sun. I was witnessing the extraordinary world of my childhood hero, Lawrence of Arabia. On one occasion, however, a more chilling silhouette presented itself in the form of a long line of Israeli tanks which emerged over the summit of a sandy ridge. Although they were only on an exercise, their huge guns trained in my direction filled me with momentary terror.

Deserts are always potentially dangerous. When Diana and I were hitching a lift out of Beersheba, the driver came to an abrupt halt, parked the car and took off on foot towards a distant building. 'Wait here,' he said, 'and don't get out of the car.' Nearly an hour passed and we became nervous. What could be taking him so long? Idly, we opened the glove compartment and discovered a pistol. Surrounded by desert, we could only sit tight and pray the gun was no more than a wise precaution. Eventually he reappeared and we went on our way without saying anything. Another time, when hitching across the Negev with a boyfriend who had been relegated to the back of the truck, the driver started to grope me in the cab. I pushed him away, always aware of the power he had to leave us stranded in hostile terrain.

After we had worked at the kibbutz for a few weeks, Susan and I decided to take a trip to Eilat, the southern tip of Israel on the Red Sea, beyond the desert. We hitched a lift across the Negev with a truckload of Israeli soldiers. They were our age and younger, little more than a bunch of kids. They joked and laughed and I found it hard to believe these boys and girls were members of a highly trained army. About an hour into our journey the driver screeched to a halt. 'Why's he stopping?' I asked. 'The engine's overheating,' they replied. The soldier got down from the cab, opened the bonnet, and let out a howl as he was slapped in the face by an explosion of boiling water and oil. A party set off on foot to seek help from a desert kibbutz and eventually the injured driver was despatched to hospital.

Later that day we rolled into Eilat. Across the bay, the Jordanian mountains were soft in the heat haze, spread out like folds of pale pink velvet above the town of Aqaba. We stood on a crescent of white sand, which swept round the bay embracing a jewel of sparkling sea. Glimpses of brilliant fish, yellow, red, purple, glinted through the clear water. 'Paradise!' I said to Susan. 'We have arrived in paradise.'

From the minute I set eyes on the place, Eilat had a hypnotic hold over me: the warm sand against my body; the motion of a moored boat rocking gently beneath me; the whisper of the tropical sea as it lapped the shore in the starlight. The ocean was like turquoise silk, shot with pink where the reflection of the mountains seeped across the bay. I would gaze at those hills and imagine Lawrence and his Arabian hordes charging down to capture Aqaba. My life was romantic, overflowing with carefree happiness and I could not leave.

I slept anywhere, on the beach or in boats drawn up on the sand and eventually in a small youth hostel. Sometimes I visited a ruined house inhabited by Joe, a silent companion who wore a battered hat and who kept his food in a basket strung from the ceiling on a disused light flex. We would sit and stare at each other in the candlelight, chewing on dry crusts spread with jam. I cadged rides with Jojo and Henri, cheeky boat boys who hailed from Marseille. I joined the young and beautiful as they sat around beach bonfires, singing the night away. I languished in sultry daydreams – which were destined to end when the money ran out.

In those days Eilat was undeveloped. There were a couple of low-rise hotels and at the edge of the desert there was an airstrip where a small plane arrived twice a week. It wasn't the kind of place where there was plenty of work and I resorted to casual labour. To begin with I washed dishes in a large restaurant where, occasionally, I would find myself, late at night, scrubbing the vast dining room floor on my hands and knees. My co-worker was a beautiful 25-year-old Israeli mother of three. She would stand amidst the filthy dishes and pans, singing with the voice of an angel. Sometimes she would dance, pirouetting around the dining room with her mop, serenading me with *Che sera sera*. We would sing together as we worked, but I knew that her *whatever will be* would be worlds away from my own; she would work for years in that stinking kitchen earning money to support her children. Later I moved on to a smaller restaurant, but I didn't last long. I broke Jewish law by washing plates on which meat had been served, in the same water as plates sullied by dairy products. The dishes had to be destroyed.

Above left: hitching with Peter and Susan to the Sea of Galilee.
Above right: travelling – and breaking down – in the Negev desert with the Israeli army.

Left: with Israeli soldiers on the beach at Eilat.
Below: a 1964 postcard showing the 'tin birdie' coming in to land at Eilat; in the background, the hotel where I worked for a while.

Above: Hans Overbeek.
Above right: with Eilat boat boys Jojo and Henri, my leg wound still bandaged.
Right: the shack where I worked painting shell turtles for tourists.
Below: dwarfed by King Solomon's Pillars in the Timna Valley, near Eilat.
Below right: Derek and Hans in Tel Aviv.

I eventually found hotel work and donned the uniform of a chambermaid. Making-up beds and cleaning bathrooms gave me access to guests' rooms where I gleaned left-over chocolates and bits of cake. The woman I worked for was a bully and in my lunch break I was consigned to a windowless kitchen cupboard where I ate my sandwiches with the boot boys. One day, feeling dejected and tearful, I chatted to a German hotel guest. 'My plane is on the airstrip,' he said. 'I'm leaving tomorrow. You can fly back to Germany with me.' He was being kind and paternal, but I declined. I was too much in love with Eilat.

When working briefly at the only other hotel, I met an Israeli who invited Susan and me to move in with him and live rent-free. It was a temporary arrangement to help us out because we were broke. About 40, he was stocky and hairy, but handsome in a louche sort of way. His clients were the rich women who stayed at the hotel and when he rolled home drunk he would divulge inappropriate details of the services he had rendered. He lived in squalor. His friends would lounge about drunk and stoned among empty bottles and overflowing ash trays, beating vacantly on bongos. I worried about his small son who would sit in the corner eating his way through bag after bag of sweets. I disapproved of my host but he was kind and when I was bedridden with a septic leg, he scrounged plates of food for me from the hotel kitchen.

A few weeks before, at the kibbutz, I had fallen on a rusty stake and cut my leg. I had washed the wound with antiseptic, put on a plaster and thought no more about it. Eilat, however, was a place which courted infection and I knew several people with desert sores which had failed to heal. I could ill-afford medical fees and when my leg became swollen and painful, I ignored it, hoping the swelling would subside. Eventually when it reached elephantine proportions, I went to the Health Centre where a horrified doctor prescribed antibiotics and bed rest. Gradually the swelling decreased, but what had been a small cut on my leg became a hole about an inch across, with smaller holes sprouting off it. I couldn't walk. I couldn't swim. I couldn't work.

My leg's failure to heal worried the doctors. 'Maybe it's syphilis,' they said and took a swab and some blood. I was astonished; I'd only ever slept with one person. I had always divulged pretty well everything to my parents and I wrote home telling them about my swollen leg and the tests. My father simply replied by correcting my spelling of 'syphilis'. I loved him for that, for not kicking up a fuss, but in fact at home they were panicking. The results were negative and eventually the hole in my leg started to shrink. To this day I bear the scar of that sore, which never totally healed until I arrived in colder climes.

I could now hobble. I recuperated with the boat boys, towing waterskiers across the bay in the boiling sun with the spray on my face. I was happy, but all my hard-earned money had been spent on doctors. Then I hit lucky. I got a job in a shack on the beach which sold souvenirs made of shells. I could sit down as I worked, taking the pressure off my leg. My bosses were Arabs, Roget and Sarossi, who tuned-in all day to Radio Cairo and who accompanied the wailing music with their own throaty caterwauling. I loved the craziness and joy exuded by my new employers. As I sat making necklaces and turtles out of shells, they brought me freshly-fried fish and Tunisian cakes thick with syrup. Eventually I was joined by Tineke, a Dutch girl, and when our Arabs were absent, we would sing together as we worked. From where I sat I could gaze across the sea to the pink mountains I loved so much. Day in, day out, we made our shell turtles and painted them in shades of green and brown, until one morning I was aghast to see that Tineke's turtles were bright red with pink spots. 'I'm tired of those boring colours,' she announced. Why not? I thought, and followed suit. When Roget and Sarossi returned they were not amused. We got the sack.

Eilat encompassed far more than beaches and fledgling tourism. Outside town, in the desert, there were copper mines where convicts worked and where seasoned travellers and bums sought temporary employment. Beyond the beautiful coral beaches, there was also a large port which was Israel's commercial lifeline to the rest of the world. In fact, Eilat was quite a rough old place. It had a frontier feel about it, a wicked craziness contained by the desert. Unless you were rich enough to fly or take a ship, the single track road across the desert was your only way in and out.

A few of my friends from the kibbutz had been in Eilat with me, but gradually they faded away across the desert, leaving just Susan. They had been replaced by an influx of bums, hardened travellers who were rougher, tougher and dirtier. Susan and I were in awe of these newcomers. We observed them from a distance in a way that was almost anthropological, tinged with disapproval and fascination. 'Just look at that one,' said Susan. 'I don't like the look of him. He's a real bum.'

Hallelujah! I'm a bum

From the moment I set eyes on him I was smitten. His name was Hans. A tall, blue-eyed Dutchman with wild blonde hair, he was the most beautiful of ragamuffins, who ambled through life without a worry in the world. He was totally spontaneous, living in the moment and for the moment. Despite his disarming smile and gentle ways there was a roguish edge to his personality, a wickedness that made him even more enticing. He had run away from home aged 14, smuggled cars, travelled to exotic places – and he was still only 23. He was the most romantic man I had ever met and, unlike most men, he voiced his affection for me. I was spellbound. It was like running away with a pirate.

Among his friends, wearing a bizarre assortment of ill-fitting clothing was the norm. They had been on the road and acquired whatever apparel they found along the way: one guy turned up wearing a Davy Crockett hat; another, a collarless shirt which was so long it resembled a tunic, giving him the air of a medieval pedlar. Hans ambled about in striped pyjamas that had been owned by someone considerably shorter and smaller; the jacket flapped open, too narrow to be buttoned up, and the trousers ended mid-calf. A few weeks later, wearing these, he accompanied me to the British Consul where he remained oblivious to the hostile glances from staff.

The centre of our social life was Café Lerner, a bohemian place where all the bums hung out. It had saloon-style doors which resulted in dramatic entries, as if everyone thought they were in the Wild West. On one wall a large mirror provided a living mural of the clientele, a rough-looking bunch, long-haired for the times, dirty, unshaven, and mostly miners. By contrast, Roget, the café manager, looked sleek and smart. With skin-tight jeans, high boots and dark hair greased back into a quiff, he pimped about, his eyes bright pinpoints from smoking hashish. Nights at Lerner's were wild; we drank and sang and danced in pure abandonment. Susan was still around. So were the boat boys, Henri and Jojo, the latter jealous of Hans and suddenly professing his undying love for me.

Hans and I were sharing a mattress in Timna House, the digs for the miners. About 20 men slept on the floor surrounded by bottles, stubbed out cigarettes and drink. It was sordid, but there was nowhere else to sleep and nowhere else I wanted to sleep. As long as I was with Hans I was happy. There was a grubby kitchen where we could prepare food, although few bothered. My maternal streak surfaced and I started whisking up raw eggs in milk and distributing this supposedly health-giving concoction to the lads, who treated the gesture with condescending amusement.

Outside the lodgings a large stretch of sand with a single palm constituted our garden. We would lie on the ground, gazing out over the mountains and sea as we sang. The favourite in our repertoire was the folk song *Hallelujah! I'm a Bum* and different people would adapt the lyrics to reflect their own situation. *Oh why don't you work, like other folk do? How the hell can I work when the skies are so blue?* When the small plane arrived in Eilat twice a week, disgorging its cargo of rich Americans, we would refer to it as the tin birdie. 'Perhaps one day,' said Hans wistfully, 'we'll have enough money to ride in a tin birdie.' I bought a postcard of that plane flying low over Eilat, coming in to land – the keepsake of a dream.

Copper had been mined at Timna since King Solomon's times, nearly a thousand years before Christ. The ancient Egyptians had also been there and after I left Israel a shrine to Hathor, the god of mining, was excavated. Back then, however, all I knew about were King Solomon's Pillars, the dramatic sandstone formations located near the mines about 10 miles outside Eilat. Hans had promised to take me there and we set off for a morning's excursion, standing by the desert road thumbing a lift. A car stopped. 'Tel Aviv?' asked the driver. Hans shrugged. 'Yeah, why not? Tel Aviv.' He turned to me. 'You coming?' We had absolutely nothing with us, no spare clothes, no hairbrush or toothbrush, virtually no money. However, I knew that if I wanted to stay with Hans I had to be spontaneous. I hopped in the car beside him and we set off across the desert on a 200-mile journey to Tel Aviv.

We arrived late at night and made our way across the city and down to the sea. 'Where are we going?' I asked. 'To Aaron's,' said Hans, in a tone that suggested everyone knew Aaron. Just before the beach, Hans struck a match and we entered a dark bunker of a room, part of a disused complex of beachside lavatories, windowless and without electricity. 'He's lived here for 15 years,' whispered Hans. Dogs barked at our approach and Aaron, who was lying on a broken-down sofa, stirred himself, sat up and lit a candle. In his 50s, he had waist-length white hair, a long beard and a sensitive face. Slowly he got to his feet and inclined his head in our direction. 'Shalom' he said. 'Shalom. You are most welcome,' then he returned to his place of rest, turned over and went to sleep, leaving the candle still burning.

I glanced around the room. There were several beds, some consisting of springs alone, others were wooden pallets and all of them were padded with rags. Few were at floor level. They had been balanced on old furniture or, in some cases, strung from the ceiling on a tangle of ropes and wires. The entire place was a delightfully Heath Robinson affair and I soon discovered that when lying in bed I could chat to someone a few feet below, whose bed was strung up at right angles to my own.

Dominating the room was a grand piano which was used as a cupboard. The lid was propped open and inside were blankets, scraps of food, books, paintings and old clothes, topped by a sleeping cat or two.

There were three dogs and four puppies which screeched and barked when people tripped over them in the dark. Decorating the walls were sketches done by people passing through and someone had clearly been good at caricatures; one cartoon face which stared down at me had been fixed to the wall by a large nail protruding from its Adam's apple.

'Aaron hibernates all winter,' Hans explained. 'In fact he rarely leaves this room until summer.' 'What does he do all day?' I enquired. 'He reads,' said Hans. 'He reads by candlelight.' As Hans spoke I sensed a deference and respect I was to witness in others. 'He does go out in summer, though,' he reassured me. 'He strides along the beach singing opera followed by a load of kids. They all run after him, mimicking his singing.' 'Does he ever leave Tel Aviv?' I asked. 'Once a year,' said Hans 'He has a friend who lives like a hermit in the desert. He goes there sometimes in summer.'

There was no doubt Aaron was charming. A gentle soul, he spoke quietly with a cultured American accent. I would arrive to find him engaged in conversation with the most unlikely people. One day there was a British woman sitting by his bed. She had a posh accent and was wearing a conventional two-piece suit and high-heeled patent leather shoes. She chatted to him for a while and then departed. 'She's gone back to work,' explained Aaron. 'She was on her lunch break.' Another surprising visitor was Paul. He arrived out of nowhere, donned a smart business suit, and set off to attend a conference in a Tel Aviv hotel. When he returned that night, he retrieved some canapés from his brief case, tasty morsels still sticking to the silver salver on which they had been served. 'Help yourselves,' he said. 'I'll put them in the piano.' Once I awoke to find a middle-aged man suspended in the bed below me and swigging port out of a bottle. 'Have a Madeira, m' dear!' he kept saying, aping the song so popular with Flanders and Swann. Most of the people who came and went, however, were down-and-outs and bums – young people who stayed a night or two and then moved on.

I was to stay in Aaron's room again on a couple of occasions. Curled up with Hans like two mice in a nest of rags, we made love to the sound of the waves crashing on the shore outside. We had no contraception and gave no thought to tomorrow. We divided our time between Aaron's room and Café Cassid, where we met up with Tel Aviv's beats and artists, ballerinas from the nearby theatre, and a junky or two. In the midst of these extraordinary people, for a very short time, I revelled in the feeling of belonging; I was Hans' girl.

On that first trip to Aaron's however, we only stayed a couple of nights. 'Gotta blow,' said Hans in the vernacular of the day. 'Need to get back and earn some bread.' We walked out of Tel Aviv at dawn. With only enough money for a couple of bagels and a packet of cheap fags, we stole a bottle of milk and were on our way. We scrumped oranges from groves along the roadside and, sitting on the verge, we sang as we waited for the next lift.

In Rehovot we were to have a strange encounter. A man appeared and invited us to his home. It transpired he wanted to take photographs of me. He sat me down and insisted I open the buttons on my shirt revealing more and more cleavage, that I hitch my skirt higher and higher. I began to protest. 'Look at these beauties,' he said, pulling out a wad of photographs showing scantily-clad girls. The images were not explicit enough to be classed as porn, but they were certainly voyeuristic. Hans, who was leafing through them, let out a yelp of disbelief: 'That's my old girlfriend from Amsterdam,' he said! I didn't like the photographer and we departed. A few weeks later I received a note sent to Poste Restante, Eilat: *Dear girl,* it read. *The photos are ready, but I cannot send by post. Please collect.* I never did.

Back in Eilat I continued to revel in my sun-drenched idyll, surviving on kitchen work at the port. One day I was collecting my mail at Poste Restante and was astonished to receive a letter from the British Consul in Haifa. He informed me that my father had written to him expressing concern about my septic leg, and offering to pay any medical fees and my fare home. In those days telephoning overseas was complicated. You had to book a call, usually 24 hours in advance, and in Eilat I had seen no evidence of landlines, let alone public telephones. I communicated with my long-suffering parents by post, letters which would sometimes take a month to arrive. Selfishly, I had failed to let them know that my leg was on the mend and they were still worried. In addition Dad had told the Consul how concerned he was about my plans to hitchhike home by myself across Europe. *You are 21 and therefore I cannot divulge your whereabouts*, wrote the Consul, *but your father sounds like such a nice man. I urge you to write to him.* I had written a letter home the previous day, telling the folks I would not be home for Christmas, that I planned to hitch 'a little way East' with Hans. I dared not mention that our proposed destination was India.

A week or two later, Hans and I went to the British Consul in Haifa to collect my new passport. We visited Kibbutz Dovrat and received a warm welcome from my old friends. Winter had come to northern Israel and the place where I had laboured in the orchards in such intense heat was now bleak and rainy. I looked back on my former self and realised the extent to which I had changed. I wondered if it was a good thing. Sometimes I had my doubts. Hobos had been my childhood heroes. By living rough with the bums of Eilat I was fulfilling a dream that alienated me from the Establishment. In Tel Aviv, when a man in a suit shook his fist at us I was delighted; equally so when the British Consul refused to renew a friend's passport until he got his hair cut. Superficially we were giving the finger to convention, but in reality I think the lure was exploration and travel. It was before mass tourism, there were no cheap flights, and this was the only way any of us could afford to see the world.

Hans and I set off for Eilat again, reaching Beersheba at nightfall. It was too dangerous to cross the desert in the dark so we bedded down in a shop doorway, a cramped space that was cold and uncomfortable, but it fulfilled my childhood dreams of being a vagabond girl. 'I'll have a look at that petrol station over the road,' said Hans. 'Maybe there's somewhere round the back that's better than this.' He came back jubilant. 'They haven't shut the door properly,' he said. 'We can sleep inside.' We gathered up our belongings, crossed the road, and slipped inside the deserted garage. Mechanics' overalls were hung on rows of hooks and we helped ourselves, wearing one on top of the other to get warm. We spread our sleeping bags on the oily concrete floor and sunk into an intermittent sleep, awaking at dawn to discover we were soaked. Water from a dripping tap had created a puddle just where we were sleeping. My hair was wet, my face was chapped and my nose red and raw. I felt like death. Hans raised himself up on one elbow, leaned over and kissed me. 'You look so, so beautiful,' he said. I could not have been more astonished.

We were only returning to Eilat briefly. Our plan was to catch a boat to Istanbul. 'From there it'll be easy to get a lift east,' said Hans. We had been spending time with Derek, an Irish Brummy who was tough and sharp and who, despite being only 19, had already done a lot of rough travelling. He had brown Beatle-length hair, blue eyes, and a childlike cheekiness which counteracted his tendency to be harsh. It soon became apparent that Derek wanted to accompany us to India. After a week or so, however, I began to realise that Hans would stay behind. 'I'll follow on,' he said, 'I'll come later.' At the same time he kept begging me to stay: 'We're so happy here. Why do we need to go anywhere else?' For me, deciding what to do was a struggle. I was in love with him, but Eilat was no longer a challenge. I didn't want to spend further months surviving on menial work and lounging around in the sun. Reluctantly, I made the decision to leave Hans behind and go with Derek, but it hurt.

Not long before we left Israel, Derek and I went with two friends to the artists' village of Ein Hodd and on the way the lads decided to pop a few pills. In Eilat I had tried smoking dope for the first time, just a bit of grass, but there were a lot of police around and I had been nervous. Now, up in the hills in this remote village, I decided to emulate the others. To this day I have no idea what pills we took. For a while we were happy, chatting and dancing, but then I embarked on a non-stop paranoid rant. All my conventional and religious values which had been quashed bubbled to the surface and spilled over. In the morning, still part of a blurred nightmare, we hitched back to Tel Aviv, where I found Hans waiting for me in Aaron's room. He had come to see us off. I was fragile and claustrophobic. He dragged me outside and down to the beach. We sat on a step by the sea in the dark while he cradled me. 'Look at the stars,' he said. 'Listen to the waves. Stay here with me. Please stay. I'll keep you safe.'

The following day we all set off for Haifa. When Derek and I collected our boat tickets I was amused to learn we were to embark on the *SS Adana*. An hour later I was leaning over the same railing I had shared a few months earlier with the newly-arrived Israeli immigrants. On the dock below, Hans waved briefly and then turned away. With tears in my eyes, I watched my tall, ambling lover drown in a sea of onlookers. And then he was gone.

At the time I thought that was the last I would ever see of him, but 18 months later, in Amsterdam, we picked up where we'd left off. We stayed in a squat – a tall, narrow Dutch house in a row of traditional residences awaiting demolition. The windows were broken and in places the stairs were so dangerous that we hoisted ourselves to the upper storeys on a rope. We slept in the attic, where the wind whipped through the broken window panes depositing snow on the bare floorboards. We clung together in the rat-scratching darkness and fell in love all over again. And yet, despite it all, I knew I couldn't live that way, that I had to move on. For a long time afterwards I received correspondence threaded with amorous declarations: *I shall never love a woman so much or in the same way as I loved you in Eilat and Amsterdam,* he wrote. Years later, out of the blue, I received a package from Turkey containing filigree earrings and a torn scrap of paper on which he had scrawled *Golden earrings for my gypsy.* No name, nothing else, but it was his writing. I never heard from him again.

CHAPTER THREE

THE ROAD TO HINDUSTAN

Haifa to Istanbul

IT WAS MY SECOND EVENING ON THE SHIP and a Turkish man had me pinned up against the wall on the lower deck. His enormous belly protruded intimately against mine and he was trying to kiss me. Above, where steps led to the upper deck, a gaunt sallow-faced sailor was leaning nonchalantly on a railing watching; earlier that day I had refused to smuggle his illegal goods into Turkey. Struggling, I found my voice and started to shout. A gaggle of women came rushing out of a nearby cabin, screeching and flapping like crows. Derek and our Danish friend, Max, came bounding down from the upper deck to see what was going on. The fat Turk let go of me and bolted, shutting himself in the nearby dining room, pursued by Derek and Max who tried to break the door down. Pandemonium reigned, until the captain was summoned and took charge. Much to my annoyance the horrified women insisted I accompany them to the cabin so I might rest after my ordeal. They had a point. It was three in the morning.

I had only popped below for a pee when the big Turk clobbered me. On the upper deck Max had been playing the guitar like a madman while Derek and I sang and stamped and clapped, dancing round and round the masts and ropes. There were a couple more Danes as well, plus a few people I had known in Eilat. By now we were well on our way to Istanbul and those who had agreed to smuggle goods for the sailors had been rewarded with a bottle of whisky.

We awoke in the morning to find we had docked at Izmir. As we wandered the streets, shivering with cold and tired from the excesses of the previous night, we were jolted back to reality by the sight of a chain gang. Turkish prisoners, their feet heavily shackled, shuffled by so close we could have touched them. I was horrified.

That evening, back on the ship, another bottle of whisky materialised from the stewards, and the offer of a second if Derek and I also agreed to smuggle for them. We caved in. The illicit goods to be taken into Turkey were plastic raincoats, nylon bedspreads and synthetic sweaters, items that in those days were hard to come by in Turkey. I saw no association between the danger of smuggling and my encounter with the shackled convicts in Izmir. A decade later I was to watch Alan Parker's film *Midnight Express* and witness the long-term incarceration of young Westerners in Turkish jails; I emerged from the cinema with delayed shock at the risk I had taken all those years before.

All of us were culturally insensitive. I knew nothing about Islamic beliefs and it never occurred to me that Muslim passengers on the boat might object to our drinking alcohol. On the ship the stewards kept the whisky coming and my friends and I continued to sing and dance our nights away. Our favourite song was Scandinavian, *Sa lange skutan kan ga*, *As long as the boat can sail…* which ends with the words *Take a kiss or two in a beautiful waltz*. One night when the others had departed to bed, Max and I waltzed round and round the deck as he sang this song, kissing me lightly when it came to the last line. A misty rain was falling and our hair blew in the wind as the ship bore its sleeping passengers across the wintry ocean. I thought back to a few months before, treading those very same boards with Chaim in the heat of a tropical night en route for Israel.

A day later we sailed up the Bosphorus and the minarets and domes of Istanbul materialised out of the mist like a Turner painting, shot with the light of dawn. As we docked, my Turkish assailant requested a photograph of us all. Perhaps he wanted a souvenir of his torrid escapade but, whatever the reason, it was a bizarre request to which we, even more bizarrely, consented.

I stepped off the ship and into a fairy tale, a maze of unruly alleys entwined with twisted, dark wooden houses with small balconies. Stovepipe chimneys, capped like toadstools, sprouted crookedly up through pavements or floorboards, poking at right angles out of windows and doors. I was spellbound by the Grand Bazaar: the richly-dyed leather; the ornate brass trays and lamps; the jewellery and precious stones. I flitted from stall to stall, sampling sweetmeats, trying on glittering slippers with curling Ali Baba toes; marvelling at embroidery and marquetry, sandalwood, ebony and ivory. Surrounded by mosques, minarets and palaces, screened by intricate friezes, and looked down on by portraits of Ottoman sultans, Derek and I stood like paupers at the golden gateway to the Orient, about to step into its secret world.

We were staying in the wrong place. The sailors had given us the address of a hotel where we were to check in as their guests and they would collect the smuggled goods. Instead, the taxi driver who ferried us from the docks deposited us in a small, dingy guesthouse owned by his friend. When we encountered our fellow smugglers, they were emerging from a pleasant little hotel in the centre of the city, accommodation far superior to our own. However, despite the iron bedsteads and bare light bulbs, compared with living at Aaron's our hostelry was luxurious.

Wandering the streets a day or two later we were accosted by the sailors who had been searching for us and who assumed we had absconded with the contraband. Having switched from their nautical livery to old-fashioned trench coats, and even a trilby, there was now a touch of the Bogart about them which looked strangely out of place. Back at our lodgings, they locked our bedroom door, drew the curtains and spoke in hushed tones. We produced the goods and the men spread them on the beds, counting each item carefully. A whispered row ensued as they accused us of stealing two sweaters. I was furious. 'I've given you everything I had,' I insisted. Derek backed me up with his own declaration of innocence. In the end they took us out for a meal, paid our hotel bill, and we parted amicably. A few weeks later in the freezing Iranian desert, Derek pulled the missing sweaters from his rucksack. I was shocked. 'You're pleased to be warm, aren't you?' he snapped.

Each day in Istanbul we had to spend time doing what Derek termed 'business'. Apart from obtaining visas and getting passports stamped by the police, our aim was to find someone who would give us a lift to Tehran. 'You're more likely to attract a ride than I am,' declared Derek, so I began frequenting tea houses and run-down hotels where swarthy men drank tea and clicked their worry beads. I was self-conscious rather than nervous and hopeless in my new role. I managed to get one or two offers of lifts, but they failed to materialise.

In the meantime we were revelling in the hospitality provided by the Turkish people. They invited us to restaurants, treated us to local delicacies and, even when we ate in cheap workers' cafés, someone would always insist on paying our bill. It was the first time I had encountered the generosity towards strangers found throughout the Muslim world. Those of us who were on the road began to count on this, a reliance I later came to see as an abuse of the generosity and friendship being proffered. Back then, though, it came as a surprise and enabled us to travel hundreds of miles with barely any money.

We spent one day searching for a parcel posted by my parents. I had sent them a list of things I needed, the most urgent being tampons. After hours spent navigating Turkish bureaucracy, we finally located the customs depot where they slapped the parcel down before me and demanded the equivalent of £5 duty in Turkish lira – about £80 in today's money. With barely any funds and a journey of hundreds of miles ahead, I was obliged to leave without my parcel. It was nearly Christmas. I thought about the festive messages my family would have tucked in amongst the goodies and how sad they must feel that I was not returning home. Istanbul was the watershed: I could turn west and return to the comfort and familiarity of my old life or I could travel east into the unknown. I had no doubts.

Derek and I had begun to tire of the incessant chitchat which produced no lifts. We had seen the wonders of the Blue Mosque and St Sophia, had admired the embroidery, paintings and jewels in the Royal Palace, had spent hours in the Grand Bazaar and wandering the labyrinth of the ancient city. 'Time to blow,' he said, and in the freezing

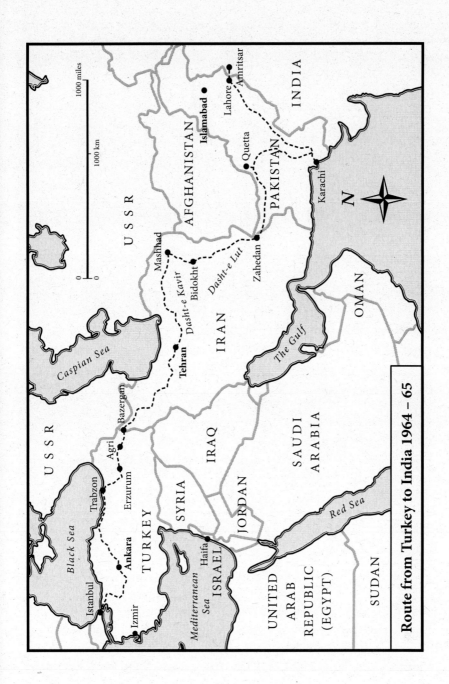

Route from Turkey to India 1964 – 65

dawn of a new day we left Istanbul and crossed the Bosphorus from Europe into Asia.

Turkish delight

A taxi driver offered us a free lift to Ankara where he was visiting his family. The Straits were behind us, but to the south there was more water. 'Is that a lake?' I asked our host. 'Marmara Denizi', he said, 'Sea of Marmara,' and I felt a small thrill at discovering a sea I had never even heard of. We drove through villages where veiled women shuffled along, bowed double beneath huge bundles of sticks, their skirts trailing in the snow. Horse-drawn carts ferried people about their business and elderly moustachioed men, some with turbans and all wearing hugely baggy trousers, stood on street corners, stamping the snow off their knee-high boots. Wooden houses formed higgledy-piggledy clusters around small mosques, and figures scuttled back and forth, Bruegel-dark against a backdrop of snow. A wintry sun splashed golden highlights on mountains and forests that lined the route. 'It's so unspoilt,' I said to Derek, 'so beautiful.'

We arrived in Ankara to find ourselves the freak show focus of dark staring eyes. Children peeped round corners and legged it as we approached. Silent men moved hesitantly in our wake, pausing when we paused, curious and nervous as cattle. Eventually one or two bolder characters detached themselves from the group, welcoming us and displaying the warmth we had come to expect. After checking into a cheap hotel we set about exploring the city. 'Not a woman in sight,' I observed to Derek, wondering how I would fare in this male-dominated world.

The following morning we left town in a dilapidated petrol lorry heading for the Black Sea. The coastline was savagely beautiful. An unpaved road, riddled with pot holes and strewn with boulders, meandered through fishing villages which had remained unchanged for centuries, and where the poorest of people treated us royally. School children wearing black smocks, their heads shaven against lice, danced along behind us giggling and staring. A man bought us coffee. 'Eighty percent of the Turkish population is illiterate,' he announced, as we sipped the sweet, grainy mixture. 'Now at last these children are in school, but what are they taught? They are being indoctrinated against Russia.' He pointed vaguely across the water. 'People here fear Russia. It is too close.' I thought back to my friends in the Russian Service at the BBC, of how our broadcasts had been jammed. It seemed strange that the Soviet bogeyman was now only a couple of hundred miles away.

When our lift on the petrol lorry petered out we resorted to public transport, haggling about the price as we entered the bus. We succeeded in reducing the fare considerably, by telling the driver we had been married for a year, that we were students and that we had very little money. On hearing this, a man stepped forward and became our host for the next two days, introducing us to his friends and providing us with meals and accommodation. With Turkish hospitality proffered so readily, it was rarely necessary to resort to such connivance, but on the couple of occasions we did so, I felt ashamed.

Our journey along the stunning coastline continued: to the north, sea sparkling in the winter sunshine; to the south, a wide alluvial plain with a backdrop of mountains. We were travelling through impoverished peasant communities, but the hospitality shown us was boundless. Their struggle for survival was visible, the hard life etched on people's faces. 'This ground is no good for crops,' we were told. 'The good soil is only finger-deep. We can grow maize and nuts; that's all.'

There was only one occasion when Turkish warmth and generosity was called into question. Trabzon was the last town on the Black Sea before we turned inland and we arrived there at nightfall after a rough lorry ride. I had been privileged to spend the journey inside the cab, whereas the two drivers had taken it in turns to travel on the roof with Derek. It had meant swapping places now and then and there had been times when one or other of the drivers was briefly on the roof alone. On arrival in our hotel in Trabzon Derek opened his rucksack and began rummaging through everything. 'There's stuff missing,' he said, surprised. 'Have a look at yours.' I opened my bag. Half my clothes had been stolen. 'My swimming costume as well,' I groaned. In the Grand Bazaar we had bought gifts for our families: 'And the presents,' said Derek. I was saddened by the theft rather than angry. Undoubtedly the truckers were the culprits, but I was aware of how poor people were and I wanted to let the matter drop. Derek, however, was out to get them and we stomped around town in the dark, searching for the miscreants. I was particularly uneasy because I knew Derek carried a knife and, although it was intended for practical purposes, in his current mood I could see the potential for a brawl. Fortunately we failed to locate the thieves and after a glass or two of Turkish tea, we returned to our lodgings.

We set off again at dawn and were picked up by a westernised young man who worked in Germany. He was charming, gave us a tour of the area in his car, bought us meals and put us up in another hotel. In the evening he drove us out of town to an isolated spot by the sea and produced a bottle of raki. It was fun and our companion was interesting, but we all had too much to drink. Since arriving in Turkey I had shared a room with Derek and most of the time a bed. When I left home, contraception had not even featured in my travel preparations. The pill was a brand new invention, medically controversial and largely inaccessible and I would never have dreamt of asking for condoms from behind the counter in a chemist shop. In Israel, because I had been in love with Hans I had taken some risks and I knew it was just possible I could be pregnant. It didn't worry me unduly; from a romantic point of view I quite liked the idea. However, it was something that held me back from consummating my relationship with Derek. In addition, as much as I liked him and sexy as I sometimes found him, any affection I felt had always been platonic. After drinking raki that night, however, I nearly succumbed to his advances and in my diary I voiced concern at my carelessness. In fact I was the ultimate prick-teaser and should not have been sharing a bed with him at all.

We moved on from Trabzon at dawn, heading inland towards the mountains. It was always a thrill to hit the road again, to savour the freedom of not knowing whom you would meet, how far you would travel, or where you would spend the night. Our day began submerged in wood chippings on the back of a truck which grumbled and creaked as it tackled the snowy mountain roads, but as the ascent grew more hazardous the driver decided to retreat. 'No going back,' insisted Derek. We extricated ourselves from our woodchip nest, clambered down from the lorry, and watched as it slithered precariously down the hill, back the way we had come.

We shouldered our packs and set off on foot up an ice-glazed road which led to the sky, our route lined by sentinel firs festooned with icicles. The forest floor was snow soft, blue-streaked with shadow, muffled by drifts. Waterfalls, frozen in mid-flow, hung like curtains of ice. After a while we rested by the roadside, singing as we nibbled on nuts, the only food we had with us. Neither of us gave a thought to being high in the mountains on a barely passable road or the fact that, come nightfall, without a lift we could freeze to death.

A dilapidated jeep skidded to a halt in front of us. There were already three men inside, but they managed to haul us and our luggage aboard. Our jovial, rotund driver was the mayor of Gümüshane, a small town in the valley on the other side of the mountain. He sported an enormous moustache and laughed and whooped as we gained the summit, before skidding treacherously down the steep incline on the other side. On arrival in town, he invited us to the mayoral dwelling, a home larger than most, where we were ensconced on throne-like chairs swathed in lengths of red velvet. A large portrait of Kemal Ataturk, father of the modern Turkish State, stared down on us, as members of the mayor's family were paraded before us. 'Now we eat meat,' announced our host in a tone which suggested such fare was a privilege.

The meal over, we were driven into the countryside to visit the town clerk who had shared our helter-skelter descent in the jeep, and who inhabited a small house fit for Hansel and Gretel: twisted stove pipes; hand-woven mats; snippets of embroidery and lace. A wooden cradle was strung from the rafters, and we dined off an ornate brass tray. Rosy-cheeked children tumbled like puppies as the latest baby swung gently in its suspended cradle. We passed a cosy night in a small bedroom with its own stove, and awoke at dawn to see large snowflakes drifting past the window.

This beautiful family offered the hospitality they would have bestowed on any stranger, be they Turkish or foreign. Such generosity imposes a burden on the host to feed the guest until he can eat no more, and there is an equal onus on the guest to show appreciation by eating everything that is set before him. The etiquette is complex. A Turk would have known exactly when to stop, but we did not. We ate our fill and more, and afterwards were devastated to discover we had gone too far; although they did their best to hide it, there was clearly insufficient food remaining for the family.

The following morning the mayor put us on a bus which navigated perilous zigzags along icy mountain roads. At prayer time it drew to a halt on a hairpin bend and the passengers descended, throwing their coats on the snow as impromptu prayer mats. 'I hope they're praying for a safe journey,' I said to Derek. 'Just look where he's parked!' We were on the very edge of the mountain overlooking an abyss. After travelling all day, we arrived in the mountain town of Erzurum, where dark wooden houses stood out starkly against the snow. There was a boardwalk lined by a couple of large stores reminiscent of the Wild West: wooden floors and counters; a stove with a tall pipe that exited through the ceiling; sacks of pulses and flour; old-fashioned tins and packaging. I hoped that one of these shops might be sufficiently well-stocked to sell sanitary protection. I entered and, beneath the gaze of a number of men, began searching the shelves. No luck. Eventually an old woman was summoned from the gloom. With my back to the stove where the men were sitting, I embarked on a charade to illustrate my needs. She stared at me blankly as if I were some kind of mad alien who had invaded her shop. I left empty-handed.

It was already nightfall. 'Perhaps we should look for somewhere to stay,' I suggested. 'No,' said Derek, gruffly. 'We'd best get on.' We followed the road out of town, but hadn't walked far when he needed a pee. He was unzipped and standing on the edge of snowy desolation when there was a staccato click and a shout. He swung round to find himself looking down the barrel of a gun. We had strayed near a military zone and were being challenged by a bear-like Turkish soldier, clad from head to toe in thick fur. We had already learnt that the Turks feared the Soviet Union, but we were unaware of Erzurum's significance in the Cold War, that it was home to NATO's most south-easterly air force base. The soldier shone his torch into our faces and looked astonished. To our relief he found the situation immensely funny and started laughing. 'Agri,' we said, pointing hopefully down the road towards our next destination, and before long our furry friend had hailed a passing truck. We were on our way again.

It was late at night when we cruised into Agri, driving along unlit dirt streets where buildings were shuttered down for the night. Our truck driver drew up in a yard outside a cow shed, took a look inside, and indicated we could spend the night in bovine company. It was freezing cold, but at least we had a roof over our heads. We curled up together for warmth on a bed of straw and slept soundly. When I awoke at dawn it was so cold that I decided to leave Derek sleeping and pop into town by myself. I found a café and after a glass or two of warm, sweet tea and a crust, I made my way back to the cow shed, only to find it padlocked on the outside!

The herdsman had arrived in my absence, collected his cattle, and secured the shed. Derek, sleeping behind a bale of hay, had escaped detection and remained ignorant of the exodus. Outside I shouted loudly and banged on the door until, eventually, he awoke. 'You're locked in,' I yelled. I began accosting people, but my sign language proved inadequate. A crowd gathered. 'Shout something,' I yelled to Derek, 'anything. Just make them understand you're inside.' Derek started banging and shouting and, as comprehension dawned, everyone became very excited. Eventually an old lady appeared, cackling wildly, and brandishing the key to the padlock. She opened the door and Derek emerged, holding up both arms like a sporting hero, as his audience fell about laughing and clapping.

We wanted to get a truck out of town, but a small boy insisted on escorting us to the bus station. When we explained that we only hitchhiked and could not afford buses, the conductor merely shrugged, and let us travel free. Something of a clown, he feigned a punch-up with the passengers, embarked on a kick-fighting spree with the children and performed a fiendish dance on the roof of the bus. He also insisted on providing us with food. The passengers laughed and shrieked and clapped. Thus, in the midst of company akin to a circus, we arrived at the last town in Turkey before Iran. As I crossed the border, I looked back at Turkey with affection. It had opened my eyes to so many things: the impoverished lives that others lived; unfamiliar music tinged with Arabic and Persian; a Muslim world of veils, mosques and muezzins. Above all, I would never forget the incredible generosity bestowed on us by the Turkish people.

Christmas in Iran

The Inoculation Officer handed me a small yellow book. The cover bore a picture of the Iranian flag – a scimitar-bearing lion-rampant, backed by a blazing sun and topped by a crown – beneath which was printed *Imperial Government of Iran*. I was to be forcibly vaccinated against cholera and this medical record, with information in Farsi, was to cause raised eyebrows over the next few years whenever I presented myself for immunisation.

The Iran we had entered was still ruled by the Shah of Persia, Mohammed Reza Pahlavi, whose secular approach, fraternisation with Israel, and gradual erosion of Islam was already causing political unrest. Only a month before we crossed the border, Ayatollah Khomeni had been arrested and sent into exile. It was another 15 years before he would return triumphant and form the first Islamic republic.

The Iranian border post at Bazergan was an island of luxury surrounded by an expanse of frozen mud. It called itself the Tourism Bureau, but its clientele seemed to consist exclusively of long-distance truckers. The immigration officer was charming. His welcome included food and accommodation, water and western pop music. 'Water!' I exclaimed, as he indicated the tap. 'Running water!'

A couple of days later we struck lucky and boarded a lorry that was travelling the width of Iran from west to east, over a thousand miles. Having left behind the bright welcome of the border community, we entered the real Iran, a drear world steeped in mud. For hundreds of miles our road was a mere furrow in the vastness of the brown steppes, terrain that was semi-desert. The land was dark, streaked khaki, ochre and chocolate; strewn with black stones and boulders. The scattered settlements were cuboid, scraped from the land, houses built of clay and straw.

Despite this bleak outlook, our lorry drivers were jovial, cheeky and funny. Our days became a charade of exaggerated gestures, used to bridge the linguistic and cultural divide: Derek farted and the truckers pinched their noses, groaned and wound down the window; they indulged in mock haggling, rubbing their index fingers against their thumbs to suggest the money they would pay Derek if he were willing to sell me. The most exhausting element of the journey was that they expected us to sing, each of their wailing performances to be matched by us. We actually liked singing and often sang as we waited by the roadside, but serenading on demand for mile upon mile became too much. Our repertoire exhausted, we resorted to nursery rhymes, Baa Baa Black Sheep being the favourite. 'Baa, baa!' they shouted. 'Baa, baa, baa!' 'Oh no,' said Derek, 'they want it again.'

One day we drew up at a dwelling where a man lay bedridden and in pain. For about an hour Hassan, our lorry driver, massaged his friend, kneading his muscles, cajoling and humouring him like a child. As in all Iranian homes, this simple room housed a vivid treasure – a richly variegated Persian carpet. As I waited for Hassan I noticed something else, a newspaper cutting of John F Kennedy pinned to the wall, an unexpected political fragment I was to see adorning walls of several homes in Iran. When we eventually left the sick man behind, our Good Samaritan had succeeded in instilling momentary peace on a face that had been racked with pain. In the weeks that followed I often thought of Hassan, crisscrossing the desert wastes and pausing to bring solace to his friend.

We reached Tehran on Christmas morning to find unpaved streets lined with rubbish-filled canals reeking of urine. A weak sun lit up a distant backdrop of mountains. We tracked down a couple of flatbreads, a tiny piece of goat's cheese and some sweets, which we washed down with warm milk. 'Christmas dinner!' I said, relishing the treat. Later Derek emerged triumphant from a shop brandishing a packet of tampons. 'Just look what I've found,' he said. 'Happy Christmas!'

After all our rough travelling we were hoping for some Christmas festivities. We had envisaged being swept up by the British diplomatic corps, being welcomed by our compatriots to their homes away from home. The sentry on the gate of the British Embassy thought otherwise. Eventually, lured like moths to candlelight, we sneaked into an Italian church where a service was in progress. Derek's boots were dirty, his jacket threadbare, and I was wearing a pair of his trousers hitched up with string. A couple of ragamuffins, we stood amidst expatriate Christmas finery, embracing the familiarity of chorister, prayer and carols.

A small girl in the pew in front was burying her head in her mother's fur coat. Suddenly I recalled that sensual childhood reassurance of fur against cheek, that feeling that came with a whisper of perfume, the sparkle of an evening dress, my mother floating down the stairs all powdery and pretty. My thoughts winged homewards. They would be gathered round the Christmas dinner table, the pudding aflame, expectantly awaiting the Queen's speech. As always, this nostalgia led to a moment of guilty introspection that I had abandoned the moral code with which I had been raised. When people started to go up to the altar for Holy Communion, I nearly followed. Later I wrote in my diary: *How could I take Communion when I might be pregnant by a Dutch bum?*

We left the light and warmth of the church wondering where to spend the night. 'Let's go to the railway station,' said Derek. 'Perhaps we can sleep in the waiting room.' When we got there it was locked, but we bedded down comfortably enough outside. It was Christmas night 1964, I was 21 years old, and I was sleeping on a railway platform in the middle of Iran. *Still no curse*, I wrote in my diary the next morning, masking unmentionable menstruation with the euphemism of the day. A few minutes later we were moved on by the police.

We had arranged a rendezvous with our truck drivers and were soon on our way across Dasht-e Kavir, the Great Salt Desert. Tired, hungry, and travelling across the freezing, rime-hard wastes, we imagined the landscape as food: 'It's like chocolate cake,' I said, looking at the mud. 'With icing,' added Derek, indicating the recent snowfall. 'Whipped meringue,' I said of the distant mountain peaks. 'Biscuits,' said Derek looking at the flat rectangular desert dwellings. As we went further east, the reflection from thicker snow rendered our days brighter, and a wintry sun glazed a honey-washed landscape. Gradually the towns became more exotic, the architecture more oriental, the turbans worn by the populace more elaborate.

We passed a night in a truckers' doss house, a single room with a raised communal sleeping platform of packed dirt at one end. There we slept side-by-side with the drivers, our bodies crammed into an ever-tighter corrugation as more of them emerged from the desert, knives tucked into turbans and belts. The only woman, I had grabbed the space on the end up against the wall, so that Derek could provide a barrier between me and the other men.

As I moved through this male world, relieving myself became more and more of a problem. Having a wee was bad enough, let alone anything else. Most of the time I walked into the desert and squatted as far from the lorry drivers as possible. In the doss house I had braved the men's limited facilities and watched male eyes pop out on stalks as I emerged. It was two or three days out of Tehran that I was finally able to make use of the tampons Derek had given me for Christmas. I was glad, but also sad. There was no longer any possibility that I was carrying Hans' child; my connection with him and with the idyll that was Eilat had finally been severed. For the next few days, with wide open desert or hole-in-the-ground lavatories, no flushing water and no disposal facilities, never had the euphemism 'curse' seemed more appropriate.

After travelling the breadth of Iran, we finally arrived in Mashhad, an attractive city near the borders with Soviet Turkmenistan and Afghanistan. We had waved off our friends the truck drivers who were travelling south, and stomped along the road through deep snow into town. We were just tucking into a mountain of rice when two Americans appeared: Dave, the teenage son of the American Consul, and Chang, a Hawaiian youth. 'Come back with us,' said Dave. 'Dad's out of town. There's beer and music.' The Consul's residence was a veritable Santa's grotto: a ceiling-high Christmas tree with lights, and a room festooned with decorations. 'Christmas at last,' I said. 'Help yourselves to drinks,' said Dave. 'There's whisky, gin, beer...' We drank and danced until the early hours, twisting the night away to Chubby Checker and revelling in the sound of western music. My chief memory of the evening, however, was a toilet that flushed, the first we had seen since Israel. 'Just look at that,' Derek kept saying and, much to the amusement of our hosts, we used it at every opportunity. Eventually, tired out, we sank into soft pastel-coloured bedding. In the morning, luxuriating in the unaccustomed comfort, I rolled over on my side and began leafing through the books piled on the bedside table. Each one addressed the threat of Communism. Reds-under-the-bed was clearly the focus of the US Consul in Mashhad.

The following day we set off to explore the city, which proved far more attractive than Tehran. After a while we bumped into a medical student called Reza, who invited us to the home he shared with four other medics. For three days they cooked for us, took us to the cinema and introduced us to their friends, including an educated young woman who spoke English. I sat drinking tea with her. 'I'm so happy to talk to a

Above left: SS Adana, Haifa to Istanbul with (left to right) Derek, Max, Inge and Jorgen.
Above right: on the road in the Turkish mountains.
Left: Derek and me with Iranian truck drivers.

Below: Reza with his turkey, Mashhad.
Right: Derek on horse and cart, leaving Mashhad, New Year's Eve, 1964.

Above: Derek on the beach, Karachi, January 1965.
Right: Derek smokes a hookah with Pakistani truck drivers, on the road to Lahore.
Below: Dancing bear, Pakistan.

Below and right: dressed for Id, Lahore.

woman,' I kept telling her. She was amused, but had no real idea of the male-dominated life I had been living. Until then I hadn't realised the degree to which I missed female company. Part of an educated elite, the medical students were polite and kind, exhibiting a naïve streak that contrasted with the Iranians who had been our companions of the road. Whereas our truck drivers had bridged the cultural divide with a bawdy charade, the medical students were inclined to giggle and attempt laboured jokes in order to communicate. One of the quirky things about the household was Reza's turkeys. There were two, probably destined for the pot, but he treated them as pets, caressing their feathers, and even bringing them into our bedroom to greet us in the morning. 'Oh God, here come the turkeys again,' I moaned to Derek, as I began yet another day with a turkey's arse suspended above my head.

We had planned to travel from Iran into Afghanistan but, despite exaggerating the money at our disposal, we were denied entry on the basis of insufficient funds. 'We'll have to go south,' said Derek. 'Perhaps they'll let us into Pakistan.' It was a detour of 500 hundred miles or so. On New Year's Eve 1964, we departed Mashhad on a small cart pulled by a horse. Sunlight glanced off the snow and lit up the distant mountains. I was caught up once again in the freedom and beauty of the moment. It was bitterly cold, yet our slow progress pleased me. The Leyland lorry we were to catch shortly afterwards was barely faster, travelling at 20mph and frequently breaking down.

A toast to 1965

It was in this ramshackle vehicle, limping south towards Dasht-e Lut, the next vast desert, that we greeted 1965. The driver handed us a bottle of arak; shivering and rubbing his hands up and down his forearms, he indicated that it was intended to warm us up. It was the best we had tasted and we gulped it down. At midnight we toasted the New Year but the alcohol had made me introspective and maudlin; I wondered where Hans was and whether he was thinking of me.

The next morning, a bright and sunny New Year's Day, the lorry dropped us off on the outskirts of a town named Bidokht. Sitting by the roadside waiting for the next lift, our tranquillity was shattered by a throng of teenage schoolboys carrying bundles and cooking pots. 'Come,' they shouted. 'Come with us and eat,' and we followed them down a desert track. At one point I hopped onto one of their bicycles and pedalled off down the trail. 'A woman on a bicycle!' they shouted, roaring with laughter. 'A woman!' We eventually arrived in a garden of spiky vegetation surrounding a deserted mud house and a ruined tower. It was a beautiful spot. We scaled the tower, munched our way through bags of nuts, and drank the sweet tea they brewed over an open fire. Then the real cooking commenced and, tearing off large pieces of naan, we dipped into a thick aromatic stew. Sixth-form students from the nearby school, these lads were the proud owners of a transistor radio, and so our day was accompanied by a cacophony of wailing music, which rose and fell, mewed and rasped, before drifting away across the sandy wastes. During the day it had been warm, but mid-afternoon the temperature plummeted and with icy breath we made our way back into town. Derek and I passed the night at the local tea house, stretched out on a beautiful Persian rug.

In the morning we resumed our position by the roadside. The sun was warm on our faces and we sat quietly, listening to the sounds of livestock and the braying of an ass. Across the road, the oriental arches and honeyed slabs of the town rose from the desert sand and, from the south, far away in the distance, a tiny figure came slowly into view. As it grew closer we made out an old shepherd herding his flock of mangy sheep. He drew level with us, paused, and rummaging amongst his clothes produced a flatbread. This he tore in two, giving half to us and retaining the rest for himself, before picking his way painstakingly northwards. Emaciated and frail, he must have given us half his day's ration. Over the years, living in Western affluence, I have often dwelt on this gesture: an old man's generosity towards strangers; the breaking and sharing of his daily crust.

For a considerable time there was no traffic and then the distant buzz of a small motorbike became louder until it drew alongside us. The rider was a policeman. 'You come with me?' he enquired. 'Visit my village?' He offered to take us pillion, one by one, so I hopped on the back and off we went. The motorbike struggled unsteadily along the sandy track which led into the desert. My mother had given me only one warning before my departure for foreign parts. She'd said nothing about medication, sunburn, contraception, rape or theft. Her only contribution to my safekeeping had been: 'Beware of white slave traffic!' Halfway to the policeman's village this bizarre piece of advice filtered into my consciousness. Could this be it?

My fears were unfounded. He deposited me in a courtyard where there were men playing cards and drinking tea, and off he went to fetch Derek. We spent a pleasant day with the policeman's family, sitting on the floor eating an enormous meal which, as ever, consisted largely of rice. There was a grate hollowed out in the middle of the floor and filled with smouldering charcoal, above which a table-shaped frame supported a thick quilt which spread out on all sides. We sat on pillows our bodies beneath the quilt, our legs radiating out from the grate like the spokes of a wheel. It was my first taste of traditional heating known as the *korsi*.

In the evening we were taken 20 miles further into the desert, to stay with a school teacher whose extended family made us very welcome. They lived in a compound with large rooms leading off a central courtyard. We were given a tour of the whole complex: the well; the stores; the village oven which was outside. There was also a room with a tiled floor edged by a gutter and drainage holes. We thought it was the lavatory, but when one of us produced a turd it proved impossible to dispose of it with the bucket of water provided. In the end we had to push it manually through one of the holes in the gutter. 'I think it's just a bathroom,' I said to Derek. 'We were only meant to wash here.'

Come nightfall, the entire family slept with us on the floor in one large room. Even with the thick Persian carpet, I found it excruciatingly uncomfortable and was kept awake by snoring adults and squealing babies. When the teacher told us we were the first foreigners to visit his village I felt really privileged. The next day they took us back to the main road and hailed a lorry bound for Zahadan. For three days we travelled south with the same truck, passing weird and wonderful rock formations in a desert as beautiful as the Negev.

Not far from Zahadan was a telecommunications base run by the Central Eastern Treaty Organisation (CENTO). The result of a pact between Iran, Iraq, Pakistan, Turkey and the UK, it had been established in 1955 to contain Soviet expansion, particularly into the Middle East. No sooner had Derek and I reached Zahadan than we encountered CENTO engineers, friendly young men who whisked us away to their living quarters in the desert. A thread of resistance to the Cold War seemed to be running through my life: BBC broadcasts to the Eastern Bloc; Black Sea children indoctrinated against Russia; the bear-like Turkish soldier in Erzrum; the US Consul's books in Mashhad; and now CENTO.

From the moment we arrived, one of them, a Canadian named John, paid me an inordinate amount of attention. The first thing he did was march me down to the *hammam*, or public bath house, where he insisted on paying for my ablutions and the required soap. After weeks of isolation in a male world, I found myself in a place that was awash, quite literally, with naked women. It was an extraordinary feeling, like rediscovering some lost tribe which had been obliterated from the face of the earth. When I eventually emerged, John expressed delight at my appearance: 'I knew you'd scrub up well,' he said. Later he produced a photo of a girl he'd been in love with, pointing out how she resembled me. I went along with the mood and dressed in the only skirt I possessed. I found his attention flattering and found him attractive. *I am trying very hard not to flirt,* I confided in my diary. *It would not be fair on Derek.*

My relationship with Derek was still a problem. I liked him immensely and there were moments when I looked at his beautiful blue eyes and felt a brief tug of love. He was a good travelling companion and I felt a fierce loyalty towards him which I don't think he ever appreciated.

Above all, I was indebted to him for having dragged me half across Asia and for having looked out for me. John, the Canadian, begged me to stay in Zahadan and it was tempting. It was suddenly quite a relief to be in the company of a conventional clean-cut man who apparently doted on me. However, his disapproval of Derek was blatant and he side-lined him at every opportunity. My loyalty remained with my travelling companion and we continued on our way, but my relationship with him had suffered and was never the same again.

The CENTO engineers ran us to the exit border for Iran, saw us through customs, and we set off across the no-man's-land in the direction of Pakistan. On maps, borders are drawn precisely between countries, as if different nations butt up to each other with no space in between. On the ground, however, this is not always the case. There is the no-man's-land which is a disputed area, the no-man's land which is a war zone and, as we found between Iran and Pakistan, the no-man's-land which is a two-mile wide ribbon of desert which appears to serve no purpose whatsoever, and where Derek and I came upon a small hut, stuck in the middle of nowhere. There was a border guard inside, and outside the hut was a wooden bench. 'Let's rest here a bit,' said Derek. 'There's bound to be some traffic crossing into Pakistan.' 'You think so?' I said, indicating the back of the bench where a warning had been carved: *John from Liverpool sat here seven days waiting for a lift.* We settled down, resigned to a long wait, but within an hour we beheld the most extraordinary sight: 'They're pink,' I said, in astonishment. 'Just look! They're both bright pink!'

Pakistan, a kaleidoscope of colour

The two identical Cadillacs bumped towards us, pink and chrome-smooth, emerging from a cloud of dust. They were being imported into Pakistan by members of London's Pakistani High Commission who welcomed us aboard. Finding ourselves cocooned in such opulence was a strange experience. The cars had tape recorders and I had never heard music in a car before. *Baby Love* by the Supremes was top of the charts and our hosts played it again and again, as well as *Haji Baba*, Nat King Cole's Persian lament.

Our first night in Pakistan was spent in a dak bungalow, an old-fashioned guest house and a remnant of colonial times. At dawn, as the mist peeled away like a transfer, it revealed a vibrant, colourful world, entwined with lush vegetation, feathered with palms, fragrant with exotic blooms. Walking along the roads and working in the fields were the most beautiful people I had ever seen. Dark-skinned, handsome like gypsies, their jewellery flashed in the sunlight. They walked tall, regal in multi-coloured turbans and drapes: a kaleidoscope of shocking pink and violet, blood red and orange; fabric as gold as the sun and blue as the sky. The women swung their hips, their skirts and dresses sparkling with mirror-work which danced in their stride. A decade later London was to be awash with ethnic goods, but back then I had never seen such rich colours, such ornate embroidery or, indeed, mirror-work. Whichever way I turned there were spangles and glitter, sequins and fragments of mirror, flashing like fireflies.

While the Cadillacs awaited customs clearance, we had to remain in the city of Quetta, an uninspiring military town which we found boring. Derek relieved the monotony by concocting exaggerated and untrue stories about our lives. It was harmless enough, a bit of a joke, but it was a game I disliked. Exchanging personal details with strangers made travelling interesting and if Pakistanis were curious about us, surely we owed them the courtesy of a truthful response. Derek was irritated. 'Why are you making such a fuss?' he demanded.

Our host, Saleem, one of the Cadillac owners, had invited us to his home in Karachi. He was a strange character, one minute serious and conventional, the next a little crazy. He located a room for Derek and me, then jumped up and down on our bed with such exuberance that it broke. 'Don't worry,' he said, 'The landlady will think you and Derek did it!' We made the acquaintance of various Pakistanis, hospitable people who invited us to eat and drink with them, including a picnic by a lake where food was washed down with a bottle of Scotch. Looking back, the abundance of alcohol puzzles me; clearly Pakistan was yet to follow a more fundamentalist Islamic path. One night Derek and I went to the park to score a little hashish, a stupidly risky assignation from which we returned unscathed.

Eventually Saleem's papers were in order and we were on the move. As the Cadillacs cruised through tiny villages, people stopped in their tracks to gawp at the surreal pink cavalcade. Churning up clouds of dust, we glided past creaking bullock carts, men on bicycles who wobbled in astonishment, groups of women who froze in disbelief. People ran out of their shops as we approached and small boys shrieked and whooped, chasing after the rosy elusive dream from another world. When we stopped for refreshment crowds gathered, flabbergasted, curious, stroking the smooth pink chrome with the tips of their fingers until Saleem shooed them away.

Five hundred miles further on, we arrived at Saleem's luxurious home in Karachi with its wrought-iron grills and tiled courtyards surrounded by tropical flowers. Servants came and went bearing trays of fruit and drinks, making our beds, sweeping our room and doing our laundry. They even cleaned Derek's filthy boots. Although they remained polite, they must have regarded our ragged clothes and unconventional appearance with disdain. One day the lady of the house came to see us looking offended. 'The servants have found a knife under your pillow,' she said to Derek. I was furious. I realised Derek had put it there out of habit rather than harbouring any malicious intent, but it was insulting to the household and implied a lack of trust.

The lifestyle of Saleem's circle was reminiscent of colonial times and of upper-class Britain. He was a charming host, introducing us to his friends, from businessmen to members of the cricket club, and we were wined and dined all over the city. Once or twice Derek and I sloped off to the beach on our own, where we watched children enjoying camel rides, a boy with a performing monkey, and a man prodding his shackled bear with a stick until it embarked on a shambling dance. When out in the city without our host, Derek and I reverted to type, hitching rides on the back of carts with long shafts, drawn by camels. Other than the knife incident, we had been on our best behaviour at Saleem's and had also been aware that we should not outstay our welcome. It had always been Saleem who pressed us to remain, but one night after a party on the roof of his house where everyone drank a lot of gin, he suddenly became drunk and abusive and made it clear it was time for us to depart. The next day we left.

With Karachi behind us, we began travelling on the ornate trucks which plied the roads of Pakistan. Hand-painted in brilliant colours, they were decorated with birds and flowers, landscapes and portraits, all entwined with intricate designs. They jingled with tiny bells and decorative chains, their windows framed by panels of embroidered cloth. We would stand by the roadside as the lorries bore down on us in all their dazzling glory, a rolling exhibition of magnificent folk art. On the rooftop at the front of each truck, projecting over the cab, there was a hollowed-out space with bedding, where truckers would take it in turns to sleep on long journeys. At night Derek and I would bed down in these cubby holes and embark on a Zoetrope journey, watching the dark shapes of the countryside slipping past beneath a star-studded sky.

On arrival in the ancient city of Lahore we were accosted by a teenage girl. 'I go to 'Convent', she announced proudly. She paused. 'It is the Convent of Jesus and Mary, but it is known simply as 'Convent'. It is a very old school, very well known.' She went on to tell us about her siblings. 'I will take you to meet Sharif, my brother,' she said. 'He will invite you to his home.' Before long we were settled in Sharif's house, surrounded by the extended family. The young people took immense pleasure in showing us their city: the tomb of Jahangir, 17th-century Moghul emperor; the Fort with its marble palaces and mosques, decorated with mosaics and gilt; the Sheesh Mahal, or Palace of Mirrors, where the guide lit a candle in the night-black interior and sparkling mosaics of mirror-work and semi-precious stones exploded into a glittering galaxy. It was a visit to the Shalimar Gardens, however, that made me feel I had finally arrived in the Orient. As we walked among the pavilions, terraces and fountains, inhaling for the first time in months the scent of freshly-mown lawns, we watched the sunset transform the lakes and decorative water channels into shining pathways of fire. High above us the muezzin wailed from the nearby minarets and I felt as if I were tiptoeing through the pages of the Arabian Nights.

It was nearly the end of Ramadan and our host family was preparing for Id. Sharif took me to the bazaar and bought me a special present to celebrate, a delicate silver ring shaped like a flower. 'Come,' said the sisters. 'You will wear *salwar kameez.*' Helping me into the traditional clothes, they added a false plait to my hair and presented me with red sequinned slippers with curling toes. 'The shoes are for you,' they said, 'a gift.' In the meantime, Derek was being initiated into the intricacies of winding a turban. 'It's massive,' I exclaimed as he emerged looking small, gaunt and white beneath his headgear. The girls were concerned at my lack of earrings and insisted I should have my ears pierced. The smaller children encircled me, sitting tailor-fashion on the floor and giggling, as one of their big sisters pushed a threaded needle through each of my ear lobes, deftly knotting the string. 'Turn the loop every hour to keep the hole open,' she instructed. 'You'll get gangrene,' warned Derek. On our last night with the family, someone appeared with a tape recorder and some beer. It was our farewell party and, as ever, we spent it twisting the night away.

On Friday, 29 January 1965, we finally crossed the border into India. We had made it! We stood on the brink of that vast sub-continent with a fiver each to our names. In two months we had travelled over 4,000 miles at the cost of £15 each, less than £200 in today's money. The extraordinary warmth of the people in every country, their unsolicited hospitality and kindness, had not only enriched our journey but had made it possible. My first experience of the generosity inherent in foreign cultures, it would influence forever my attitudes to other nations.

CHAPTER FOUR

JAI HIND

An Alchemist's Dream

W E WERE GREETED IN INDIA by a corpulent customs officer, a Sikh with a giant moustache, who found us hysterically funny. The initial cause of his amusement was the whisky bottle top in Derek's lapel, but from a little chortling he descended into bouts of childish giggles, rocking back and forth at the mere sight of us. We were surrounded by Sikhs, all of whom joked and laughed; it was more like a party than a border crossing.

Our first Indian city was Amritsar with its magnificent Golden Temple, the holy of holies of the Sikh religion. I stood on the marble walkway which surrounded the sacred Pool of Immortal Nectar, and gazed in awe at the iconic temple across the water. A square, solid edifice topped by an ornate parapet with a cupola on each corner, the building rose dreamlike from the centre of the pool, where it rested on a marble platform approached by a long causeway. Its glory, however, lay in the fact that it was gilded with pure, burnished gold. It shone as if it had absorbed the rays of the sun, its brilliance spilling over into a reflection which turned the water as gold as an alchemist's dream.

Derek and I joined the throng crossing the causeway and entered the hallowed hall. The priests sat beneath a jewel-encrusted canopy, chanting verses from the Guru Granth Sahib – the holy book – and the wooden walls were inlaid with gold and silver. That evening a Sikh boy invited us onto the roof of his house from which we overlooked the nightly removal of the holy book from the temple. Below us the crowd surged past and the religious tome, accompanied by chanting, drum rolls and the discordant blowing of horns, was borne on its ceremonial passage to the Sikh Parliament. It was like something from the Old Testament; I felt as if at any moment the walls of Jericho might fall.

The temple lay at the centre of a larger complex, surrounded by elegant milky-white buildings, one of which housed a museum, where we came upon graphic paintings of Sikhs being murdered by the Mughals and also by the British. Until then I had never heard of the 1919 Amritsar massacre at Jallianwala Bagh, an attack on a nonviolent gathering of unarmed civilians, including women and children. In contravention of martial law imposed by the British, Sikhs had been celebrating their *baishakhi* festival when General Dyer arrived and ordered 50 riflemen to shoot into the crowd. Trapped within a walled garden, hundreds were slaughtered. Once again, I found myself appalled by British colonial history.

Shortly after our arrival in Amritsar, when Derek had lit up a cigarette in a street near the Golden Temple, a crowd of growling Sikhs had appeared, incandescent with rage and brandishing ornate axes on poles – smoking was proscribed by the Sikh religion. Later, when we had moved into the free hostel provided at the *gurdwara*, or temple complex, we were relaxing in our room when Derek announced that he needed a cigarette. 'You can't smoke here,' I protested. 'We're inside the temple precinct.' 'There aren't any windows,' he said. 'If we shut the door and have a fag, nobody will be any the wiser.' What we had failed to notice was a miniscule hole in the wall. A Sikh in the adjacent room saw a thin line of smoke emanating from this pinhole and called the guards. Once again we were confronted by a group of men brandishing staves and axes. We feigned innocence, were forgiven and issued with a warning.

Although monotheistic, Sikh theosophy aims to embrace all faiths and to provide free accommodation and food for all pilgrims. After a good night's sleep on a *charpoy* – the ubiquitous Indian bed consisting of a wooden frame strung with rope or string as a mattress – Derek and I joined the people standing in line for food. We were handed a metal bowl containing lentil dal and a chapati each. At that time we were the only foreigners eating, although these days, with mass tourism, the

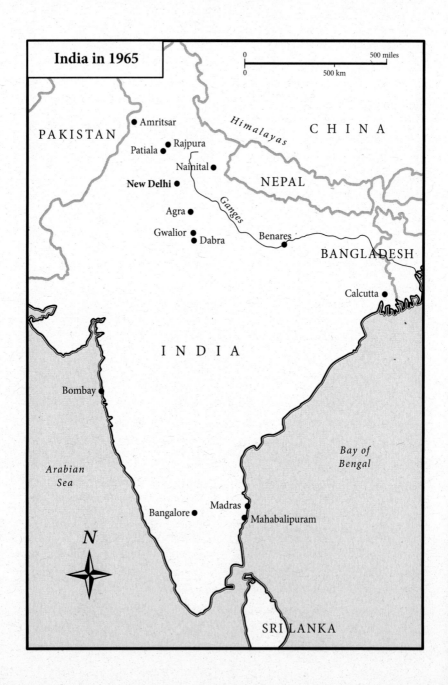

India in 1965

temple's community kitchen caters for thousands daily. Our meal over, we had to help with the washing up. I began to sluice the shiny, metal bowl with water and was instantly reprimanded for not being thorough; for the first time I was taught how to use grit from the ground to scour pots. I was to stay in other gurdwaras in India, and a decade later in east Africa, but none was ever as ethereal as that first glimpse of the Golden Temple, rising from the Pool of Immortal Nectar in a morning mist shot with gold.

A day or two later we hitchhiked to Patiala and entered a world we had assumed no longer existed. Our elderly Indian hosts were the well-off, cultured product of the Raj and they harked back to days long gone. 'When Edward, Prince of Wales, came here in 1922,' said our hostess, 'they lit up the pleasure gardens in his honour. It was a beautiful sight: brass bands, parades, so much pomp and ceremony.' 'Polo matches, shooting and pig-sticking,' added her husband, 'and the maharaja held a banquet in the Prince's honour.' Later Derek and I visited the park where a giant statue of Queen Victoria still dominated: *Queen of India, Empress of India, beloved of her people,* read the inscription.

Various relatives of our hosts were delegated to entertain us, first stop Patiala Flying Club, where we were taken up, one at a time, in a small plane. After a bird's eye view of the city we circled low over the maharajah's palace. 'The present maharajah's father was the first man in India to own an aircraft,' the pilot told me. 'He had a plane brought from the UK as early as 1911, a Wright Brothers model, and had an airstrip built.' We had lunch at a sports club, where there was a billiard room and a cricket match in progress and, later, in borrowed finery, we attended a Rotary Club dinner where the guest speaker was the Australian High Commissioner. The press had been invited to cover the event, but the journalists were far more interested in Derek's Beatle-style hair. 'Are you a yeah yeah yeah man?' they enquired. Derek shrugged: 'It's just the uncut look,' he replied.

After a day or two, we were introduced to Autar Singh, the son of our Patiala hosts, who whisked us away to his farm at Sardargarh, outside Rajpura. A handsome man, a decade my senior, his partner worked in the law courts at Patiala as the Punjab's first female lawyer. An unconventional Sikh, whose lifestyle was frowned upon by his relatives, Autar had flouted religious rules by cutting his hair and shaving off his beard. His turban, ready-wound like a hat, was kept on a hook by the door against unexpected callers. 'I'd better put this on,' he'd grumble, bunging it on his head as he went off to town on his scooter. Despite coming from a wealthy, aristocratic family, he had opted to live simply, away from the Anglophile trappings of his class. He described himself as a gentleman farmer, but he lived in a small house with only basic amenities. Meals were frugal, consisting largely of dal, home-grown vegetables and chapatis. The land surrounding his home was flat and fertile, the main crop being sugar cane which meant an abundance of snakes. More than once, as I sluiced myself down double-quick in Autar's primitive bathroom, I came across sloughed-off snake skins.

'Come with me,' said Autar one afternoon, 'I want to show you the farm.' He threw a Punjabi shawl loosely across his shoulders and, accompanied by his teenage niece, Gopi, we set off to check the wells and crops. Along the way we called on neighbours and chatted to farm labourers. Eventually we came across a group of agitated people; one of the workers had poured pesticide on his head to rid himself of lice. 'He's gone blind,' Autar told me, exasperated. 'I've warned them again and again about the dangers of pesticide. They know they must only use the tiniest amount on the crops, and yet he doused his entire head with the stuff.' Autar's workers lived in a cluster of dwellings near his house and he showed a paternal interest in their welfare. 'I've arranged for someone from the family planning clinic to come and talk to the women about contraception,' he told me. A couple of days later when a man was sent to undertake this task, Autar was furious. 'How could they be so stupid?!' he fumed. 'The women aren't going communicate with a man about such intimate matters.'

For a few days Derek and I relaxed with Autar on the flat roof of the farmhouse, reading, eating, playing gramophone records and talking long into the night. Our host was interesting, well-read, and was the first person to enlighten me regarding conditions in British India. 'No dogs, no Indians,' he told me. 'That's what they wrote up outside their clubs.' He talked about Partition and the inept carving up of the sub-continent by the British. 'Here, read this,' he said, handing me a copy of Khushwant Singh's *Train to Pakistan*, a novel which highlighted the division and horrors of that time.

Autar's only form of transport was a motor scooter, so when the time came for us to depart, he hitched a trailer to a tractor and put two large armchairs inside the trailer. 'Get in,' he said. 'We'll go to the station in style!' Sinking into the upholstery we bumped along the country tracks, Derek and I laughing at the eccentricity of our latest transport. We hadn't gone far, however, when Autar was stopped and quizzed at length by the police. 'We have to return to Sardargarh,' he said grimly. 'There's been an assassination.' Later we were to learn that Partap Singh Kairon, one of the architects of Independence, former Chief Minister of Punjab, and an iconic but controversial statesman and politician, had been shot dead on his way from Delhi to Chandigarh.

The following day we set off again. As we boarded the train for Delhi, Autar pressed another book into my hand. It was John Masters' *Bhowani Junction*. 'Good for a train journey,' he said. Another story which featured the turbulence of the British withdrawal from India, it portrayed the divided loyalties of the Anglo-Indian community which ran the rail networks.

Our days at Sardargarh had been golden. Autar and I had enjoyed a silent empathy which was to manifest itself in correspondence over the next 46 years, letters which he always signed off in the same way: *With that peculiar affection, Autar of Sardargarh.*

A parting of the ways

In New Delhi, Derek and I sat in the park writing letters and postcards thanking all the people between Turkey and India who had offered us hospitality. 'We can't afford this,' protested Derek, but I insisted. I could imagine the picture postcards being treasured, shown to neighbours, pinned to walls – such a small token for the generosity that had been showered upon us.

In those days travellers used Poste Restante to hold mail for collection at post offices in different countries. American Express offered a similar mail-drop service which, in this instance, we were using. The first time we called there I found a letter from Canadian John with whom we'd stayed in Zahadan, asking me to meet him in Bombay. On subsequent visits, there was a second then a third letter from John. I also picked up a lot of correspondence from family and friends. Derek was in a filthy mood, partly because of my letters from John, and partly because he had not received any mail himself. I wrote to John saying I would meet him in Bombay and then immediately tore up the letter making Derek furious at my prevarication. The next time we ambled along to American Express, there was John in person, hanging about in case I turned up. He had flown from Iran to Bombay and from Bombay to Delhi in search of me. What's more, Autar turned up at exactly the same time, bent on showing us around Delhi.

Derek loathed John and didn't want me to spend any time with him. 'But he's travelled nearly 2,000 miles to see me,' I said. Ignoring Derek's fury I set off with John to explore Delhi for an hour or so, after which we enjoyed a romantic meal in a restaurant. However, we hardly knew each other. *I think I've knocked about too much to be with someone as straight as John*, I wrote in my diary. After dinner we went a walk in the park. It was dusk and I allowed him to kiss me briefly. We were sitting on a bench chatting, when a policeman popped up from behind a bush, frantically blowing his whistle. 'I am arresting you for kissing in public,' he announced. We were astonished. Apart from the fact there was nobody in the vicinity, about half an hour had elapsed since our so-called misdemeanour which had been not only brief but chaste. 'You come with me to the police station,' said the cop, full of self-importance. The three of us set off at a brisk pace through the park. However, when he discovered the exit nearest the police station was padlocked, our captor merely shrugged and let us go.

By now it was dark and I needed to return to the Hindu temple where Derek and I were staying. 'Travel round India with me,' begged John. He had booked a vacation in order to spend time with me, but still I declined. 'You promised to travel with Derek to India,' he protested. 'Well, you're here; you're in India.' However, I remained loyal to Derek. I couldn't leave him suddenly, just like that, after all the things we had been through together. I felt guilty about both men and wondered how much of it was my own fault. I was flirtatious by nature and I had written John an affectionate letter after leaving Zahadan, but his dedication in pursuing me had taken me by surprise.

The following day Autar put us on a bus bound for Agra and we travelled south, having rows all the way. At Agra we slept on a balcony at the back of a small Sikh temple. Above our heads was a washing line hung with enormous Sikh drawers, the long loose undergarments required by their faith. Despite the intermittent chanting I slept well, awoken only once by a large hairy Sikh looming over me stroking my face. The next day Derek was less angry and we went to see the Taj Mahal. I had been bowled over by the Palace of Mirrors in Lahore and the Golden Temple in Amritsar, but the Taj Mahal, so familiar from photographs, was something of an anti-climax. Then, inside the tomb, came the shock. 'Here,' said the guide, pointing to a hole, 'here there was once the largest precious stone in the world. It is now in Britain.' The subject of the British looting jewels from the Taj Mahal and elsewhere in India is controversial and has been vehemently denied, but the guide had no doubt the British were guilty. No matter who was responsible, it was evident that rubies, emeralds and all kinds of gems previously inlaid in the walls of the Taj Mahal had been stolen over the years.

Two days later, hitchhiking outside Shivpuri, we were picked up by a gentleman in a large expensive car. He was HK Srivastava and, although we didn't realise it at the time, the son of Sir JP Srivastava, an arch loyalist of the British Raj, a member of the pre-Independence Council set up by the Viceroy, and one of the most influential men in India. HK, as he was known, ran several of his father's industries, and was on his way to his sugar plantation and processing factory in the village of Dabra. He invited us to stay in the factory guesthouse, a colonial-style bungalow with comfortable beds, where servants turned down our freshly laundered sheets. Our hosts were charming and, once again, old school; it was as if the Raj had never disappeared. We were treated to a splendid dinner, sparkling conversation, and luxury.

Early in the morning I wandered through the grounds of the factory. Elephants were pushing wagons of cane, the chimney was smoking, the cane juice bubbling. Bales of crushed stalks, drying in the sun, smelled sweet like hay. I stumbled on tiny waterfalls and irrigation channels, statues of Hindu gods, and trees in blossom. At the end of the drive, as the bullock carts creaked past, I saw the drivers stop and prostrate themselves before a grave. 'That's where my factory manager lies,' HK told me, 'a Dutchman, the man who created the gardens you saw. The workers loved him.' In the bungalow, tucked away in a dark corner, I came across a blue-and-white Delft tile and a tiny painting of Amsterdam.

It was in Dabra that HK introduced us to a Peace Corps volunteer called Tim who was in charge of a poultry project. The brainchild of President John F Kennedy, the American Peace Corps was calling upon the youth of America to promote world peace by living and working in developing countries. By the time I washed up in India, the organisation had been officially established for four years and the volunteers who were to befriend me were the first wave of idealistic youngsters recruited for the programme. With Tim, Derek and I caught the train to Gwalior, where we stayed with a Peace Corps teacher named Phil. A typical Indian settlement and sufficiently large that I thought I might find work, Gwalior seemed the ideal place to stop awhile.

As for Derek, Gwalior was the parting of our ways. I was sad, but also relieved. We were an ill-matched couple and I had not always treated him well, but we'd had some unforgettable experiences. Our journey on the road to India had changed my life.

Above left: Autar Singh
Above right: Derek, Autar, his brother Tari and *(left)* me, on the rooftop of the farm, Sardargarh, Rajpura, Punjab.

Above: Derek, me and Tari at Rajpura station.
Below: elephants and bullocks working at the sugar factory at Dabra.

Peace Corps Phil with one of his students.

Life with the Peace Corps volunteers Phil and Tim, at Gwalior, Madya Pradesh, India, 1965.
Above: *The new cook! Outside the kitchen with Phil's dog.* ***Right:*** *early morning shikar, Tim, centre, with rifle.*
Below: *with Walter Wenner and his monkey.* ***Far right:*** *Tim and Phil hauling water up to the roof.*

'Zis India,' moaned Walter, as we bumped our way along the jungle road on his scooter, 'Zis India, it is vun big latrine.' In addition to this daily mantra, brought on by the sight of peasants defecating by the roadside, Walter would repeatedly bewail local inefficiency, particularly power cuts: 'Poor India!' he would say, and then, acknowledging the Prime Minister's burden, 'Poor Shastri!'

By 6.30 every morning, I was on the back of Walter's scooter, riding the rough track to the moped factory where we both worked. The company, Saund Zweirad Union, which manufactured a variety of scooters, was the result of a German-Indian collaboration. Most of the factory workers were men from the surrounding villages. In addition, there were two or three German supervisors, one of whom was my friend, Walter, and the bosses were Sikhs who had trained in Germany. After spending a couple of weeks walking the streets of Gwalior in search of a job, and attending a couple of unsuccessful interviews at a textile mill and the gas company, I was finally employed as a secretary in the office of the moped factory, mostly because I had O-Level German and could get the gist of the correspondence involved.

I had another job as well. When I had arrived in Gwalior, Phil, the Peace Corps volunteer, had just sacked his cook. Even though I had little experience of cooking, I agreed to take over this role in return for temporary accommodation and a small contribution towards my food. I was installed in the tiny outhouse which had been my predecessor's bedroom. 'He might come back in the night and get you!' taunted Phil. 'After all, you have stolen his job.' In the room I had a string bed, or charpoy, and Phil squeezed in a chair and a small bookcase. There was no fan and at night I lay sweltering in a pool of sweat, but it was a joy being resident in one place after months of living out of a rucksack.

Kherapati Colony, where Phil lived, consisted of a dirt road lined by middle-class Indian homes. Basic in their amenities, they were nonetheless solidly built and spacious. The Peace Corps house, which had a flat roof, consisted of two bedrooms and a fairly large living space. There was a narrow hallway at the entrance to the house with a latticework window, open to the elements, which permitted air to circulate. The back yard, which formed the hub of the household, was lined on one side by outhouses consisting of my bedroom, a toilet, and a tiny room which served as a bathroom where we sluiced ourselves down with buckets of water.

At the end of the yard, the kitchen comprised little more than storage space and a couple of rings for cooking. There was no fridge, no proper sink, and water had to be fetched in buckets from a tap in the yard. The entire room was caked in black grease. As the new cook, it was clearly my responsibility to make the place more hygienic and for two days I scrubbed and scraped and swept, as legions of ants, cockroaches and other creepy-crawlies teemed across the floor fleeing my intrusive brush. 'You've done a great job,' said Phil, as I emerged exhausted, rivulets of perspiration running down my filthy face, and I felt that, for the time being at least, I had earned my place in his home.

Producing meals was baptism by fire. There were frequent visitors. Tim, who had introduced me to the household, often stayed over, as did others who drifted through Gwalior: Peace Corps volunteers and officials and the occasional traveller. Sometimes we entertained Indian teachers from Phil's school; at other times I cooked for friends and neighbours. I had to learn how to haggle in the market, how to turn local ingredients into acceptable meals, how to pluck poultry, gut game and skin rabbits. For someone who had cooked little but the occasional sausage or pork chop, this was a huge challenge. The kitchen was a sweatshop and the work a grind, but the lads for whom I prepared food were relaxed and fun and I enjoyed trying to please them. As for the dishes I produced, they gradually improved through trial and error. Once when I bought some berries in the market intending to stew them with sugar to make a dessert, I simmered them so long that they turned into jam. I accepted the resulting accolade without letting on that I had made the jam by accident.

Keeping the kitchen clean was a nightmare. It was so hot that within a few hours everything was transformed into a palette of degradation that was a constant surprise: bread turned bright blue or yellow; vegetables became red or orange slime. Any tea leaves left in a cup, or stray grains of rice, would attract armies of insects within seconds. One day I discovered the kitchen floor seething with ants the size of wasps. 'We'll have to burn them,' said Phil. He sloshed kerosene across the floor and dropped a lighted match onto the throbbing mass. The ants' bodies popped as they burnt.

Undertaking domestic chores was a fair way of paying for my accommodation and meals, but once I started work at the moped factory my duties seemed more onerous and exhausting. Most days I would be up at 5.30am to prepare breakfast before my departure for the factory. I would often work a 12-hour shift in the office with only 15 minutes for lunch. Then, as soon as I arrived home, there was cooking to be done, dishes to wash and the kitchen to clean. I was working too hard as well as feeling debilitated by the extreme heat. I slept badly.

The tiredness was accentuated by partying. There were magical Indian evenings when we would sit in the moonlight, drinking beer and singing. We were close friends with the family across the road, the D'Cruzes: Poppy, the Anglo-Indian mother; Pat, the Burmese father who worked for the Indian Air Force; and their two children. Burly and amusing, Pat was the focal point of all the fun and games. He played the guitar and roared out songs, his favourite being *When the saints go marching in…* Sometimes we would dance, twirling around the yard to Pat's strumming.

There were also quieter interludes when Phil and I would sit on the flat roof of the house where it was cooler, talking long into the night and putting the world to rights. All down the street we could see the silhouettes of neighbours relaxing in a similar fashion, escaping the stifling interior of their homes. A quick-witted, lithe-limbed young man, a couple of years my senior, Phil came across as exuberant and as crazy as everyone else, but an underlying conventional streak meant he could always be relied upon to be sensible. He taught me words and phrases in Hindi and talked about Indian gods and Indian history. When he brought up the war in Vietnam, I was embarrassed by my ignorance; it had been going on for a decade, but had barely crossed my radar.

Gwalior was a microcosm of Indian life and I grew to love the place with a passion. It was dominated by one of the largest and most famous forts in India, including a palace which housed a maharani; her husband, Jivajirao Scindia – the last ruling maharaja of Gwalior – had died in 1961. He had been known for his keen interest in model railways, and had employed a silver toy train which trundled around the palace dining table serving dishes, wines and chutneys to his guests. Sometimes the royal elephants were exercised in town, their swaying bulk, adorned with regalia, taking ponderous steps through the crowds. On a couple of occasions I witnessed a *sadhu*, or holy man, preaching from an elephant in the *maidan*, the main square.

In the markets, cobblers sewed shoes by hand, butchers held knives between their toes, and ancient men wearing Gandhi caps sat on big-wheeled carts selling their wares beneath huge black umbrellas. There were spices and sweetmeats, glittering fabrics and mirrorwork, vegetables, fruit and an array of potions sold by quacks. Wherever I went I was accompanied by a cacophony: metal workers bashing out pots and pans; the whirring of sewing machines; the cries of hawkers; the whine of the toy sellers' miniature stringed instruments; the tinkle of temple bells.

I was caught up in the turmoil of teeming humanity, a whirl of vibrant colour, noise, perfume and stench. Mud-coated wild pigs and water buffalos picked their way through the rubbish and chaos, together with emaciated sacred cows, their horns painted red and gold. There were country women in swinging skirts, arms and ankles heavy with bracelets, dwarfed by huge bundles of hay carried on their heads. Holy men brandished tridents and staves, their hair wild, faces daubed with paint, and bodies scantily covered with saffron-coloured cloth. Contrasting with the saris and silks, the silver and precious stones, were the rags worn by beggars, who whined and tugged and poked, exhibiting their deformities to foster sympathy. There was a beggar king who organised his followers, placing them where they could acquire the most alms. The saddest of these had a life-sized male head on a body little bigger than a baby's, and was deposited daily in a basket on the steps of the temple. I knew many of Gwalior's citizens: the tellers in the dusty bank; teachers and pupils from the school; the dhobi who beat the hell out of my clothes, slapping them against river rocks until the zips and buttons burst; and my friends at the scooter factory. I was caught up in a love affair with India and I felt part of it all.

I had embarked on a sporadic relationship with Tim, the Peace Corps volunteer we had met in Dabra, and who often stayed at the Gwalior house. Phil wasn't entirely happy about such goings-on in a Peace Corps residence; when Phil was away Tim would be attentive and affectionate, but on Phil's return he would become aloof, as if nothing had happened between us. Our favourite haunt in Phil's absence was a seedy bar in town where individual booths had been constructed out of packing cases and where privacy was provided by a piece of filthy sacking strung across the entrance. We would sit in our booth drinking beer and he would talk of the farm where he and numerous siblings had been raised in poverty. A stocky, blonde cornflake-packet lad, he was the embodiment of that farm boy image. When he showed me dog-eared photos of his family I thought how proud they must have been of his role in the Peace Corps; how introducing poultry farming to India would be an initiative they would appreciate.

At the moped factory I had my own problems. In order to employ a woman, they had been forced to obtain permission from head office in Delhi. Once again I was operating in a male world and, as ever, lavatories proved a problem: I was prone to walk in on men having a pee, none of whom bothered to lock the doors. The fact I had to complain highlighted me as an intruder in their male environment. I shared an office with Chandra, a bony clerk, officious and full of self-importance. 'These letters must be written again,' he admonished. 'Your English is extremely bad.' After that I taught myself to write the obsequious language required, correspondence straight out of Victorian England. Later he was to tear up some letters I had written regarding delayed orders. 'You have told them the truth,' he pronounced angrily. At the time I disliked the man and the way he treated me, but with hindsight I can understand how upset he must have felt at being usurped by a foreigner, particularly a young woman. In no time I was promoted over him, working for senior personnel, while he was relegated to mundane everyday business in a small back office. I was paid more than he was and my arrival must have scared him, an impoverished family man who needed job security.

The office servants were at my beck and call. Their job was to staple and clip things together, fetch files and make cups of tea. In between the power cuts, which would occur several times a day, I would regularly forget to use paperweights, and the whirring ceiling fans would whisk my correspondence skywards. Chandra would scowl and the staff would run around the room, leaping to rescue my paperwork. Many of the requests I made of the servants fell outside their remit, particularly rat hunts. My crusade against vermin in the office was deemed pointless and as they ran around armed with rulers and swatting at rats, they were reduced to giggles. Rodents were not the only wildlife. Snakes and scorpions were frequently found in or near the factory.

Ram Kishon, the senior servant, was the proud possessor of a pair of huge black lace-ups which he only wore when absolutely necessary. He would squat in the corner, picking his feet and smoking a bidi, a cigarette made of rolled leaves and tied with string. When the buzzer rang from the boss's office he would rise wearily, don the shoes, and shuffle off to answer the call of the Sahib. A few minutes later he would return, remove his footwear and start to relax, only to hear the infernal summons again. The shoes came on and off many times a day and caused him endless trouble, but they were his pride and joy, his status symbol. Much later I was shocked to learn that he had completed several years of education, more than the average Indian villager, and yet he was condemned to menial work, treated as the lowest of the low, and rewarded with incredibly bad pay.

One day the managing director arrived from Delhi. An elderly Sikh with an enormous paunch and huge temper, he shouted angrily at everybody, especially his two sons who were the factory managers. He decided to extend his visit by two weeks to oversee the smooth running of the business. The place was transformed. Everyone crept silently from room to room, whispering and glancing nervously towards the great Sahib's door. A meeting was arranged and we sat around the table, wilting in the heat. 'Respected Papa Sahib,' whined the sons. 'You shut up,' he yelled, and swore profusely in Punjabi. The session continued with ranting and raving: some spoke Hindi, some Punjabi and the German supervisors whispered to each other in German. 'How can Miss Steele take the minutes if you don't speak English?' he yelled. The meeting reached a crescendo when he brought his fist down on the table, knocking over a glass of water. The papers on the desk swam and everyone tried in vain not to laugh.

Eventually the time came for his departure. We said our farewells and as his jeep roared away in a cloud of dust everyone let out a sigh of relief. My best friend in the office was a gentle Sikh, a young man who was usually reticent and quiet. To my amazement he started mimicking his boss who had just departed. He banged on the table, jumped up and down on the sofa shouting 'Miss Steele, Miss Steele, take the minutes please!' In the midst of this someone yelled 'Smoke! Smoke!' The factory was on fire. 'Thank goodness it is after the big Sahib's departure,' they laughed, as they ran to and from the well, filling small buckets to douse the flames.

I came to love working in that factory and I had to deal with clients all over India. To contact them I had to dial the local telephone exchange: 'Operator, operator,' I would shout and eventually someone would come through on the crackly line and dial the number I requested. 'I'm phoning about order number so and so...' I would say, but nobody used the familiar Alpha Bravo Charlie Delta, but rather the names of Indian cities: Agra Bombay Calcutta Delhi… I had got into the swing of doing things the Indian way and I had become firm friends with most of the factory staff. Even Chandra had come to accept me.

Sometimes there would be a factory football match with teams made up of the workers and their German supervisors. I knew nothing about football, but occasionally I went and watched the matches. 'Miss Steele can be the referee,' they announced one day. 'Memsahib, memsahib, will you be our referee?' I had to admit my ignorance of football and the fact that I was merely a groupie.

I socialised quite a lot with Walter who lived just around the corner from me and the Peace Corps boys. He was round and pink and his conventional manner belied his 28 years. He would cook amazing meals and ply me with alcohol, but my visits were rarely relaxed; Kuni, his pet monkey, would attack me, leaping onto my head, screeching and tugging my hair. One evening the monkey leapt over the wall and into our midst dragging a sari behind her. It took Walter a day or two to locate the irate owner of the garment. Despite the overpowering heat, Walter could occasionally be seen in his national costume: Bavarian lederhosen with embroidered braces. He was a strange companion, not least because he seemed to retain a lingering admiration for the Nazi regime. The Germans at the factory were mostly scathing about the competence of their Indian workers, but there was a young lad working with Walter who was an exception. 'A very good boy,' said Walter, 'clever, efficient…' He decided to honour this young man with a public presentation; he would bestow upon him the medal which had been awarded to his own father for service to the Third Reich – a medal with a swastika, which he knew the lad would revere as a religious symbol.

Besides Walter and the Peace Corps boys, I socialised with an extraordinary range of people. I was entertained by the bank manager and his family, by big-wigs from the factory, by people from the Indian Air Force and by HK Srivastava and his wife, who hosted an overnight dinner party for me and Tim at the guest bungalow in Dabra. Sometimes teachers from Phil's school were our hosts, one couple honouring us with a performance of Indian classical music.

On one occasion an Indian army officer took me to the cinema to see a film about the Sino-Indian border conflict which had taken place a couple of years previously. To my astonishment, the audience found the movie hysterically funny. Despite the soldiers on-screen bursting into song, and my host overwhelming me with tedious details of the tactics employed, I thought the film was fascinating. It was April 1965 and the catchphrase *Hindi Chini bhai-bhai* – Indians and Chinese are brothers – was being bandied about, as China once again amassed troops on India's northern border and broadcast the slogan over loudspeakers. Also heading for a war with Pakistan, India was in a precarious position. All leave for troops had been cancelled and trains were packed with soldiers. 'Surely China wouldn't dare attack India,' I observed to Phil, 'India would have the backing of Britain and the USA.' 'India's more likely to go to war with Pakistan,' he replied. 'Well, if we go to war, the British High Commission might give me a free passage home!' I said flippantly.

Sometimes with Phil and Tim, and with people from the factory, I went on picnics to lakes in the countryside. My swimsuit, which had been stolen by the Turkish truck drivers, had never been replaced and I shocked my hosts by leaping into the water fully clad; the German matrons married to the factory supervisors were clearly put out by my lack of decorum. Occasionally we set up camp in the lee of ruined Hindu temples. Laced with lianas and occupied by monkeys and parrots, they were similar to those depicted a couple of years later in Disney's *Jungle Book*. A favourite haunt was the lake at Tikanpur where a maharajah had built a palace in the shape of a ship. I was told that in its heyday it had been the site of exotic parties and debauchery and that the maharajah had suffered a premature death caused by wine, women and song. I found the palace and its fables romantic.

In those days, little thought, if any, was given to animal conservation and it would be a decade before the question of animal rights was raised. Nearly everyone we knew in Gwalior went on *shikar*, hunting, and to me it felt like being caught up in an amazing Indian adventure. The surrounding countryside, referred to as jungle, consisted of miles of arid soil interspersed with small rocky outcrops. Dried-up thorn bushes and brush dominated, but now and again we would come across a flame tree flaunting its blaze of brilliant orange blossom. Sometimes we would set off at dawn; at other times we would travel into the jungle at night, the lights on our jeep picking out the odd panther, as well as deer, porcupines, jackals and hyenas. We shot fowl of various kinds, deer and rabbit, all of which found their way to the cooking pot. I even served up a delicious roast peacock, a target we should have boycotted, it being a sacred bird. It was tiger country and from time to time villagers reported the theft of livestock. On one *shikar* our Indian companions suspected a tiger in the vicinity. I joined the beaters and started thrashing the undergrowth, but thankfully none materialised. One day, after a picnic at a fortified farm house in the jungle, the men set up old cans for me to use as target practice. I was firing a rifle and just becoming adept at hitting my target, when a breathless man appeared. 'Dacoits!' he shouted. 'Dacoits are coming. Go! Go now!' Dacoits were bandits who were rumoured to murder, rape and pillage. We made a quick exit.

And always there was the ever-increasing searing, shimmering heat. The temperature climbed daily reaching well over 37°C in the shade. In a letter home to my parents I mentioned that it had hit 43°C. They wrote back that in colonial times the British had escaped to the hill stations when it was hot and enquired why I had not done likewise! At the factory the servants threw water on the cuss-cuss grass matting which covered the windows so that any air passing through the mats would render the interior cooler. With excessive heat our thirst increased and boiling water became a time-consuming daily occupation. Stored in earthenware pots which sweated, the water remained surprisingly cool.

One week we revelled in freak weather. It was as if the heat had reached its zenith and could do nothing but explode. Electric-blue lightning sliced the sky and then the rains came, a deluge like nothing I had witnessed before. Through the latticework window in the hallway we watched our portly neighbour, Pat D'Cruze, wearing only his striped pyjama shorts and brandishing an umbrella, dancing joyfully in the rain. Later that night I followed suit, pirouetting on the rooftop as the rain fell, whirling in ecstasy with Phil's little dog. A day or two later the respite was over. The world steamed and returned to normal.

By now I was undertaking other activities in the Peace Corps household, particularly when Phil and Tim went on leave. I lent out library books to Phil's students, sweet little boys who would arrive at the house keen to practise their English, and I sold Tim's eggs to people who came to the door. There were also Tim's poultry deliveries. 'Over 500 chickens arriving tonight,' he would say. 'Wanna come to the station with me?' When I accompanied him on a poultry mission I was of little help, but poultry management was all part of life at Kherapati Colony. If Indian teachers from Phil's school turned up when he was out, I would enjoy providing them with cups of tea and talking to them, and when Phil departed for a vacation in Nepal he left me instructions regarding deliveries: 'A bookcase,' he said, 'a table, and possibly a baby monkey.' 'A monkey!' I exclaimed, but to my relief the animal never materialised; I suspect it had been put on Phil's list as a joke.

After a few weeks in the Peace Corps house I moved into a rented room next door, an arrangement deemed more appropriate than living with two young men. I had arrived in Gwalior penniless and despite cooking for Phil and working at the factory, money remained incredibly tight. I budgeted carefully, even counting the cost of my weekly airmail letter home. I had to pay rent for my new lodgings, rent for an electric fan, and a small contribution towards my food. My concern was how I would eventually fund my journey back to England. I continually checked out shipping, charter flights and even transport overland, but I never had any prospect of raising the sum required. '*I could work my passage on a Scandinavian ship,*' I proposed in one letter. '*Only Scandinavians take on women as crew.*' I didn't want to go home anyway; I was far too excited about India to abandon my adventures. In letters to my parents I was continually postponing my return.

I had just celebrated my 22nd birthday – in honour of which Phil and Tim had decorated the room with peacock feathers and lighted candles – when I began to have problems. One of these was the inappropriate behaviour of my boss at the factory, a Sikh manager married to a German woman. The factory being way out in the countryside, I was reliant on people from work giving me a lift home and when he kept insisting that I stay behind with the men and drink I had no option but to remain. Much as I liked a party, I rarely wanted to stay on after such a long day's work. One evening he tried to kiss me. I beat him off furiously, but after that my role as his personal secretary was awkward. The next disaster involved two Lipton Tea salesmen who invited me for a picnic at a dak bungalow, a guest house in the countryside. I knew them quite well and was astonished when they lunged at me simultaneously. I screamed, and when a servant appeared they let me go and took me home. Despite these events, I still failed to see what was coming; the majority of Indian men I knew had been friendly and respectful and had introduced me to their families.

When the shit hit the fan, I was caught by surprise. Walter, as he had done many times, invited me to a picnic with his friends, both Indian and German. One man declined, saying his wife would not permit him to go if I were to be one of the guests. Another followed suit. Reluctantly, Walter passed on this information. It was serious. To cap it all, an Indian woman who lived nearby had started inviting me to drink tea with her. She lived in a poor, mud dwelling and, although she spoke no English and we could barely communicate, I was flattered. 'Why are you visiting that woman?' enquired Walter sternly. 'She's a prostitute.' I'd had no idea of her profession and would not have really cared had I known, but it was another log on the fire.

I had earned a reputation which, as far as I was concerned, I did not warrant. I had occasionally succumbed to Tim's attentions, but that was in the privacy of my own home. I had partied a lot and drunk too much, but not in public. I racked my brains to think of what else had caused this dilemma: wearing skirts and dresses that were too short for India;

leaping into lakes fully clothed; socialising with men unchaperoned. I began to realise I had behaved inappropriately for a woman in India. It wasn't surprising. In the space of a few months I had gone from living with bums on the beach in Eilat to mixing with conventional Indian society. I had failed miserably to make the transition.

I sat crying in my room trying to decide what to do. Part of me wanted to sit it out, to continue my life in Gwalior until my bad reputation was obliterated; to run away was to appear guilty. However, my concern was for the good work of my Peace Corps friends. I knew their endeavours and reputations would suffer through their association with me. I also knew they thought it better if I moved on. In the end, it was because of them that I left.

At the factory I told them my father had summoned me home, a lie I thought they would comprehend. On the day of my departure they arranged a party. We sat in the office eating sweetmeats and drinking cokes. Other than my bosses, they had all become good friends. 'We have arranged a photographer,' they said. We sat in stiff rows outside the factory. The camera was poised. 'Stop!' someone shouted. 'Where is your bouquet?' They had forgotten to give it to me! Phil and Tim threw a goodbye party for me as well. Pat D'Cruze played his guitar and we all sang *When the saints...* The next day I set off to Delhi, riding pillion on a scooter Tim was delivering to a friend. The last thing I saw was Walter, dressed in his lederhosen, pursuing his monkey down the street.

I never went back. Months later I was walking down the street in New Delhi when a man accosted me. I hesitated; I had no idea who he was. 'You're that woman from Gwalior, aren't you?' he said and he and his companion giggled.

Delhi

The walls were lined with ancient military tomes. All the 19th-century trappings of the British Raj remained untouched: the high-ceilinged room with its heavy furniture; the massive paintings in their gilt frames;

the heavy fans which had cooled many a British officer as he indulged in a chota peg. I stood ill-at-ease in my borrowed sari, as young Indian army officers clicked their heels and bestowed upon me the old-fashioned charm befitting a lady who had entered their mess.

I had met these young men within a couple of weeks of arriving in Delhi. Tim had deposited me in the hostel for Peace Corps volunteers, but I had quickly found lodgings with an Indian widow. The army officers were friends of the Indian girl who rented the room adjacent to mine. Our landlady felt responsible for the two young women in her care and tried to ensure we mixed with the right company. I found her concern stifling, but these escorts apparently met with her approval. We went out with them on several occasions, dining and dancing and visiting the theatre. They were charming, but I found them a strain. Similar outings followed in the company of a suave and handsome young Indian, one of the directors of the General Electricity Company in Delhi. He was interesting and attentive and wanted to spend more time with me, but all these dates were a throwback to a world I had left far behind. I could be ladylike and charming if I had to be, but I was moving in elite circles. It was all too conventional.

Two days after arriving in Delhi I had landed a day's secretarial work for publisher Prentice Hall, work for which I had been well paid – *fifty chips for doing virtually nothing*, I wrote in the vernacular. However, I needed a proper job. In Gwalior a woman from All India Radio had seen me in the bazaar and wound down the window of her car. 'What on earth are you doing here?' she'd asked and, interested in my story, she had stopped and interviewed me. 'Come and see me if you're ever in Delhi,' she said. She was out of town, but I decided to pop into All India Radio anyway to see if there were any jobs going. On arrival I found the radio station surrounded by barbed wire and a soldier in a sentry box denied me entry. 'But I'm from the BBC,' I lied. 'Please tell them there's someone here from the BBC.' I gained admission and could truthfully say I had been a former employee of the BBC. As luck would have it they were about to conduct auditions for announcers and within 10 minutes I was sitting with 15 hopefuls, most of whom spoke heavily-accented Indian English. There was one other English applicant, a Geordie whom I could barely understand and whose accent left the Indians present nonplussed. I got the job, and during the months which followed broadcast folk tales for the All India Radio English Service.

My next port of call was IBM where I had heard there was a vacancy for a senior secretary. After three long interviews, a shorthand and typing test and a rigorous medical, I started work organising training schools for IBM personnel.

By now I had reverted to intermittent socialising with Peace Corps volunteers, and so it was I landed a voluntary job as well, working in the Peace Corps egg shop at weekends. Together with Carl, a Hawaiian volunteer, I graded, sorted and sold eggs and totted up the accounts at the end of the day. It was incredibly hot and I worked hard, believing that I was doing something useful for India. I loved being part of a street of Indian shops, dealing with the customers, chasing off scallywags who would creep up behind me and try to nick coins from the money drawer. Sometimes I rode pillion on Carl's scooter through the Delhi traffic, collecting and delivering eggs. We would weave in and out of bullock carts, horse-drawn tongas, bicycle rickshaws and handcarts piled high with goods, skidding to avoid the sacred cows which wandered at will. 'Why do you sell eggs?' asked my colleagues at IBM, waggling their heads from side to side in that Indian way, bemused at this menial occupation. 'Which came first?' they would ask, giggling. 'Was it the egg or was it the chicken?'

I had only been in New Delhi a month. I had landed on my feet, but I pined for Gwalior and it had been sad seeing Tim off at the railway station, particularly as I was forced to do so twice. Delhi Station was teeming: beggars and hawkers; *chai wallahs* with trays of sweet milky tea served in disposable clay cups; porters clad in knee-length scarlet tunics, loping along with towers of suitcases on their heads; opulent travellers with servants, and the not-so-rich who were to travel third class. The latter had a trick. They would hike along the track until they found the stationary train in a siding, then climb inside the third class carriages and bolt the doors from the inside. By the time the train arrived at the station the compartments were packed. Sometimes the only way to board was to throw your luggage through the window and then follow suit, providing you had someone to give you a bunk-up from the platform, or haul you up from inside. The first time I tried to see Tim off, he had failed in this attempt and had to try again the following day.

I had experienced Indian trains myself and on a couple of occasions I had opted to travel in the women's carriage where I sat on the floor amidst breast-feeding mothers, livestock, bundles, pots and pans. On one journey I had even managed to clamber up into the luggage rack which had proved more comfortable. Many passengers tried their luck on the roof. Once I was on a long distance train, squashed up against the door, when I heard tapping on the window and an urgent voice saying: 'Memsahib! Memsahib! Please be letting me inside!' Our train was travelling at speed and there was no way I could open the door. It was terrifying seeing the distraught man clinging to the outside. Eventually I saw his feet swinging wildly in mid-air as someone on the roof hauled him to safety.

With Tim gone, my last connection with Gwalior was severed and I embraced city life to the full. The IBM courses were run from a suite in a large hotel. I was dropped off in the morning by a driver and collected by the same vehicle in the evening. During that first month, my boss, Devesh, and I worked closely in an environment far removed from a conventional office set-up. We shared lunch and multiple coffee breaks, relaxing on the sofa in the hotel suite and talking nineteen to the dozen. A shy man, a decade my senior, he had studied in Europe where he had been subjected to racism which had imbued him with bitterness. Before long, he began bringing me newspapers, articles and a variety of literature to read and discuss. Like Autar before him, he seemed bent on feeding my intellect. 'I can't believe a girl like you never went to university,' he kept saying. I lapped up this attention. I found his conversation stimulating and his gentle manner attractive.

Street scenes in Gwalior.

Above: *working for the IBM Application School, New Delhi, aged 22; still showing an inappropriate amount of leg for India.*
Left: *Dancing with Indian Army officer, New Delhi.*
Below: *diplomatic encounters, August 1965.*

Right: pony-trekking, Nainital, in the Himalayas.
Below: temples by the sea, Mahabalipuram, Madras.

Below: paddyfields, Southern India. *Below right:* Paul, SS Devonia, Bombay to Genoa, December 1965.

I worked hard for that first training school. There were 16 students, friendly and appreciative young Indian men who attended the conferences and lectures. I prepared the paperwork, helped select film clips, ordered refreshments, dealt with correspondence and wrote the final report. At the end of the course there was a dinner during which I was thanked formally for my contribution. A professional photograph was taken of the participants with me sitting in the centre of the front row. My boss was subsequently reprimanded for inviting me to appear in the picture. 'It's because you're a woman,' he explained. However, looking at the photograph now, I am not surprised at IBM's displeasure; I am, still, inappropriately dressed for India and showing rather too much leg.

The first training school completed, I set about preparing everything for the next course. 'We'll be travelling all over India,' I was told. 'You'll be flying to Calcutta, Madras, Bombay...' I couldn't believe my luck. *I would be mad to return to England,* I wrote to my parents, *when I can see the whole of India at IBM's expense.*

I was spending most of my time in New Delhi, rather than in the old city. I loved the elegant colonial architecture of the Government Secretariat, the lawns and lanes radiating out from India Gate. Gazing across that large open space, I would imagine days gone by: the Viceroy, potentates, soldiers in their livery, elephants in full regalia. A couple of months after I arrived in Delhi I was to spend an afternoon in elevated circles myself, when I attended the president's Independence Day garden party with an IBM delegation. I milled about in the company of ambassadors, politicians, and the high and mighty from across the sub-continent. Everyone drooped in the oppressive heat, perspiration creating unsightly dark patches on their finery. When I finally shook hands with Prime Minister Shastri, his size belied his importance; a miniature man, he barely came up to my shoulders.

I lived in a social whirl: from IBM dinners in posh hotels and dates with Indian army officers, to cheap meals with Peace Corps volunteers. I was taken to the cinema, to the ballet, and to the theatre. My friend

Kumar ran an art gallery where I listened to poems and folk music, ancient songs of the wandering minstrels of Bengal, and with Carl from the egg shop, I attended a concert by Ravi Shankar. Things came to a head when my landlady's cook threatened to resign. 'He is woken up by your coming in late every evening,' she complained. 'He has to get out of bed and unbolt the door.' 'Perhaps you could give me a key?' I asked tentatively. 'A key!' she said. 'Oh no, that's out of the question.' Given that I was being exceptionally polite and careful in my lodgings and was always home well before midnight, it was frustrating. Nonetheless, I was comfortable in the widow's home where my rent was cheap and I was provided with a delicious breakfast which always included fresh mango. She was a kind woman who had fallen on hard times and was trying to keep up appearances. Her disapproval of my nocturnal socialising was tempered by the fact I was picked up daily by the IBM chauffeur.

As the summer progressed, the temperature rocketed. At the end of June the early morning average was 41ºC in the shade. Four people in the city died of cholera in one week and there was talk of typhoid. I rushed off to the IBM doctor to get my jabs updated. My hair was dank and my face and neck permanently mottled with an unsightly heat rash. In time, the skies turned leaden and towering dust-laden clouds obscured the relentless blue, before disintegrating into sand storms which clogged the urban pores of the city. When the monsoon brought relief I ran barefoot through the park with my Peace Corps friend, Jim, dancing in the downpour until we were both soaked to the skin. But with the rains came bugs and insects, and an army of cockroaches invaded my bedroom. The monsoon was short-lived, resulting in famine: rice was rationed and people in the east were reduced to eating jute leaves.

After I had been in Delhi a few weeks, I was invited to live with Devesh and his family. Initially, I was reluctant, but he was persuasive and because it was an IBM residence I could live rent-free. He and I were spending more and more time at IBM dinner parties and functions, where he sometimes made speeches and I was introduced to visiting executives. The venues were luxurious and I no longer dressed in the shabby, faded clothes I had worn in Gwalior. With my IBM salary I had been able to order tailor-made outfits in the bazaar: an array of everyday cotton dresses; a lightweight suit; a saffron-coloured evening dress with a high collar; a cream outfit made of wild silk. Rather late in the day, I had also bought salwar, the modest leggings Indian women wear beneath tunics, and occasionally I wore a sari. I enjoyed socialising, was efficient at my job, and I thrived on the additional responsibility. However, looking back, I realise I was being given more focus than was appropriate.

At the height of summer, I joined my boss and his family on holiday in the foothills of the Himalayas. Although none of us had ridden before, we spent hours every day on horseback exploring the steep mountain trails, accompanied by cheeky pony boys who ran beside us, swatting our horses' backsides with sticks. We were staying in Nainital, a pretty little town with houses stacked up the hillside above a lake. On the shoreline there was a temple where women poured squashed banana on a phallus-shaped stone, the lingam dedicated to the god Shiva. There were flowers, garlands and incense, and temple bells that tinkled in the bright thin air. Not far from the temple, the townsfolk set up a *mela*, a small country fair, with colourful stalls and a wooden, hand-cranked Ferris wheel. Gradually the mountain people began arriving in town in their party clothes. Small of stature, with elvin features and eyes more reminiscent of Tibet than India, the men wore skull caps and embroidered waistcoats; the women, bangled and bespangled, had heavy rings through their noses. Stalls overflowed with fruit and sweetmeats, treats and titbits. At night coloured lanterns were lit and music floated towards the distant mountain peaks. It was a goblin market from a children's storybook.

I enjoyed the reprieve from the heat, the Himalayan mists, the forests and cool mornings. One day I rose early and was walking around the lake alone when a holy man, virtually naked, with matted hair and a painted face, jumped out from behind a bush almost on top of me. I started, then, pulling myself together, I folded my hands in a nervous greeting: 'Namaste-ji,' I said, inclining my head. There wasn't a soul in sight. I knew that rogues and charlatans sometimes posed as holy men and I was scared, but the sadhu approached in silence and laid his hands upon my head, producing in me a feeling of utter calm.

Eventually we set off for home and arrived in Delhi at night to find everything in darkness. At first we assumed there was a power cut, but then we were flagged down by the police. 'Turn off the car lights,' they said. 'There may be air raids. We are at war.' From April 1965 there had been skirmishes between Pakistan and India. Now, as a result of Pakistan's attempt to infiltrate Indian-administered Kashmir and foment insurgency, the tensions had escalated into a full-scale war. The Kashmir issue wasn't new. It was the second major conflict between the two countries over the status of an area which had been disputed ever since Britain created India and Pakistan in 1947.

I had never lived in a war zone before. There were air-raid warnings every night. A local civil defence warden was appointed and a list of do's and don'ts issued: *during bombing put cotton wool in your ears and a rolled-up handkerchief between your teeth; lie flat on the ground with your face downwards; keep all baths filled with water for firefighting.* India had bombed Karachi, Rawalpindi, Lahore and Dacca and a Pakistani plane had been shot down over Delhi. The press wrote about a Pakistani spy who had been arrested and of Pakistani parachutists landing in Punjab. My thoughts turned to Autar on his farm: 'He'll probably round them all up, give them a cup of tea and discuss Chinese philosophy,' I joked. Mosques were now heavily guarded and Hindu-Muslim riots broke out in Calcutta. Land forces were engaging in huge tank battles at Chawinda and even the navy had joined the fray. It was full-on combat.

Foolishly, I was excited. What an adventure! There were no international flights and therefore no mail from overseas. I sent my parents a telegram informing them I was safe and telephoned the British High Commission to ensure I would not miss out on any evacuation. 'There are plans in place,' they told me. 'We'll contact you if things get worse,' but I never got that free trip home. One of the things I found frustrating was that the air-conditioning – 'eskishion' as the servants called it – drowned out the sound of the nightly air-raid sirens. While I was sleeping through all the drama, other people, ignoring civil defence advice, were on their rooftops listening to the anti-aircraft guns and watching the searchlights picking out Pakistani planes.

In October, when the fighting was over, the Hindu festival of Dussehra was celebrated – an occasion when good triumphs over evil and the killing of certain demons from Hindu mythology is enacted. That year the crowds added their modern enemies to the cast of evil: effigies of China's leader, Mao Tse-Tung, together with President Ayub Khan of Pakistan and his supporter, President Sukarno of Indonesia, were set alight alongside the traditional villains. As for the war, the supposed cessation of hostilities was drawn up during international negotiations in Tashkent the following January, but the conflict had rendered Kashmir an intractable issue and enmity over the region continues until this day.

At the beginning of October, a fire in the IBM house where we lived caused considerable damage and we were evacuated. I returned temporarily to the Peace Corps hostel where I had stayed on arrival in Delhi. One day I was walking down the street when an Indian woman started chatting to me over her garden wall. 'My name is Ramita' she said. 'I'm a secretary at the Italian embassy.' 'Do you know of any lodgings?' I asked. 'I'm looking for somewhere to rent.' 'Come and live with me,' she said. 'I have a spare room. You can move in immediately.'

Pushing 40, Ramita had given her best years to an Italian boyfriend who had dumped her and returned to Italy; I had inadvertently landed myself with an inappropriate companion, at least in Indian terms. My biggest problem, however, had nothing to do with Indian morality: it was the fact that her servant belonged to an inferior caste and was forbidden to touch her food, whereas I, the casteless one, was expected to sit for hours in the back yard, grinding up spices. My new landlady proved garrulous and exhausting. She was also bossy. 'You are washing in cold water,' she exclaimed. 'This is a very dirty habit.' Despite the oppressive temperature, I was forced to heat up water on the stove in the kitchen.

One evening I returned home to find that Ramita had invited me to a dance at the Italian Embassy. We were to be accompanied by her latest Italian boyfriend. She decked me out in a sari and before long a car arrived to collect us. I was good at ballroom dancing and when her escort invited me to dance we whirled around the floor in perfect unison. Ramita was jealous. When we arrived home she went berserk, her fury directed not at me, but at the man concerned. She screamed and tore at her bed sheets, ripping them with her teeth. She ground her jewellery into the floor with her heels, and threw her belongings across the room. She looked old for her years and pathetic and I felt genuinely sorry for her. 'Can I do anything to help?' I enquired nervously. 'Fetch my tranquillisers and a glass of water,' she demanded, but when I handed them to her she smashed the glass against the wall. I was astonished, upset and inadequate. The next day she behaved as if nothing had happened and she never lost control again, at least in my company. I went on living with her, despite the requisite grinding of masala.

Meanwhile, the IBM education department had been moved to a small, private house and, because of the war with Pakistan, all the courses we had set up had been cancelled. My job had become virtually redundant. On top of this, my boss was in hospital seriously ill and I was working intermittently for someone else. I kept the work going, optimistically making plans for courses that might take place the following year, but my job had become mundane.

One day I came across Meghraj, one of the servants, poring over an English text book written in Hindi – a book which subsequently proved to be full of mistakes. He had never been to school, but had taught himself to write English script and to speak enough rudimentary English to run small errands in an office. I decided to help him. Every day, an hour before I started work, he would settle down at my desk for an English lesson, overwhelming me with the smell of garlic and coconut hair oil. Emaciated to the point of near-starvation, his stunted growth, protruding teeth and pockmarked skin were the hall-marks of poverty. At 20 years old, only two years my junior, he highlighted the lottery of birth, the yawning chasm between his world and mine. He was keen, so keen that in the office I no longer enjoyed a spare moment to myself. He hounded me for more lessons and begged for extra time at weekends and holidays. However late I stayed out the night before, I always ensured I didn't disappoint him, arriving promptly for his early morning lesson. When I finally left IBM and was being served the usual farewell coke and cake, the door opened and Meghraj appeared, accompanied by his family, who bestowed upon me garland after garland of marigolds.

When Devesh recovered and returned to work, he expressed regret that the courses had been cancelled and that I would no longer be able to travel throughout India at IBM's expense. 'Would you like to visit my family in Calcutta?' he enquired. 'They would show you the city.' I was delighted. 'Maybe I could even stop over at Benares on the way?' I asked. Also known as Varanasi, Benares was India's oldest city, its spiritual capital, a place I had long wanted to visit. Within a few days he handed me an air ticket acquired in his name. 'Are you sure it's ok for me to use this?' I asked. 'Yes, of course,' he said, 'no problem.' Other than one domestic flight from London to Glasgow in 1962, I had never flown anywhere in my life, so I assumed he knew what he was talking about.

I flew to Benares where I stayed with two Peace Corps volunteers who lived in a big old house in the city centre. I wandered the alleyways and visited ancient temples and ruins overrun by monkeys. A Hindu who dies in Benares is believed to attain instant *moksha*, or release, followed by a state of *nirvana*. I was aware that people travelled from all over India to die in the holy city, but when I actually stumbled on the sick and dying it was a shock. They formed long queues which snaked their way towards wide flights of steps, the *ghats*, which descended to the sacred waters. Lepers, cripples and people who were barely alive, crawled, shuffled and dragged themselves along the ground, or were carried, in the direction of the great Ganges and their ultimate demise. When their time came, their corpses were loaded onto funeral pyres, set alight and pushed into midstream on a flaming raft. They did not always burn; either the relatives lacked funds for sufficient fuel, or else the river doused the flames before the cremation was complete. From a rowing boat, I watched limbs floating past, birds pecking at the flesh. A baby and then a man sailed by, face downwards, their bodies translucent, white below the waterline and a putrid yellow above. The boatman croaked rhythmically the only three English words he knew: 'Body, flesh, crow.'

Those who washed in this water, drank it, or bathed in it, could count on absolution from their sins. And so they gathered, the naked holy men, the women wrapped in brilliant saris, chanting and praying, scattering petals across the surface of the river. Men filled tiny brass pots used for ablutions, sluicing away their sins. Young boys splashed and played, ducking each other and diving from the ghats, as the dhobis washed laundry, spreading a brilliant patchwork of garments on the steps to dry in the sun.

I bought holy necklaces of knobbly sandalwood beads that I might remember the strangeness. I watched the early morning mists rise over waters which had begun their journey over a thousand miles away, ice cold and glacial pure, before acquiring the filthy debris of death. I looked on and waited until the noonday sun scorched the sky and the religious chanting from the bathers seemed to fade away wraithlike in the heat. Then I turned away from the filth and the crowds and sought out the lawns and cloisters of Benares Hindu University, which had spawned India's freedom fighters and politicians, poets and lawyers, scholars who had shaken up the world order. As those who had passed on were borne down the River Ganges towards the ocean, those of us whose time had not yet run its span, drank tea on the manicured lawns of a seat of learning that was the pride of India.

The next day at Benares airport I checked in and boarded the plane for Calcutta. I was beginning to wonder why we were running late, when the airport police entered the plane in search of me; the discrepancy between the name on my passport and that on the ticket had been reported. My experience of Indian police had always indicated that they played an officious game, but that they couldn't care less about implementing regulations. Rather than pleading my genuine innocence regarding non-transferable tickets, I decided to behave like an arrogant memsahib. I told them I was recently married to the person named on the ticket but that my passport had yet to be updated. 'You can stay on the plane,' they said, 'but you may be arrested at your destination.' The plane, which had been delayed because of me, took off. Throughout the nail-biting flight I contemplated the possibility of being arrested in Calcutta. This unhappy state of affairs was enhanced by a Canadian businessman sitting next to me. 'In a spot of trouble?' he drawled. 'Let me help you.' I thought he was being kind. 'I'll sort out the police and then you can stay with me at my hotel. You can earn a bit of money.'

There were no police awaiting me when we landed. I got shot of the predatory Canadian and was just hailing a taxi when I beheld a sight I would never forget: rickshaws being pulled by men, their skeletal frames straining between the shafts as they ran. Having assumed such practices had long been outlawed, I was horrified. 'They die,' said the taxi driver when I questioned him. 'They live until they are 25, and then they die.'

I enjoyed Calcutta. British colonial architecture lent the city a shabby grace. I was shown the memorial to the infamous Black Hole, the botanical gardens, and, to my delight, the house of writer and philosopher Rabindranath Tagore. Inside the temple at Khalighat, where I was invited to join in a ritual *puja*, I encountered the most terrifying of all India's deities: Kali, the dark mother, with her black face, staring eyes and protruding tongue.

Throughout my time in New Delhi I continued to work in the egg shop and to spend time with Peace Corps volunteers, mostly young men, who came in from their postings to seek respite in the capital. Sometimes we left the sophistication of New Delhi behind, wandering the alleys of Chadni Chowk, the heart of the old city, where I delighted once again in markets and stalls, free-range holy cows and the reality of India's teeming masses, filth and poverty. When we stayed late we would see people sleeping in the road wrapped in rags, and yet in the midst of this squalor we experienced the hospitality so readily offered by those who could least afford it: street musicians who invited us to join them and drink tea; impoverished people who invited us to share food. Back in the new part of town, we would occasionally treat ourselves to a meal in a restaurant, often sharing a dish to keep the price down. Struggling to articulate our new-found experiences, we talked of India and politics, books and art; shared our hopes and dreams. When the boys returned to their posts they wrote to me: a letter from a lad in hospital with amoebic dysentery; how to use buffalo shit as cooking fuel; a Parisian postcard from a volunteer who had fled India; notes and jokes, poems and love letters, I kept them all.

At the end of November, 1965, I decided the time had come to leave India. I was still only 22 and I had spent nearly a year mixing with every stratum of Indian society. I had made some serious mistakes, but I had worked incredibly hard. I was deeply in love with India and my sojourn there was to influence my entire life. I updated my passport, gave in my notice at IBM, queued for a day to obtain a tax clearance certificate and booked my passage by sea from Bombay to Genoa.

Before leaving India, however, I wanted to take a brief look at Madras. In Delhi I boarded a train travelling south, a journey of over 1,000 miles. Late at night when we drew into Gwalior railway station I sat there staring at the platform where Tim's poultry had been delivered, where I had greeted visitors and sent them off with fond farewells. I thought of the moped factory in the jungle, of Walter in his lederhosen, of all the people I knew in that town. I didn't get off the train. I just sat there staring sadly into the night.

The train journey was a joy. In the restaurant car, where I ordered meals and snacks, I felt at home, like an old India hand. I chatted to the other diners, men and women from India as well as Ceylon. A Sikh joined me and began to tell me about his customs and I found I already knew everything he had to tell. On that long journey south I made so many friends. I noted in my diary that I would travel forever; that I could envisage myself as a really old woman, still exploring the world.

At Madras I was entertained royally by IBM staff. We drove along the palm strewn coast, through stunning countryside, to Mahabalipuram, the site of ancient temples by the sea. Today it is a World Heritage tourist centre, but back then we were alone except for small children who shouted 'white woman' at me in Tamil as we drove by. In some dank caves in a nearby village, we entered an underground temple where we executed various *pujas*. Decked with garish painted gods, it seemed a primitive place, mired in something dark from times long gone. For a moment I reverted to the Christian roots I had rejected: How pagan, I thought. How primitive! At the very second this thought entered my head the priest turned and stared into my eyes. In perfect Oxford English he said: 'Don't think of this as a pagan ceremony. Imagine you're worshipping your Lord Christ.'

From Madras I boarded the train for the last lap to Bombay. India, that great, teeming, colourful continent, was soon to slip from my grasp. In some ways I had been an innocent abroad, in love with the people I saw, with the sights and sounds and smells. Overflowing with youthful passion, I had failed to even notice the fine lines I had crossed. I had approached people and situations without subtlety, caught up in a whirlwind of enthusiasm, embracing them with exuberance without considering the outcome.

On 3 December, 1965, I boarded the British India Steam Navigation Company's *SS Devonia* bound for Genoa. As the ship eased out of the port of Bombay, the great soulful moan of its horn reflected my heartbreak and loss. In India I had received attention, both wanted and unwanted, from more men than I would encounter in the rest of my life, but my love affair had never been with them. It was India that I loved.

In the Jingle-Jangle Morning

I was the only white woman on the ship. The minute I stepped on board the British members of the crew began teasing me and chatting me up. 'Look at her eyes,' said the barman to one of the sailors. 'Just look at her beautiful eyes!' It wasn't until the end of the 17-day voyage that they admitted they had taken bets as to which of them would win me. None did. In my diary I likened them to plump pink-and-white cherubs.

After the initial sadness at leaving India, a great peace descended on me, the contentment unique to that time capsule which exists between departure and arrival. I spent much of my time with Paul, a young traveller who had been working at a mental hospital in Australia. At a time when there was no proper awareness of mental health, he made me think about the causes, the mitigating circumstances, the varying degrees of aberration. He had a poetic turn of phrase and we discussed books, poetry, religion and philosophy. The voyage across the Indian Ocean was warm and lazy. I played deck quoits with the other passengers, chatted and read, and revelled in the frequent sight of flying fish and dolphins.

On 9 December, 1965, six days out of Bombay, we docked at Aden which was in a state of emergency and controlled by the British army. We could disembark at our own risk and I duly signed a form accepting liability for anything untoward that might occur. Once on land it was unbearably hot. Together with one or two others, I wandered the deserted sandy streets, past flat-roofed houses. On every corner there were British soldiers, guns at the ready: 'What you doin' 'ere, love? If I was you I'd get right back on that boat.' I didn't stay ashore long.

Slowly the ship sailed north, up the Suez Canal, the desert squeezing us on either side. Inevitably, my thoughts turned to Eilat, so near and yet so far, tucked away up the eastern arm of the Red Sea. On our last peaceful tropical morning in the Suez Canal, I heard Paul playing his guitar on the deck and singing in a strange cracked voice. '*Hey Mr Tambourine Man*', he croaked, '*play a song for me.*' It was the first time I heard the name Bob Dylan. It was a jingle-jangle morning that would last for decades.

The winter Mediterranean hit us like a shock. The wilder the sea became, the fewer passengers turned up in the dining room. When the storm was at its height, I was the only one left, everyone else remaining below or throwing up. For a couple of days I dined with the crew who made a fuss of me and invited me to join them for a film show. With the deck at 45 degrees and waves crashing over the ship's rail, I sat cocooned with the lads, roaring with laughter at Lee Marvin in *Cat Ballou*.

On 20 December, 1965, we docked at Genoa. Fourteen months after I had left Europe, I stepped ashore a totally different person. I boarded the Trans-European Express and the next day, after crossing the Channel, I arrived at Victoria Station. Lacking winter clothes, I had borrowed a pair of old trousers from someone and a dirty sweater. Grubby and dishevelled, I walked across the platform to meet my parents. I had made it home for Christmas.

CHAPTER FIVE

MAN AND HIS WORLD

Inside the Tin Birdie

MICHAEL HUNKA, the Canadian father of the family across the road, was hurrying up my parents' garden path. 'I've got a proposition for Jenny,' he said. 'Something urgent.'

His brother, Dymie, was one of the people setting up Expo 67, the World Fair to be held in Montreal the following year. His remit was to fill the DuPont Auditorium with lectures by famous scientists and a complementary programme of science films. Peter Morris, the director of the Canadian Film Institute, was in charge, with a colleague as organiser. In the midst of negotiations with the International Science Film Association in Paris, the latter had been taken ill. 'Do you know anyone who could take on the job at short notice?' asked Dymie. 'Remember Jenny,' enquired Michael, 'the girl across the road? She used to work for the BBC and knows a bit about film. Maybe she could do it.'

A few days later, en route from Paris to Ottawa, Peter Morris broke his journey in London to interview me. 'I've worked on film productions,' I told him, 'but I know nothing about science.' 'Tell me what you've been doing since you were at the BBC,' he said. I regaled him with tales of my travels and working in India, hardly the credentials necessary to organise an international science film festival. 'If you can travel rough overland to India and then just walk into a variety of jobs, I'm sure you can cope with Canada,' he said. 'You'll need to start as soon as possible, though.'

A month later, in October 1966, I was on a plane to Canada. The man in the seat next to mine woke me up. 'Sorry to disturb you,' he said, 'but I couldn't let you miss this wonderful sight.' The Aurora Borealis had transformed the sky into shimmering emerald, shot with lime and turquoise, tinged pink. I gazed on it with awe, but as I watched this flickering gateway to my new world, it was the bums of Eilat who were on my mind. Scrubbed up nicely for my new role, I looked down on the past reflection of myself, a vagabond girl standing on the beach near the Negev desert, gazing skywards. Now I was on my first international flight. I've made it, Hans, I thought. Here I am, inside the 'tin birdie'!

Galoshes Galore

'This little thing,' drawled the motel owner, her arm encircling me protectively, 'This little thing came by herself all the way from London, England!' Everyone in the diner looked up. 'And because she's English,' she added, 'I've made tea. Not coffee, but tea! My husband was over there in the war and he says the English drink tea all day.' My hostess sat me down before a pile of doughnuts with lurid green icing. 'Hallowe'en doughnuts!' she said. 'Enjoy your breakfast, dear.'

Breakfast over, I prepared to visit the Canadian Film Institute, my new place of work just across the road. I popped back to my room, slipped into my high boots and shiny green PVC mac and crossed the snowy highway. As I walked into the main office all activity ceased. 'Oh my God,' said someone. 'Swing-ing London! Just look at that coat. It's so London!' Peter did the rounds, introducing me to my new colleagues. No wonder they had found my clothing fashionable. *Canadian women are such frumps,* I wrote home. *Their clothes, their hair! Such prim styles – so old-fashioned!* This was borne out that evening when I paid my first visit to downtown Ottawa. People were scurrying along in coats and hats reminiscent of the 50s. With so much snow, most of them were wearing old-fashioned rubber galoshes over their shoes. Clearly Canada's capital was some kind of backwater. *Grim architecture,* I wrote home, *and galoshes – galoshes galore.*

What made Canada foreign and exciting was the snow. Day after day it fell, overwhelming the city in a vast white drifting mass,

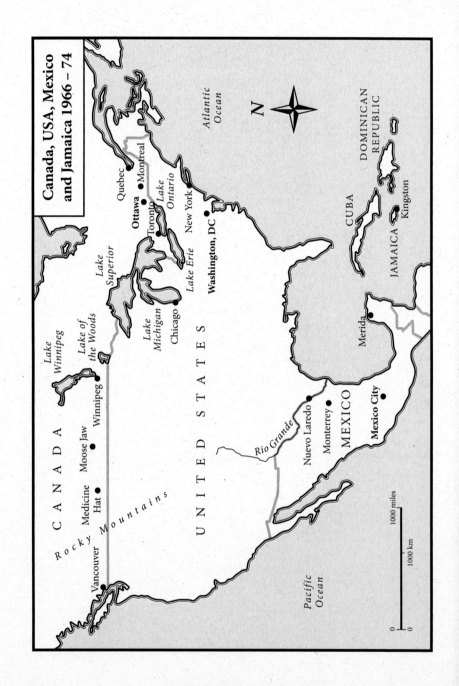

Canada, USA, Mexico and Jamaica 1966 – 74

CANADA

UNITED STATES

MEXICO

Rocky Mountains

Pacific Ocean

Atlantic Ocean

Vancouver

Medicine Hat

Moose Jaw

Winnipeg

Lake Winnipeg

Lake of the Woods

Lake Superior

Lake Michigan

Chicago

Lake Ontario

Lake Erie

Quebec

Montreal

Ottawa

Toronto

New York

Washington, DC

Rio Grande

Nuevo Laredo

Monterrey

Mexico City

Merida

CUBA

JAMAICA

Kingston

DOMINICAN REPUBLIC

N

1000 miles

1000 km

0

0

muffling sound, softening hard edges. People were galvanised into action: shovelling, digging, scraping, etching lines of survival in the relentless Arctic spillage. The whirring of snow ploughs and bursts of light punctuated my sleep, as outside a convoy battled the environment. Finally the temperature plummeted, the blizzards petered out, and I found myself inhabiting the ice-hard northern rim of the world.

I stayed in the motel a few days, courtesy of the Canadian Film Institute, and then moved downtown into a YWCA dormitory while I sought accommodation. Night after night, when my day at the Film Institute ended, I walked the streets of Ottawa, answering small ads, knocking on doors. I wanted somewhere cheap to live, but above all a place with character. My colleagues kept advising me to live in a modern apartment block. 'There'll be a swimming pool, a laundromat, a janitor to fix things,' they said. 'You'll feel safe.' No one could comprehend why I was trawling the more run-down areas of town.

Eventually I found a flat overlooking the Byward Market with its little French-Canadian stores, market stalls and junk shops. It was also the red light district. My future home consisted of a tiny bed-sit, a miniscule kitchen and bathroom, but through the windows I could watch the hustle and bustle of the market below. The walls of the apartment were grubby, the floor thick with grease and dirt and the furnishings tatty. I scraped away a patch on the floor and found parquet flooring beneath the grime. The place had potential and I fell in love with it instantly.

My new landlord and landlady were aloof, but once they realised I wanted to do the place up, they warmed to me. Together with their small daughter they occupied the ground floor apartment. Pale and skinny with bad complexions, they looked underfed and worn down by life. Despite this, they were kind. When I had eventually cleaned and decorated the flat I heard a knock on the door. 'Here's a little gift for you,' said the landlady. 'We thought they were real cute.' She handed me plastic bathroom curtains decorated with large sparkly poodles. I didn't have the heart to hide them away. I hung them up, invited the family in to admire them, and tolerated them for the rest of my time in the flat.

The hallway outside my door was cavernous, uncarpeted, brown and dingy with a further staircase leading up to the roof. I had two neighbours. Next to me, in a flat nearly as small as my own, lived a dumpy little English woman with her partner, a huge and silent Canadian Indian – First Nations, as Indians were to become known later. Their room was dominated by a cage containing a raucous macaw. A few days after moving into my apartment, I came across the Indian sitting on the kerb outside the building swigging beer from a bottle. I breezed up to him, bent on making neighbourly conversation. 'And what tribe do you belong to?' I asked in my naïve way. He looked up, surprised. 'I belong to the tribe of drunkards,' he said quietly, and took another swig. The only other time he spoke was when I acquired a kitten. 'It'll get my parrot,' he said. The kitten was to disappear mysteriously.

On the other side of the hall, a New Zealander inhabited a large apartment. Decorated in shades of pink and lilac, it was draped with frills and lace and cluttered with satin cushions and china figurines. A pretty woman in her forties, she wore a lot of makeup and dressed in exotic kimonos. She was friendly and we chatted and drank wine together for months before it dawned on me she was a prostitute. When I moaned about decorating my flat she laughed. 'You think yours is bad,' she said. 'The previous tenants here had an orgy. They rolled naked girls in green paint and pressed their bodies against the wall. I was surrounded by breasts and bums when I moved in here.'

Gradually I scraped and cleaned and painted my rooms. I bought a carpet and curtains, a rocking chair from a junk shop, and a poster of a Chagall painting entitled *Rabbi and Book*, because the greens and yellows complemented my colour scheme and because I was amused by the rabbi's bright green beard. Within a very short time I had made friends with a weird assortment of people from all over the world. One day, during a small gathering to celebrate my new abode, a German guy said, 'You know what this place is like? A New York, East Side, Puerto Rican tenement!' I was delighted.

The Film Institute was housed in a nondescript two-storey building on Ottawa's Carling Avenue and was run by a small but dedicated team, headed up by Roy Little, with Peter Morris as director. It comprised a film collection, a small reference library, and was the umbrella organisation for the National Film Archive and the National Film Theatre. Individual members of staff produced booklets on film and film makers, and the Institute held film seasons dedicated to different genres. I had washed up in an interesting friendly environment and, as it transpired, an organisation which was to kick-start my entire career.

By now I was 23 years old and the official organiser of Insight 67, a programme comprising 1000 science films to be screened in the DuPont Auditorium at the World Fair, and designed to tie in with lectures by some of the world's leading scientists. I was to work closely with the International Science Film Library in Brussels, the International Science Film Association (ISFA) in Paris, as well as organising the 21st ISFA Congress and Film Festival at the University of Montreal. My work load was overwhelming and was even more onerous because everything had to be bilingual, not only to accommodate French Canada, but to ensure French and English, international languages, were available at Expo.

I had two personal secretaries. The first, a young man, was a French-Canadian graduate of about my age, who was surly and regarded me with contempt. Although I could easily read the letters I received in French, my language was not up to error-free replies, particularly when dealt with at speed. The Frenchman's role was to translate and type them for me, as well as fielding phone calls from the French-speaking press. By contrast, my English-speaking secretary was a sweet old-fashioned woman who approached me with deference and asked if I minded being addressed by my first name. In addition to film screenings and general correspondence, I had to deal with publicity and with the English-speaking press.

During the months which followed, the Film Institute was

overflowing with films from all over the world and it was up to me to screen the lot and make recommendations. I decided to begin with entries for the medical category, the first of which proved something of a shock: a man's penis had been cut off by a jealous lover and the film highlighted the process by which Jugoslav surgeons had fashioned him a new one. The detail was graphic, right through to the grand finale when the lucky fellow could once again get an erection and have a pee. I ticked the *Yes* box, accepting the film for screening and adding it to the pile of the day which featured a heart operation and a Japanese entry entitled *I will not eat, no!*

One day I was confronted by a pile of Russian language films with no subtitles. I telephoned the Soviet Embassy who sent me a translator, a charming man with whom I sat amongst the film cans discussing Soviet propaganda and his views of the West. He was handsome, funny, and as we watched films of the Russian tundra he kept shouting, 'Reincows! You see, you see, more reincows!' India's submissions were science Bollywood-style, with hundreds of traditional Indian dancers twirling across the screen representing atoms. For a while about 30 Japanese films went missing, until they turned up hidden behind a stack of Hungarian movies meant for the National Film Theatre.

During these early days I accompanied Peter Morris on regular trips to Toronto and Montreal. Eventually, much to my relief, we arranged for a doctor in Toronto to double-check the medical films submitted, and we also held 35mm screenings at Toronto's Shell Centre. Toronto proved to be a fairly modern metropolis, more the kind of city I had expected to find in Canada, and French-speaking Montreal with its narrow streets, boutiques and bistros exhibited style which was more reminiscent of Europe. Our frequent dealings with the National Film Board of Canada were peaceable enough, but at the University of Montreal, where we were initiating arrangements for the International Science Film Association's Congress, I brushed with my first separatist, a man who belonged to a burgeoning group of French-Canadians who wanted the Province of Quebec to secede from confederate Canada. He demanded that the

Quebec flag alone be prominent at every ISFA meeting. We had barely begun to discuss this request, when he leapt to his feet yelling, 'Fuck all English Canadians. Fuck Ottawa!' At a time when profanity was not as prevalent as it is today, this outburst reduced us to stunned silence.

In December 1966 Peter Morris visited Europe and on his return I joined him at a meeting in New York. My first view of the USA was an eye-opener. I had not anticipated poverty and I was shocked at the sight of black beggars on 42nd Street. 'It's like being back in India,' I told Peter. My next surprise was the fallout shelters, in stores, hotels, galleries and public places. Their presence was indicated amidst commonplace signage – Rest Room, Elevator, Fallout Shelter – as if the threat of nuclear war was the most normal thing in the world.

New York City enthralled me. I visited the Empire State Building and Frank Lloyd Wright's iconic Guggenheim Museum. I wandered through Greenwich Village, relishing glimpses of the bohemian society that was so lacking in Ottawa: people holding forth on soap boxes; unconventional clothes; musicians, bars and cafés. I visited the famous White Horse Tavern, where Dylan Thomas supped his last before dying in New York – and I sampled American pizza. Until the first Pizza Express had opened in London the previous year, pizza as we know it today was unavailable in Britain. At Peter's instigation, I ordered a margherita and was flabbergasted at the 14-inch pizza set before me. 'How on earth am I expected to eat all that?' I asked.

As Canada was preparing to welcome the world to Expo 67 and to its centenary celebrations, the world itself was on the boil: more and more African nations were seeking self-rule; Israel was gearing itself up for its first major conflict; the US was sending ever more troops to Vietnam, and protest movements were erupting across America and Europe. I spent Christmas with Dymie and his family at Pointe Claire, Quebec, where we watched the extraordinary sight of car-racing taking place on a frozen lake. To my surprise, he told me that his nephew, my childhood friend Martin Hunka, would be working at Expo's DuPont Auditorium where my Insight 67 films were to be screened.

'You have committed a crime against the Canadian State.' The immigration officer was serious. He regarded me suspiciously. 'And why is your passport restricted?' I explained that it was a replacement for one that had been stolen in Israel. He turned the pages slowly. 'And why were you visiting all these countries?' He frowned. 'What were you doing there?'

Because I had been recruited urgently, on the advice of the Canadian Film Institute I had entered the country on a visitor's visa. The CFI had assured me they would regulate my immigration status but, although I reminded them frequently, they had failed to do so. Now my visitor's visa was due to expire and I had gone to Immigration to try and effect the regulation myself. Peter Morris was summoned from the Canadian Film Institute and confirmed that I was essential to CFI's preparations for Expo 67. Reluctantly Immigration awarded residency.

New Year's Day, 1967, heralded the inauguration of year-long festivities to celebrate the Centenary of the Canadian Federation, kicking off with messages from Prime Minister Lester Pearson and from the Queen. According to the French-Canadian press the Queen spoke far better French than her English-Canadian Government ministers, but this was clearly a dig at the politicians concerned, rather than a royalist accolade. Jubilant bands marched through Ottawa in the snow waving Canadian flags, and the Centennial Torch, destined to be pulled by huskies from the parliament buildings to every province in Canada, was lit. During the year which followed, citizens were imbued with a new pride, a Canadian identity which overwhelmed art, politics, culture and individuals with a collective euphoria. Beautiful ice carvings sprung up all over the city – bears and moose, igloos and trappers – and *Les Feux Follets* performed Inuit hunting dances and First Nations religious ceremonies on stage. When they were not advertising for bilingual bunny girls – apparently necessary for the millions expected to visit the world fair – radio broadcasts were punctuated with self-congratulatory cameos extolling the virtues of Canada and culminating with a child drawling, 'We gotta country that's free.'

A feeling of freedom was certainly paramount during this celebratory year, but not everyone saw it that way. French Canada was going through a period of intense change, the populace divided into federalists and those who wanted sovereignty for Quebec. France's General de Gaulle who, together with other heads of state, had received an official invitation to visit Expo 67, delivered a speech in Montreal in which he shouted, '*Vive le Québec libre*' – long live free Quebec. The speech caused a furore and was deemed a breach of diplomatic protocol. Prime Minister Lester Pearson sent a letter to De Gaulle: *The people of Canada are free*, he wrote. *Every province in Canada is free. Canadians do not need liberating!* De Gaulle responded by returning to France without even visiting Ottawa and his speech, having emboldened the Quebec sovereignty movement, went down as a milestone in the schism between French and English Canada.

With the advent of the New Year, the Film Institute went into crisis management. Expo 67 was due to open in April and Peter and I began working from early morning until very late at night. By March I had three girls typing for me all day, plus a boy packing and mailing publicity, while I continued to screen and assess hundreds of films.

As if all the work for Expo wasn't enough, the Film Institute was hosting an International Festival of Laughter with films selected by a poll of critics from 40 countries. It was an enjoyable, if exhausting, interlude, as Peter and I shot off in a limousine to Ottawa airport to pick up various celebrities. Eleanor Keaton, widow of Buster Keaton who had died the previous year, proved to be a great asset to the festival and when we took her out for dinner we enjoyed her down-to-earth lively company. 'At 15 I became a night club dancer,' she told us. 'Six Blondes from Hollywood, we called ourselves. We toured the world.' At 20 she was a Munchkin in *The Wizard of Oz* and a year later, when a contract dancer at MGM, she'd met Buster, more than twice her age, who was working as a gag man supplying comic routines for the Marx Brothers. 'Talkies had come in,' she told us. 'There was no longer any interest in Buster's silent films; he was at an all-time low.' At our Festival of Laughter we screened *The Railrodder*, which Keaton had made in Canada in 1965, the year before he died, followed by *Buster Keaton Rides Again*, the behind-the-scenes documentary about the film, introduced by Eleanor and in which she featured.

Hal Roach, a pioneer producer who had made movies with Harold Lloyd, Laurel and Hardy and many other famous stars, was another of our dinner guests. At the British Embassy I also chatted to Norman Wisdom when a reception was held in his honour. The Festival of Laughter was an immense success, but it was the old favourites with the Marx Brothers, Chaplin, Keaton and Harold Lloyd which pulled the biggest crowds. There were a couple of world premieres as well, including Canada's *Amanita Pestilens,* produced by Crawley Films and starring a very early film performance by Geneviève Bujold.

As Expo grew closer, there were numerous problems in getting the World Fair up and running. Winter lingered longer than usual and snow made it impossible to lay the turf by the planned deadline. The St Lawrence River had not completely thawed and there were fears that when it did, the site would be flooded. There were threats of demonstrations and bombs outside the Soviet Pavilion and the press reported that the Mafia had moved into Montreal big-time. A letter from my mother in England bewailed the fact that a television programme about Expo had failed to be relayed successfully by what she called 'that Stelstar thing', and the British kept complaining that Canadians had hung the Union flag upside down. In the end, by hook or by crook, it all came together. With 62 nations participating, the 1000-acre site became the home of cutting-edge design and architecture. Millions of people gawped at the breathtaking innovations, attended the outstanding theatrical offerings from the Bolshoi to La Scala, and stood awe-struck before massive multi-screen film presentations. The motto for Expo 67 was *Man and His World* and the world did indeed come to Montreal.

The official celebration of Canada's centenary took place on

Above: *newly arrived in Canada in 1966, aged 23.*
Above right: *Expo 67 World Fair, Montreal (April – October 1967) showing the Ontario, Western Provinces and Canada Pavilions and the mini-rail transport link. Photo courtesy of Laurent Bélanger (CC BY-SA 3.0).*

Left and above: *Peter Morris, Ottawa, 1968.*

Above: *Peter (second left) at the founding conference of the Canadian Science Film Association, May 1968.*
Right: *with Peter in Ireland, spring 1969.*

With Pat Crawley at Stoneacres, the Crawley family ranch at Old Chelsea, Quebec, in 1969. **Above right:** *cooking maple syrup in the snow.*

Below: *two award-winning Canadian film-makers;* **(left)** *Judy Crawley, Pat's mother, a pioneer for women in the industry;* **(right)** *Cameron Graham, TV documentary producer, and my boss at CBC from 1969 to 1974.*

Dominion Day in July, when there were garden parties, fireworks and dancing. Only a year after hobnobbing with the great and famous at Prime Minister Shastri's garden party in New Delhi, I was repeating the experience at City Hall in Ottawa in the presence of the Queen, Prince Philip, and a horde of women in 19th-century dress. Cars sounded their horns from midnight until 4am to welcome Canada's second century and I sang the Canadian national anthem with the best of them.

Even though Expo had opened, Peter and I went on working night and day. Many of the films from overseas had been delayed and a last-minute selection process continued. Copyright had to be cleared, and mountains of film cans shipped back and forth between Ottawa and Montreal. *Insight 67* proved a success and our film shows and lectures went pretty much according to plan. I even got through the terrifying experience of having to go on stage and introduce two of the visiting scientists, a difficult task for someone who had no understanding of the scientific content of their presentation. By the end of October everyone was completely and utterly exhausted.

The culmination of *Insight 67* was to be a closing reception at the DuPont Auditorium. Peter and I worked all day, putting out tables and chairs, dealing with caterers, cleaning and tidying the room where the function was to be held. We also had to remove huge piles of heavy film cans, a task which left us weary and sweating profusely. There had been someone else who was meant to help us, but she had failed to turn up.

In June, half way through Expo, a new member of staff had come to CFI, a beautiful Pakistani girl who spoke English, French, Urdu and Japanese and who had a science degree. 'Come and have lunch with me,' I said, befriending her on her first day. 'I'm just popping over to the diner across the road.' 'No thank you,' she replied. 'Daddy will be picking me up any moment now.' Her father, the Pakistani High Commissioner, would arrive with his chauffeur daily and whisk her home for luncheon. It was she who had been scheduled to help us prepare that final reception.

Peter and I just managed to get everything done in time. We shot off to the rest rooms for a wash and brush-up and I slipped quickly into a dress, ran a comb through my hair and rushed back to greet our guests. As I arrived, the Pakistani girl swept into the room wearing a glamorous sari, her long hair sleek and shining, her makeup perfectly applied. 'Where on earth have you been?' we demanded angrily. 'I was getting ready for this evening, of course' she said. 'I had to have my hair done.' The dignitaries and guests surged around her, complimenting her on *Insight 67*, on the wonderful lectures, on the variety of films screened. She'd had virtually nothing to do with it, but she smiled, shook hands, oozed charm –and hijacked the accolade that was rightfully mine. Back at the Canadian Film Institute Roy Little called me into his office. 'Congratulations, Jenny,' he said. 'You did a fantastic job,' but his praise didn't make up for my disappointment at being side-lined at the final reception.

Canada had moved on during 1967. It had become less old-fashioned, more sophisticated, and Pierre Elliott Trudeau was in the wings, waiting to transform the country into a buzzing youthful culture. I, too, had changed. I had taken on a huge amount of responsibility and successfully brought three international projects to fruition. I had also become more politically aware, better informed and better read. Courtesy of my mentor, Peter Morris, I was on my way.

Flores de Noche Buena

'Are you engaged?' demanded Dr Haight, a middle-aged woman whose name was pronounced *hate*. Her tone was uncompromising. 'If you're not even engaged, then I cannot possibly give you any contraception.' I had approached the doctor's appointment with temerity, as it transpired with good reason. She took down a tome from her bookcase and opened it on a page with diagrams illustrating human reproduction. 'Have a look at this,' she said, 'and don't come back again until you're engaged or married.' I escaped her suffocating office with its heavy furniture and trudged despondently through the snow.

I hadn't realised that in Canada at that time, the only legal methods of birth control were natural ones – abstinence or the rhythm method. Contraception could be prescribed for therapeutic reasons only and any doctor who bent the rules could be prosecuted. Birth control campaigners had defied the law and set up clandestine clinics across Canada, but it was to be 1969 before contraception was legalised and the pill more openly introduced. It wasn't that different in Britain where, since 1961, the pill had, in theory, only been available for married women. In 1967 that UK law was relaxed, but during the so-called swinging 60s, getting hold of the pill could not be taken for granted. As in Canada, it involved searching for a sympathetic doctor.

It was Peter Morris, with whom I was now in a relationship, who hunted down such a practitioner. Probably in his late 30s, the doctor was handsome, jocular, arrogant and sexist. His surgery was bursting at the seams with women of all ages, the older ones seeking injections for an early version of hormone replacement therapy. When one of these women emerged from a consultation and fainted gracefully away in the waiting room, the doctor came out of his office, chortled and declared, 'Just look at that! They see me and they swoon!' I found him smarmy and unprofessional, but he fixed me up with the only pill available at the time, a high dose combination which much later was withdrawn. To all intents and purposes I was a pill 'guinea pig'.

Peter had left his wife and family and, to my eternal remorse and shame, I was the catalyst for that separation. At the time I came up with various justifications for the affair, but whether they were valid or not, I was largely to blame. An Englishman, he had moved to Canada to undertake post-graduate studies but, once qualified, he immediately abandoned the sciences to pursue a career in film.

Peter and I had been toiling under immense pressure. We sometimes worked 16-hour days in the Canadian Film Institute, as well as travelling to Montreal and Toronto for meetings, dining out and attending social functions linked to films and festivals. While preparing for Expo 67 we frequently spent entire weekends screening films; he was rarely at home. Our empathy was instant, and intellectually and practically he took me under his wing. He was gentle and kind and somewhat enigmatic. While he worked hard at educating me, I focused on drawing him out of his shell. The result was a liaison which was intense, close, creative and fun, an alliance I interpreted as being in love, when really it was largely about my own coming of age.

Because I had never been to university I was reticent about expressing opinions. In a room full of people conversing on any topic Peter would always say, 'And what do you think, Jenny?' forcing me to participate. Although only six years my senior, he was a far cry from my previous boyfriends. With his receding hairline, glasses, short stature and conventional dress he was neither cool nor laid back, but rather a busy little person who bustled from place to place with short purposeful steps. Despite this, I found him attractive and was lured, above all, by his brain. He made me regard the world afresh, often through literary, philosophical or political allusions which, for me, were brand new concepts.

The fact that we were working such long hours meant that moments snatched for ourselves were rendered exceptional by their urgency. We would rush down to the canal and watch fishermen lighting small fires on the frozen surface as they fished through holes in the ice. We dashed up into the hills to see the maple trees tapped, watching the sap boil in giant cauldrons until someone ladled the syrup onto the snow where it solidified into sticky toffee. Once the winter ice had melted, he showed me timber floating down the Ottawa River to the saw-mill and later, in summer, we made brief forays into the Ontario countryside returning with armfuls of wild flowers. One evening he whisked me off to a rundown ballroom, just the other side of the river in French Canada, where the punters still dressed like Elvis and women danced around the proverbial handbags.

Once Expo 67 was behind us, and I had returned the films overseas and tied up administrative details, my contract with the Canadian Film Institute was at an end. Totally exhausted from our hard-working summer, in December 1967 Peter and I set off for Mexico, taking trains to Chicago and from there a single bus ride through to Laredo on the Mexican border. Sleeping on trains was comfortable enough, but four nights and days non-stop on a Greyhound bus proved cramped and debilitating.

The Chicago I glimpsed was dirty, industrial and unappealing. It was a hostile place where anyone who nodded off on a bench in the bus terminal, was prodded with a truncheon by one of the cops – a harsh measure to prevent vagrancy. Travelling south down the length of the United States, small-town America appeared cosier than I had anticipated: pretty communities, dominated by old white clapboard houses with verandas. Texas was the state which seemed the most foreign. There were far more black people than I had expected and the entire population, black and white, wore Stetsons and smoked giant cigars. Each time the bus ground to a halt and we sought refreshment in a diner, I felt self-conscious; the laid-back pace and languid drawl rendered me small, uptight and immensely British. During the half-hour break in San Antonio I rushed into Woolworths and purchased a gold band that resembled a wedding ring, a sop to the Catholic hotel owners I knew we would encounter south of the border.

At midnight, on the fifth day of our journey from Canada, we disembarked on the American side of the border and crossed the bridge over the Rio Grande to Nuevo Laredo. We entered a large, dimly-lit Mexican customs shed where we were overseen by a crazy crone who was collecting money in a plastic pouch. There were no formalities, no uniforms, no receipts and she was clearly pocketing bribes. When she came to our holdall she unpacked it to about half way down, then cackling wildly she put back our belongings. I nudged Peter. 'I think she's tucked her money pouch under our clothes,' I said. 'No, that's the one with our plastic raincoats,' he replied. I dived into the bag, retrieved the pouch and opened it. As I had predicted, it was full of cash. I handed it to the old woman who screamed with laughter, waving it in the air and shouting at our fellow passengers in a babble of Spanish. To be fair, it might have been a genuine mistake, but the potential for us going off with her money and the police being tipped off seemed highly likely.

Eventually we squeezed ourselves inside the waiting Mexican bus, sandwiched between enormous brown paper parcels belonging to Mexicans returning from an American shopping spree. We arrived in Monterrey at dawn – a cold, wet, poverty-stricken city, peopled by urchins selling newspapers – where we ate chicken stew in a shack full of early morning workers. The ride to Mexico City took a further 12 hours, crossing hundreds of miles of semi-desert spiked with giant cacti. Scattered about were a few mangy sheep, and villages clustered behind tall cacti stockades. Men with droopy moustaches, sombreros and ponchos rode by on mules. It was traditional Mexico as portrayed in Westerns.

In Mexico City, at our request, the taxi driver deposited us in the cheapest accommodation he could find, a room infested with bugs and cockroaches. The city was a magnificent juxtaposition of the ancient and the new: modern architecture incorporating mosaics and murals and courtyards, next to old Spanish houses and churches; wide highways alongside narrow alleyways; people with fashionable clothes mingling with peasants clad in blankets. I stood on the brink of a whole new cultural experience. I knew nothing about Aztecs and Mayans and I had never even been to Spain. In the Museum of Anthropology wide eyes from the past stared at me from unfamiliar clay statues, as I marvelled at jade masks and feathered head dresses. In the evening I watched the huge pyramids of Teotihuacan lit dramatically for a *son et lumière* show. As ever, Peter was my guide, showing me churches and parks, murals by Diego Rivera; introducing me to refried beans, chicken and chocolate, and tequila.

'The men are leering at you,' exclaimed Peter on the second day. 'It's that skirt of yours!' Mini-skirts had arrived in Canada with Expo 67, where the hostesses from the British Pavilion had caused a furore with their 'indecent' hemlines designed to reflect swinging London. The skirt I was wearing in Mexico was only about three inches above the knee, barely 'mini' at all, but Mexican skirts were considerably longer. I bought some scissors and hacked away at the stitching on my hemline, dropping it to a respectable length.

From Mexico City we took a slow train to Merida, two sweltering sleepless nights on wooden seats. The countryside was lush with banana trees, palms and the ubiquitous cacti. Some villages consisted of straw huts made from palm fronds, while others boasted more substantial stone housing with thatched roofs. Two fellow-travellers befriended us, boys bent on practising their English. 'You like the monkeys?' they enquired. 'Oh yes,' said Peter. 'We love them. They're so small and their fur is almost yellow.' The boys regarded us scornfully. 'The Monkees!' they admonished. 'Pop group!'

Merida, the capital of Yucatan, with its colonial architecture, white houses and numerous squares was still relatively small and rural. In our budget hotel, we were surrounded by seedy elegance: a ceiling adorned with flaking cherubs; an open, tiled hallway dominated by huge columns; a wide marble staircase with chipped steps. We visited the home of the Conquistador Montejo who was portrayed in a statue over the doorway, his feet resting on the heads of the Mayans he had subdued. We explored the Mayan ruins of Chichin Itza and climbed the great pyramid in the centre, with no more than a couple of other tourists in sight. We visited markets full of chillies and spices, corn and earthenware, where women wore white dresses with embroidered borders.

I should have been in my element, but I longed for the freedom of the road. The vagabond girl had gone. I stood on the hotel balcony overlooking the square and watched half-a-dozen long-haired young people sitting by their rucksacks. Dear sweet Peter with his generous ways and kindness to me was not as free as they were. The people in the square would soon pick up their bags and bum their way north or south with no particular destination in mind, while he would be back in his office in the Canadian Film Institute dressed in his straight clothing, adhering to routine. Briefly, I felt trapped.

Slowly, by a roundabout route, we made our way back to Mexico City, gorging ourselves on tropical fruit and staying in small towns where women wore ankle-length skirts and braided their hair. We travelled through inland settlements with a backdrop of blue mountains and visited fishing villages with white strands, where brightly-coloured nets lay drying in the sun. We watched turtles stacked on their backs in baskets, open-mouthed and gasping in the heat, and on a river bank surrounded by swamps we discovered stuffed crocodiles for sale.

Finally we were back in Mexico City for Christmas. Small backstreet bars were invaded by moustachioed men in enormous sombreros, their gleaming brass instruments blasting revellers to their feet. On Christmas Eve, in the dead of night, the popular mayor of the city lined every road with pots of poinsettias: '*Flores de Noche Buena*,' we were told, flowers of the holy night. 'He drove the lorry himself,' they said, 'a good man, this mayor.' Apocryphal or not, I enjoyed the image of the mayor driving round the city in the dark like some errant Santa Claus. As soon as Christmas was over, trios of Wise Men began to appear, Spanish-style, round every corner, until I began to feel I was seeing triple. It was an interesting interlude. We ate and drank well, but I was not relaxed. It was Peter's first Christmas away from his family. 'You shouldn't be here,' I told him. 'You should be with your children.' I felt guilty.

From Mexico City we flew back to the USA. Disembarking in Chicago we found ourselves wading through a sea of what looked like negatives on the tarmac. Curious, we stooped and grabbed a handful. 'Soldiers,' said Peter, squinting at the peeled-off Polaroids. 'Off to Vietnam; fond farewells.' On our bus journey back to Canada, two soldiers, apparently just home on leave, were sitting behind us exchanging war stories. 'We picked up a couple of gooks,' said one. 'Took 'em up in the helicopter, then on the way back to camp, we just ditched 'em.' He paused. 'Pushed 'em out the back!' His tone was matter of fact. They both laughed. A few stops later we watched them step off the bus into small town America. 'They'll get a hero's welcome,' I said wryly.

It was no coincidence that the brief interlude on our return journey was dominated by the spectre of Vietnam. During 1967 American casualties had rocketed. US protests, which had kicked off with a few thousand college students, had now escalated into massive demonstrations, and across the USA conscripts were gathering en masse to burn their draft cards. The whole world had the Vietnam War in its sights and anti-war, anti-American sentiments were burgeoning into huge protests across Europe.

I arrived back in Canada to find I had landed a job with the British Industrial and Scientific Film Association and was to report to their offices two weeks later. On 15 January, 1968, I returned to England.

The Horror of Helical Strakes

I saw the Canadian maple leaf on a young man's rucksack and pursued him down Regent Street. 'You're Canadian,' I said, stating the obvious. 'I miss Canada so much.' Taken aback, the lad drew to an abrupt halt, put down his rucksack on the pavement and sat on it. 'Whoa!' he said. 'What's all this about?' I felt foolish, but we chatted a bit, about Ottawa, about Expo 67. He was kind and smiling. 'You can go back, can't you?' 'Of course,' I said. 'Yes, of course. I can go back.'

It was the helical strakes that had driven me to the end of my tether; helical strakes and vortex-induced vibration on industrial chimneys. No wonder I was missing Canada. I had spent the entire day assessing industrial and building films. It wasn't always that bad. Occasionally there were beautiful natural history productions, but there were an awful lot of films about buildings, paint and chemicals, and I found myself regularly incarcerated in screening rooms at Shell and ICI. Everything I viewed had to be analysed and listed in a brochure. After viewing so many films for Expo 67, working for the British Industrial and Scientific Film Association was a doddle, but exceedingly boring.

During my time in Canada, swinging London had come into its own. Round the corner from my office, Carnaby Street was awash with new fashions, crazier and wackier by the day. Conventions had been smashed, laws relaxed and British class barriers breached. The Beatles and the Rolling Stones had turned everything on its head and produced a counter-culture. Even the pirate disc-jockeys who had broadcast from Radio Caroline had been welcomed into Auntie's bosom and were revolutionising the BBC. The dingy post-war London I had inhabited five years previously had blossomed into a vibrant colourful world bent on hedonism and freedom.

I was living at my parents' home in Dorking and commuting to London. Every night when I arrived home I would find letters from Peter awaiting me, pages of handwritten adoration, poetry filled with passionate declarations. There were telegrams and phone calls and talk of marriage. His attentions were welcome and I felt immense affection for him, but I was being smothered. It was too much, too soon.

He came to England for a science film conference and we shot off to Paris for a few days together. My abiding memory of that trip was turning a corner and being met by hundreds of riot police, shields up, visors down, coming straight at us. There had been a minor student demonstration, a precursor of the massive riots which would unfold two months later. We sought refuge in a café as wave after wave of police charged past.

On arrival in England, Peter had been jubilant. The Canadian Film Institute had been awarded funding to establish a Canadian Science Film Association. I was to be offered the job of running it and also of compiling and editing a monthly CSFA Journal. By the end of March 1968, just after my 25th birthday and after only three months home in England, I found myself back in Canada.

You Don't Need a Weatherman

I elbowed my way across the crowded room and squeezed into the kitchen in search of a drink. Sitting on the floor in the corner was Pierre Elliott Trudeau, the prime minister of Canada. He smiled, we said, 'Hi', and I poured myself some wine. Like most of Canada I had been swept up by Trudeaumania, a political equivalent to the popularity of the Beatles. He was young for his 49 years, good-looking and accessible. Infamous for his crazy behaviour – pirouetting by himself in Buckingham Palace while other guests walked off to meet the Queen, or sliding down the bannisters at an international conference – he was equally renowned for his intellect, his radical views and legal reforms. I wanted to sit beside him on the kitchen floor, but I resisted. 'I think it would have been intrusive,' I confided to my Film Institute friend Alison. 'He'd probably think I was after his autograph or something.' 'I felt the same,' she replied.

Peter and I were renting an apartment on Echo Drive in Ottawa, overlooking the Rideau Canal. We were happy. We had furnished our flat with cheap furniture: modern wicker tables and chairs with thin black metal legs. Juxtaposing bright colours was all the trend and we went over the top, painting our walls and bookcases bright orange and purple. With cheap rush matting on bare floorboards we considered our nest stylish.

That year the Canadian winter seemed endless, blizzard after blizzard. *White, white, white,* I wrote home. *I yearn for colour.* Then, almost overnight, everything melted. The banks of frozen snow which had dominated the sidewalks for months thawed into wet mush, leaving behind the flotsam imprisoned by winter – dog shit and bits of litter. The Ottawa River appeared to boil as steam rose through the cracks in the ice. We removed the snow tyres from our car and put on wheels with summer treads. The landlord relieved us of our double glazing and clipped on screens to keep out midges and mosquitoes. Within a few days it was not just warm, but hot. I missed the subtlety of the English spring with its warm fragrance. I thought of primroses pushing through the mossy banks, the woods full of bluebells. Peter, ever concerned, brought me flowers in a pot. 'That's the best I can do,' he said. 'You'll never get any spring in this country.'

On hot days we relaxed in the gardens on the banks of the Rideau Canal or on the beach at one of the nearby lakes. I passed my driving test, purchased a beaten-up, second hand Chevy II, and became more independent. My relationship with Peter blossomed. Our life was full, packed with interesting events and encounters, and finally I felt able to commit. We became engaged, although future plans were dependent upon his divorce.

Expo 67 had brought change to Canada. The fusty old-fashioned Ottawa where I had arrived only three years before was all but gone. The flamboyance and youthful approach of the Trudeau regime made individuals feel empowered. Despite being leader of the Liberal Party and from a privileged background, Trudeau had previously been interested in Marxism. He'd been blacklisted and barred from the United States for subscribing to left-wing publications and for attending a conference in Moscow. He was also a friend of Cuba's Fidel Castro. Later, as a lawyer, he had specialised in cases which focused on labour and civil rights. For someone raised within the conventions of French-Canadian Catholicism, his reforms regarding homosexuality, contraception, abortion and divorce came as a surprise. His slogan was *a just society* and he worked tirelessly to achieve this. I was a huge fan; like many others I felt I was being listened to – that, should I wish to do so, I could effect change.

South of the border, however, everything was in turmoil. Returning US troops were being met with antagonism, and disillusioned veterans were joining in the demonstrations. Hot on the heels of this turbulence, came the assassinations: Civil Rights campaigner Martin Luther King Junior; JFK's brother, senator Bobby Kennedy; and in Canada, Quebec lawyer and politician, Pierre Laporte, targeted by the Front de Libération du Québec. From Australia to Amsterdam, Mississippi to Madrid, there was a tide of protest against the Vietnam War. Caught up in disorder and upheaval, the old order was being turned on its head. Everything was being questioned and everyone wanted a slice of the action: anti-war protesters, Black Power groups, people advocating rights for women. Fringe organisations and anarchists jumped on the bandwagon, including the militant left-wing group known as the Weathermen. *You don't need a weatherman*, sang Bob Dylan *to know which way the wind blows.* With this ferment came a newfound feeling of international solidarity and many genuinely felt that if people worked together they could make the world a better place. Positive, empowered and full of hope, they coined the phrase *love and peace*, soon to become the hippie mantra of the next decade.

The official inauguration of the Canadian Science Film Association had taken place in May and I was busy organising a CSFA Symposium of about a hundred people from all over Canada, plus trans-Atlantic telephone hook-ups with Europeans. I was working with all kinds of creative people, from a sound technician who had helped with special effects on Kubrick's *2001: A Space Odyssey* to an elderly Californian who was pioneering the very beginnings of computer animation. I was also writing, producing and editing a monthly bulletin for the Canadian Science Film Association, probably the part of my job I found most fulfilling.

Peter and I spent a lot of time socialising with our good friends, Alison and Dennis Reid. Twiggy-like, tall and beautiful, Alison worked with us at the Canadian Film Institute, while her husband, Dennis, was the curator of Post-Confederation Art at the National Gallery of Canada. Through him we were invited to private views of new art exhibitions and met many eminent artists of the day. Like the world surrounding it, art had become subject to radical change: sequences of hard-edged lines creating an illusion of movement and deemed psychedelic; pictures consisting of nothing but stripes or squares; a painting of spaghetti with a rose plonked on the top; above all, packaging. Everyday objects were suddenly being interpreted as art, and Warhol's work was spilling over into Canada where the gallery proudly displayed his Brillo boxes. I was privileged to see those exhibits first hand, but they left me cold. However, I did enjoy the gallery's more conventional exhibitions to which we were always invited, and the wonderful parties held in Dennis and Alison's home. It was with them that Peter and I were to share the greatest event of a generation.

On 20 July 1969, the four of us squeezed in front of a small television with a couple of friends to watch a 20th-century miracle: Neil Armstrong and Buzz Aldrin walking on the surface of the moon. In the space-saturated years which followed, the world looked up in awe and focused on the moon, but for the astronauts themselves, their most mind-blowing experience was looking back, seeing the reality of Earth as a tiny planet. John Borman of the Apollo 8 mission described how from out in space all nationalistic traits blended; how he grasped the concept that Earth really was just one world. *Why the hell can't we learn to live together like decent people?* he wrote in *Newsweek*.

Back on earth, a view which complemented the sentiments of the astronauts was being expressed by Canadian Marshal McLuhan, the philosopher of communication theory. Coining the phrase *the global village*, he suggested that technology would soon reduce the world to one small community. An extraordinary man, he predicted the World Wide Web 30 years before it actually came into being and his famous saying *The medium is the message* was on everybody's lips.

Another who shot to global stardom at that time was the Indian musician, Ravi Shankar. To many in the West, world music as we know it today was a new experience, and the likes of Shankar and Bob Marley were just beginning to penetrate the collective consciousness. When Peter and I visited Stratford, Ontario, we attended an informal afternoon lecture by Shankar. Having seen him on stage in New Delhi, where he'd played all night until his audience was satiated, I now found myself sitting a mere arm's length from the great man as he highlighted for his Western audience the chasm between East and West. 'In India I prepare for a concert with peace and quiet, with meditation.' Shankar's demeanour was gentle, his voice modulated. 'In the West you have a different approach,' he said. 'Rigid time-slots are not conducive to freedom of expression. Imagine my arrival at Woodstock...' He grimaced. 'They landed me in the middle of the festival by helicopter! It was raining. There was mud everywhere and thousands of screaming fans. My sitar strings went limp. It was a terrible experience.'

With music, politics and art shaken up, there was no reason why fashion should be immune. Swirly patterns were in: lime-green juxtaposed with shocking pink; yellow, purple, red and orange. While other men wore psychedelic ties and paisley shirts with wide collars, Peter stuck to conventional dress. As for me, skirts had become so short that I wrote home: *I cannot possibly wear suspenders with miniskirts. Nobody wears suspender belts any more. There's this new invention, pantie stockings. Have you heard of them, Mum? They're the most comfortable, wonderful invention.*

I had long been a fan of Marlene Dietrich. In August 1969, when she agreed to a live concert in Ottawa to complement the Film Institute's festival of her films, I was excited at the prospect of seeing the *femme fatale* in the flesh. It didn't take us long to discover who was boss. Despite being 69 she was determined to project a glamorous, youthful image. At the brand new National Arts Centre in Ottawa she issued precise instructions to the stage crew: every move, every angle had to show her to best advantage, and her stipulations regarding lighting meant she was bathed throughout in a pink rejuvenating glow. All photography was forbidden under threat of her stopping the show. The fact that her performance was so controlled eliminated some of her old spark, but someone was impressed: a young man dressed in a white toga tossed roses onto the stage throughout the performance.

An alternative venue for poets and musicians was Ottawa's Café Le Hibou. A shabby room with a stage at one end, it played host to an extraordinary array of poets and musicians, some already celebrated, some destined for fame. Squashed around tiny tables we listened to poets and some of the great musicians of the day. On one occasion, at a table cheek-by-jowl with the performers, I witnessed the legendary American blues singer, Howlin' Wolf, rolling on the stage, his massive shoes within a few inches of my nose. 'Here in Ottawa,' he told the audience, 'people stare at me because I'm black. There just ain't no black people here.' This may have been the case, but he was absolutely huge. 'Of course they stare at him,' whispered Peter. 'He's a giant!' I have never been musical but I loved the creative atmosphere of Café Le Hibou where I also saw live performances by Muddy Waters and Taj Mahal. Numerous well-known performers such as Joni Mitchell, Jimi Hendrix, Neil Young and Buffy St

Marie, frequented Le Hibou around that time.

Peter and I were living in a domestic bubble. We experimented with cooking and talked long into the night over meals and bottles of wine. Under Peter's tutelage I was gaining a whole new perspective on the world; he opened my eyes to working-class politics, philosophy, as well as all things Canadian. We indulged in a cosiness that became routine and somewhat bookish. I was becoming more confident intellectually, I had a good job, I was at home in Canada and I was truly cherished. Superficially I was blooming, but lurking in the back of my mind there was a twinge of resistance. I didn't even admit it to myself, but I wasn't really ready to settle down. The whole wide world was still out there.

As luck would have it, my life was about to change. My contract with the Canadian Science Film Association was just coming up for renewal when the Canadian Film Institute received a phone call from Rod Holmes, a television producer with the Canadian Broadcasting Corporation, CBC. 'We're planning a series entitled *The Conquest of Space*,' he said, 'and we're wondering if you know a suitable film researcher for the project.' 'We've just the person right here,' said director, Roy Little. 'Jenny screened hundreds of space films for Expo 67.' Within a couple of weeks I was working at the CBC on my very first job as a television film researcher.

A Break for Freedom

Working for the Canadian Broadcasting Corporation was liberating after the quieter environment of the Canadian Film Institute. Suddenly I was surrounded by the bustle of producers, film editors and camera crews. I had been working closely with Peter for the best part of three years, as well socialising with him and, eventually, living with him. A certain amount of routine and stagnation had crept into our relationship but now, working at CBC, my horizons suddenly widened again.

The Conquest of Space focused on the years since 1957 and Soviet Sputnik 1. My science film contacts from Expo 67 stood me in good stead as I trawled film from Britain, France, the Soviet Union and the USA. The theme tune for the series was Simon and Garfunkel's *The Sound of Silence* and for months, as I worked long periods in the studios and cutting rooms, that song was the backdrop to my life.

The scriptwriter for the series was an Irishman called Noel Moore. 'I was in Malaysia with the British army,' he told me. 'They were my John Wayne days! I had some strange assignments: once I was asked to guard a hippopotamus from terrorists!' Noel loved quasi-scientific experiments. One evening at our house we discovered him stringing up a container from a light bulb. 'What on earth are you doing?' I asked. 'I'm trying to manufacture ozone,' he replied. Another time I was sitting in a packed CBC canteen when Noel's thick Irish accent came booming over the tannoy: 'It's God here,' he said. 'Can we be havin' a bit o' hush?!'

He invited us to a party at his farmhouse outside Ottawa, an event which, to our amazement, was attended almost exclusively by Russians. They emerged from the snowy wastes, tall dark figures with fur hats, high boots, long coats, trudging towards the house like Cossacks, clutching bottles of vodka and a samovar. They stood on the wooden veranda, stamping the snow off their boots, before crossing the threshold in stockinged feet and making for the kitchen where they installed the samovar. Members of the Soviet Embassy in Ottawa, they were only allowed to travel a limited distance outside the city, and Noel's home was located beyond the permitted zone. Consequently, their demeanour was rebellious, as if they were playing hooky. The ensuing vodka-induced revelry lasted all afternoon and well into the night, including in the bedroom, where I glimpsed a Russian in diplomatic relations with a Canadian woman. By the time Peter and I left, these latter-day Zhivagos had become maudlin and the old clapboard house resounded with song as deep and mournful as an Orthodox liturgy.

Shortly after working on *The Conquest of Space* I began undertaking the Canadian research for a BBC series on the British Empire as well as working on a CBC programme called *What's Left?* The latter was an eye-opener: I watched archive film of 'Big Bill' Haywood on the march in New York with the International Workers of the World, known as Wobblies, and witnessed the 1919 Winnipeg Strike including Bloody Saturday when the Royal Canadian Mounted Police charged the strikers. It was the first of a decade of occasions, when I found myself totally immersed in one area of interest, sometimes for weeks on end. Sitting day-after-day in a darkened room, screening film about the same subject, can eventually overwhelm reality and suck you into the lives and times of others.

Because there was so much work I was now frequently catching the 7am breakfast flight from Ottawa to Toronto, returning 12 hours later on the dinner flight. My new job was beginning to erode the cosy routine I had with Peter. At CBC I was being exposed to an inordinate amount of flattery. The cameramen were begging me to register as a contestant in the forthcoming Miss CBC contest. Whilst decrying the event as sexist, I was secretly delighted at their insistence I might win. Feminism had only just entered my consciousness; prior to that I had never given it a thought.

Together with my friend, Alison, I had joined the National Gallery of Canada women's group. Women's rights regarding education, employment, reproduction and health were brand new concepts to us all. We read books on sexual politics: Gloria Steinem, Kate Millett and Germaine Greer. It was a time when women were coming together for mass demonstrations causing the media to focus on the new sexual revolution. On Mother's Day in the USA the National Organisation for Women demanded *rights not roses*, a phrase that summed up what became known as the second wave of feminism – the first being the fight for women's suffrage back at the turn of the century.

Half-a-dozen members of our women's group met up one weekend in an isolated lakeside cabin. At the time, women were being encouraged to accept their bodies as they were, rather than striving for stereotypical notions of beauty. We sat around, stark naked, drinking wine, and taking it in turns to say what we liked or disliked about our appearance. 'I'd like bigger breasts and smaller thighs,' I said. 'I'm too fat,' said someone else.

One woman had been born with six nipples and had scars below her breasts where four had been removed. 'In the old days I'd have been burnt as a witch,' she joked. Each declaration was met with a positive rebuttal along the lines of: 'But you're beautiful as you are.' Discussions continued all afternoon, as we exchanged confidences about sexuality, menstruation and relationships. Being transparent about intimate women's issues was a new experience and it created a close bond between those present. The day ended with exuberant skinny-dipping in the lake.

Consciousness-raising sounds clichéd now, but I was discussing issues I had never considered before. Being part of the women's group changed my life and also caused me to reappraise my upbringing. There is no doubt my brother, Philip, and I had been equally adored by our parents, but I began to realise that his education and development had sometimes been given priority over my own. I was also becoming aware of sexist advertising and sent frequent letters of complaint to companies guilty of objectifying women. Strangely, I never extended feminist attitudes to my own sense of fashion and I continued to dress provocatively in the scantiest of miniskirts.

At the Canadian Broadcasting Corporation I was now working for executive producer, Cameron Graham. A charming, accessible man who was to become a lifelong friend, he was nonetheless very much part of CBC establishment and already a high flyer. Over the years which followed he was to award me numerous contracts. I would contact him long-distance from England and elsewhere: 'Got any work for me, Cam?' I'd ask, and he always fixed me up with something.

With production work looming on more than one television series, the CBC leased some offices and cutting rooms at Crawley Films, a family-run company, headed by the iconic patriarch, Budge Crawley. I found myself working in a new, dynamic environment, packed with young filmmakers who were interesting, unconventional and fun. I began spending lunch hours and breaks with Pat Crawley, one of Budge's three sons; I was attracted to him and enjoyed his company. One week, when I had work to do in Toronto, he invited me to stay in the house he shared with friends. One of the bizarre things I remember about that visit was a conical lump of soap in the bathroom: three or four feet high, it was an end-piece Pat had removed from a production tube when filming in a soap factory. The idea was to embrace the block of soap, rubbing one's wet body against it, before returning to the bath!

I was devoting more and more time to friends from Crawley Films and the CBC and gradually drifting away from Peter. However, I didn't know how to end the relationship and I failed to discuss my misgivings with him. I felt guilty, and I stayed with him longer than I should have done. In the end I took the coward's way out: I packed my bags and drove off in a blizzard to Stoneacres, the Crawley family ranch in the Gatineau Hills, leaving Peter for good. He was utterly devastated and refused to believe I wasn't coming back. 'Why are you throwing it all away?' he kept asking. 'We were so happy. Such happiness is rare.' He was right. We were compatible and we had been incredibly happy. However, I had finally faced up to the fact that I wasn't ready to settle down.

Running away, almost on the spur of the moment, was a shocking way to sever an engagement and a relationship of three years. I had hurt him terribly and it would be a decade before he found his true soul mate and partner. He went on to become Canada's primary authority on cinema with numerous prestigious publications to his name.

CHAPTER SIX

LAND OF THE SILVER BIRCH

Crawley Films

DANNY WAS OUT OF IT. He'd been snorting coke and had flaked out on the cutting-room floor. I was carefully navigating my way around this sprawling figure when a young man with shoulder-length curly hair stuck his head round the door. 'Southern Comfort upstairs, Jenny.' I hesitated. 'Come on,' he insisted. 'It's the end of the week. Come and join us.' I knew there would be a fair number of spliffs doing the rounds as well. Friday afternoon at Crawley Films had a tendency to be a write-off.

Other than the occasional trespasser such as stoned-out Danny, the CBC enclave was an oasis of convention surrounded by the creative hippie mayhem that was Crawleys. Even within our own ranks, however, eccentric behaviour manifested itself occasionally. Jim Williams, our film editor, was inclined to have tantrums and more than once I was forced to duck a metal film can as it zoomed over my head and crashed against the wall. Jim was diabetic and his outbursts usually erupted late afternoon when his insulin needed topping up. He had other reasons for his frustration: once a bush pilot, the onset of diabetes had forced him to stop flying. His temperament was geared to the great outdoors and being caged in a cutting-room had rendered him bitter.

Many of the Canadians I knew were at home in the wilds. Seemingly effete city-dwellers would arrive at their lakeside cabins and become instantly transformed into bush men, wielding axes and navigating rapids. Sally Macdonald, a film director at Crawley's and elderly by the time I met her, would frequently disappear into the wilderness by herself on long canoeing expeditions. A couple of years later when I went to see the American thriller *Deliverance*, I came away convinced that the entire Canadian population consisted of bushwhackers; throughout the screening most of the audience had discussed, rather too loudly, the merits or otherwise of the paddle strokes.

Going out with Pat Crawley and getting involved with his family was a far cry from being with Peter. Despite his years in Canada, Peter remained essentially English and devoid of the more muscular Canadian approach. Life with him had been gentle and academic. With the Crawleys it was non-stop 'doing': shooting films, writing scripts, recording sounds, playing music, ploughing snow, riding horses. Sure, there were academic discussions as well, but usually related to whatever piece of creativity was in progress.

Over the next four years I was to spend a lot of time at Stoneacres, the Crawleys' ranch-style estate, situated in the Gatineau hills near Old Chelsea, Quebec. There had once been cattle there, but these were long gone. The exterior of the house was nondescript and functional but, once inside, the focus was outwards, towards the land. The large sitting room had a stone fireplace, a slate floor, and picture windows. It extended into a dining area with a long refectory table where hospitality was extended to an extraordinary array of guests. Behind that, in a small kitchen, rows of burnished copper pots contrasted with the generally muted shades of the interior.

Downstairs, leading off a large room, was a conservatory and it was there that Pat had rigged up his bed so he could fall asleep looking at the stars and surrounding wilderness. Lying in that bed with the thick snow piled just beyond the glass, I felt like a small hibernating animal, cocooned in the vastness of what I saw as the real Canada. There was only one intrusion, a wedding band, suspended from the roof on a thread, which swung gently back and forth above my head. It belonged to Pat's ex-wife who lived in New York, and he seemed to regard the ring with injured reverence, like an amulet which protected him from the reality of the estrangement. Years later, when I slept in a chief's hut in the African bush with a dead juju bug suspended on a string above me, I was reminded of the wedding ring in Patrick's conservatory and the hex it had cast on my peace of mind.

Pat had five siblings and the sprawling house was overflowing with young people: the family, their partners, friends and children, plus anyone who happened to be working at Crawley Films at the time, including those who, these days, might be deemed celebrities.

By the time I came on the scene, Budge Crawley, father of the family and celebrated film maker, had taken a second wife and absented himself from the household. His first wife, Judy, still inhabited Stoneacres, and was a delightful woman with whom I formed a lasting friendship. A pioneer cineaste, she had started shooting films with Budge in 1938, working as a camerawoman and in every field of production. Towards the end of my time in Canada, she was writing the screenplay for *The Man Who Skied Down Everest*, a film about Japanese extreme skier Yuichiro Miura which was to win the 1976 Academy Award for best documentary. Although I was the same age as her son Pat, I thought of Judy more as a contemporary than as a mother-figure. She would confide in me, discuss ideas with me, and I loved her. When my relationship with Pat had fizzled out and I was returning temporarily to England, one of Pat's sisters came to me: 'Judy is terribly upset you're leaving,' she said. 'She keeps asking me "How can we make Pat marry Jenny?" ' She wasn't serious, of course, but the sentiment was flattering.

My relationship with Pat only lasted a few months. His focus was elsewhere. Handsome, physically large with a temperament to match, he was coming into his own as a movie maker and he would shoot footage wherever we went. It was Pat who instilled in me a love of the Canadian wilderness. He led me along forest trails in deep snow, where I discovered that wearing snowshoes was an acquired skill and not as easy as it looked. On a couple of occasions we slept outside in an Arctic sleeping bag and, lying quite still, he made me listen out for the rhythmic thumping of winter animals communicating in the snow. He also introduced me to wolves, but they weren't in the wild; they were in the backyard of his friend, Bill Mason!

Dubbed the patron saint of canoeing, Bill had explored the furthest reaches of Canada, including the Arctic. Artist, animator, movie-maker and author, he was a true environmentalist, blazing a trail long before such issues became fashionable. His award-winning films included a series about wolves and behind his house he kept three of them in a pen. On winter weekends, I would sometimes accompany Pat and his family on a visit to the Masons. Beside their simple house Bill had flooded a small area, providing a mini ice rink where we used to play broomball, a homespun version of ice hockey which involved slipping around on the ice and whacking at a ball with household brooms. Sometimes the wolves would start to howl and I would creep round the corner to observe these magnificent creatures baying at the moon. They were eventually returned to the wild, but not before causing ructions at Ottawa airport when a worker heard strange noises emanating from a crate. On tracing the owner he enquired what was inside. 'It's a wolf,' said Bill nonchalantly.

From boiling up maple syrup on a stove outside in the snow, to lounging in the summer heat serenaded by young musicians, or haymaking in the big paddock in front of the house, life with the Crawleys was never dull. Meal times were special. Not only was the food delicious, but one never quite knew who would turn up at the dinner table. One time it was Michael J Pollard who, three years before, had appeared in *Bonnie and Clyde.* Another time it was Howard Alk, celebrated editor, cinematographer and collaborator of Bob Dylan. At the time I met Alk, Budge Crawley had hired him to direct and edit *Janis,* a film about the singer which was to rack up big grosses in America. I had talked to Alk in the cutting-rooms during Crawley Films Friday afternoon parties, but I was far too straight to connect with him; he made me nervous.

The young film-makers who surrounded me at work were a dynamic bunch and sometimes their interests rubbed off on me in quirky ways. I remember Bruce Nyznik, then a sound man, admonishing me: 'Jenny, you just don't listen properly.' He marched me off to a neighbourhood supermarket and proceeded to walk along the shelves, vigorously shaking packets to demonstrate the different sounds made by the contents. 'Use your ears. You're missing out on an entire world,' said the young man, who went on to win numerous film awards for sound as well as directing.

In the CBC unit I was embarking on my most prolific years as a film researcher. Over the next four years I was to undertake research in Ottawa, Toronto, Montreal and New York, as well as back in England. The executive producer was always Cameron Graham, known as Cam, but I was answerable to directors, Munroe Scott and Brian Nolan: two men, chalk and cheese. Munroe was even-tempered, efficient and easy to work for. His instructions were precise, his scripts ready on time, and his research requirements listed down to the last detail. There was no confusion, but also little leeway for creativity on my part. Brian was the opposite: enigmatic and cool, he wore well-cut jeans and crisp open-necked shirts. He had been in the US Army in Korea, worked as an international correspondent and, despite his love of all things Canadian, he came across as more American in style. His research needs were less specific than Munroe's which meant I had more fun locating material, but the ratio of film selected to footage used was probably less efficient.

Various film editors came and went in the CBC Unit, but it was Jim Williams who became a friend and who was always there for me. Blonde, handsome and in his 40s, he was the ultimate clean-cut outdoor type. He was my rock and he was to help me in many ways: moving impossibly heavy pieces of furniture into my apartment; providing a deep male voice on my phone in an attempt to repel a spate of dirty phone calls; assisting me with the physical removal from my flat of a wild-eyed, mentally disturbed girl who'd run away from home. Ever grounded, amusing and affectionate, Jim was something of a tragic character for whom things never seemed to go quite right.

There were three researchers assigned to the unit: Anne Acland, aloof and efficient; Bobbi Turcotte, smart, fussy, her desk orderly; and me, the antithesis of the others, possibly too casual. Whereas Bobbi would work through research lists methodically, I would give priority to subjects that interested me, leaving the boring items to Bobbi. 'Have you done this one yet, Jenny?' she'd enquire politely. 'No,' I'd say. 'I'll do it later in the week.' When the time came, I often found the more mundane footage had been located and ordered by Bobbi. Despite this, I took my research seriously, locating unique visual material and approaching each piece of research with enthusiasm and pride.

During my time with the Canadian Broadcasting Corporation I was to work on five television film series totalling 42 episodes, as well as contributing to other movies. Returning from a visit to Canada, my brother's friend told him, 'Your sister's name is always on the television.' It was. I was working with a prestigious team on prestigious productions.

The Days Before Yesterday

Being a researcher on a lengthy television series was like doing a massive jigsaw puzzle. Each fragment of discovery contributed to the overall picture, little gems which injected something dynamic into lives and times: film and photographs; maps and paintings; songs and voices; unexpected witnesses with fascinating stories. The script was the skeleton. I added the contours, fleshing it out with detail until it was whole. My work gave me a privileged entrée into the most fascinating places. One week I'd be sitting in a warehouse in New York chatting with a news film buff; a week later I'd be in the Glenbow Foundation Archive in Calgary looking at photographic glass plates depicting pioneers in western Canada – wagon trains, log cabins and Indians in full regalia. Once I spent an entire afternoon with a psychic medium who had been the mentor of Mackenzie King, former prime minister of Canada, and who, unbelievably, had influenced his political decisions.

One unforgettable visit was to the Ottawa Archive. I was after a rare gramophone record, the only copy of the recording in existence. The archivist was reluctant. 'Go on,' I wheedled. 'I'll be really careful. I'll whip it up to our sound department, they'll record it, and I'll have it back to you inside a couple of hours. No one need ever know.' The archivist caved in. I nearly hugged him. It was a real coup. He slipped the record gently into a protective envelope and away I went. On reaching my office, I gingerly opened the package, and there lay the precious record – cracked in half. I had treated it with immense care. It was so old that, had it remained in the archive, the same thing could have happened. However, it wasn't in the archive. It was there on my desk. The subsequent phone call was excruciating.

For long stints in other cities I was put up in comfortable hotels. When I first contacted the CBC travel department about a hotel in New York, my film editor friend Jim wound me up. 'Tell 'em you want to stay in the Waldorf Astoria,' he drawled. Gullible as always, I had no idea it was one of the poshest hotels in New York. I phoned the CBC travel man. 'George,' I said, 'I think the Waldorf Astoria's probably best.' 'You bet it is,' he snorted, and you're not staying there!' Nonetheless, he did once arrange for me to stay in New York's historic Algonquin Hotel, celebrated in the 1920s as the meeting place of well-known literary figures and resplendent with art nouveau décor.

Screening and selecting archive film was always the highlight of my job. It was the glimpses of people from long ago that thrilled me – wealthy women in fox furs and cloche hats; dustbowl victims of the Great Depression, fixing on me hollow-eyed as the tumbleweeds blew past; soldiers who stared into the camera as they marched off to die in distant lands. For days on end I would be closeted in the dark, observing this flickering carnival of life long gone.

When I had made my selection, the editor would order the prints and I would catalogue them. When working on a series, the director might ask for a shot he had seen months before, and out of all the cans stacked from floor to ceiling, I had to know exactly where to find it. Occasionally mistakes were made. 'Hey, Jim,' I remember saying. 'Take a look at this. Those soldiers aren't wearing German helmets.' 'Oh, hell,' he said, 'They're Spanish. How on earth did they get cut in with the Germans?' Once a production was complete, every frame had to be logged; film, stills, sound and music paid for.

During my years with CBC I worked on various productions about Canada's political history. Aired in the years which followed Expo 67, when Canada was reassessing its identity, these were deemed ground-breaking documentaries for which producer Cameron Graham won well-deserved awards. *The Days Before Yesterday* was my favourite series: '*Where are the days before yesterday? Where have the golden days gone?*' went the theme tune, and I would sit in my apartment when the programmes were aired, singing along and watching all the fragments I had chosen, expertly slotted into place; the finished jigsaw was fulfilling.

Overseas film director

In May 1970, after my first stint as a film researcher for CBC and only six months with Pat Crawley, I returned to England to set up the location filming for a series about Lester Pearson who'd been prime minister of Canada from 1963 to 1968. The offer of work in London could not have come at a better time. I had been happy with Pat, but he had spent more and more time away filming and had clearly lost interest in our relationship. I was sad to leave him behind and desperately upset at the loss of his family, all of whom I had grown to love.

Lester Pearson had also been a professor, historian, statesman and diplomat, and had won the Nobel Peace Prize for organising the UN Emergency Force to resolve the Suez Crisis. I was to focus on his life towards the end of the First World War, when he had joined the Royal Flying Corps (which preceded the RAF) at Hendon. Prior to that, he had been trained with the Officer Training Corps at Wadham College, Oxford, where Robert Graves had been his company officer and had recommended his promotion. A shell-shocked poet at the time, Graves had gone on to become the celebrated scholar and writer everyone knows. In the early 1920s, when Pearson returned to Oxford to study at St John's College, he discovered Graves had also returned; they were fellow undergraduates.

Cam had asked me to interview Robert Graves about his years with

Lester Pearson. I wrote to Graves who lived in Spain, and discovered he planned to be in London that July. What I didn't know was that, aged 75, he had begun to lose his memory. When I eventually filmed him we were forced to shoot take after take; every time he was meant to say Canada, he said Australia. It was embarrassing for me and frustrating for him. A handsome, distinguished-looking old man, he sported a traditional, flat-crowned Spanish hat, his curly white hair protruding from beneath the wide brim. His manner was conceited and he was outrageously flirtatious, even on camera. In between shooting, we shared an entertaining lunch in a local pub, during which he reminisced about Augustus John. 'That man could never resist women,' pronounced Graves. 'My mother, my wife and my daughter have all been chased round my kitchen table by Augustus John!'

When Cam and Lester Pearson eventually arrived in England, we spent a couple of days shooting scenes about the Royal Flying Corps at the RAF Museum in Hendon. The curator had kindly taken a First World War aircraft from under wraps and put it out on the field. Pearson described his first lesson, over half a century before. 'I went up with the flight instructor,' he said. 'We circled the airfield a couple of times while he showed me the controls and that was that! Then I went solo.' Our location may have been a museum, but it was still very much Royal Air Force. At lunch we all piled into the officers' mess for refreshments, whereupon members of the film crew were asked to retire to a room next door reserved for other ranks. They had been working really hard and I was furious. 'I'll go with them,' I insisted, but was told, 'No, stay here. This room is for officers and ladies.' Apart from the fact I disliked the designation of lady, I considered myself part of the crew. 'It's ridiculous to apply RAF rules to people who aren't even in the Forces,' I growled at Cam, but he hushed me up. 'Let it go,' he warned. 'They've been so helpful. Come on now, have a drink.' Cam knew me well. I would have had no compunctions about having a fight with the RAF officer who was our host.

The next location for filming was at Oxford during a couple of idyllic summer days. It was strange to wander across the lawns and through the cloisters of St John's College in the company of Lester Pearson who had studied there in the 1920s. We filmed him reminiscing with his old tutor, William Conrad Costin, author and scholar, who went on to become president of the college. One of my fond memories was shooting in the library where ancient tomes were attached to the table with chains.

During these days on location, Lester Pearson insisted I ride with him in the back of the large Austin Princess. I liked him and we chatted away without reservation. Slight of build and cosy in demeanour, he seemed an unlikely person to have been prime minister and to have influenced international politics. As the car purred along, he kept humming to himself and singing the popular tune from *Butch Cassidy and the Sundance Kid*. 'Raindrops keep fallin' on my head,' sung the Nobel Peace Prize winner, the ex-prime minister of Canada, 'Those raindrops keep fallin' on my head, they keep fallin'…' Once, when I was sitting on the jump seat opposite, he leant forward and said unexpectedly, 'If I were still prime minister I'd have you in my office.' Cam always vowed the double entendre was intentional, but I like to think otherwise; I don't think he would have been inappropriate.

Pearson and Cam returned to Canada leaving me in charge of further shooting. Richard Bedford Bennett, Canadian prime minister during the Great Depression, eventually retired to Britain and was the only Canadian prime minister ever to be awarded a peerage. He lived in Cherkley Court, a stately home in Mickleham, Surrey, not far from Dorking. In 1947 he had a heart attack and died in his bath. I managed to track down an elderly couple who had been servants up at 'the big house'. With their cockney accents they were perfect for a Canadian audience. Apparently the water in Bennett's bath kept running after he'd had the heart attack and got hotter and hotter. 'Boiled in 'is bath, 'e was!' the old man kept saying. ''E were bright red. Imagine that. Boiled! '

Bennett was buried at Mickleham church and Cam had said I should direct the filming of the servants and of the grave and churchyard. It was a simple shoot and with a superb cameraman and crew, I just let them get on with it. I was pleased with my credit, *overseas film director*, but with hindsight, perhaps it was a wasted opportunity; I should have shown more initiative with both that and the Robert Graves filming. During all the years I worked for Cam he was forever trying to propel me towards greater things, but I never took up the bait. In Mickleham churchyard the cameraman had shot one or two cut-aways of me. When Jim Williams viewed the rushes in the CBC Unit at Crawley Films he sent me a message: *Good God, Jenny, what has happened to you? Your hair! You look like a wild woman.*

My contract with Cam over, I continued to freelance from the CBC London office. As I worked, non-stop breaking news from Reuters and other agencies was relayed over loudspeakers; although I had nothing to do with news, having a heads-up on world affairs made me feel at the hub of things. My most interesting assignment was a six-episode series with the working title *The Politics of Fear*, produced and directed by David Rabinovitch, a specialist on terrorism. My task was to find interviewees. I spent a lot of time on the phone to Cyprus trying to get hold of Archbishop Makarios who had survived four assassination attempts and was in the throes of dealing with the guerrilla organisation EOKA. I very nearly got him, but Cyprus was in turmoil and my sources prevaricated. A hunt for so-called terrorists was proving difficult. Eventually, after trawling underground contacts in London's Irish community, I arranged a clandestine meeting with an IRA man who fitted the bill. I spent the afternoon with him in a pub and eventually he agreed to an anonymous interview. I went zooming off to producer Jeff Anderson. 'I've got someone,' I said, 'a fantastic Irishman. He's perfect.' 'What are his credentials?' enquired Jeff, sounding less than enthusiastic. 'If we interview him, he can't be anonymous, you know. 'He has to be,' I insisted, 'otherwise he'll be arrested. He puts the freedom fighter's perspective perfectly.' 'No,' said Jeff. 'It can't be done.' I was furious. 'You're only going to portray one side of the argument, aren't you?' I protested. 'Sorry,' said Jeff. 'We can't use him, and that's final.'

At the time I was living in a small rented room in the home of the celebrated Polish artist, Feliks Topolski. One of the Nash houses in Regents Park, the elegant facade belied the shabby interior. The stairwell was papered with Topolski's sketches printed on newspaper and featuring people from all over the world. I saw virtually nothing of Feliks who had separate quarters within the house, but he did invite me to his studio beneath a railway arch near Waterloo. I liked him. He made me welcome and showed me his work.

While working in the CBC London office I had met a young Canadian called Tim Wilson, a freelance radio reporter who had just arrived in London from Switzerland. We were to embark on a relationship that, in August 1971, would lure me back to Canada. In the meantime, however, I had heard there was a researcher needed at the film unit attached to the Slade School of Fine Art. I applied for the job and got it.

The End of a Golden Age

Entitled *Peacemaking 1919*, the film was about the Treaty of Versailles – the most important of the negotiations that brought an end to the First World War – and was a collaboration between the Slade Film Unit and Visual Programme Systems.

My first port of call was the British Institute of Recorded Sound. 'Make yourself comfortable, dear,' said the curator. 'Back in a mo'. Just listening to an aria!' He disappeared into a sound booth while I waited. Eventually he emerged beaming. 'Splendid,' he muttered, 'absolutely splendid! Now, how can I help you? Mistinguett wasn't it?' Born in 1875, the French *femme fatale,* singer and actress had been an entertainer at the Folies Bergère and Moulin Rouge, as well as a silent movie star. By the 1920s her flamboyance and risqué routines had made her one of the world's most highly-paid entertainers. Back at the Slade I sank into a worn leather chair in the study of my boss, Thorold Dickinson. 'I saw Mistinguett when I was young,' he announced unexpectedly. 'She descended the stairs, feathers in her hair, a feather train, and those long, long legs...' He paused, lost in the past. After a moment he stood up

Above: radio reporter Tim Wilson; (right) interviewing former Canadian prime minister Lester Pearson, London, 1970. Below: with Tim and Marx in Highgate cemetery; white trash, aged 28.

London, 1971-72 (below, left to right): with Lutz Becker, film-maker and artist at Slade Film Unit; Jenni Pozzi, fellow film researcher at the Slade; with Val at Crown Cassette Communications.

Above: Tim Wilson at Clearwater Bay, Lake of the Woods, Canada, summer 1972.
Below: George Timko, on the back stairs to my apartment on Wellington Street, Ottawa, winter 1972.

Left: George and his new hat, Jamaica, March 1973.
Above: a last visit to Old Chelsea, Quebec, Boxing Day 1973, just before leaving Canada for good.

and went to the cupboard to fetch a glass. 'Now,' he said, 'have a sherry. How's the research going?'

Thorold was Britain's first university professor of film and, by the time I met him, he seemed weary of this role. *Peacemaking 1919* was to be his last production and he retired at the end of that year. A charming old-fashioned gentleman, he had worked as a director, screenwriter and producer from 1928 to 1955. His involvement with film had taken him all over the world: from Paris in the 1920s to the USSR in 1937; from the Spanish Civil War to head of film at the UN. As he held court behind his antique desk, books stretching from floor to ceiling behind him, he expressed genuine interest in the young people who worked for him. He made me feel worthwhile.

The director of *Peacemaking* was Charles Frend who, only the year before, had been second unit director on David Lean's *Ryan's Daughter*. A doyen of the golden age of film, he had started his career in 1931 as a film editor for Hitchcock. He went on to direct some of the Ealing comedies and classics such as *The Cruel Sea*. Charles shared an office with me and researcher, Jenni Pozzi. Smartly turned out, usually with a tweed jacket and tie, he was gentle, kind, good humoured and, as it transpired, utterly confused. It didn't take us long to realise that he forgot things from one day to the next. For a while Jenni and I ignored the problem, but in the end we had to advise Thorold. It was embarrassing to voice reservations about one of Britain's cinema greats, and heart-breaking to witness Charles' dawning realisation that he couldn't cope. Shortly afterwards, he was diagnosed with a brain tumour.

Into the midst of this fragile situation and the Slade's fusty environment charged our collaborators, Visual Programme Systems producers Sandy Lieberson and David Puttnam. Entering Thorold's office, where he sat behind his desk with a bow tie and a velvet jacket, they were casual, speedy and entrepreneurial. Sandy, an American, had just produced *Performance*, starring Mick Jagger and notorious for explicit sex and drug scenes. Puttnam was about to produce the rock musical *That'll be the Day* and a decade later would become well-known for his Academy Award-winning film *Chariots of Fire*. Forceful wheeler-dealers, they were the antithesis of Thorold and everything he stood for, but despite the setbacks and an understandable lack of harmony between VPS and the Slade, *Peacemaking 1919* eventually got made. It was directed by David Mingay who went on to work on *A Bigger Splash* with David Hockney.

Researcher Jenni Pozzi and I became close and were to remain friends for decades to come. We cruised about in unison wearing high boots, calf-length midi-skirts and long cloaks. Once, when we were visiting the sound archives at BBC Broadcasting House, there was wet paint. As we flounced along behind the curator he was concerned: 'Don't swish, ladies,' he admonished. 'Do be careful. Please, please don't swish!' The CBC offices, which I still visited from time to time, were located in the rag trade district, where Jenni and I used to glean scraps of material for patchwork. We would arrive late afternoon as the workshops closed, to find discarded bin bags filled with cut-offs from machine-made garments. One day, carrying two of these sacks apiece, we boarded a packed tube train. In the middle of our journey the bags burst, spilling a sea of fabric across the floor. We got off at the next station, leaving commuters ankle-deep in scraps of cloth.

Having worked so long in north America, I was now familiarising myself with the British film libraries, exploring a golden age that had waned. The way the footage was catalogued reflected the era in which it had been shot: *Natives run amok*; *Britannia rules the waves*. Sometimes I would come across a film can that had slipped through the net, a dusty remnant lying forgotten in a corner. Prising it open was exciting; what would I find inside? If the newsreels were a treasure trove, the film librarians were national treasures: John and Pat at Movietone, the wonderful Larry McKinna at Pathé, and ETV's Stanley Forman, a specialist on Soviet and left-wing footage. There were others besides film researchers who frequented these libraries: politicians watching historical speeches; actors observing mannerisms of those they were about to portray; students and historians.

In addition to film libraries there were newspaper and picture libraries to visit, as well as the British Library. The British Library reading room, located in the British Museum, was extraordinary. Access was restricted to registered researchers and I was aware I was treading in the steps of Marx, Gandhi, Orwell, so many exceptional minds. To obtain a permit I had to stand at a hatch opening onto a small office that looked Dickensian. My name, company and purpose were hand-written in ink in a giant ledger; the only thing that seemed missing was a quill pen. The library occupied a circular domed room with desks radiating from a central hub. The stacks reached to the ceiling and there were walkways, high up and at different levels, inhabited by librarians who looked like distant pin figures.

To be allowed inside this sacred enclave was a privilege. I barely dared breathe for fear of disturbing the pursuit of great minds. Then, one day, I was to witness an unusual disturbance. On the highest walkway, up near the domed ceiling, a man started to twang a Jew's harp. The sound reverberated round and round the dome, startling the readers far below, who began to whisper in astonishment. A couple of people were seen running around the top level and the unfortunate musician was accosted and whisked away. I never had the facts verified, but rumour had it that the miscreant had waited years to listen to the effects of his Jews' harp being played in the dome.

The London I had returned to from Canada had changed drastically. The harsh Mary Quant and Twiggy looks of the 1960s had softened into hippie fashions: long swirling skirts, embroidered waistcoats, Afghan coats, big-brimmed hats and patchwork. The mirror-work I had first seen in Pakistan was now everywhere, as were Indian dresses, ethnic beads and earrings. Men had very long hair, which made them look romantic. Jeans were flared and patched, boots were high, and lots of people walked around with bare feet. Any combination was acceptable.

When my contract with the Slade ended, I got a job with Crown Cassette Communications, a company which had just begun to buy up rights on films for use on the newly-released Phillips video cassette recorder – the first viable VCR for home use. We discussed excitedly how video cassettes might be played on buses, trains and aircraft, at sports centres and schools. 'Everyone will have one in their home,' said George Wightman, our director. It was a situation we could barely envisage.

George, my new boss, was gentle and amusing and, at heart, he was a poet. I always felt that being involved in business, let alone an entrepreneurial escapade with VCRs, was not really where he belonged. A pillar of the Poetry Society, he was also a scholar who published translations of classical Arab poetry. My friend and colleague, Val, was to write in a letter: *I had to work at George's flat last week. He served me coffee in china urns on Qing Dynasty plates!*

There were four of us, all young women, negotiating the VCR rights on films and we were pretty successful at tying up deals. However, what we, and particularly George, thought people would watch in the years to follow, turned out to be a far cry from the reality. We focused on alternative movies: art films, foreign titles, classics. We approached the Arts Council and the British Council for advice. Popular culture was simply not contemplated or catered for. These days, when I watch an in-flight movie, I think back with amusement to the menu of highbrow films we had planned to offer passengers.

It had been a strange year. I had started off dealing with old-timers such as Robert Graves and Charles Frend, and had ended up working on projects which would cause a worldwide visual revolution. None of us, however, had grasped the enormity of what was to come.

Tumbleweed Trails

In the early 70s protest was alive and kicking. Young people were engaged rather than apathetic. A mistrust in authoritarian society prevailed and everyone was on the march. Left-wing groups dominated, many concerned with world issues: the Irish Troubles; apartheid in South Africa; the Vietnam War; South American resistance movements such as the Tupamaros. In addition, thousands of workers took to the streets to demonstrate against the new Industrial Relations Act. The first ever Gay Pride march got underway and women were also demonstrating for control of their bodies and their lives. The IRA and an anarchist group, the Angry Brigade, were letting off bombs in London. Although I wasn't very political, I went on quite a few demonstrations. I stuck anti-apartheid stickers on South African oranges in supermarkets, and anti-Vietnam War stickers on tube station walls. While my brother was deadly serious about his protests, actually getting arrested, I remained on the sidelines.

I was distributing the political stickers at the instigation of my Canadian boyfriend, Tim Wilson. We had been going out for several months, while he continued working as a freelance reporter out of CBC London. Professional, focused and erudite, his notable interviewees included Hitler's chief architect, Albert Speer, as well as John Lennon and Yoko Ono. He had also taken the opportunity of interviewing Lester Pearson when we were filming him in England. Tim had a cultured modulated voice, blue grey eyes and finely chiselled features. His wavy blonde hair was self-consciously fluffed up and he wore a wide-brimmed suede leather hat. His style was casual and classy and despite the hat and hair, he was no hippy.

On Tim's press pass I gained access to some interesting events. When the public was queueing round the block to see the Tutankhamun exhibition at the British Museum, I gazed on the magnificent golden mask and other artefacts unimpeded by crowds. Tim also covered the London visit of the African American activist Angela Davis, and I found myself part of an audience where everyone raised their fists in Black Power salutes. An interview with a young man who had set up the first-ever computer dating agency was less controversial. 'Well, that's not going anywhere,' I said to Tim afterwards. 'How's that supposed to work when hardly anyone owns a computer?'

With Tim things were always interesting, verging on the academic, rather than spontaneous or wild. His prime focus was his work, in which he excelled, and although our relationship was full of affection and fun, a part of him always seemed to hang back, retaining a journalist's objectivity. This was enhanced by the fact he was a good photographer, seeing the world, including me, through a lens. From an outing to Highgate cemetery to shots that were more intimate, his photographic legacy includes a portrait of our times together and of me, aged 28, strutting the streets of London in my fashionable knee-high boots.

For a short while we rented a room in a house in Stockwell where Canadian Kathleen McCreery and her partner, Richard, lived with members of the Red Ladder Theatre. A founder of this agitprop company, Kathleen was passionate about taking theatre to the working classes, often performing in factories. The large house in Stockwell was run according to a strict rota which involved a lot of cleaning and which Tim ignored. As a result I often took his turn as well as my own. I never told Kathleen and the fact that I continued to do his share meant that I was undermining the egalitarian politics of the household as well as my own beliefs about liberated women.

We took holidays in Cornwall and Paris and Tim often visited my family in Dorking, where his easy manner and charm made him popular, particularly with my grandmother, by then in her 90s. However, back home in Winnipeg, his own family was undergoing some problems. When he decided to return home neither of us was certain what would happen to our relationship, but after prevaricating for a couple of months he invited me to join him in Canada.

I chucked in my job at Crown Cassettes and arrived in Winnipeg mid-summer, eventually moving into Tim's family home in an affluent leafy suburb. I got a temporary job in the Television Operations Department at CBC Winnipeg, where I was astonished to run into my old friend Pat who'd been my colleague at BBC Bush House a decade before. Newly-married to a Canadian, she was working at the same television station.

Winnipeg, my first experience of the prairies, had a wide open feel about it. There were street parties with fiddlers and square-dancing and, outside town on an open plain, we attended a pow-wow. The day was a scorcher and crowds milled around inside a huge marquee, drinking beer and sodas and listening to music blasting from speakers. Men in checked shirts, jeans and cowboy hats and women with old-fashioned full-skirted dresses looked as if they'd stepped out of the musical *Oklahoma*. Standing together, beaded and feathered, were groups of First Nations people, the bells around their ankles tinkling as they shifted, waiting for their dance. The pop music stopped and the Indian drumming began. The men set up a rhythmic stamping, circling round and round the marquee, their voices whooping and chanting. It was exotic and exciting but I felt I was watching the death throes of a culture, the MC's commentary rendering the event a performance rather than a spiritual ceremony. Next up was line-dancing for the white folks. Here our man came into his own as he slipped into the role of caller: 'Take your partners, swing 'em up, swing 'em down, round you go, and round and round. That's it boys and girls, up and down and round and round.'

In downtown Winnipeg I was excited when I came across a shop selling First Nations handicrafts: beautiful beadwork, moccasins and pipes. I wanted to buy some as presents to send home, but I was met with surly passive resistance. The Indians sat behind the counter, eyes lowered, and said absolutely nothing. Even when I picked up individual items and expressed interest, they steadfastly ignored me. Perhaps the outlet had been set up by the government to benefit the reserve. Whatever the reason for its existence, it seemed to be serving no purpose and I left without my souvenirs. I sympathised with the vendors and was reminded of the silent First Nations neighbour I'd encountered on arrival in Ottawa. Their rebellion was working; I was being frozen out.

Around that time Tim got press passes for *The Ecstasy of Rita Joe*, a play by George Ryga, which had been adapted for dance and was being performed by the Winnipeg Ballet. The theatrical version had been an immense hit and had opened people's eyes to the plight of First Nations people: Rita Joe, the heroine, had left the reserve for a better life in the city, only to be raped and murdered. The Winnipeg production had been commissioned by the Manitoba Indian Brotherhood to commemorate the centenary of Indian treaties signed in 1871.

The theatre was packed and, as a prelude to the performance, a spotlight was trained on Canada's most celebrated First Nations son, Chief Dan George, who was seated in the audience. In the stage production he had acted the part of Rita's father but, this being a ballet, his participation had been relegated to a filmed backdrop. A poet, author and actor, he was at the height of his fame, having just received an Oscar for his role in *Little Big Man*. Silence fell and the chief was introduced, whereupon he rose to his feet and sang a rendition of *Send me the Pillow that you Dream On*, a performance I found embarrassing and inappropriate. The ballet which followed was good, but the lack of First Nations dancers in a show that was meant to be entirely about Indians meant it failed to ring true.

Afterwards there was a reception. Expensively-dressed white people crowded into a room where they were served champagne and canapés. There was a self-congratulatory air about the gathering which, after such a harrowing story, made me feel alienated from the crowd. In the midst of the chatter I noticed a drab little man standing isolated in a corner. The representative of the Manitoba Indian Brotherhood, he wore a shiny suit and looked ill-at-ease. I spent the next half hour in his company. Later, as Tim and I left the theatre, we passed a drunken Indian lying in the gutter pissing himself. The theatre-goers walked by chattering without so much as a glance.

One of the places I loved in Winnipeg was the Hudson's Bay Company shop. The company had first operated in wilderness outposts in 1670 where beaver pelts and furs were traded for goods. Stepping inside HBC's modern department store, the first thing that confronted the shopper was blankets piled high on a counter. Once the main commodity traded, I was delighted to see they were still on sale; I would inhale the smell of wool, reflecting on the unbroken line of tradition that had brought them to this place. My other indulgence was fur. It was to be two decades before people boycotted the fur trade and the Hudson's Bay Company ceased trading skins. Nowadays it is impossible to imagine that we failed to object to the slaughter of animals for their pelts, but it had never really been brought to our attention. At the Hudson's Bay store I would stand amidst rows of glamorous coats, revelling in the variety of natural patterns and stroking the soft fur. I bought a hood made from Canadian lynx for my mother and sent it home.

Just over a 100 miles from Winnipeg, at Clearwater Bay on Lake of the Woods, Tim's family owned a lodge. It was an idyllic retreat, perched a little way up a hill amidst silver birches, and overlooking the water. On leaving the highway, we would drive a few miles down a sandy track between pines and, arriving on the shore, take a dinghy across the lake to the cabin. It was a tranquil place: dawn with the sound of lapping water and the haunting cry of the loon; sunset when the lake turned to fire as the heat of the day died. Sometimes we took picnics to a bay about ten miles away where I had a go at water-skiing. It is how I like to remember Canadian summers: the sun glancing off the lake, the sound of canoe paddles dipping into the surface, and the smell of pine.

When the long hot summer was over and the maple leaves turned red, Tim and I headed west. In his small open-topped car we drove across Saskatchewan and Alberta, speeding across the prairies under vast skies. I thrilled to romantic place names, such as Moose Jaw, and Medicine Hat. I loved the drawn-out throaty whistles of passing trains. We had travelled at a steady pace along a dead straight road for hundreds of miles when, on the outskirts of a small town, we encountered strange restrictions requiring vehicles to travel at a specific speed between two points. Having failed to do this, we were flagged down by the police and taken into a tiny settlement with clapboard houses and raised wooden sidewalks. The community had clearly been by-passed by the main highway and the anomaly of the speed restrictions was raising income by way of compensation. The cop got out of his car and demanded a fine, in cash, which he pocketed.

As we approached the far west and the Rockies, the weather suddenly changed. In under an hour, fall turned into winter. We started to climb the mountain road and a blizzard of unseasonal snow began to settle. We were ill-prepared; lacking tyres with winter treads it was impossible to continue. Eventually we slipped and slithered down a side road to the entrance of a lodge where we sought refuge. We were greeted by an old man. 'Shall I take your bags, ma'am?' he asked Tim cheekily – a comment on the length of Tim's hair – and proceeded to laugh at his own joke. We had happened on Num-Ti-Jah Lodge, built by the legendary mountain man Jimmy Simpson in the late 1930s. Jimmy, the old man who stood before us, had emigrated from England in 1896 and washed up in the Rockies where he had become a trapper and a guide. In his 90s, he remained spry and was living out the last of his days at the lodge he had built. A year later the legendary old man was dead, but we had brushed briefly with the last and arguably greatest of the Canadian mountain men.

There was very little accommodation at the lodge and Tim and I were the only guests. My main memory of the place is of a woman shrieking non-stop abuse at a man on the other end of a radio telephone. The next morning the snow had stopped and the sun shone. Although we had been warned not to venture beyond the front of the lodge, I ignored the advice. I had only gone a few yards when round a bend in the pathway I encountered a bull moose. It towered above me with massive antlers. Quietly I beat a retreat, thanking my lucky stars I hadn't met a bear.

With the freak snow gone, we journeyed on across the Rockies to Vancouver. Back in the 60s the United States had made plans for underground nuclear weapons tests in tectonically-unstable Amitchka, an island that was part of Alaska. Protesters had been frightened the tests would start a tsunami. 'Don't make a wave,' they'd chanted and 'It's your fault if our fault goes.' At the time Tim and I arrived in Vancouver, a chartered ship, renamed Greenpeace for the protest, had set sail from Vancouver to oppose the latest Amchitka island tests. Turned back by the US Coastguards and hounded by bad weather, it returned to Vancouver to discover that support for its cause had burgeoned. Tim and I stood among crowds holding Greenpeace banners, and protesters handing out leaflets. There had been demonstrations before, but this one was different. We were witnessing the birth of Greenpeace, a movement which was to awaken environmental awareness worldwide.

After our interlude in Vancouver we returned to a wintry Winnipeg. Summer days at Lake of the Woods seemed long gone and our relationship was on the wane. Tim, always dynamic and affectionate, seemed confused and preoccupied. It wasn't surprising. His mother and father had split up and he was questioning parental allegiances, the direction his career would take, as well as his life with me. He decided to leave me and join his mother in Chicago. I phoned Cam. 'Got any work?' I asked. 'Of course,' said Cam. 'Come to Ottawa.'

Two years later I was to spend Christmas with Tim, his father and brothers, at a lakeside house in Kenora, from where we walked across the ice and saw the distant summer cabin shut up for winter. On Christmas Eve the washing machine broke down and I walked through thick snow into town to the laundromat. Stamping the snow off my boots, I stepped into the soapy warmth and bright lights within. There was music playing, not the pop songs I would have anticipated, but angelic sopranos singing *Silent Night*. The place was packed with women and children doing their washing and every single one of them was First Nations. I have always thought it fitting that my final farewell to Lake of the Woods should feature those who were once its indigenous custodians.

Every Day and Every Night

'Mike's got malaria again,' said Donna. A skinny 19-year-old with black, curly, waist-length hair, her small, pale face was drawn with worry. I followed her up the dingy staircase and entered the apartment opposite my own. In a darkened room a delirious youth was lying in a pool of sweat. Keeping vigil at his bedside were three or four lads. Donna fetched a cold, damp cloth and started mopping the sick man's brow while the young men whispered in worried tones. Barely 20 years old, they were Midwest American farm boys, draft dodgers hiding out in Canada. I had spent some mellow moments with them and, despite their naivety, I liked their gentle, friendly manner. Mike, the sick boy, was different. He

187

was a deserter who had already done his stint in Vietnam as a medic. His bouts of malaria would recur every six weeks or so and, although they only lasted a few hours, their onset would throw everyone into a frenzy, particularly on the occasions when he passed out. However, as illegal immigrants doing casual labour on Ottawa construction sites, they had no legitimate access to health care. Each time the malaria struck they considered risking repatriation and jail in order to get Mike treated, but then he would recover and everyone would continue as before.

As a medic Mike had dealt with many atrocities in Vietnam, the majority of them perpetrated by South Vietnamese allies, rather than the enemy. 'We were supposed to be there to help them,' he said, 'but they hated us. They hate all Americans.' One of the most frequent medical procedures involved GIs whose drinks had been spiked with ground glass. 'We had to slice the lads open from their throats right down to their stomachs,' Mike told me. 'After that we had to try and pick out individual glass fragments.' Another popular atrocity was executed by prostitutes who would pad the upper side of a razor blade or piece of glass and insert it in their vaginas. 'I had to assist with the restoration of so many pricks,' said Mike wearily. 'It wasn't what I had been trained for, but then…' He shrugged.

Back in Ottawa and working for CBC again, I had located the type of rundown apartment block I favoured, just round the corner from Crawley Films. Living above a Chinese take-away and overlooking a Jewish bakery and a junk shop, I felt at ease. Down below at street level, a couple of winos made themselves at home on the bottom stairs, swigging from their bottles and greeting me drunkenly as I squeezed past. My friends had long since given up urging me to live in a more salubrious neighbourhood.

When I moved into my flat it had been gloomy and unfurnished, but I quickly slapped on white paint throughout, bought and painted junk furniture and tossed a couple of raffia mats onto bare floorboards. The result was a large, bright room, uncluttered and simply furnished. I also acquired a huge wooden storage unit being discarded at Crawleys and which nestled nicely into my window space. Sanded-down and partially painted bright blue, it served as a high desk where I sat on a stool for hours, writing and drawing and watching customers lined up in the Jewish bakery opposite. My film editor friend, Jim Williams, had nearly killed himself helping with my removals, the massive piece of cutting-room furniture from Crawleys being the final straw. 'That's it, Jenny,' he groaned. 'No more! Never again!' In addition to the large living room, I had a double bedroom, a small kitchen and a bathroom with a crawl space, where I discovered the previous tenant's stash of porn. At the back of the house there was a small platform, from which a wooden fire escape descended to a dirt parking lot, and a backyard overflowing with cartons and packaging from the Chinese takeaway.

Busy with my film research and located only five minutes' walk from my office at Crawley Films, I had stepped back into my old life at Ottawa with ease. On one of my trips to New York to locate archive film and liaise with the CBC New York office, I decided to look up one of the young Americans I had met in London. Lying on my bed at the Algonquin Hotel, I dialled his number. 'Come on over this evening,' he said, surprised. 'We've got a writers' group meeting, but I'm free afterwards.' That night, in an Upper West Side apartment, I sat in a circle of aspiring writers and listened to them reading their work. Beside me, a nervous young man called George kept dropping his pencil and bits of paper. Incredibly handsome, he had longish straight brown hair and a gentle, shy demeanour. For the next couple of days as I went about my business in New York I could think of nothing but him. Then the day before I was due to fly back to Canada, the phone rang in my hotel room. He had taken two days to pluck up courage to ask me for a date. We met up and, for me, it was love at first sight.

George was of Czech descent. Although his grandmother had been in America 35 years, she couldn't speak a word of English. 'She's still like a peasant,' he told me. 'She cooks watery chicken stew and sometimes she even pees in the garden.' He'd never known his father and was no longer in touch with his mother. Twenty-five years old, he had already engaged with some admirable projects, such as counselling challenged teenagers in New York City and manning a mobile library in Newark which played music to attract ghetto kids. His enthusiasm had been dampened when he realised black children were being provided with white middle-class literature, rather than books by black authors. He had ended up doing odd carpentry jobs in New York in order to finance his writing. Sensitive, incredibly shy and quite unnecessarily self-effacing his approach to life filled me with admiration. Reluctantly I returned to Canada. 'Come back soon,' he said, and in the vernacular of the time, 'I really dig having you here.'

We exchanged so many letters in those early days. *Some of my thoughts are so romantic, such dreams, that I'm afraid to air them,* he wrote. Enclosed with his letters were poems, some by him, some by authors he rated. Our correspondence was romantic in the widest sense and the images he conjured were of the time: Woody Guthrie in an old shack; a war correspondent watching the bombers head home. His letters, his words, his love-making were imbued with a tenderness that was unique.

Who is this George you keep mentioning? wrote my mother in January 1973, sad that I had found yet another man who lived far away from England. It was a bleak time for my parents. My brother was in Amsterdam, about to hitchhike to India, I was still overseas, and my ailing grandmother, now 96, required a lot of attention. Two or three months later, they had something more to worry about; Philip had been taken ill in Delhi, where doctors had failed to diagnose the problem. Eventually he rallied enough to travel home, but he ended up in hospital with a large abscess in his neck. Having lived in India, I began to dwell on potential diseases, and ended up even more concerned than Mum and Dad. I was gloomy about something else as well; I had just turned 30. On my birthday, drunk and maudlin, I had phoned Jenni Pozzi in London, bewailing my advancing years. In England it was the middle of the night; sleepily she reassured me there was life after 30.

In the meantime, George and I had been travelling back and forth between Ottawa and New York until, with some trepidation, he had moved in with me in Canada. 'I'm not sure about leaving New York,' he said. 'I'm really worried about quitting therapy.' I didn't take much notice. I had never encountered anyone who was in therapy and I regarded it as a self-indulgent American habit. A year later I was to fully comprehend the effort and sacrifice required of George to leave his life in New York and join me.

At the end of March, 1973, George and I went on holiday to Jamaica. For the first 10 days we stayed at Strawberry Fields on the northeast coast near a small village called Robin's Bay. Situated in an idyllic setting, it was a small campsite which was destined to become a hippie haven later in the decade. There were beautiful beaches, exotic foliage and a backdrop of mountains.

I had left England before Jamaican culture had become popular and I was unfamiliar with a West Indian accent. Bob Marley and the Wailers had only made their first visit to London the previous year and I had never even heard of reggae. George and I were picked up at Kingston airport by the campsite taxi, driven by a couple of crazy guys with beaded dreads. The road wound through the Blue Mountains, crossing river beds, wending its way through tiny villages overwhelmed by lush vegetation, and finally dipping down into Robin's Bay. I didn't understand a single word spoken by our drivers. 'What language are you speaking?' I asked politely. One of them threw me a disinterested backward glance. 'English!' he said.

Next morning we awoke to find a cool dude wearing shades lurking outside our tent. 'Masha,' he said with a broad grin. 'My name, it like de masha potato!' and he offered us dope, rum and coconut milk for breakfast. His mantra was 'Cool, man, cool,' undermined by his frequent use of *likkle* for the word *little*. With Masha we explored the countryside, following river beds and trails through groves of banana trees and coconut palms. We scrambled over rocks and up the side of giant waterfalls which tumbled hundreds of feet into deep pools where we swam. Eventually we descended to the shore, passing through small farms, where we ate guavas and drank coconut milk. A goat stood in the shade suckling its kid, butterflies alighted on gaudy flowers, and lizards scuttled into the undergrowth as we approached. On the beach an army of small boys shimmied up palms to knock down coconuts. 'I want you to meet someone,' said Masha. We entered a shack where a man lay on a bed, looking out to sea through the doorway. 'The pipe-maker,' announced Masha, and the man rose from his bed and greeted us. Gleefully he pointed to a postcard pinned to the wall. 'Houses of Parliament,' he said, 'Westminster. Sent by my brother from London.' 'Cool, man. Cool,' responded Masha, nodding enthusiastically, but I imagined the brother standing in the rain in gloomy London and wishing he had never abandoned the paradise that surrounded us.

One day Masha took us snorkelling in his dugout. I had a brief glimpse of the coral and the brilliantly coloured fish before I began to get stings from fire coral. He guided me to another area but my legs were hurting and I had lost my nerve. I sat in the canoe, while he and George swam further out and, inevitably, I began to think about sharks. Masha returned briefly to sling some fish he'd speared into the boat. 'Sharks?' I enquired tentatively. 'Are there sharks here?' He laughed. 'A shark come, you just hit him on de nose, man,' he said, and swam away laughing. I stayed in the boat, not because of sharks but because, although I was a strong swimmer, amongst sea creatures and coral I was out of my comfort zone.

Back at Masha's home we were welcomed by his mother, Doris, who showed me how to cook the fish we had caught and who served up a meal in his room – fish chowder, yams, breadfruit and dumplings. 'Now you go home and tell your friends about eating in a Jamaican man's house,' said Masha proudly. Throughout the meal we fought to make ourselves heard above a cricket match being broadcast on the radio. 'Queen's Park Oval, Trinidad,' shouted Doris. 'Australia and West Indies.' Jamaica was cricket crazy. When walking up the street to Masha's we had heard test match commentaries blaring from every shack and wherever we went we saw small boys playing cricket.

By Western standards Masha's household was poverty-stricken, but what we saw as a shack served as a comfortable two-roomed home. Starving dogs and cats hung about the door hoping for scraps, and babies crawled in the dirt outside. 'I want my room to be fashionable,' Masha told us. To this end he had carved ornaments from coconut shells and pinned his own childlike drawings to the wall: a reindeer, a boat, and a man with Caucasian features. He proudly showed us the small patch of land he owned, financed through picking oranges in Florida. He had also worked on tourist boats in Ocho Rios, where he had earned little and been ripped off by his boss. As I helped Doris with the washing up she told me about Masha's sister: 'In hospital having a baby,' she said. 'She already got eight!' It was time for us to go. Doris was about to embark on a programme called *Pot o' Gold* on the radio, and the afternoon was drawing to a close. As we left she was trimming the wick on the oil lamp in preparation for the night. The glass shade was inscribed with the words *Home Sweet Home.*

One Saturday night George and I were driven to a nearby community hall for a dance. Inside it was pitch dark with distorted reggae blasting out of the village's sole piece of stereo equipment. In the backyard giant spliffs and bottles of rum were passed from person to person. Inside, the hall was packed with sweat-stained dancers locked in intimate clinches. In every direction I was surrounded by blatant sexuality. I danced with a couple of guys who started rubbing their pricks against me. Then a boy of about 12 approached: 'Please, missee,' he kept whining. 'Please missee, I pay you money.' Shortly after that someone sloped up to me and informed me how well endowed he was, followed afterwards by a guy who said, 'Come with me. I not hurt your pussy.' The evening was turning into a nightmare while George, oblivious, continued to dance with the same beautiful girl. Eventually, to my relief, a young man appeared at my side and danced with me at length. He was flirtatious but no more than that, and I was finally having fun. Suddenly George dashed over with the Jamaican friend who had brought us to the dance hall. 'We gotta go,' he said urgently. I didn't want to. The initial hassles behind me, I had started to enjoy myself. 'Now,' he insisted and he and our host dragged me into a waiting car. We sped off. Unbeknownst to me, my dancing partner had a girlfriend whose brother was on his way to get me. 'He's got a knife,' said our friend.

Our evenings at Strawberry Fields were tranquil. Exhausted from walking and swimming in the heat of the day, we would light the oil lamp in our tent and sit quietly, writing diaries, drinking rum, smoking a bit of dope. The occasional song drifted towards us through the night and we departed early to bed. I was in love with George and full of wonder at his attention to detail: how he focused on the shape of a leaf, the mark left by an insect, or the life inside a shell.

Having extended our stay by a couple of days, we finally wrenched ourselves away from Strawberry Fields. Our farewell to Masha was sad. 'Send me a likkle letter,' he said, 'And photos. People always promise but de photos never come.' I was to send him photos and correspondence for the next couple of years.

George and I decided to hitchhike along the north coast to Montego Bay, from where we would take a train to Kingston to catch our return flight. Getting lifts was easy. We travelled in clapped-out lorries and cars and met fishermen, builders, a couple of Canadian water engineers, and a parish councillor. All the talk was of Michael Manley, the prime minister elected the previous year on the slogan *better must come*. A staunch trade unionist, he was a proponent of land reform, redistribution of wealth, a minimum wage, free education, and literacy for all. He moved easily among his people, filling them with hope, and they loved him. Just outside Ocho Rios our travelling companions started talking about Ian Fleming. 'Goldeneye! Goldeneye!' they shouted, pointing out the track which led to the villa once owned by the writer. 'James Bond! You know James Bond?' *Live and Let Die*, starring Roger Moore, had been filmed in Jamaica only three months before and they were full of it.

Ocho Rios proved to be the end of our rural idyll. People on the streets shouted abuse at us. Everyone was aggressive and extremely nasty. I didn't blame them. At one end of town there were luxurious hotel complexes incorporating Ocho Rios Playboy Club. Rich white people sat on beaches surrounded by high wire fences topped with barbed wire and the only Jamaicans permitted inside the enclosures were waiters and litter pickers. George and I were disgusted. We went off to explore the slums and shanty towns, but nobody could understand why whites would want to be that side of town. 'Ganja?' they enquired. Dope was the only reason they could possibly envisage for us being in their neighbourhood. I remembered a girl back in Anotto Bay shouting after us surprised, 'You like blacks, then?'

A few days later in Montego Bay it was worse. We tried various lodgings, but were told, 'No whites.' Eventually we checked into a hotel, where a man led us along a corridor offering clean but simple accommodation, to a filthy room with a broken-down bed, its sharp springs poking through a thin mattress. 'Your bed,' he said pointedly. Then he swung the door which was dodgy on its hinges. 'And the door doesn't lock.' Having found somewhere to stay, we went into a packed bar and sat at a table. We tried to attract the waiter's attention, but he averted his gaze. When we stood at the bar, we were studiously ignored. We returned to our table, where eventually a man joined us. 'No drinks?' he asked surprised. 'They don't want to serve us,' I said, at which he went up to the bar and smashed his fist down angrily on the counter. 'Bring beer for my friends!' he said. He was a teacher and we passed an interesting hour with him discussing Jamaica. That man's friendly gesture has remained with me, reminding me that there is always someone who will restore one's faith in human nature. As for the brief racial discrimination I experienced in Jamaica, I felt hounded and frightened. However, I knew I could leave it behind whenever I chose, unlike people the world over who are subjected to it daily with no means of escape.

We were to find peace in Falmouth, situated in the parish of Trelawney, a small market town steeped in history. One-time centre of the slave trade and a busy port for shipping sugar and rum, Falmouth's colonial architecture and quiet streets provided us with a welcome refuge from the tourist mayhem elsewhere. For me, with its Cornish connections, its Georgian houses with roses in the garden, it was a nostalgic glimpse of home. On the outskirts of town, however, they were in the process of constructing a large hotel complex. Falmouth was clearly destined to go the way of Ocho Rios.

On the beach we encountered Joshua, a 50-year-old fisherman who took a liking to George. I sat on an upturned boat watching how the two of them interacted, both sensitive and quietly spoken. Joshua talked about boat-building and how his canoes were hewn by hand. As he and George ran their fingers across the surface of the boats, I revelled in the sight of an old Jamaican fisherman talking to a young New York carpenter about the properties of wood. Joshua reminisced about his childhood, told how a British ship had towed in the carcass of the largest shark he had ever seen. 'The sailors cut open de shark,' he said, 'and inside we see a gold tooth and a gold watch!' At another beach a group of wild-looking Rastafarian fishermen pointed to a smudge on the horizon. 'Cuba!' they said. They explained how they travelled long distances in their small boats. 'Big big waves, man, but big sea no problem. Jah keep us safe.' Back on the street people cautioned us. 'Don't talk to Rastas,' they said. 'Crazy men, bad men.' But I liked the Rastas. They were funny and friendly and incredible handsome in their wildness.

From Montego Bay we travelled second class on a train through the centre of the island to Kingston. A hot, dusty four-hour journey on hard wooden seats, it gave us a view of the most spectacular countryside. At small stations market women got on with baskets of fruit and vegetables. Finally, three evangelists boarded and distributed prayer and hymn sheets to those who could read. Everyone but George and I prayed loudly and burst into song. The preacher man was displeased. 'Being educated,' he said pointedly, 'and being able to read, is far less important than following the Lord Jesus.' In Kingston, we had one luxurious night in a hotel before our flight. We swam in the pool, read and drank a little rum, but it was a far cry from Strawberry Fields.

Returning to a Canada still blanketed by snow was depressing. Despite sparkling snowy walks and skating on Ottawa's Rideau Canal, life was proving difficult for George. Each morning I departed for work leaving him to walk the streets seeking employment. He had assumed his librarian experience would stand him in good stead, but the Ottawa libraries weren't interested. After several weeks he still had no job.

When the snow eventually melted, on summer weekends we would canoe down the Rideau Canal to the luxurious Chateau Laurier hotel to purchase the New York Times. Sometimes we went picnics by lakes or attended barbecues. George busied himself with the minutiae of our surroundings, keeping vigil over birds nesting at the back of our house and requisitioning the corner of a flower bed which encircled a public war memorial, where he nurtured a few plants. He made me incredibly happy. Loving, considerate, gentle, creative, he seemed the ideal partner. At home we talked of books, wrote poems, and sketched each other. He would leave me notes adorned with little sketches: *Gone boating. Will be back with some beer* – in the corner a man paddling a canoe and a childish drawing of the sun. Sometimes the notes simply said, *Hello,* or *Psst* followed by some kisses. Once I came home to find a rough sketch labelled *Jenny's radio.* It was a paper-trail of intimacy. When I went to Montreal to undertake film research George came too, and while I was incarcerated in the National Film Board he would explore the city. The first thing he did on arrival in our hotel room was to turn all the pictures round to face the wall. 'You can't do that,' I protested. 'There's no way I'm going to look at that hideous art for the next two days,' he said. 'It'll make me unhappy.'

I continued to adore the man, but he had no work and I knew he missed the stimulation of New York City. For a few weeks he got a night job frying chicken. He would arrive home at 1am with burnt fingers and reeking of fat. 'Don't bring your clothes into the bedroom,' I'd wail. 'They really stink.' His shoes were even worse and he had to discard them before entering the flat. He loathed the job, but was amused by his French Canadian colleagues and found them fun.

At the end of summer 1973 George returned to New York for good. I wasn't surprised, but I was devastated. *I miss you and the good things we did,* he wrote; *I dreamt you were in a relationship with a guy...and I was jealous.* Three months later, on the anniversary of the day we'd first met, his letter bore the reminder *It's a year now!* Why was he writing these affectionate letters? I didn't understand – until I got to New York.

A bite of the Big Apple

I had been living in New York City a few weeks, undertaking film research for Cam Graham's four-part series, *Flight, the Passionate Affair.* After years of political and historical documentaries, narrowing subject matter down to the history of aviation was a welcome change. The research itself didn't justify an extended stay in NYC. It was merely that I had packed up my belongings and left Canada behind. I was on my way home, via Manhattan.

I was living in an apartment on the Upper West Side with a group of women I had met through George. My room was large, bright and sparsely-furnished with bare floorboards and big windows. My arrival was a bit weird. No sooner had I put down my rucksack than my flatmates appeared and started fussing. They were friendly and welcoming, but seemed concerned about me. 'Are you anxious?' they asked. 'I'm fine,' I said, surprised. 'Really happy I can stay here' 'But you must be feeling a bit crazy,' they said, 'a bit worried...'

The apartment had several bedrooms, a huge entrance hall and a reasonably large kitchen which was the hub of all communication. Stuck all over the fridge door were abandoned hair-rollers – large plastic curlers symbolising the conventional trappings relinquished by the residents. Weekly house meetings, held around the kitchen table, consisted of a prolonged analysis of the household and its occupants. To create as little work as possible, people took it in turns to prepare the same two meals, served cold: chicken cooked in soya sauce one day, tuna and mayonnaise the next. The apartment was also home to a couple of cats which were monitored for anxiety and if they looked particularly skittish were administered valium crushed up in their food. I loved my new surroundings and the people I lived with, but it didn't take me long to realise that this was not your run-of-the-mill New York apartment.

A few weeks before George left Ottawa, he had given me a well-worn copy of *The Conditions of Human Growth* by Saul Newton and Jane Pearce, based on the work of the late Harry Stack Sullivan. The authors, controversial psychotherapists, had set up an unorthodox therapeutic community on New York's Upper West Side. Its adherents held that the nuclear family was the root of all mental illness and participants were persuaded by their therapists to sever family ties, particularly with their mothers. Falling in love and monogamy were taboo, whereas multiple partners were encouraged. Members of the group were expected to live in sex-segregated apartments and it was suggested that children be sent to boarding school or raised by other members of the group in order to limit parental bonding. In fact the therapists controlled everything. Outsiders referred to members of this group as Sullivanians. Without intending to, I had ended up in the midst of a cult.

The first thing I found tricky was the lack of spontaneity. I had to make an appointment if I wanted to see anyone and most people were booked up well in advance. I even had to make dates to spend time with those in the same apartment. Dates were categorised: therapy, study, work, writing, art, meals and sleepovers. I had assumed that on arrival in New York I would pop in and see George, but popping in anywhere was not an option. I had to wait two weeks until he was free for a date. I arranged to go round to his apartment at nine in the evening, the first slot he had free. At midnight, when I was about to leave, he said, 'But you arrived after nine. That normally means a sleepover.' He was put out when I refused. As far as I was concerned, he had left me in Canada, breaking up a loving relationship, and yet he seemed to think I would sleep with him because it was a sleepover slot. I was being subjected to an abnormal system of controls which were outside my experience.

As I submerged myself in Sullivanian practices, George's departure from Canada and his subsequent correspondence were gradually put into context. By living in a monogamous, therapy-free relationship with me in Ottawa, he had been breaking all the taboos. Strangely, during our time together, we had rarely discussed psychoanalysis and until he gave me *The Conditions of Human Growth*, I had never even heard of Sullivanians. After George had left me I had been surprised at the frequency of his letters and at the affection they contained. He described us as being emotionally close and full of empathy. He wanted to know about everything I was doing, everything I was thinking. His fond sentiments had seemed at odds with someone who had just ended a nine-month relationship.

Then gradually the language in his correspondence had begun to change. The word *anxiety* cropped up again and again. *I've been in a state of near-terror lately,* he wrote. Suddenly he was worried about everything, particularly about how he was going to raise enough money for the amount of therapy prescribed. Coming from someone who, in Jamaica, had chatted so easily with the locals and made friends in foreign places, this temerity was hard to fathom. His new job – teaching youngsters in a rough area – was deemed appropriate by his therapist, he wrote, because it was good for him to work with kids who were more 'beat-up' than he was. In his letters he referred to advice from his new therapist, Michael Cohen, whom he liked.

Thirteen years later the *New York Times* reported a trial involving custody of a child. As I read the story I realised I had known the mother in 1974, and that one of the witnesses, therapist Michael Cohen who had quit the group, was undoubtedly the one referred to by George. The court case resulted in a lot of adverse publicity. The Sullivanians were vilified by anti-cult organisations, psychotherapists, and the families of those who had been sucked into the group. In those early days, however, when I was briefly in the midst of that community, I found its members creative and fun. Writers, dancers, teachers, artists and photographers, they were supportive and caring. I simply accepted their somewhat unorthodox way of life and became very fond of them.

I adored New York. As I went about my work I felt as if I'd been slapped in the face, woken up by this vibrant, crazy, over-the-top city. I never knew what would happen next, what strange situations or people I might encounter. I was swept up by the pure energy of the place. In a short time I knew everyone in the shops near the apartment. I would stride down Broadway in US Navy bell-bottoms which were sold in Army & Navy surplus stores and were considered fashionable. Made of thick blue-black woollen material, they were tight around the bum and instead of flies the front had a large rectangular flap that buttoned on three sides. They were beautifully-cut and looked great.

When I wasn't working, I would wander the streets for hours, amazed at the juxtaposition of wealth and poverty. One minute I'd be in a street that was affluent; the next I'd turn the corner and step into the middle of *West Side Story*. It was the same with my work: I moved between the flash CBC offices located in a skyscraper on Park Avenue and the dingy warehouses which housed archive film. My favourite film librarian was Movietone's Nick Leary who would chat to me with his heavy Bronx accent as we scoffed plates of meatballs balanced on a dusty packing case. Situated in a loft at West 54th, the fading slogan on the wall outside proclaimed: *Movietone News, The Mightiest of All*.

I visited a Manhattan warehouse one Saturday morning, where a friend took her child for so-called art classes. 'It's for adults as well,' she said. 'It's about self-expression.' Everyone in the class was issued with a large roll of rough paper, paints and brushes. I looked around me. Some people were stamping in paint with their bare feet, splashing colourful puddles everywhere, before walking across their paper. Others were doing handprints and small children were actually rolling in paint. I picked up a brush and drew what I considered to be loose abstract lines. The next moment I felt the presence of the teacher, a massive black guy, standing behind me. 'Ma'am,' he said, staring at my artistic endeavours and shaking his head in disbelief. 'Ma'am, you are so fucked up!'

I continued to see George when his tight schedule permitted. We were close, but his attitude towards me had become platonic. One day he invited me to visit him at Hostos Community College where he had recently begun teaching. A relatively new establishment it had been set up to cater mainly for Hispanic and Puerto Rican students. 'You get the Number 2 train uptown to 149th and Grand Concourse,' said George. 'Don't get off before or after. It's not safe.' By mistake I took an express which didn't stop at the designated station. I'd blown it. Instead of making my way back underground, however, I ascended to street level. It wasn't far; I would walk. The neighbourhood looked rough and there wasn't a white face in sight. The latter didn't worry me in the slightest, but it did concern a local taxi driver who, the minute I set foot on the sidewalk, screeched to a halt beside me. He wound down the window. 'Ma'am,' he drawled, 'You're on the wrong side o' town!' I climbed into his taxi, zoomed along a few blocks, and emerged into a different world. 'You'll be OK here,' said my saviour, declining any payment. Maybe I was over-confident. A couple of times I had walked home by myself along Broadway at 3am without any problems. No doubt there's an element of luck in doing such things and remaining unscathed, but I have always believed that paranoia increases one's chances of being victimised.

Before leaving New York, I had work to do in Washington DC. I was to spend five days undertaking research at the Library of Congress, the National Film Archive and the Naval Photographic Centre. Film archivist Bill Murphy and CBC's Nancy Wolfe showed me the sights and I spent a few happy days ensconced in the Hotel Washington. Situated on Pennsylvania Avenue, a stone's throw from the White House, it was an elegant hotel which was the haunt of US Senators. One evening, dining by myself next to a large table of politicians, I overheard them being dismissive about Canada. Having spent nigh on seven years working there, I felt a degree of loyalty for my adopted nation. Hearing it discussed as if it were a 51st state of the Union made me furious and I intervened in the conversation. I was immediately invited to join the senators at their table, where we drank wine and enjoyed a heated discussion on Canada and world politics.

Later, back in my room, the phone rang. It was my flatmate, Nancy, phoning from New York. 'I've got a little rocker here,' she said. 'A little rocker!?' 'Yeah. A small guy,' she said. 'All leather and rings. His name's

Pete.' A longstanding friend of my brother, Pete stayed a couple of days with me in the New York apartment, where he proved reticent about entering the kitchen. 'They keep asking me if I'm anxious,' he complained.

I had a lot of fun in New York with my Sullivanian flatmates. My favourite was Nancy with whom I did some writing, developed photos and drank a lot of wine. She was always bewailing the fact that she hadn't time for more dates with me, but then, male or female, you were meant to spread your affection rather than focusing on one person. On Saturday nights a group of us would sometimes go to parties, gatherings where every guest would be a Sullivanian. Running down Broadway or boarding a bus, the girls would yell out a checklist of readiness: money; wine; diaphragm (as in contraceptive); date book...

The more I became familiar with the city, the more I wanted to stay on. I regretted not having moved there years before. Sullivanian friends were beginning to suggest I get a therapist. I wasn't even that averse to the idea; it had become so much part of the everyday life and conversation which surrounded me. However, my CBC contract was at an end and, although Cam had offered me a couple of months' work in California, I stuck to my plan of returning to England.

In February 1974 as I flew out of JFK Airport my handbag contained a postcard of a simple painting by Canadian artist LL Fitzgerald. It depicted a scene through a window, a snowy urban landscape. It could have been the view from my last Ottawa apartment, the view I would forever associate with George. On the back of the postcard I had written the second verse of Rupert Brooke's poem *The Wayfarers*:

Do you think there's a far border town, somewhere,
The desert's edge, last of the lands we know,
Some gaunt eventual limit of our light,
In which I'll find you waiting; and we'll go
Together, hand in hand again, out there,
Into the waste we know not, into night?

About six months later at a party in London I met a woman who was talking about New York. We had friends in common, American students who had studied in London. 'New York,' she sighed. 'I slept with the most beautiful man I've ever met in my life. George...'

'Yeah,' I said sadly. 'Yeah. I knew George.'

CHAPTER SEVEN

JAMBO AFRICA

London Again

'HOW'S MY BREAKFAST COMING ALONG?' demanded Don. He was sitting in the bath stark naked, holding court. There were usually half a dozen of us in the kitchen, relaxing with our Saturday morning tea and fags and chatting with Don as he sluiced his body and dispensed quick-witted banter. No one felt inhibited by his nakedness, least of all Don. It was not unusual to have a bath tub in the kitchen; landlords who converted run-down properties saved money by utilising plumbing already in situ. Don's tub, like many others, was fitted with a hardboard lid which at other times served as a table over which the taps protruded at one end.

A tall, dark, man, striking and with a receding hairline, Don was a tailor for Biba, the fashion giant which had just taken over Derry and Toms department store on Kensington High Street. He regaled us with amusing gossip about everyone in the company and I was to meet the subjects of Biba intrigue when he gave me a private tour of his workplace.

Run by the celebrated Barbara Hulanicki, the new Biba consisted of several storeys of goods sold to as many as a million customers a week. Its success hinged on the way its merchandise was displayed. Dominated by art deco surroundings, and dimly lit so you could barely see what you were buying, the lofty halls were heaped with garments in colour-coordinated piles: T-shirts in mulberry, blackberry, aubergine and violet; skirts and dresses in rust, terracotta and burnt sienna. There were flowing garments for tall Twiggy-figures, striped trousers with enormous flares, tottering towers of wide-brimmed hats, ostrich feathers and leopard-spot fabric. A cornucopia of fashion, Biba was an experience which indulged the excesses and moods of the time, yet on the rare occasion when I bought anything, I would end up disappointed; once isolated from its exotic surroundings my purchase would seem rather drab. On an upper storey, the Rainbow Room restaurant, with its multi-coloured recessed lighting and pink marble floor, was the haunt of rock stars. Above that, topping off the whole extravaganza, were the Kensington Roof Gardens, graced by real live flamingos.

Don occupied the ground floor of a crumbling Victorian house in Perham Road, West Kensington. I lived upstairs in accommodation that was considerably smaller: a high-ceilinged bedsit, with a large window overlooking the street, and a small kitchen opening onto a balcony, surrounded by a balustrade and supported by the front porch below. I loved that balcony. I would sit there with friends observing the goings-on in the street. When my mother visited, she would step hesitantly onto the protruding stonework as if dipping her toes into icy water. 'I don't quite trust it,' she'd say. 'Are you sure it's safe?' My father, after descending to inspect the supporting columns in the front porch, proclaimed them dangerously cracked.

After the crisp dry cold of North America, the dank English winter seemed to seep into my bones. Mould crept across peeling wallpaper. People used bits of newspaper as draft-excluders, and rags to soak up condensation which trickled down the inside of the windows. I was back in the land of paraffin heaters, popping gas fires, and electricity meters with slots for coins. New York with its big airy rooms and central heating now seemed sophisticated; coming home after so long I discovered my comfort zone had become more North American than I had realised.

The drawbacks were counteracted by the pleasure of getting to know my brother, now Phil rather than Philip, and his friends. As a young teenager he had been away at boarding school and he was still there when, at 19, I had started work. By the time he had finished school and was at university, I had gone travelling. Previously our lives had overlapped during his school holidays, but now we were both living in London. The five-year age gap had closed, we had friends in common, and I felt closer to him than I had since he was a small boy. He had long curly hippie hair, wore shades and was more druggy than I was; actually, compared with the norm, I wasn't very druggy at all. Phil had just landed a job at Hodder & Stoughton which would kick-start his career, decades of prestigious work for well-known publishers for whom he wrote and edited children's non-fiction. I was a bit in awe of him and his friends; they seemed so much cooler than I was.

With the coming of spring and warmer days, life at the Perham Road house blossomed. I had lived in the same bedsit briefly before joining Tim in Canada. Now I was back at the heart of a household which filled me with exuberance. Extraordinary people came and went, spilling over into each other's flats, climbing through the skylight to play guitars among the chimney stacks, partying and dancing. Don had constructed a large sleeping platform in his front room which, when necessary, accommodated an overflow of several people and a cat or two.

There was so much coming and going that the line between temporary and permanent residents blurred. There was Angus with his long blonde hair and high-heeled boots who was involved with the rock band, *Hatfield and the North*, and Shah, a Pakistani friend, who was struggling with the expectations of his conventional family. Tim, one of my brother's inner circle, had morphed from cavalier curls, velvet jackets and lace, to the epitome of leather-coated cool. He spent time with Kaye, a journalist from the *New Musical Express*. Pete was a musician, an R&D man at Polydor, who lived with his girlfriend Lil who came from St Helena. Patrick, an aspiring artist, could not afford art materials and became adept at switching the price tags on tubes of paint. Garnett, a tall Barbadian friend of Don's, wore wide-brimmed hats, flew gigantic kites and rigged the house's pay phone so he could call Barbados free. Marjan, who was Dutch, was working illegally, packing condoms for the Family Planning Association. In the midst of all this, in a room off a half-landing, there lived a bespectacled conventional woman with long greasy hair and old-fashioned clothes, who scuttled nervously through the mayhem that surrounded her.

Our Asian landlady put on airs and graces as if she were letting out a palace rather than a crumbling edifice. 'There are burn marks on my furniture,' she complained, as if the lack of an external wall to the bathroom was of no consequence, when all that protected naked bathers from the neighbours' prying eyes was a polythene sheet. Occasionally, when she collected rent early on a Saturday morning, she appeared more accessible, even sitting on the beds of her sleepy lodgers and chatting. 'She reeked of gin,' said my brother, by way of explanation. The poor woman was peeved when Tim sawed the legs off her furniture for aesthetic reasons, but on the whole she was good to me, and I corresponded with her about potential accommodation for several years.

It was not a salubrious neighbourhood and you never knew what would happen next: the man two doors up going berserk and being carted off by the cops; an IRA bomb factory discovered in the next street; thieves blatantly nicking things or dismantling bicycles in full daylight. However, as in Manhattan, I knew many of the characters in the nearby shops, including the local butcher whose window featured a pig with sausages coming out of its bum.

All visitors to the house at Perham Road were welcomed, including my middle-aged relatives. I remember Aunt Phylly perched on a high stool, sipping a large gin, as the spliff smoke swirled around her. 'Cool!' she said. 'That's what you all say, isn't it? This is cool!' My parents reciprocated our hospitality in even greater measure. On many a hungover Sunday, car-loads of us would travel down to their home in Dorking to partake of Sunday lunch. Afterwards everyone would lounge around on the lawn before returning to London laden with pots of homemade marmalade and flowers from the garden. I was proud of the warm welcome offered by my father and mother and my friends must have appreciated it, too, because, when Phil and I were absent overseas, they continued to visit.

I was in the last throes of my London research for CBC's *Flight, the Passionate Affair*. Specialists in aviation history proved to be an eccentric breed, often housed in opulent surroundings, such as the Royal

Aeronautical Society in Mayfair and the MOD's Air History Branch in Queen Anne's Chambers. Beaumont's Aviation Bookshop, founded in the 40s, was another port of call, where aeroplane fanatics met in a cellar surrounded by thousands of back issues of aviation magazines. In his office at the Science Museum, curator Bruce Lacey sat amidst piles of books, papers, pictures and bits of aeroplane, his conversation peppered with adulation for aviators in general and Blériot in particular. 'The first cross-Channel flight,' he whispered. 'That Blériot! What a character!,' then chuckling, 'He had a mistress over here, you know. No wonder he flew back and forth across the Channel!' I have since searched unsuccessfully to find evidence of such a liaison.

During this period I also worked for Visual Programme Systems, run by Sandy Lieberson and David Puttnam whom I'd first encountered during my time at the Slade. I occupied a desk next to journalist Ray Connelly, who was bashing out a screenplay for *James Dean, the First American Teenager*. Ken Russell's *Lisztomania* was also in the making and *Brother, Can You Spare a Dime?* for which I did some film research. Visual Programme Systems and its sister company Goodtimes Enterprises operated out of a busy office on Great Titchfield Street, where all kinds of people buzzed in and out, including Terry Gilliam of Monty Python fame.

My remit from VPS was to research a film with the working title *War Babies* and I spent days incarcerated in the film department of the Imperial War Museum. I was searching for movies of the home front, not just in Britain, but also in Germany, Italy, Japan and Russia. Comparing civilians in different countries coping with the same conflict highlighted the futility and tragedy of warfare. After viewing a film telling British citizens to be hygienic and to clean their teeth for the war effort, I understood the previous generation better. The population had spent the war years being told what they had to do, down to the last personal detail. They were expected to be obedient for patriotic reasons and the freedom being exploited by my generation was a luxury they now found hard to fathom. It was what their generation had fought for, yet youth demonstrating against the Establishment and overturning conventional norms seemed to be taking things a bit too far. I remember my brother growling 'Fascists' when referring to the cops who had roughed him up at a demo and my father, normally quiet, saying angrily, 'You have no idea what real fascists are like.'

It was 1974, a whole decade after my journey to India and, from April that year, family planning advice and contraceptives were to be provided free of charge by the NHS, irrespective of age or marital status. For me, as well as for officialdom, it had taken all that time to break down mental and physical taboos regarding extra-marital sex. In Canada I had been in long-term relationships. Now, with contraceptives free and readily available, like most of my friends, I became somewhat promiscuous. I genuinely believed in free love. The spectre of AIDS had yet to raise its head and giving of oneself physically and mentally to someone for a brief interlude was more than just fun; it was treasured intimacy with no strings attached to spoil the intensity of the moment. I saw such liaisons as truly romantic.

The previous decade's turmoil regarding feminist politics was coming to fruition. For the first time financial and legal independence for women were being enshrined in legislation and awareness of women's rights was very much on the national agenda. The Equal Opportunities Commission was established, and the following year the Sex Discrimination Act. I was an avid reader of *Spare Rib,* the magazine which professed to provide alternatives to the stereotypical roles of women; it seems unbelievable now, but when the publication first emerged in 1972, it was considered so controversial that WH Smith and some other major outlets refused to stock it. My diary entries for one month find me on a women's march from Charing Cross to Hyde Park, at a one-day conference on Sex Discrimination in EEC Countries, at an exhibition of women's art, and participating in a women's workshop.

I had so many friends at this time, but the two I loved the most were my Dutch friend, Marjan, and Jenni Pozzi who had been my fellow film researcher at the Slade. These women were the antithesis of each other.

Above left: brother Phil, on the roof of the
house in Perham Road, West Kensington.
Above right: Marjan, Phil's Dutch girlfriend.
Right: a promotional photograph for the
opening of the new Biba department store, in
September 1973, with Don on the far right.

Below: lazy Sunday afternoons relaxing in
the garden of 'Clovelly', Dorking. From left to
right: Patrick, Mum, Marjan, Phil, Dad.

Above: market in Tanzania, June 1974.
Left: bus breakdown in the Serengeti National Park, en route to Musoma.
Below: waiting for the ferry, Kendu Bay.

Below: Ogada family, neighbours at Kendu Bay; Chacha and Joseph; with law student O' Kello at Nakuru.

Pozzi, as she was known, was intellectual, extrovert, fun, and prone to exaggeration. Marjan was a down-to-earth, precise, no-nonsense person with a dry sense of humour, who always said exactly what she thought. Both women were arty: Marjan loved print and design and eventually ended up at the London College of Printing; Jenni, who had been at art school before becoming a film researcher, was a truly creative person in every sphere. Both gave me a new perspective on all things visual.

Those were halcyon youthful days spent in the company of crazy, wonderful, talented friends who used the shabby Perham Road house as their hub. I had interesting work in a world that was vibrant with change, and yet I was ever restless, always hankering after more travel. Eventually, unable to control my yearnings, I shot off to an East End airline bucket-shop and bought a dodgy one-way air ticket to Dar es Salaam. On 29 May, 1974, with only £250 in my pocket, I was off again.

'Bring me some African soil,' demanded Don, who had spent part of his childhood in Kenya.

'Before you go, I've got something to tell you,' said Shah, my longstanding Pakistani friend. 'I'm gay.'

'Say goodbye to Banana,' said Patrick, and handed me his wonky cat, which lacked ears, claws and a tail, having fallen from the top storey of the house and hit the pavement.

'You wear one and I'll wear the other,' said *Hatfield and the North* Angus, removing a pendant earring from one of his ear lobes and inserting it in mine. And I did, until it was taken by the Maasai.

A Tanzanian Utopia

My first letter home from Dar es Salaam was an inventory of people I had met during my first two days: insect catchers from London's Natural History Museum; merchant seamen from Israel; a soldier from Zambia and a well-driller from Holland. From the indigenous population I listed a couple of education inspectors, hotel workers and an old man selling roots to repel ants. I had also encountered an Asian smuggler-cum-poacher who had enquired what contraband he could ship from Dorking to Tanzania. *Gin and tonics spring to mind,* I wrote to Mum and Dad.

Having turned up in town from the airport with no accommodation arranged, I had ended up staying with a Danish aid worker. During the day, when he was at work, I set about exploring the city where I found the populace instantly welcoming; '*Jambo!* Hello!' greeted me on all sides. If I sat in any bar or café, within a few minutes I would be embroiled in a conversation with someone. Most people spoke some English and, above all, they loved discussing politics.

There was unanimous enthusiasm for Mwalimu, or teacher, the name by which Julius Nyerere was known. Although he had been president of Tanzania for 13 years and worked in Government House, he lived in a small residence on the outskirts of town. His socialist policies were apparent at every turn and I was impressed by his determination to eschew elitism. Professional people, from politicians to bank managers, were required to do an annual stint of agricultural labour, and uncultivated land, including private gardens, could be expropriated by anyone to grow crops, becoming their property from planting until harvest.

Nyerere attempted to treat his nation of disparate tribes as one extended family. His one-party government was the Tanganyika African National Union, TANU for short, and *ujamaa* villages, run as collectives, were the cornerstone of his policies. Each settlement boasted a health centre and a school, and education was compulsory and free. Everywhere I went I saw peasants, women, soldiers and children reading. When I visited the national museum in Dar es Salaam, entry free, it was packed with barefoot visitors, including children, staring at the exhibits and trying to read the labels.

Tanzania was officially non-aligned in the Cold War. Where Sino-Soviet rivalry was concerned, however, it had sided with China and the Chinese influence was evident. Medical models in the windows of clinics and chemist shops had Chinese faces. Stalls offered Great Wall spam, Chinese toothpaste and Lotus Blossom toilet paper. There were Chinese people on the streets and Chinese road builders.

Wherever I went I was asking questions and making notes. On my second day in Dar es Salaam I telephoned *Umoja wa Wanawake wa Tanganyika*, the National Council of Women of Tanganyika, and was told that if I called in the following day I might be able to talk to someone. Unable to afford a taxi, I walked miles along dusty roads until I came to the imposing colonial building which housed the Women's Council. Dressed in jeans, sweaty and covered in dust, I was nonetheless admitted by the doorman. I asked to see the Secretary General of the organisation, Mrs Thecla Mchauru. After a while her assistant appeared. 'Mrs Mchauru wants to know which newspaper you represent,' she said. 'I'm not from the press,' I answered, unabashed. 'I just thought it would be interesting to have a chat with her!' Looking back I am embarrassed by my presumption, but I like to think I was naïve rather than consciously arrogant. 'She's a very busy woman,' said the assistant sharply, and disappeared down the corridor. After a while she returned and ushered me into the Secretary General's office.

The woman behind the desk was wearing spectacles and, ironically, smoking Sportsman cigarettes. 'How do you pronounce your first name?' she asked. 'Ah, Jen-nee. I shall call you Jenny then.' To begin with she was hesitant; she was pressed for time. Then, as she realised how interested I was in Tanzanian women, she warmed to me. 'This organisation was founded because so many women, literate and illiterate, contributed to the struggle for Independence,' she said. 'Having achieved our goal, we began to drift apart. We needed the women to come back and participate in government – and we've done it!'

Each village, city and district, every regional and national organisation, had working and executive committees where women adapted and enforced government directives. Every male minister in the Government had a female counterpart. 'There are absolutely no barriers for women in this country,' declared Thecla Mchauru.' As she went into detail, I was astonished. I thought of the marches in London, the women's group meetings in Canada, the consciousness-raising, the workshops, the conferences. I had discovered a country where equality for women was not only enshrined in governance and legislation, but where it was carried out at grass-roots level. Mrs Mchauru gave me a full half hour. 'Right, I must rush,' she said eventually. I have a meeting about power – electricity is such a problem.' *'Kwa heri,'* I said, *'Asante sana*, thank you,' and she was gone, shooting off down the corridor laden with files.

For five days I wandered the streets, getting a feel for the city. I frequented backstreet shacks where I ate goat curry, knocked back a beer or two and chatted with people from all walks of life. Dar es Salaam had been a gentle introduction to Africa. A few days before, as I had flown down the African continent, landing in Cairo, Entebbe and Nairobi en route, I had looked out of the plane window with trepidation. My return journey overland would cover thousands of miles and, even in those days, £250 was a paltry sum for such an undertaking. Reluctantly I decided it was time I got going on the long trek north. The following morning found me at the Nkrumah Road bus station ready to embark on my first ever African journey.

'Dar es Salaam to Moshi, 12 hours,' they'd said at the bus station. It was to take 17! The road was paved, but our vehicle was dilapidated, its suspension shot. Nobody, including the driver, had any sense of urgency. We spluttered to a halt at various villages, where neat mud dwellings were surrounded by spotless compounds and the only concrete buildings housed schools and clinics. At each stop we dropped off passengers, acquired new ones, and dallied in the market place while the roof of the bus was reloaded with goods and belongings.

We travelled across plains planted with bananas, sisal and maize, shadowed by a backdrop of blue African mountains. For the first time I saw laterite, the deep red soil of Africa that Don had regarded with such nostalgia. As the bus rumbled sluggishly north, we entered Maasai territory where tall, handsome warriors appeared, clad in red robes and carrying staves and spears. Many of them wore plugs in their ear lobes,

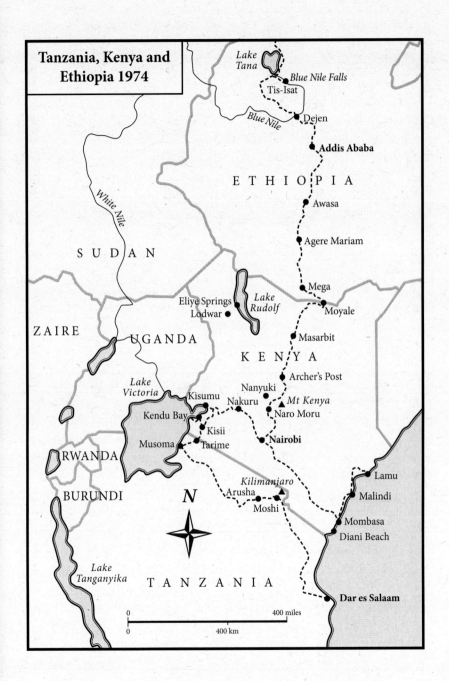

Tanzania, Kenya and Ethiopia 1974

Lake Tana

Blue Nile Falls

Tis-Isat

Blue Nile

Dejen

Addis Ababa

E T H I O P I A

Awasa

Agere Mariam

Mega

White Nile

S U D A N

Moyale

Eliye Springs

Lake Rudolf

Lodwar

Masarbit

Z A I R E

U G A N D A

K E N Y A

Archer's Post

Nanyuki

Lake Victoria

Kisumu

Nakuru

Mt Kenya

Kendu Bay

Naro Moru

Kisii

Nairobi

RWANDA

Musoma

Tarime

BURUNDI

Kilimanjaro

Lamu

Arusha

Malindi

Moshi

Mombasa

Diani Beach

Lake Tanganyika

T A N Z A N I A

Dar es Salaam

N

0   400 miles

0   400 km

flat and circular like draughts pieces, and often bigger in diameter. In cases where the discs had been removed, loops of ear lobe hung down like fleshy pendants.

My fellow-travellers were noisy and exuberant. I had been welcomed aboard enthusiastically: *'Jambo mama, jambo*! *Karibu*, welcome!' The passengers flung their arms around me and offered me food. It was my first taste of the intimacy of African hospitality. I was overwhelmed by warmth and by a kaleidoscope of colour: the strong shades of the landscape; the brilliance of the cloth worn by the women. It was an African journey filled with song and laughter, the first of many down the years.

By the time the bus limped into Moshi it was nearly midnight. Towering more than 5,000 metres above the town was Mount Kilimanjaro. I had flown over its crater a few days earlier, but now I stood in awe at the foot of the highest mountain in Africa, its snowy summit gleaming in the moonlight. There had been one other foreigner on the bus, a young Canadian who had politely passed the time of day, but kept his distance. I had been relieved at his reticence; I wanted to mix with Africans. However, when the young man saw me leave the bus and wander off alone into the night, he caught up with me. 'Have you got somewhere to stay?' he asked, concerned. 'No, not yet,' I said. 'I'll ask around.' 'I'll walk with you,' he insisted, and he remained my chaperone until I had located a cheap hotel in one of the backstreets, where he deposited me and departed.

My lodgings consisted of a single-storey concrete building with about a dozen basic rooms leading off a corridor. A communal bathroom consisted of a couple of cubicles with taps and buckets. It was a lodging house for men who worked in town. I was the only white person, the only woman, and dwarfed by the other residents who seemed exceptionally tall and black. Unlike my rowdy companions on the bus, they moved about silently, loose-limbed, nodding to acknowledge my presence. The lock to my bedroom door was nearly hanging off. I was slightly nervous, but after my exhausting journey I slept well enough. I didn't really expect to be molested or robbed. Unlike many Third World countries I had visited, Tanzania had so far been hassle-free. The following night I moved to the Presidential Hotel which was more central and which, despite its name, was cheap and shabby. There the African clientele was vibrant and friendly. *Wherever I go I seem to be the only white person*, I wrote home. *It feels quite strange to be a white woman alone in a world populated mostly by black men.*

The next day I took the early morning bus to Arusha, a couple of hours away, but by then I had a streaming cold and felt ill. It was pouring with rain and the hills and fields steamed in the heat. The bus made numerous stops, collecting and dropping off villagers, and suddenly the world was full of bananas: unripe and green, curling upwards symmetrically from stems; ripe and yellow, spilling from roadside stalls; piled on people's heads like exotic millinery; stacked sky-high on the roof of the bus. Combined with bread and vitamin pills and washed down with water, bananas were an affordable meal for my meagre budget.

In Arusha, the gateway to the National Park, I enquired about the possibility of a trip to the Ngorogoro Crater, but it cost too much. Then it dawned on me that there must be a local bus; I discovered that, without paying safari fees, I could take local transport which went through the centre of the Serengeti National Park.

Our Maasai bus conductor excelled in humorous patter. I couldn't understand a word, but he moved up and down the aisle, shouting asides, pulling faces, causing mayhem, until all the passengers were in stitches. Near the beginning of the journey, trees festooned with Spanish moss loomed out of the morning mist like an enchanted glade. I had never seen anything like it and I pointed it out to the woman next to me. Her response was magical: 'It is not animal, mama. It is not vegetable, mama. It comes and goes with the mist.'

Gradually the sun rose until, inside the bus, we were roasting. The engine choked and belched and our bruising progress across ridges and potholes did not instil confidence. We passed isolated clusters of dwellings, Maasai tribesmen herding cattle, and then big game began to appear: zebras and elephants, gazelles and ostriches, as well as hundreds of wildebeest, migrating amidst clouds of dust. The bus gave one dying explosive cough and stalled. Please, God, no lions, I thought.

The mad bus conductor kicked us all out. Everyone wanted to pee and while I pissed puddles in the dust with the other women, the men relieved themselves on the other side of the bus. None of the passengers appeared nervous or even mildly annoyed about the breakdown. For half an hour the conductor kept up his entertaining banter while the driver tinkered with the engine, until once more we were underway, lurching across the never-ending plain in the direction of Musoma. After a 14-hour journey, we reached the shores of Lake Victoria. The bus ticket had cost a few shillings and I had seen as much game as I would have done on an expensive safari.

There had been one white man on the journey, an Englishman who looked a bit like Prince Charles, and who had just climbed Kilimanjaro. In his early 20s, he seemed old-fashioned and was arrogant towards Africans. *Prince Charles keeps stuffing his face in front of starving locals,* I observed in my diary. However, my cold was worse, and when he suggested we share a twin room to save money I reluctantly agreed. Having scrubbed my dirty clothes under a tap in the yard, I went inside and collapsed on my bed, only to be bombarded by geckos which, uncharacteristically, kept losing their grip on the ceiling.

The following day I felt better. We travelled to Tarime near the Kenyan border, where we waited hours for a bus to Kenya which never came. It was still pouring with rain. Prince Charles, who had caught my cold and felt ill, was preparing to bed down for the night in his one-man tent. I had spent all my Tanzanian currency in readiness for crossing the border and was well and truly stuck. I began chatting with some young Tanzanians. 'Come with me,' said one of them. 'I live in Kenya. I'll take you to my family.' He squashed me into someone's overloaded van, guided me through the border post, and we caught a bus to Kisii.

I was sad to leave Tanzania behind. Kenya was to be very different. *How can the East African Community ever succeed,* I pondered in my diary, *when there are such disparate characters in the equation*? Idi Amin, Jomo Kenyatta and Julius Nyerere had seemed unlikely bedfellows and that proved to be the case. As for Nyerere, his agricultural programmes were set to fail. Whereas great strides were made in literacy and health care, his project in its entirety never came to fruition. A decade later he stepped down voluntarily and capitalism returned to Tanzania. I was heart-broken. I had treasured my glimpse of an egalitarian society and had admired the man who had created it. Despite his rigid political views and the failure of his dream state, Nyerere went on to be revered worldwide for his moral authority; he was described as the 'conscience of Africa'.

Obama's Kenya

The young man who had taken me under his wing in Tarime was called Chacha. 'Your name is a dance!' I told him. 'Did you know that? The Cha-cha is a dance!' 'A dance?' he said in disbelief. 'I love to dance.' He grinned. 'Joseph,' he shouted, summoning his older brother, 'Chacha is a dance!' They requested a demonstration. The limited steps of the Cha-cha-cha, back and forth, side to side, seemed lame without the music, but Chacha threw back his head and laughed. 'My name is a dance!' he kept saying.

He was 20 years old, tall and handsome. He wore tight purple flared jeans, a plum-coloured T-shirt and a sombrero, whereas his grandfather, he told me, still wore tribal dress. The night before, after knocking for a long time on the door of his relatives in Kisii, we eventually discovered they were away. 'We have to stay in a hotel,' he said and led me to a cheap lodging place. Initially I was nervous about the arrangement, but it proved no different from staying in a twin room with Prince Charles. Chacha looked after me well and the following day, in torrential rain, we boarded a bus that skidded along the flooded mud tracks to Kendu Bay, a village on the shores of that vast inland sea which is Lake Victoria. Chacha was staying there for a while with his older brother, Joseph.

221

They welcomed me into their home and I loved them both instantly. Intelligent, funny, hospitable young men, their thirst for education and betterment had been instilled in them by their father, a member of the Kenyan police prior to Independence.

Chacha already had his East African General Certificate of Education and was about to start a job as a primary school teacher. Joseph, also immersed in studies, was an employee of the Maize Control Board, storing the crop in large barns against times of famine. His accommodation, rented from the Board, was part of a long breeze-block building with a corrugated iron roof. Inside, the large gap between the top of the dividing walls and the roof, permitted the most intimate sounds of living to be transmitted between the homes: loving and tears; laughter and music; and at night time the rasping asthmatic breathing of unhealthy children.

Joseph occupied one sparsely furnished room which provided the living space; another, even smaller, housed a kerosene burner for cooking and one or two pots. There was a single communal tap outside, at the end of the compound, and two latrines shared by several families who lived there. On the first day, contemplating their tiny house, I wondered where they were expecting me to sleep. There was one big bed which Chacha and Joseph shared – my first exposure to the fact that in Africa it is common for all kinds of people to share beds. Come nightfall, there was no sign of Joseph. 'Where's Joseph gone?' I enquired. 'He's sleeping outside in the reeds,' said Chacha. 'You will sleep with me in here.' 'OK,' I said, 'but no sex.' 'I've never slept with a white woman,' he said plaintively. 'No sex,' I reiterated. He agreed, hesitantly, and was as good as his word. I slept soundly, curled up with him in the big bed without any interference.

Chacha and Joseph were good hosts. We discussed their tribal customs, Kenyan politics, and the minutiae of their lives. They came from a typical African family which comprised their father, his three wives, 11 brothers and five sisters. They were the offspring of different mothers. Joseph was more down-to-earth, whereas Chacha was a dreamer. He would sit on the jetty by the lakeside, staring into the water which rippled between floating islands of reeds. 'Look,' he said, pointing skywards at a flock of passing birds. 'Where are they flying? Which countries will they see?' The sight of a plane high in the sky would fill him with longing. 'Tell me about America,' he pleaded. 'Tell me about London. Is it true that trains travel beneath the ground?'

When I first arrived, Chacha and Joseph had expected me to cook, but I'd been unable to recognise a single ingredient. My inept efforts in the kitchen not only caused hilarity but also called into question my competence as a woman. After my failure, Joseph did the cooking and we would sit down nightly to plates of *ugali*, maize flour cooked with water, and beaten into a dough-like mound. My hosts had little money to feed another mouth and I needed to reciprocate in kind. At a nearby kiosk I purchased some odds and ends, including a bottle of Tree Top orange squash which was received as if it were the finest champagne. 'Tree Top!' they told the neighbours. 'Jenny has given us Tree Top!' I had unwittingly hit on something they considered the height of luxury.

One day Chacha and I caught a bus to Homa Bay, another village nestling in the reeds. Fishermen in canoes and small dhows drifted timelessly on the water, silhouetted against the glare. Flocks of cranes flew overhead. Girls crowded round me squabbling over who would braid my hair African-style. We feasted on fresh fish from the lake served with the ubiquitous *ugali* and, with Chacha as my guide, I learned about the local Luo tribe. 'No teeth!' he indicated, as the women grinned at me displaying a gap in their lower incisors. 'They remove them during initiation ceremonies, six from each woman.' I learned, too, that the Luo were a political force to be reckoned with, always vying for power with members of the dominant Kikuyu tribe.

When the time came for me to leave Kendu Bay, Chacha offered to accompany me to Kisumu. All day we sat on the jetty with other villagers awaiting a steamer which failed to appear. For a young boy called Thomas, it was the first leg of his solitary journey to Nairobi where he was to undergo surgery. Spruced up for the occasion, in a clean white shirt, grey shorts, and a jacket, he looked uncomfortably hot. Eventually Chacha and I gave up on the steamer. 'We will take car express,' he said, the local name for a communal taxi. Squashed between bulky women in the sweltering heat, I cuddled small children, held babies and joined in the jocular atmosphere of a crazy ride. *I am at one with these people,* I wrote in my diary. *I am beginning to feel part of Africa.*

In Kisumu Chacha and I stayed in the Sikh *gurdwara*, the first I had encountered since India. During the day we sat in shack cafés drinking endless cups of sweet milky tea and talking. Our backgrounds were worlds apart, but we shared a natural empathy. 'Why won't you have sex with me?' asked Chacha eventually. 'Because I'm only with you for a few days and because we don't have any condoms,' I said. I discovered he knew virtually nothing about contraception and after I'd given him a lecture about birth control and STIs he seemed genuinely surprised and grateful. We spent our last evening in a bar, drinking beer and dancing the night away. At dawn I watched him board the steamer and sail away across Lake Victoria, through the morning mist and out of my life. We parted with tears in our eyes.

Chacha was the first of many Africans to befriend me. His brother Joseph wrote the following year: *The sun has just set and as usual I am cooking ugali. I wish you were near and I could invite you for dinner, but you are far indeed. I hope someday we will sit again at the table of friendliness.* As for the sleepy village of Kendu Bay, it was but a stone's throw from the birthplace of the late Barack Obama Senior. The future President of the United States of America was to be born half Luo, a situation which must have thrilled a tribe that was driven by such massive political aspirations.

An Ozzie Soulmate

Since crossing the border into Kenya I had only seen Africans. Now I climbed on a bus bound for Nakuru and found myself surrounded by East African Asians. On arrival, I stumbled on a Hindu temple which

I knew was likely to offer accommodation. As I made my way through a garden adorned with tropical flowers, white doves and Hindu icons, I was transported back a decade, immersed in the sights and smells of India. An elderly man wearing a Gandhi cap emerged to greet me. '*Namaste-ji*' I said, folding my hands, and he led me to a simple white-washed room with a single bed. The tariff, scrawled on the back of a small poster of the god Krishna, was cheap, a token contribution to the temple's upkeep. That night I lay between pristine sheets, the fan whirring overhead, and thought of Chacha and Joseph. I was tempted to return, to relive the charm of Kendu Bay. *Not a good idea,* I reprimanded myself in my diary. *No going back.*

The following morning, refreshed, I was hitchhiking in the direction of Lake Nakuru, famous for its flamingos, when a coach pulled up and I was welcomed aboard by students from the Law School of Kenya. On an outing to Nakuru National Park, they happily included me in their party. It was a day of stimulating conversation and an uncountable number of flamingos – shifting shades of coral, rose, peach and salmon, stretching into the distance, as far as the eye could see. I thought of the sad Biba rooftop flamingos, confined to gloomy, urban isolation.

The next day, whilst thumbing a ride to Nairobi, I met Jenni, an Australian hitchhiker. A Sikh picked us up and, driving like a maniac, played fast and loose with the gangly giraffes which swayed along the roadside. In Nairobi it was raining and the modern muddy metropolis was a shock. After the warm welcome I had received in the countryside, I found urban Kenyans aloof and unfriendly. Perhaps it was understandable: there were a lot of white people around, including fake big-game hunters, who wore bush hats and safari fashion and who drove vehicles printed with zebra stripes.

The first thing I did was look for Thomas, the young lad from Kendu Bay bound for Kenyatta Hospital. I had promised to visit him, but I arrived to find the corridors jam-packed with mothers and sick children, all squatting on the floor in the hope of seeing a doctor. A nurse walked with me through the crowd: 'Thomas! Thomas!' she called. 'Anyone called Thomas?' I trawled the hundreds of hopeful upturned faces but I never found him.

Jenni and I had checked in at Nairobi Youth Hostel which had huge, noisy mixed dormitories and was a hub for travellers in East Africa, including one or two Japanese. Attractive young men with shoulder-length hair and bandanas, they seemed to transform the youth hostel kitchen into the set of a Samurai movie. Whereas the rest of us had breakfast on the hoof, scoffing a hunk of bread and knocking back a few cups of tea, the Japanese embarked on their day in a more elaborate fashion. Each item they cooked was arranged on the plate in a manner deemed aesthetically pleasing. I watched astonished as they nudged a vegetable or piece of fruit into an acceptable angle. Having achieved perfection, they produced chopsticks from their pockets and approached their meal with the reverence merited by such preparation.

Australian Jenni was 25 years old, a sharp, intrepid, feminist, wild and full of fun. A teacher and a traveller she found everything in the world accessible rather than daunting. 'I'm thinking of getting hold of a truck,' she said casually. 'There's bound to be someone who wants goods shifted. I'll drive it down to South Africa, sell it, and then catch a ship from there.' In Nairobi it continued to rain non-stop, turning the unpaved streets into mud, the potholes into ponds. We copped out, escaping to the Kenya Coffee House, a modern café where, with caffeine-induced energy, we spent hours debating African and feminist politics and exchanging travellers' tales. Despite the fact I wasn't cut out to be a long-distance trucker, we had a lot in common and in a short time were firm friends. 'The coast's the answer,' she said, gazing through the window at the dreary, sodden vista which resembled Redhill on a wet Sunday afternoon. 'We gotta follow the sun.' A couple of days later, having changed money on the black market from a man selling African carvings, we were on our way to Mombasa. In my pocket was the purchase that had enabled our illicit currency exchange: two small Makonde men chiselled out of dark wood, squatting on their haunches, smoking pipes.

Our first lift went as far as Emali where we sat for a while at a shack with a small bar. All kinds of people turned up at this way station: Indian merchants; fat cat Kenyans in smart cars; nomads herding goats; Turkana with their high beaded collars. It had finally stopped raining and dust thrown up by passing trucks stuck to the sweat on our faces as we indulged in ice-cold Tusker beer. The landscape was from a Gauguin palette: deep red earth, purple hills, green and yellow roadside vegetation with flashes of red and orange canna lilies. As promised, I scooped up some red earth to take home for Don, a small bag which would remain tucked away in my rucksack for thousands of miles as I crawled up the face of Africa.

I was still wearing Angus' earring, the one he had given me as a farewell present. Sitting outside the shack with Jenni, I watched two Maasai emerge dreamlike from a cloud of dust. 'Just look at them,' I said. 'Lion hunters, warriors – they're magnificent!' They walked tall, holding their spears, red cloth draped casually across perfect bodies, their braided hair dressed with red ochre. Seeing me, they stopped in their tracks, their eyes riveted on Angus' earring. They pointed at it and one of them stepped towards me, his palm extended. He was already covered in beadwork, as well as makeshift urban jewellery made of bottle tops, corks and bits of plastic, but apparently that was not enough. He wanted the earring. I took it off and slipped it onto his outstretched hand, whereupon he inserted it into his ear lobe and was gone. I thought of Angus far away in London wearing the other half of the pair – Angus, the hippie musician, with his long blond hair, high-heeled boots, tight jeans and pale green eye shadow, now sharing his jewellery with a Maasai warrior.

In Mombasa we had our first glimpse of a Swahili world where African and Arabic cultures were fused. We explored Fort Jesus and the narrow alleys of the old town with its Arab antiques and junk shops. After a couple of days we set off again, hitching north towards the Lamu archipelago. Neither of us owned a guide book: *Lonely Planet* had only just been published, and it would be another eight years before the

Rough Guide appeared. I was making my way north, just as Jenni was travelling south, but within those parameters we went with the flow, following whims, washing up in unexpected places. I had never even heard of Lamu until I reached Nairobi.

In Malindi we stayed in the countryside with a hospitable school teacher who cooked fresh fish for us on an open fire, but after that the coast road north became rough. We were given a lift by two Asian salesmen, though when we queried what they were selling they were evasive. After a while I developed a splitting headache and with every jolt I thought I was going to throw up. Between Malindi and Mokowe, just over 130 miles, we had four punctures, but our drivers were well prepared with a boot full of spare tyres. They addressed each blow-out with resigned nonchalance while we waited by the roadside. There was no shade, only thorn trees. My head throbbed. 'Lions around here,' said our salesmen, as they retrieved yet another spare from the boot. 'We're not joking. It really is lion country.'

At nightfall, when we reached Mokowe, the villagers could see I felt ill. They were concerned and kind. 'The mama is tired,' they kept saying. *Lala nzuri, mama.* Sleep well.' We checked into a faded colonial rest house with broken floorboards, a dilapidated veranda and peeling paint. Outside my window there was a swamp surrounded by palms and frequented by acrobatic monkeys. I wondered what wild beasts might be lurking in the darkness beyond. I drank several pints of water, swallowed a load of pills, and collapsed on the bed, leaving Jenni to party with an African boyfriend she had acquired en route.

Lamu – Paradise Island

In the morning, although I still felt fragile, my headache had gone. On 22 June, just under a month since I'd arrived in Africa, Jenni and I boarded a ferry bound for the island of Lamu. After 45 minutes, chugging across the strait and alongside mangrove-choked creeks, we saw the white buildings and palm-lined waterfront of Lamu Old Town.

As the boat docked and we disembarked, a group of lads surrounded us, grinning and chanting rhythmically: 'Beau-ti-ful to look at, dan-ger-ous to touch!'

Constructed of coral stone and mangrove timber, Lamu had once been an important trading centre for East Africa, a mini-Zanzibar. Whispers of past glories were everywhere, a mosaic of Indian, Persian, Arabic and African fragments, an amalgam that was also reflected in the features of the inhabitants. Traditional dhows still plied the waters, each with its single lateen sail shaped like the wing of a bird.

Couched in a labyrinth of bewitching donkey-wide alleys, the town lured us into its heart with a dreamlike magnetism. We sought out the shade of verandas and balconies, oases of privacy shielded by lacy screens and friezes. We tiptoed under archways which revealed dark stairwells with stone steps spiralling to rooftop dwellings. We passed doors which hung heavy-hinged, carved and studded, slammed shut against centuries of prying eyes. Here and there vegetation trailed over high walls enclosing courtyards: serpentine branches laden with exotic fruit, or garlands of jasmine and purple bougainvillea. A rich bouquet permeated the passageways: fragrant blooms, over-ripe fruit, sandalwood and spices, merging with a whiff of sewage and donkey dung. Every so often this torpid warren would fan out like a breath of fresh air, widening into a sandy space where there was a small market, or the pristine sacred area fronting a mosque.

I was staying at Shamouti, a simple lodging house with half a dozen rooms, one of which Jenni and I shared with a Yorkshireman called Alan. There weren't that many young foreigners on Lamu, so I was surprised to encounter Georgina, a childhood acquaintance from Dorking. Our stay on the island only overlapped briefly but, because of our shared Lamu experiences, our friendship was to flower on our return home. One of the most vivacious friends I made was Arlene from Tucson, Arizona – a wild-haired freckly woman who was holed up with a beautiful black youth called Tito. 'I couldn't stand suburbia,' she drawled. 'One morning I packed my bags, walked out on my husband and came to

Africa.' There was Joseph, an Italian Australian, who ended up with Jenni; a Japanese guy who had built himself a sleeping platform up a tree; Ursula, a politically serious Canadian partnered by a Spaniard on the run from Franco; and a large tattooed American known as Dragon Lady who spent all her time dropping acid. I spent one evening in the company of a few rich Kenyan tourists who spoke of the government's intention to develop Lamu as a resort, but apart from that I met no African sightseers.

It wasn't long before I was drifting with the languid pace of the island. Jenni and I hung out in the New Star Restaurant, an outdoor yard surrounded by a palisade and roofed, here and there, with palm fronds. Presided over by the plump proprietor, Bangladesh, who was as inscrutable as he was stoned, we whiled away our time, talking, drinking chai, and treating ourselves to jelly halva, and doughy sponges known as half-cakes – despite being whole. Sometimes we would walk to the beach and lie on the warm white sand, isolated specks on a strand that meandered miles backed by dunes. We swam and read, sliding slice upon slice of slippery mango into our mouths.

Morning would find me inching my way along the narrow streets of the old town: squeezing into doorways to avoid passing donkeys; pausing to peep into the dark interiors of small, shuttered shops. Men ambled past in their traditional white tunics or brightly coloured *kikoys* and skull-caps. Women scuttled by in their *bui-buis*, black-robed and veiled like errant nuns. Occasionally a patrol of convicts would pass, prisoners interred in the old fort with its bulbous crenelated tower which dominated the town. 'Look out for the Spaniard,' someone told me. 'There's a Spaniard incarcerated in there.' Jenni and I saw him once; his sad eyes flicked towards us and we pondered his crime.

Slowly, slowly, *pole, pole*, we got to know some of the islanders. Ali, handsome and westernised, took a group of us out on his dhow to a coral reef. Tanned and scruffy, our limbs draped lazily over the side of the boat, we felt piratical and free. Omar, more traditional, took us by boat to a tiny sandy island where we cooked fish and ate coconut. From

Above: *the waterfront, Lamu island.*
Right: *girls in bui-buis, Lamu.*
Below left: *Lamu street scene.*
Below right: *Bangladesh, boss of the*
New Star Restaurant, Lamu.

Above: *Australian Jenni, Lamu.*
Above right: *sailing trip on a dhow with Ali.*
Right: *with Balo in The Passion.*
Below: *Haji Shobolo and his family.*
Below right: *Richard's rooftop terrace, Lamu.*

Lamu town we made small forays inland, meeting people at work on their *shambas* or smallholdings, recognising them later as they hailed us in the market place.

One day Jenni and I stumbled across Haji Shoblo, an elderly man, snoozing in the shade of a palm beside a pile of lush paisley-shaped mangos. He gave us a tour of his *shamba*: three coconut palms, two mango trees, and a series of dunes where his goats foraged on reeds and thorns. Stringy, stooped and worn, the old man was a rascal. He liked to spin a yarn, create a scene, gather an audience. With a curt word he would silence his wives or send the children packing, but having established his authority, he would rock back and forth with devilish laughter. From crack of dawn he could be found in the market place where he worked as a butcher. The job had its perks; gristly leftovers could be boiled into broth by his three wives, all of whom we met.

The oldest spouse, ostracised because she was barren, lived alone in a filthy mud hut. The second resided in Matandoni, a village on the other side of the island, where a few of us were invited to meet her. Having twisted my ankle, I rode Haji Shoblo's donkey, while he walked behind whacking the donkey's backside with a stick. Rain soaked our Biblical cavalcade as we waded through dunes, circumnavigating mango trees and palms bent double in the wind. Wife number two was bright and attractive, despite which her conjugal visits were limited to one night a week after Friday prayers. Her adobe dwelling was more spacious than most, and we were proudly shown a couple of china plates bordered with roses. However, she, too, had failed to live up to expectations, bearing daughters rather than sons. Sitting on the ground outside her hut, we shared potato broth from a tin bowl while the village schoolmaster played his flute in our honour. The next day, tired and flea-ridden, we slogged our way back to Lamu town, my stubborn steed frequently digging in and refusing to budge.

Haji Shoblo's youngest and third wife had produced the long-awaited son. The house was full of laughter, as children tumbled in the dirt and played with the scabby cats in the alley outside. 'Baby Shoblo!'

announced the proud father, grinning from ear to ear and bouncing the baby boy up and down on his knee. Months later, back in England, I was to receive correspondence scribed by a letter writer: baby Shoblo was dead. *My heart is broken,* said my old friend, *but it is the will of Allah.*

Shortly after I first met the old man, I saw that one of his knees had swollen to immense proportions and I feared he might have elephantiasis. I urged him to accompany me to the health centre, but pointing to a piece of magic string tied just above the knee, he said, 'Swahili medicine.' On my second attempt to lure him to the doctor he created such a scene that the market stopped trading. Instead, he took out a knife and began to make small incisions in the infected area. 'Swahili medicine,' he observed again archly.

Bwana Ndegi – Birdman

My life on Lamu changed when I met Richard Bonham. Only 19, he was slim and boyish, with wavy blond hair and slightly slanted eyes which I found seductive. We had passed each other one night in a dark alley, stopped and said, 'Hello', then awkwardly moved on. It wasn't long before we bumped into each other again and started talking. I fell in love.

Richard had been raised on a coffee estate outside Nairobi. From a tender age he had been immersed in bush craft; he knew how to use a gun, how to survive in the wild. A white Kenyan, he spoke Swahili and worked and socialised with black Africans. What I loved most about him were his laid-back, madcap qualities, combined with a recklessness which, to some extent, I shared.

A couple of months before I met him, Richard had qualified to fly a light aircraft and had become a bush pilot. He collected fish from the neighbouring islands, storing it in a freezer on Lamu until it was collected by a frozen food company. Whenever possible, I flew with him to the islands. Before landing, we had to clear the airstrip by dive-bombing errant livestock, and on islets where the landing space was little more than a clearing, we sometimes screeched to a halt barely making it.

Once we had landed, islanders would appear with the fish and load up the plane. One fishermen's camp was only accessible by boat. 'See those sacks?' said Richard as we circled above the island. 'Shove 'em out the back for me, will you?' 'What's inside?' I asked. 'Ice,' he said. I watched as the bags plunged earthwards and small figures below ran to retrieve the ice which would chill their fish on its journey across the sea to Lamu.

Sometimes, when swooping and soaring in the tiny aircraft, I felt as if we had spread our wings; as if we were flying free, wheeling like a giant ethereal bird above the world. 'The Swahili word *ndegi* means bird as well as aeroplane,' explained Richard. I loved the fact the islanders referred to him as *Bwana Ndegi*; birdman or pilot, it was all the same. Far below the sea unrolled before us like shantung, rippling from azure to aquamarine to indigo, studded with tiny islands which shone like gems.

By now I had left Shamouti Lodge and was living in Richard's house: a simple roof terrace, a tiny bedroom, a bathroom and a dining room which was rarely used. We spent all our time on the rooftop, talking, drinking and smoking, sleeping beneath the stars. We were awoken at sunrise by cockerels, the braying of donkeys and the muezzin's call to prayer. The terrace was shaded by a canopy of palm fronds which lifted and rustled in the breeze, and from our perch we overlooked other rooftops where neighbours talked quietly in the night. It reminded me of India, of the families who socialised on the rooftops of Gwalior.

People were always popping in. '*Hodi? Hodi?*' they would shout, mounting the narrow staircase from the street. 'Anyone at home?' It would be Omar, Balo or Ali, or one of Richard's other workers. Or it might be Gwyn or Freddy, who flew similar aircraft and worked for the fish company, or maybe Australian Jenni.

The fishermen would congregate on the rooftop to discuss business. They were kind to me, teaching me Swahili, and one of them gave me silver earrings that had belonged to his mother. It was Ali Soo who coveted the red and white gingham shirt I had inherited from my lover, George, in New York. It was my favourite garment, a tactile souvenir.

Now, as I handed it over to Ali Soo, I dwelt on the random trails left by belongings: a Maasai warrior with Angus' earring; a Swahili fisherman with George's shirt. When Richard was in Nairobi, the fishermen took me by dhow to Matandoni where I was served coconut and fish and the village women decorated my hands with henna. 'Like a bride,' said Omar, the one who translated everything into English. The men giggled. 'They are saying you and Richard must marry,' he told me. They fetched garlands of jasmine which they twisted around my wrists, an unforgettable heady fragrance of paradise.

I had met Omar when I first arrived. A tall, quietly spoken young man who lacked an eye, he had shown me round his *shamba* and taken me out in his boat. The foreigners referred to him as Omar-One-Eye, to distinguish between him and the numerous other Omars on the island. Now I got to know him as Richard's assistant, the one on whom he relied to communicate with the fishermen and keep track of deals. Despite Omar's help, things were not always plain sailing: 'Balo and the Kapini boys have stolen each other's boats,' wailed Richard. 'One lot has buggered off with all the prawns; the others have gone to the police. The police! Now I have to get involved with them.'

The police on Lamu were unpopular. They were Kikuyu, the same tribe as Jomo Kenyatta, the president. Although Kikuyu made up the largest ethnic group in Kenya and could rightfully expect substantial representation in public life, they wielded economic and political influence beyond what was appropriate. On Lamu, where the majority was Swahili and Muslim, Kikuyu police and politicians were doubly resented. They were also corrupt. All kinds of illegal shenanigans unfolded on the island and the police were either part of it or turned a blind eye.

The café on the waterfront sold coconut drinks and tropical juices. Passion fruit was such a favourite that the café was referred to as The Passion. 'See you later in The Passion,' we'd say. The owners' real passion, however, had nothing to do with fruit juice; it was the smuggling of ivory and skins. Tucked away on an island, with herds of elephant on the nearby mainland, the café was an ideal front for such activities. In one letter home I wrote: *The ivory poacher (who doesn't know I know) is sitting at my feet. He's keen on me, and he sends his salaams to my honourable parents.* When I enquired about the ivory smuggling, I was told 'There's nothing you or anyone can do. Mama Kenyatta's behind the whole operation.' Apocryphal or not, the president's wife was renowned as the ultimate wheeler-dealer.

Omar would boast openly about selling drugs to the cops. On the island there was no shortage of substances to smoke, sniff and chew. The popular local high was provided by *miraa* or *mirungi,* narcotic stalks and leaves which were shipped in from the mainland. People hung banana leaves outside their dwellings or shops to advertise availability. I only chewed *miraa* on a couple of occasions: once with the Lamu fishermen and another time when travelling in Ethiopia, where truckers chewed the form known as *khat* to keep awake on long journeys. The drug was supposed to act like speed, but I didn't feel particularly hyper after either experience.

Everyone on Lamu smoked a lot of weed, which only served to heighten the whimsy of a place where people materialised out of nowhere and faded away like will-o'-the-wisps into shadows and secret courtyards. The strongest marijuana was supplied by an American who lived on the island and who incorporated it into shakes whisked up from milk powder. For me, one glass of his potion proved enough; I lost an entire day focusing on the colours of a single trader bead. I didn't mind the occasional spliff, but I disliked being out of control and wasting so much time.

'There's a wedding,' said Omar one day. 'I can arrange for you to join the women's celebration.' It was held in the evening in a courtyard, open to the sky and behind locked doors. The only men permitted inside were the musicians and, to my surprise, a couple of transvestites. When I arrived, young women who were normally swathed in *bui-buis,* were putting on their finery in an upstairs room, chatting, laughing, smudging their eyelids with kohl and applying lipstick. The two transvestites sat in front of mirrors, giggling and ladling on the make-up. Anticipating a traditional Muslim wedding party I had dressed demurely, only to find myself looking quaintly old-fashioned as everyone squeezed into skin-tight miniskirts and sexy tops. Exuberant and welcoming, the girls lounged around, smoking cigarettes and trying to communicate with me in their few words of English.

When the drumming started, everyone descended to the courtyard where there was food and soft drinks. 'Where's the bride?' I enquired. 'The bride? Oh, she doesn't come,' I was told. There were about 30 young women present, dancing, and wiggling their backsides provocatively. Young men gathered outside the high walls, shouting comments and trying to peer through slits in the large, wooden door. The drumming got faster and louder until, hours later, at four in the morning, we ended with a massive conga, everyone snaking around the yard, writhing seductively until the bitter end. It was raining as I sneaked home up the dark alleyway to Richard's. I crept up to the rooftop and, cocooned cosily in his bed, I watched the rain dripping off the palm-fronds and listened to the muezzin's call to early morning prayers.

The girls I had met at the wedding began to invite me into their homes and I remained astonished at how open and modern they were behind closed doors. The wedding parties continued for four days, the drumming and music emanating from various courtyards around town. Then came the big day when we were permitted to view the bride. Omar brought me a garland of jasmine and accompanied me to a packed hall where, on a raised platform, a plump young woman sat on a large red plastic sofa. She was heavily made-up, unsmiling and stiff as a Barbie. The groom was nowhere to be seen.

Lethargic Lamu days slipped by. Richard took me by boat to a deserted island where we swam, ate lobster and coconut, and slept the night on the beach. I continued to fly with him to different islands, collecting fish, returning to my starlit idyll on the rooftop. Occasionally, when he was away, I flew with Gwyn, who also collected fish and who flew my mail up from Nairobi. Larger-than-life characters came and went, dropping into island life, then disappearing again. One was a flying doctor, a substantial butch-looking woman, who was in a relationship with the man who ran Lamu Museum. *Another new moon*, I wrote in my diary, *I should be on my way.* But I stayed.

Richard was going to Mombasa for a couple of days on business and said I could fly down with him. 'The muezzin needs a new cassette tape for the mosque,' said Balo. 'You could buy it while Richard's in the meeting.' He gave me directions and, on arrival in Mombasa, I went to a street which consisted of rows of shacks that sold music. I had the name of the call-to-prayer written on a piece of paper in Arabic – or so I thought. 'Which one?' asked the shop keeper. 'This one,' I said, waving the piece of paper in front of him. He laughed. 'We have many of those,' he said. 'Too many!' He played various cassettes, but the wailing all sounded the same. 'That one,' I said finally, taking pot luck. I never knew whether my choice proved appropriate, but I received no complaint.

That evening Richard and I flew down to Diani Beach and stayed in the old seaside home that belonged to his family. As the house came into view, we dipped down to alert the sole remaining servant, who ran out waving a piece of cloth to acknowledge our arrival. Situated on the edge of a white strand that stretched for miles, the house was a time capsule of its colonial past. Everything was enveloped in dust sheets. People from times long gone stared out from silver-framed photographs. 'As children we were brought down here quite a lot because of the Mau Mau,' said Richard. 'We were always finding snakes in the store room.' As the sun set, we strolled the length of the deserted beach until we came to a restaurant and a bar. Later, as we ambled slowly back to the house, the sea lapped gently on the shoreline and the stars shone.

Back in Lamu, the dream was fading. I had been there just over a month but, cocooned in the timeless magic of the island, I felt as if I had been there for eternity. My friends had gone to Nairobi. The police were cracking down: they had taken away The Passion's licence and were hassling people at Shamouti Lodge. The rains were at their height, a daily tropical deluge which forced us to sleep inside, and the road on the mainland was closed. Richard was gloomy: the fish company was shutting down and he would have to sack the fishermen. The time had come for me to move on. Haji Shoblo invited me for a farewell potato curry at his house. At the New Star I bad farewell to Bangladesh. Omar-One-Eye and the fishermen came to Richard's roof terrace: Ali Faya, Faridi, Ali Soo wearing George's shirt, and the rest. 'Why don't you marry Richard?' they asked for the umpteenth time.

Richard took me to Nairobi. For a while we were flying over the bush, looking down on herds of wild animals. 'I've got a gun in the back,' he said, nodding towards the rear of the aircraft. 'We'd need it if we ended up down there!' Later, he said he was thirsty. 'I'll just get that coconut from the back,' he said, and handed me the joystick. I was terrified. 'Don't move it at all. Hold it steady, just as it is,' he said. 'I'll only be a second or two.' He sat down and began hacking at the coconut with a *panga*. 'Come back,' I begged. 'Come back now!' He came and took over, but we hadn't gone far when the stall-warning indicator began to flash. 'Too much fish,' declared Richard, unfazed. 'We're rather overloaded: 90 kilos overweight!' The little plane struggled to gain the altitude required to get over the hills. I was relieved when we were finally circling above the East African Flying Club in Nairobi. '5 Yankee Alpha Charlie Papa,' repeated the control tower, giving us permission to land. We were met by Freddy, a friend who'd been on Richard's rooftop in Lamu the very first night we got together. 'Good heavens, Jenny,' he said in surprise. 'You're still here!'

Richard departed for the family coffee estate at Kiambu, and I went to Catch 22, a travellers' hang-out, where inevitably I connected with friends. 'His lordship's not introducing you to the family then?' said Alan sarcastically. Working class and very Yorkshire, Alan had never minced his words regarding Richard; he considered him a spoilt little colonial rich-boy. 'That twat and his bloody plane,' he would say, as Richard zoomed above the sunbathers on Lamu beach, coming in to land at Manda. 'He's a bush pilot,' I would protest. 'He's working.' In Lamu, when I sloped off home to Richard's meagre rooftop, Alan would growl: 'Off to the penthouse then, are we?' Alan had a point. Richard was from a wealthy colonial family who could afford to send him off to Texas to train as a pilot and to set him up with a plane. Nonetheless, the Richard I knew wasn't snobby or pretentious. He was a crazy, laid-back, alternative person who was happiest out in the bush or mixing with black Africans.

My friends were staying at the Abbey Hotel, a cheap run-down establishment that overlooked a rubbish dump. For the next few days I slept on the floor of different people's rooms. Amidst the petrol fumes and hassle of Nairobi I longed for the smell of jasmine, the familiar faces and languid pace of Lamu. I spent most of my time with Australian Jenni. In the evenings we would smoke dope and she would play the guitar and sing. Miriam Makeba's song, *Malaika*, had just been released and was being played everywhere. Sitting on the floor of that grubby hotel in the candlelight, Jenni would sing in her sweet voice: *Malaika, nakupenda, Malaika: My angel, I love you, my angel.* It was how I would remember her. Meanwhile I ached for Richard. Alan's gibe had hit home and I was full of doubts. Why hadn't Richard taken me home with him? Just when I had given up hope of seeing him again, he turned up and took me back to the coffee estate where I stepped into a pre-Independence world.

Richard's family home was a colonial bungalow set in a leafy garden with manicured green lawns. It would not have been out of place in rural Surrey. Inside, the sitting room looked very English, with its huge open fireplace, in front of which two large, floppy dogs relaxed as we drank afternoon tea. There were several servants in livery, as if Africa had stood still and *Uhuru* had never happened. Richard's mother was charming and welcoming, but she was of her time. 'You travel on buses!' she exclaimed, horrified. 'On buses, with *shenzis*!' 'What's a *shenzi*?' I asked, innocently. 'Yes, mother,' said Richard, annoyed, 'What exactly is a *shenzi*?' A derogatory term meaning trash or uncouth people, she was using it to refer to Africans.

I stayed four nights at Richard's home. We had some happy moments together but, on the whole, I was ill-at-ease. In the morning a servant would appear while I was still in bed, pull back the curtains, and present me with my morning tea on a silver salver, alongside a single rose in a vase. I smiled, thanked him, tried to engage, but he resolutely averted his eyes and said nothing. However, I enjoyed wandering along the rows of coffee bushes as Richard told me about production. Everyone greeted him warmly; as a child his playmates had been the children of the plantation workers.

Just as I thought my time with Richard was drawing to a close, he announced, 'We're going to Rudolf.' Lake Rudolf, later renamed Lake Turkana, was 154 miles long, 20 miles wide, and the world's largest permanent desert lake. Situated in northwest Kenya and southwest Ethiopia, its more romantic name was the Jade Sea. With two American passengers, Mike and Carol, we set off from Nairobi, flying over beautiful scenery and lakes to Nakuru, and then north, over the mountains, until we hit the desert. Navigation with Richard could be hit and miss. He often flew using road maps, but the desert lacked roads and there were no substantial landmarks. He had set a course, but in a single-engine plane with no instruments we could have done little in bad weather. Below us lay mile upon mile of desolation, interrupted only by the fragile thorn *bomas* which encircled bivouacs belonging to nomads. Mike was poring over the map trying to work out our exact location. He was nervous. 'Lodwar has to be somewhere round here,' said Richard unperturbed. 'I hope so anyway. We could do with some fuel.' About ten minutes later the outpost appeared, its buildings spread below us.

The main settlement for Turkana territory, Lodwar was so inaccessible that, in 1959, the British had kept Jomo Kenyatta there under house arrest. A couple of years after that, missionaries flattened a small piece of land for use as an airstrip and brought in a plane and a couple of flying nuns to do outreach work among the Turkana. A decade later, we were met by the bizarre sight of a nun in full habit, guiding us in on the landing strip with the small, circular bats used for marshalling aircraft. 'Sorry,' she apologised, as Richard disembarked, 'we're right out of fuel and supplies. You'll have to go on to Eliye Springs.' Eliye Springs had always been our destination, but it was a further 30 miles to the east. I was secretly worried that we might not have enough fuel to make it.

We took off again and, before long, there below us lay the emerald lake, a long beach with palms, an airstrip and a tiny tourist lodge. We flew along the shoreline radioing for permission to land. 'Have you got fuel?' enquired Richard. 'Fuel, yes,' said a very British voice, 'and will you be requiring dinner, sir?' 'No thanks,' said Richard. Our plan was to camp on the beach.

Our first day was dreamlike and timeless. I sat mesmerised by the heat and glare. The air seemed leaden, the buzzing of insects loud in the silence. I found myself focusing on minute detail: the pricks in the sand left by tiny creatures; the webbed footprints of birds; individual grains of sand glistening on our faces and bodies. Each movement appeared to be in slow motion, suspended briefly before it followed through. I killed an ant and almost expected it to scream.

A young Turkana woman broke the spell, emerging from the desert, padding softly between the palms and down onto the beach. She had a thick collar of beads and bare breasts with scar patterns. I was wearing a swimsuit and she ran her hands approvingly over a scar on my thigh, the result of a childhood vaccination. She stroked my hair as if I were a cat. She offered me a hard, round dried fruit and began to chip pieces off it using her Turkana knife-bracelet. I gave her a couple of coins for a necklace she had made out of fish bones from the lake.

We awoke each morning to a massive sun, a ferocious red ball of fire, which rose over the lake until gradually the desert mountains turned pink and the day began. In the evening we lit fires and lay around in the moonlight, awaiting the nocturnal wind which blew off the desert. One night, as we ambled along the shore, we saw log-like shapes in the distance and Richard backed me slowly up the beach to the edge of the dunes. 'Just in case they're crocs,' he said. He threw a stone to see if they moved, but nothing stirred.

For a short while during those few days, Richard retreated into a silence I found upsetting; we had so little time left. Once he disappeared into the desert for hours on end, while the rest of us swam near the shore, pointlessly keeping an eye out for crocodiles. Briefly, I sought respite from the heat in the tourist lodge. There was nobody staying there and I quenched my thirst in solitude watched by Freddy, an evil-looking baby croc in a tank. On the wall there was a photo montage of limbless people, crocodile victims. I relaxed in a chair, swigging my coke, and the barman turned on the BBC World Service. There was talk of a crash on the M1 and of IRA bombings, followed by a programme about armour through the ages and how armpits were especially vulnerable.

On our last evening, Richard came out of his shell. 'Come with me,' he said, taking my hand, and leading me up from the lake shore onto a high ridge. Below us the sun was setting over the beach and the lake. Above, the moon was rising over the desert. The sand had been blown into intricately ridged waves, patterned like the seabed. There were thorns, small bleached animal bones, and dried-up bushes. We stood close, isolated on the bald edge of the globe. Barefoot, and wearing only swimsuits, we walked further into a desert where the bones of *homo sapiens* and *homo erectus* had been discovered; a 200,000-year-old skull, and the oldest stone tools ever found. We lay together on a small flattened mound, and when we arose I saw the marks our bodies had left alongside those of other creatures. And then we ran down from the ridge, slipping and sliding in the sand dunes, down, down, down, and dived into the Jade Sea. Later that night, sitting around the camp fire and talking of primeval man, Mike said, 'There are those who believe this lake is on the site of the Garden of Eden.'

We left early the next morning and flew down the desolate eastern shore where, disturbed by the noise of the plane, crocodiles slid into the water, flamingos took flight and ostriches started running. Turkana people looked up and waved. 'When I was a child I used to camp down there with my father,' said Richard, and I finally understood his relaxed attitude towards being lost or potentially running out of fuel. Had we been forced to land, he would have been quite at home.

We were to drop off Mike and Carol at Nanyuki about 260 miles to the south. 'That's odd,' said Richard, as we came in to land. 'This used to be a grass airstrip. Now you could land a jet!' He called up the control tower. 'There's no response,' he said, 'how strange.' We landed, not at Nanyuki civil airstrip as intended, but at a Kenya Air Force base, where we were interned for three hours in a yard surrounded by high whitewashed walls topped with barbed wire. Richard had no ID with him, no licence, no log book, nothing. 'It's back at the house,' he said vaguely. 'Heaven knows where.' Eventually the two Americans' passports were confiscated as security, and we were released. My own passport was back at the coffee estate in my rucksack.

Richard's mother collected us from Nairobi, and in a short time we were back at his home. My last evening consisted of a candlelit, cut-glass dinner, peppered with inappropriate comments from his mother. It was pointless trying to counteract her views about Africans and modern Kenya; she had lived through the Mau Mau uprising and had watched the disintegration of a colonial way of life. Clinging on, and steeped in the old ways, I saw her life as an anachronism, but to me she was hospitable and kind. She was also more astute than I had realised. When Richard left the table briefly, she looked me in the eye and said, 'You really care about him, don't you?'

In the morning I got up early and walked around the gardens. The mist was rising, the dew was heavy, and the workers were already in the coffee plantation. After breakfast I collected my dirty old rucksack and, as we went to the car, I was horrified to find half a dozen servants lined up outside anticipating tips. I had barely enough money to crawl up the face of Africa. All I could do was express my inadequate gratitude verbally: 'Asante sana,' I said, 'Thank you so much for everything.' They stared at me blankly and I departed overwhelmed with guilt.

We flew to Nanyuki to take Richard's licence and log book to the Kenya Air Force, this time landing on the civilian airstrip. Richard radioed for someone from the air force to come and collect him. While he was gone I tried to concentrate on reading my book. For me, it was the end of the line; once he returned, I was to go on my way. A few days before, at Lake Rudolf, he'd said, 'Don't let's drag it out, Jenny. Don't let's spoil it.' In my diary that morning I had written: *I've made myself pretty. I want him to remember me laughing in the Kenyan sunshine and making love in the sunset.* Now there was an ache in the pit of my stomach and my eyes kept welling up.

On Richard's return, I discovered the Kenya Air Force saga had worsened. The commanding officer was back at the base. 'He thinks I was taking aerial photographs,' said Richard. 'He believes Mike and Carol are American spies. He said if he'd been on duty when we landed, he'd have slung us all in jail and impounded the plane!' The matter was to be referred to senior Kenya Air Force officials. Inevitably Richard didn't seem that concerned. 'We'll just have to wait and see,' he said, shrugging. 'I'll be in Lamu anyway.'

Our farewell was stilted, brief and unemotional. I walked off, my rucksack on my back, and set off south along a deserted tarmac road which shimmered in the heat. A few minutes later the plane dipped overhead on its way to Nairobi. I watched until it was a speck in the distance and only then I broke down and cried my eyes out.

Wanki-Wonki Ranch

'Have you heard of a Mrs Kenealy?' I had asked Richard's mother. 'She lives at the foot of Mount Kenya.' 'Mrs Kenealy!' I was clearly adding another name to the list of inappropriate people to associate with. 'She used to be married to a District Commissioner,' she replied. 'Then along came Mr Kenealy, an Irishman, the maddest man in Kenya, and she ran away with him. She's a tough old stick; a bit crazy.'

Now I was on my way to see Mrs Kenealy, a widow, who allowed travellers to stay on her farm. I hitched a ride on a Guinness truck to Naro Moru, bought some supplies, and found a lad to act as a guide. 'Wanki-Wonki?' I asked him. 'You know Wanki-Wonki ranch?' I'd been told *wanki-wonki* was what the locals shouted when herding zebra. 'Yes, mama,' said the boy. 'I take you to Wanki-Wonki.'

Mrs Kenealy was a tiny old woman clad in giant baggy trousers and wearing a battered, wide-brimmed straw hat. Parked outside her house was a beaten-up Volkswagen. Inside, her home resembled an Irish farmhouse: a dining room with a heavy refectory table and a dresser crammed with blue-and-white china; a large, open, stone fireplace; a wood-fired antique kitchen range. Oil lamps were the only source of lighting. Basic and unadorned, the house had an old-world charm, a warmth that, like its owner, was welcoming and unfussed. Outside, farm buildings nestled in pastoral countryside. A stream gushed down the hillside between verdant banks and Mount Kenya rose up in the distance, hidden by clouds.

I had arrived at Wanki-Wonki, tear-stained, to find several people I knew in residence, including Australian Jenni who was covered in tropical sores. Mrs Kenealy wandered about, pleasantly scruffy, appearing oblivious to our presence. There was a local boy who chopped wood for the kitchen stove and another who helped a bit in the kitchen, but they – and everyone else – seemed to be part of an unconventional migrant community. In the evening an ever-changing group sat around the candlelit dining table as Mrs Kenealy and the kitchen boy served up something akin to thick Irish stew. Afterwards everyone lounged about in front of a large log fire, putting the world to rights. It was a good place to get over heartache.

For several days I was lovelorn, then, one morning, I woke up angry at my self-indulgence. I needed to get out into the real Africa again. I walked into Naro Moru and hitched a couple of lifts up to Isiolo, a desert town 60 miles north, where I spent the day with Samburu and Turkana people, haggling over jewellery: flat beads stamped out of ostrich egg shells; small metal beads made from bullets; large round yellow beads, supposedly amber but clearly fake. I drank chai and had a stimulating conversation with a Kikuyu musician and a Swahili poet, then I hitched back to Wanki-Wonki refreshed and determined to pull myself together.

Most of the others left Wanki-Wonki before I did. One day Mrs Kenealy squeezed four of them into her Volkswagen and spluttered off in the direction of Nairobi. One of her passengers was Jenni. I never saw her again; three years later she died of cancer.

I needed a visa for Ethiopia, a doctor's appointment, and possibly a companion for hitching north. Reluctantly I returned to Nairobi on the back of an army truck. I knew Richard would be on Lamu. I was desolate without him. In the 60s, *Island of Dreams* by the Springfields had been my favourite. Now, walking round Nairobi, it haunted me.

I wander the streets
And the gay crowded places
Trying to forget you
But somehow it seems
My thoughts ever stray
To our last sweet embraces
There on the beautiful island of dreams
High in the sky is a bird on the wing
Please carry me with you…

Wherever I went in Nairobi, there were people I knew: fellow-travellers, old colonials, resident white people. I frequented the Belle-View drive-in cinema, the Kenya Coffee House, the Nairobi Theatre Club, The Thorn Tree and the old colonial Norfolk Hotel. I visited Freddy and helped him deliver fish cakes round Nairobi for the frozen food company. The city had become easy and good fun, but my acquaintances were white, not black. I knew none of the black Africans who passed me on the street. It was a long way from Chacha and Kendu Bay.

As for Richard, he went on to become a safari legend, co-founding the Big Life Foundation to protect East African wildlife and support the Maasai community, winning prestigious international awards for conservation, and earning an affectionate accolade from the locals who called him *Enkasi* – the White Maasai.

Above: Richard and *(right)* refuelling at Eliye Springs, on the shores of Lake Rudolf.
Right: Richard's family home, Kiambu.

Below: Mrs Kenealy, her battered VW and friends at Wanki-Wonki Ranch, Naro Moru.
Below right: Turkana woman at Archer's Post

Above: with Patrick and Arlene at the Norfolk Hotel, Nairobi. ***Above right:*** Vincent, Addis Ababa, Ethiopia.

Above: travelling with Michael by truck in Ethiopia.
Below: boys knitting at the roadside. ***Below right:*** monastery ferries on Lake Tana, the source of the Blue Nile.

Above and **left:** *at the Tis-Isat Falls, on the Blue Nile, Ethiopia.* **Below:** *with Saad (on left) and fellow truck drivers, Khartoum to Shendi, Sudan.*

Below: *Saad's family and Saad (centre) with friends, in Shendi, Sudan.*

Above: *fourth train breakdown en route to Wadi Halfa.* ***Above right:*** *Abdul Aziz, on paddle steamer to Aswan.*

Above right: *travelling north by old paddle steamer across Lake Nasser, Egypt, past Abu Simbel* ***(left)***.
Left: *Kitchener's Island and gardens, Aswan.*
Below: *postcard of the pyramids of Giza, Egypt.*

CHAPTER EIGHT

THE LONE AND LEVEL SANDS

ONE OR TWO MEN had offered to hitch to Ethiopia with me, but I had rejected them. I was angry at my dependency on travelling with others, particularly the opposite sex; I saw it as a cop-out. Rationally I knew it would be unwise to travel too far north alone – the roads deteriorated into rough tracks which traversed desert – but I was on the point of risking it. Then one of my friends showed me a map: 'Look at this,' she said. 'The word *bandits* is actually printed across parts of Ethiopia!' That settled it. I set off, hitching north, with a young German called Willy, a gentle, practical guy who was kind and considerate, but who hardly said a word.

A couple of days later, I was sitting by the roadside at Archer's Post. A dust-blown village a couple of hundred miles north of Nairobi, it had a frontier feel. With hardly any traffic, our journey had been slow. There were rarely any lodging houses, we had very little money, and we slept rough. The evening before, we had spent the night sleeping in a cemetery attached to a tiny mission church. Now Willy had headed off to wash in the river and a small boy was standing in front of me. 'Abdi Adan,' he announced. 'I am nine.' He wanted to practise his English. 'Lions!' he warned. 'Lions come here. Steal goats.' As the village was situated in the Samburu-Isiolo Game Reserve, this was hardly surprising; we had already heard tales from a truck driver of livestock and camels being taken. At this point Willy returned from the river. 'Crocodiles!' he said.

While I was talking to the boy, I had been aware of a group of Samburu warriors preening themselves nearby, admiring their reflections in tiny pocket mirrors. They turned their heads this way and that, adjusting their beaded collars and jewellery, fiddling with their long braided hair which was dressed with red ochre. They toyed ostentatiously with their spears, sizing them up, testing the blades.

We had entered an area formerly known as the Northern Frontier District, carved out by the British in 1925 from what is today's southern Somalia. It was a wild place which, during the colonial administration, had been a no-go area. Now local leaders were demanding reunification with the Somali Republic and had been detained by the Kenyan authorities. As we made our way north, we noticed that the features of those around us were changing; they were Somalis.

From Archer's Post, the road deteriorated into corrugated dirt ruts. Missionaries took us on the next leg of our journey, their truck jolting along for hours through beautiful desert scenery until, reaching Masarbit in the dark, we stepped from the lorry into a blinding storm of red dust. Screwing up our eyes, we struggled through the wind towards a cluster of mud dwellings. 'I think it's safer to sleep here,' said Willy, 'near to people.' We lay on the ground in the lee of a small mud house. 'This is someone's garden,' I said, feeling the bumpy remnants of cultivation beneath my back. Still buffeted by the storm, our eyes, mouths and nostrils were clogged with sand. 'I've got some net,' I said, rummaging in my rucksack. It was my rudimentary mosquito protection and it always came in handy. We wound strips of netting around our heads and across our faces, until we resembled a couple of mummies.

We slept intermittently. It was still dark when a woman emerged from her hut with a torch. Seeing our bodies trussed up on the ground, she let out a terrified scream. 'Speak to her,' said Willy. 'Say anything at all, so she can hear it's a woman's voice.' I greeted her and she ran inside to fetch her husband who appeared carrying a paraffin lamp and approached us looking totally astonished. They invited us into their home, but by then it was almost dawn and we only stepped inside briefly.

The world had turned red! There was an eerie light. The wind had dropped, and people were moving like shadows in a fog of red dust. In my diary I likened them to the reddleman in Hardy's *Return of the Native,* the man whose trade – marking sheep with red ochre – had turned him red from head to foot. We made our way to the town centre and found a well. After washing my face, I decided to rub some moisturiser into my desiccated skin. Within a few minutes dust particles stuck to the face cream, coating me with a red mask.

We left at noon on a particularly filthy truck. When Willy insisted I ride inside the cab I was grateful for the comparative comfort, yet frustrated that I warranted gentlemanly behaviour. My diary was full of analysis about my role as a woman in a world of rough travel: anger at the dependency my body imposed on me; at the practical complications and temporary weakness caused by menstruation. Later that night, after arriving at a village where we drank a lot of *chang'aa*, a lethal local brew, we slept on the floor of a ruined concrete hut, partially roofed with corrugated iron. When the owner stopped by in the morning he shook his head. 'No good here,' he admonished. 'Many many snakes!'

A day later we reached the border town of Moyale with its huge camel market backed by distant mountains. I was full of heartache at leaving Kenya. During two months in the country I had seen unforgettable landscapes and wildlife, met so many wonderful people, black and white. However, by now I had quickly reverted to being quite feral. I was a vagabond girl again, travelling rough as I had with Derek a decade before on the way to India. Despite any discomfort and potential danger, there is nothing that matches the freedom of the road.

Just as Willy and I were going through the border post, ten young French travellers appeared, aiming to travel to Addis Ababa by bus. 'Ethiopia! We've made it,' I said to Willy, elated at having reached another milestone.' 'It's safe to split, now,' was his response. 'You'll be OK with the French.' I was stunned; I felt as if I were a chattel being transferred to French jurisdiction. All the misgivings expressed in my diary about being a woman traveller sprung to mind. Clearly Willy had regarded me as an encumbrance. The French kids were already boarding a bus. I picked up my rucksack and joined them. '*Cet Allemand*,' said one of the girls, '*il est vraiement doux*.' 'Yeah,' I said, 'Yeah. Willy's a sweet guy.'

'His Imperial Majesty, Haile Selassie,' announced the man, indicating a statue shrouded in a sheet. The Emperor had been detained, but there had been no coup and nobody knew what would happen next. To tear down the statue might have been premature, but it was not advisable to have it on display. Ras Tefari, the Lion of Judah, Emperor of Ethiopia for the past 44 years, was hidden beneath a sheet awaiting his destiny.

Ethiopia was in turmoil. For several months students, workers, peasants and the army had been in revolt and, in the north, the Eritrean Liberation Front had waged war seeking independence. With a backdrop of famine, violence had erupted throughout the country. Everyone was talking politics. The population was edgy and protest had not yet resulted in any concrete resolution.

The five-day bus journey from Moyale to Addis Ababa was uncomfortable. Within a few hours, my French companions and I were crawling with fleas. There was so much dust that my streaming eyes became raw and itchy. The people who boarded the bus were hungry. They pushed and shoved and quarrelled, quickly resorting to fisticuffs. The markets, bustling with camels and colourful, handsome people, lacked food. In Africa I had become used to hopping off a bus and stocking up with provisions in the nearest market, but in the semi-desert of southern Ethiopia there was nothing available. Ragged urchins ran at us chanting, 'Give me! Give me! Give me!'

I didn't go hungry. Any stereotypical views I might have had of the French proved spot on; their rucksacks were laden with tins of gourmet delicacies which they produced in private, along with the odd bottle of wine and the inevitable Gallic shrug. Despite being filthy and flea-ridden, they also managed to look fashionable. They were generous and kind, but as the discomfort increased, so their tempers became frayed and one or two of them lost patience with the Ethiopians.

In Mega, one wearisome, flea-scratching night, we were given a brief reprieve. An Ethiopian family invited us into their home, a large, circular adobe hut lit by an oil lamp. There, accompanied by a stringed instrument, they serenaded us with Ethiopian songs, a gathering mirrored by elongated shadows dancing in the dim light. On the way to their dwelling, we had been astonished to come across a young Englishman who carried a rolled umbrella and who would not have looked out of place in the 1950s. When the Ethiopians had finished singing they indicated it was the turn of the foreigners. The French contribution completed, it was my turn. 'English songs! English!' called everyone. Performing fills me with dread; I just couldn't do it. The Ethiopians waited. The French waited. I was filled with shame. The Englishman stepped into the breach: 'I have a song,' he said and embarked on a lengthy ballad about cricket!

At Agere Mariam, we hit tarmac, the first paved road in five days – no more violent jolting. It was a dreamlike moment, when suddenly the road turned smooth and silent, like gliding on ice. With a proper road, came a little comfort: limited electricity; a splash or two of water; one or two food stalls in the market. Eventually the desert gave way to sporadic higgledy-piggledy cultivation: bananas, maize and coffee bushes growing cottage-garden-style around small settlements ringed by cactus fences. At Awasa I washed in hot water for the first time since Nairobi. But the fleas lived on.

On arriving in Addis Ababa, the first thing I noticed was a giant hoarding displaying a poster split down the middle: one side showed Emperor Haile Selassie feeding steak to his dogs; the other, emaciated peasants. The juxtaposition summed up the political situation at a glance, but the photograph depicting famine wasn't needed; it was all around us. Starving people had come into the capital from the north, particularly from the most severely affected provinces of Wollo and Tigre. An army of cadaverous beggars had overtaken Addis: on every street corner there were skeletal malnourished people dressed in filthy rags. Barefoot children with swollen bellies and protruding ribs had flies crawling around their eyes, clustering on the catarrh which clogged their nostrils and on the suppurating sores on their legs. I was witnessing the flotsam of the previous year's famine when an estimated 300,000, mostly the rural poor, had died.

On my first day in Addis I went exploring on my own. After five days of travelling in a group I sought isolation. I wanted to get my bearings and glean an overall impression of the city. It didn't take long. Addis was one of the foulest filthiest places I had ever set foot in. It was the rainy season. The maze of unpaved backstreets and shanty town slums were ankle deep in mud. Sewage overflowed onto the streets. Everywhere smelt rank. A tide of ragged citizens ebbed and flowed through the alleyways, in and out of packing-case shacks. Pools of water formed in sagging ceilings made of plastic sheets. Rain drummed rhythmically on scraps of torn metal used for shelter. The people were friendly in their destitution and smiled warmly as I passed.

I was in poor shape. I had an upset stomach, problems with peeing and a menstrual cycle which had gone awry. I was still crawling with fleas and was unable to sleep for scratching. Exhausted, I nonetheless knew I had to obtain a visa for Sudan, the next country on my itinerary. It was a long walk to the Sudanese embassy, and by the time I got there I was fragile and shaky. En route I had discovered a strange phenomenon: my armpits had started to swell! *Oh God,* I wrote in my diary. *Do they have bubonic plague in Ethiopia?!*

The next day I was to meet dear sweet Vincent. With his blue-black skin he was the darkest African I had set eyes on. Whereas Ethiopians have thin fine features, Vincent had the flared nostrils and full lips of his native Togo. A young man in his 20s, he was tall, gentle and very sad. He had left Togo hoping to find employment in another African country. After a difficult journey of nearly 3,000 miles, he had washed up in Addis where it was impossible to find work in all the chaos. His opportunities were also limited because he spoke French; in Ethiopia he needed Amharic, or maybe a bit of Italian or English. He had latched onto me as a fellow foreigner and, being familiar with the city, he delighted in giving me a tour. We walked for hours around the town centre, where there were ugly modern buildings, paved streets and wide open spaces, as well as older architecture such as St George's Cathedral. Finally Vincent led me to the highlight of his tour: 'Le Palais!' he said with a verbal flourish. I wondered if the Emperor was inside the building; whether he was under house arrest or locked up elsewhere?

It was a strange time to be in Addis. Caught up in the maelstrom of a creeping coup, the old order had not quite vanished. Sometimes a well-heeled woman, wearing a pristine white dress draped with an embroidered *shamma*, would stride through the beggars like the Queen of Sheba and, despite Marxist-Leninist steps to get rid of the Orthodox church, robed Christians would gather bearing Coptic crosses.

The next Africans to take me under their wing were Ethiopians Johannes and Mbebe. Johannes ran a small tourist shop as a front for his political activities. He had led a student revolt, been shot in the leg, and jailed for six months. He and Mbebe offered me non-stop hospitality which was well-intentioned and utterly exhausting. My bowels were liquid but, despite my protests, they plied me with Ethiopian food. It was my first taste of *injera* and *wot*, the food prevalent throughout Ethiopia and which I loathed. *Injera* is a flat spongy bread made from a grain called *teff*, but unlike most unleavened bread, it is sour and rubbery. *Wot* is a spicy stew of meat or vegetables, but in the impoverished Ethiopia of 1974 it lacked either and was more like spiced gruel.

One night Mbebe and Johannes took me to watch folk dancing at a rundown hotel on the outskirts of town. We ate Ethiopian food and drank Ethiopian mead, known as *tej*, and *tella*, a local beer. All over the city the army was on the streets; there were tanks and a curfew. As the evening progressed, I kept saying, 'Surely we should leave now. We'll miss the curfew.' 'Plenty of time,' they insisted, and kept downing drinks. Finally, when curfew time was past and we were unable to leave, they booked a room. I trusted them and liked them and I don't think their intention was to seduce me; they were just drunk. The three of us slept African-style, sharing a bed for the night. Initially they tried to touch me up, but they accepted my refusal and quickly rolled over and went to sleep, whereas I was so uncomfortable I didn't sleep a wink.

Throughout my time in Addis I stayed at the shabby, rambling Shoa hotel which, like most cheap African hotels, doubled as a brothel. The rooms on the ground floor were set aside for prostitutes; those on the upper storeys were occupied mainly by foreigners travelling rough. Tucked away upstairs there were some interesting characters, old hippies who had holed up there for a considerable length of time. Advice was scrawled directly onto the walls in various languages: places to stay in Sudan or Kenya; where to hitch a good ride or to change money on the black market. John, from Arizona, planned to fix up a rendezvous in San Francisco for all the people he had met on the road. An open invitation was written on his bedroom wall, but he also gave out personal invitations scrawled on scraps of paper. I still have mine. *Rendezvous: 7.7.77 at 7.07pm, San Francisco, China Town, Universal Café.* I have often wondered whether anyone turned up.

Hidden away in Room 61 in the upper labyrinth, I was to find my next travelling companion, a quiet Austrian named Michael whom I was to love dearly. From the moment I met him, we spent nearly all our time together. Blonde, with very blue eyes, he had a face that was interesting rather than classically handsome. I found him easy to get on with and an endless source of new thoughts and facts. In the midst of the rain and squalor of Addis, he provided a warmth and cosiness which kept me going. Ultra-left-wing, he talked politics nonstop.

With Michael I wandered the backstreets of Addis Ababa, drinking in squalid *tej* bars frequented by the destitute, places which were advertised by means of a blue plastic kettle strung up outside like an inn sign. Lit by paraffin lamps and with dirt floors and rough wooden tables, these Fagin's kitchens included some unlikely clientele – stray students or educated dissidents desperate to talk politics. *The tej house tonight was like a robbers' den,* I wrote in my diary. *Someone tried to pick my pocket, but the political talk was fascinating.*

There were prostitutes everywhere, some mere children, 11 or 12-year-old girls who sat in doorways with their legs splayed or who leant against walls with a provocative stance. During our wandering,

Michael and I entered what we assumed was the usual *tej* house, only to find the rare luxury of electric lighting and a proper bar. Dominating the room was a large television, airing a NASA space film. We made ourselves comfortable at a table and waited, anticipating *chai* or *tej*. Two or three teenage girls hung about the room, one of them pregnant, and at one end a matriarch sat knitting. We had inadvertently stumbled into a backstreet brothel where, with much giggling, we were welcomed with tea. Every so often the door would open and a ragged man would appear and prop up the bar for a while, before departing to a room out the back with one of the girls. These men found our presence incredibly funny and they began to linger at the bar, talking about us and laughing, rather than focusing on the girls. We were bad for business and the madame decided we should leave. We stepped out into the rain and mud, leaving an astronaut on the television screen, floating weightless above a squalid, poverty-stricken world.

Michael and I had had enough of Addis. We set off for the bus station, and caught a bus north. Once out of the city, we abandoned the bus. On a beautiful twilight truck ride, climbing higher and higher into the mountains, we were overwhelmed by the fragrance of the roadside herbs and fresh air. Our first stop was in a small village, where locals invited us into a room and served us coffee. The floor was carpeted with sweet-smelling hay. 'Wie eine Almhütte,' said Michael, and I thought of Heidi climbing up the mountain to visit the Alm-Uncle, one of my favourite children's stories. Later that night, after another ride, we stopped in Dejen, a town swirling with incense. We had arrived in the land of frankincense and myrrh.

We had become adept at dealing with fleas and bedbugs. As soon as we were shown our accommodation we would spray the mattress with repellent and vacate the room for an hour or so. On our return we would dispose of all the dead critters which had risen to the surface. We travelled together well, happily talking for hours on end. Michael enlightened me about African liberation movements such as Mozambique's FRELIMO and Angola's MPLA, members of which used his home as a safe house

261

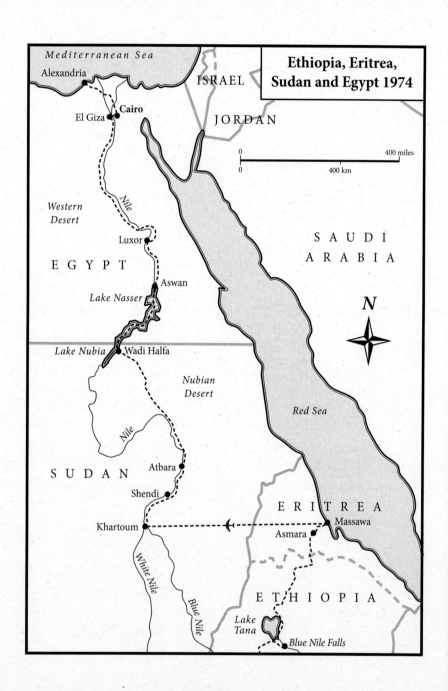

Ethiopia, Eritrea, Sudan and Egypt 1974

in Vienna. Compared with him I was politically naïve, but he was never condescending and I found our discussions stimulating.

The journey north took us along terrifying switchback roads through range after range of spectacular mountains. Sometimes our heavily-laden vehicles crossed rickety bridges which spanned vast chasms. I felt like a hostage to fate; I would gaze into the abyss and wonder whether this time my number was up. When it wasn't mountainous, the landscape was lush and pastoral, rolling hills reminiscent of Tuscany, which probably made the Italians who occupied Ethiopia in 1936 feel very much at home. Italian influence remained much in evidence, particularly further north in Eritrea which had been a colony for nearly 150 years. Not being fans of Ethiopian food, Michael and I were initially relieved to find spaghetti available, but piles of pasta without sauce began to pall after a while.

The lush countryside belied the starvation we had seen in Addis. We were witnessing a 'green famine' which occurs when the rains come too late. Successive droughts, the high death rate of people and livestock, and a system ruled by feudal overlords, meant that despite the pastoral scenes, those who had survived the famine were still malnourished. Poverty in the city had appeared more desperate, but our Arcadian progress was still haunted by scrawny flea-ridden people swathed in dirty rags. Incongruously, among their number, were urchins who knitted – little boys who stood by the roadside chatting to each other, their knitting needles clicking. In places where lifts were few and we had to wait a long time, people would encircle us in hollow-eyed silence. Even though their faces were drawn, the exceptional beauty of their race was evident in their fine features. There was curiosity in their gaze rather than resentment, but after a while their focus would render us claustrophobic and struggling to communicate would become a burden. The further north we travelled, the more food became available. Apart from the dreaded *injera* and *wot* and the inevitable spaghetti, there was the occasional egg, and as we drew nearer to Eritrea there was sometimes *ful*, a paste made of mashed fava beans. Another relic of Italian influence was the preponderance of red wine, a luxury we could ill afford but to which we occasionally succumbed. Meat was becoming available as well. When our truck driver purchased a sheep, he insisted Michael hold it on his lap, where it peed on him throughout the journey.

We travelled through places of historic interest, but there was little evidence of tourism. On Lake Tana, the source of the Blue Nile, where islands harboured ancient monasteries, remains of emperors and hidden treasure, only Ethiopian males were permitted access. However, we gazed in wonder at the Tis-Isat Falls, a curtain of Blue Nile water over 300 metres wide, which thundered into the chasm below and where, in a nearby village, I purchased magic blue glass rings to keep away the evil eye. The nearer we got to Eritrea, the cleaner the towns became. The sun shone on fields of wild flowers and we passed healthy-looking women washing clothes in the river.

In Asmara, the capital of Eritrea, we found a *tej* bar and struck up a conversation with the locals. We were now in the land of the Eritrean Liberation Front, the ELF, a guerrilla movement which had been fighting for independence from Ethiopia for a decade. Ethiopian troops were in control of the towns and highways, but the guerrillas had the countryside. 'Everything's quiet now,' we were told. 'Fighting will start up again in about a month.' It was from Eritrea that I planned to go over the border into Sudan. 'It's closed,' one of the young men told me. 'They're trying to stop ELF fighters from crossing.' 'You'll have to fly the border,' said Michael. 'It's only a short distance.' 'I haven't enough money for flights,' I protested. 'There is a smuggler's route,' said our companion. 'I can arrange for you to cross with the guerrillas. They go, one by one, in the boot of a car.' Reluctantly I declined his offer. It was far too dangerous but, ever after, I wondered if I'd missed out on the adventure of a lifetime.

Asmara was beautiful. Its high altitude gave it a pleasant warm climate. There were palm-lined streets and parks, Italianate architecture, sophisticated restaurants and cinemas. 'Piccola Roma,' the colonial Italians had called it, 'our little Rome in Africa.' Michael and I discovered an Italian restaurant called Rino's where we gorged ourselves on steak and lasagne, drank wine and endless cups of cappuccino. We went to the cinema and watched a strange assortment of films, mostly dubbed in Italian with Amharic subtitles. We were relaxed, well-fed, and the sun was shining. It was like being on holiday.

After a rather unsuccessful overnight trip to the coast, we spent our last two nights together in a small, comfortable hotel. We dined at Rino's and talked non-stop. 'I'll miss you,' Michael said, and I knew that our parting would be a wrench. He had lent me the money for the short flight to Kassala in Sudan, just 275 miles away, and he was heading south to Kenya. In the spice market we set up meetings with black market currency dealers who came and went from our room. I enjoyed the buzz of the clandestine dealing. A couple of months later, at home in England, I received a Kenyan bank note in the post. Michael had glued his head over the spot where Kenyatta's face should have been.

His bus south departed at dawn. Accompanied by an inter-faith dirge of muezzin and church bells, we said our fond farewells. 'I'm sure we'll meet again sometime,' he faltered. I was certain we would. I thought I had found a friend for life.

Sudan – the Lone and Level Sands

I was surprised when the Sudan Airways clerk drove me to the airport free of charge and gave me a packet of cigarettes. 'You are the only passenger who wants to land in Kassala,' he said, shaking his head sorrowfully. Clearly it was a real hassle for the plane to land in such a remote place just for me. 'If you would like to go to Khartoum,' he ventured, 'I can send you there at no extra charge.' I couldn't believe my luck. The plane proved cavernous, more like a military transport vehicle. There were less seats than in a normal aircraft and few passengers. Only a few hours after bidding farewell to Michael, I found myself nearly 500 miles away, exploring Sudan's capital.

Khartoum was an oven, a city that baked at over 40°C. I walked about slit-eyed in the blinding light. The desert had made inroads into the city centre, choking alleyways and dusting wide open spaces with sand. Unpaved avenues were lined by elegant colonial buildings. Majestic in crisp white cotton robes, their faces scarred with tribal allegiance, the men seemed to glide along in the dazzling light. Stifled, and at times rendered dizzy by the temperature, I was overwhelmed by the same sense of freedom and wellbeing I had felt in Tanzania. The citizens were gentle, welcoming and approachable. I was unafraid, and relaxed.

On my first foray into the city, a charming young man offered me a tour on the back of his scooter. Under his tutelage I trod in the footsteps of Gordon and Kitchener, the Victorian heroes of British imperialism. Artefacts which had belonged to General Gordon lay in dusty neglect inside the house where he had lived. My host led me along the sandy streets of Omdurman, talking of the famous battle that had taken place nearby, the conflict in which Kitchener had slaughtered the Mahdist hordes in their thousands. Before me, the dome of the Mahdi's tomb glinted in the sunlight. A tribute to the self-styled messianic Muslim, the nemesis of British imperialists, it had been rebuilt by the Mahdi's son in 1947. 'The original tomb was opened up by Kitchener,' my companion told me. 'He removed the Mahdi's body and cut off his head.' I flinched, but the information had been delivered factually, without malice. 'After Kitchener's victory here at Omdurman,' he added, 'you British remained for the next 57 years.'

For the rest of the afternoon I rode pillion around Khartoum. At Al Mogran I was shown the confluence of the White Nile and Blue Nile, rivers which retain their distinct identities for a short distance on account of the silt they carry. I could just make out the White Nile which had emerged from Lake Victoria, and I thought of Chacha at Kendu Bay gazing dreamily into the water. I could also see the Blue Nile which had flowed from Lake Tana in Ethiopia, and which had thundered over the Tis-Isat Falls where I had stood in awe with Michael. Now these two rivers were about to merge into one mighty torrent which would accompany me on my journey north to the Mediterranean.

I was only in Khartoum a couple of days but Sudanese friends were easily come by. Various meetings were scrawled in the margin of my diary: *Lunch at Al Sharg Hotel; 6.30 Egyptian Consulate, meet up with road engineer afterwards; 10am phone the television guy; outing with man from tourist office.* My companions, who were all male, behaved perfectly. They took me to their homes, I met their families, we drank tea, and they drove me around in the sweltering heat. This initial Sudanese welcome reflected the experiences which were to follow in the most hospitable country I have ever visited.

Sitting by the Nile in the evening, drinking beer, the road engineer talked politics. 'President Nimeiri is fickle,' he told me. 'He's gone from the military to socialism, and now he's moving towards capitalism; Chevron Oil has just been granted concessions in Sudan.' A decade later, the capricious Nimeiri was to embrace fundamentalism and Sharia law; near the very spot where we were sitting, Sudan's entire liquor supply would be ceremoniously tipped into the Nile. The road engineer went on to talk about his job. 'I prefer working with the Chinese,' he explained. 'The Russians have to refer to Moscow all the time and it slows everything down. The Chinese make decisions on the spot. They achieve miracles.'

In Khartoum I had stayed at the youth hostel, a comfortable enough place where my fellow lodgers were friendly. However, I didn't want anything to do with them. I had a long journey ahead and I was determined to travel alone. I needn't have worried. From the moment I left Khartoum until I arrived in Egypt, I only met indigenous people.

Early in the morning I went to the lorry park in Khartoum and set about finding a truck heading north. I was no longer with the educated elite. The truckers spoke no European languages and all I could do was shout out the name of my destinations: 'Shendi? Atbara?' Within a few minutes I had been hauled up onto the roof of a lorry. I was to travel with three men, two below in the cab, one on the roof with me. My map had indicated a major road heading north for about 120 miles to Shendi. Nothing had prepared me for the rough journey that was to follow, a slog of several hours surrounded by nothing but desert. I only had a small metal army flask of water and a few dried dates. I still had my *kikoy*, the length of cloth I had worn in Lamu. Now I wound it around my head creating a giant turban, looping the end across my face against the dust. The lorry swayed along, its progress inhibited by sand. Every so often the drivers would stop and brew small glasses of tea, but a thimbleful of liquid did nothing to quench my thirst. Late afternoon we limped into Shendi, a historic trading centre on the banks of the Nile. Despite its importance in days gone by, it was little more than a village, a pretty place with friendly people.

Saad, one of the truck drivers, took me to his home where his extended family welcomed me with open arms. We entered a large oblong room, its bare mud walls lined by beds which doubled as seating. Everyone grinned, but we could only communicate by miming. I adopted my usual ploy, hamming it up with the children, cuddling babies, international gestures everyone could understand. Saad's wife appeared with a tray of tiny glasses filled with sweet red liquid. She looked surprised when I swigged it down; clearly it was meant to be savoured and sipped. I pointed at some water in a bucket and they brought me a cupful. I could no longer keep up the polite pretence; I demanded water and more water. I gulped it down with no regard to its cleanliness or safety. I was gasping. Eventually, finding the situation highly amusing, they furnished me with my own personal bucket. The children giggled and mimicked my drinking.

My thirst slaked, everyone became curious about my possessions. Most of my belongings were in my rucksack, but I kept a few odds and ends in a small bag. One by one they scrutinised the contents, passing them round the room. There was a pocket mirror, a hair brush, a bit of makeup. Then they came across my Tampax. An old man removed one tampon from the box and looked at it curiously. He turned it round and round, sniffed it and passed it on. Everyone followed suit, perplexed by the tampon and apparently discussing what its purpose might be.

Eventually, after sharing an evening meal, I was given a bed outside so I could sleep under the stars. Laughing, they put another bucket of water at my side. I passed the night in bloated discomfort, tossing and turning. I broke into a sweat, had a splitting headache and felt ill. I awoke at 5am feeling better. I had survived the dehydration but, had I been in a city hospital, I would have undoubtedly been put on a drip.

Early in the morning I helped the women washing dishes and played with the children. Some of the small girls wore short dresses and no knickers and when I caught a glimpse of their genitalia, I was puzzled. There was something abnormal. I knew about male circumcision, but in those days I had never heard of female genital mutilation. Apparently in northern Sudan infibulation, the most drastic form of FGM, is practised, and sometimes this is performed on girls who are little more than infants.

Throughout the morning, Saad paraded me before the populace, like some exotic creature he had discovered. We strolled beneath the palms on the banks of the Nile, exchanging greetings, accepting tea and sweetmeats. I felt immensely privileged. By mid-afternoon they had located a lorry bound for Atbara, and I embarked on the next leg of my journey, travelling through the desert with three new and charming truckers.

En route they paused to point out some distant pyramids. They couldn't communicate with me, but later I realised I had been looking at the Pyramids of Meroe, the tombs of over 40 kings and queens. Meroe had been the capital of the Kingdom of Kush which, from 712 to 657 BCE, had ruled much of Egypt, its trade extending as far as India and China. Now its glory was submerged in the shifting sands.

We rolled into Atbara late at night and the truckers deposited me in a lodging house, entrusting the manager with my care and safety. I slept soundly in a yard packed with beds occupied by about 30 men. I awoke at dawn to the sound of ritual ablutions and prayer, after which women began to appear, waiting on the men and serving them breakfast. I thanked my host, who declined payment, and set off to explore. I needed to find out about catching a train across the desert to Wadi Halfa.

In the souk I was accosted by Magdi who worked for the State Bank for Foreign Trade and who invited me home to stay with his wife and small child, and where he showed off his upholstered furniture and an electric fan. All day his friends and relations arrived to inspect me. My favourite was his larger-than-life neighbour. 'I am Lotfi,' he bellowed, 'the fattest man in Sudan. Tomorrow you will come to my house for breakfast.' He introduced me to his family, all as rotund and noisy as he. 'I'm a railway man,' he said. 'Everyone in this town used to work on the railways. We had 20,000 workers here; machine shops, rail yards, it was so busy...' He paused, looking nostalgic. 'In 1948 I was working for the British. It was the year of the railway workers' strikes. We set up the first trade union in Sudan and it was because of us that the Government brought in labour legislation.' Later he told me that President Nimeiri had once frequented Atbara. 'For a while it was a communist stronghold,' he said. 'That's why he came.' Apparently, that fickle president had also flirted with communism.

That night I was taken to dine in some beautiful gardens attached to a colonial rest house. Magdi and his family were generous, but I was worn out. Back at his home, we were to sleep outside on the roof terrace. I was surprised when he produced one enormous bed to be shared between him, his wife, his child and me. Yet again, I attributed this bed-sharing to African hospitality but, unlike further south, I was among Muslims. It didn't feel quite right, but I told myself we were to sleep fully-clothed and that, with his wife and child in the bed, nothing would happen. Once in the night he did try to sneak a kiss and I pushed him away, but after that any potential intimacy was thwarted by my upset stomach. The bed was adjacent to a lavatory. All night, every few minutes, I leapt from the bed, rushed to the toilet, and provided my hosts with the most graphic sound effects, together with a stench that pervaded the entire area. The next day as I boarded the train, I wondered how I was going to cope with the toilet facilities.

According to Lotfi, the train I was taking to Wadi Halfa was the original, taken out to Sudan in 1906. True or not, the engine had certainly been struggling far too long. It was to break down four times, delaying our journey by 24 hours. It travelled so slowly that it might have been quicker to walk. Each time it gave up the ghost, we waited hours until it was mended. On one occasion the guard produced an ancient bicycle and cycled back alongside the railway tracks to search for a mechanic at the previous halt.

Inside the train, it was like a roasting tray where passengers sweated like basted chickens. At the rear of each carriage there was a huge earthenware jar of water which, at intervals along the way, was replenished with Nile water the colour of tea, fed through a hose. When the train ground to a halt in the evening, the night wind whipped up a dust storm, funnelling it through the windows and coating everyone in a fine layer of sand. The sleeping passengers gleamed in the moonlight like grainy petrified statues, washed with a pearly glaze. If a long delay was expected, everyone climbed out and relaxed in the desert, brewing spiced tea, eating refreshing cucumbers and singing songs. We slept on the sand, the chill night breeze a balm to our daytime fever. I lay under the stars and thought of Saint-Exupéry, T E Lawrence, Wilfred Thesiger, my personal desert heroes. I looked around at the other passengers. We were vulnerable, miniscule creatures scratching our trails across a vast, hostile expanse. With a bad cold, an upset stomach and my period, which had inconveniently started the minute I boarded the train, I felt brittle, but also ecstatically happy. I loved these gentle, friendly Sudanese people. With so few belongings, so little money, they sat singing their hearts out beneath the stars.

During one breakdown there was a water crisis. People scoured the length of the train locating the earthenware pots, all of which were empty. Dwelling on my recent dehydration, I prayed the train would be mended within the usual nine hours; thankfully, it only took seven. I consulted my map and was relieved to see *good water* and *oasis* written by halt number 6 and, sure enough, when we arrived there we found two enormous tanks of water: one for washing; the other, for drinking, was clear, rather than Nile-brown.

Eventually, after four days, we creaked and clunked into Wadi Halfa, the railhead on the shores of Lake Nubia. For me, the only foreigner on the train, the journey had been unforgettable.

Ozymandias

Lake Nasser, a reservoir 350 miles long and 22 miles wide, had been created in the 60s through the construction of the Aswan High Dam. The southern, Sudanese part of this artificial sea was known as Lake Nubia where, moored just offshore, I saw for the first time the extraordinary vessel on which I was to travel to Egypt. The *10th of Ramadan* was a Heath Robinson affair; it had plied the Nile between Wadi Halfa and Egypt since before 1919 and was probably of a similar vintage to the train I'd just taken. The boat was a paddle steamer, with two barge-like appendages, one on either side, making it look weird and cumbersome. Once on board, I stood aghast as the boat shuddered into motion, powered by the most beautiful, big, black engine. During the journey I kept returning for another peep at this impressive remnant of the steam age. 'I can't understand why you're enjoying it so much,' grumbled Mohmoud, a fellow passenger. 'This boat is the disgrace of Sudan!' Nine years later, the *10th of Ramadan* burst into flames and sank, drowning more than 300 of those on board.

On the deck it was chaos: babies rolled around amidst pots and pans; elderly people slept; people brewed tea and mashed fava beans into *ful*. In the night, picking my way across recumbent bodies, I stepped on an old man who leapt to his feet, shrieking and kicking me until other passengers calmed him down. Every evening noisy youths sang Arabic songs or played poker, but most of the time they wanted to engage me in conversation. 'What do you think of our War?' they asked again and again. Whether Sudanese or Egyptian, the 1973 conflict with Israel was fresh in their minds and they were certainly not happy about the Disengagement Agreement that had just been signed between Egypt and Israel.

Shortly after boarding the steamer I had met Abdul Aziz and his companion El Sir, Sudanese students who were studying at Cairo University and who were about to start their new academic year. Gentle, educated young men they were kind and protective towards me, although Aziz, the more Arabic-looking of the two, delivered his concern with a good measure of flirtation.

I still didn't feel well. I had blocked sinuses, a sore throat and swollen glands, but although I had pushed my body to its limit, nothing could eradicate the joy and beauty of that journey. At daybreak, after my first night on deck, I had opened my eyes to find Pharaoh Ramses II looming over me in the dawn. I stared in awe and disbelief – Ozymandias, right there, before my very eyes! I'd seen Abu Simbel printed in tiny letters on my map, but I knew little of the temples and gigantic statues which had been relocated when the Aswan Dam was built. Shelley, I thought –the lone and level sands!

My name is Ozymandias, King of Kings;
Look on my Works, ye Mighty and despair!
Nothing beside remains. Round the decay
Of that colossal Wreck, boundless and bare
The lone and level sands stretch far away.

There was just one tiny boat anchored nearby; not a tourist in sight. As for our steamer, it was merely ferrying locals between Sudan and Egypt. It had no reason to stop and examine antiquities.

I spent much of the day sitting on the prow of the ship, in the shade near the anchor. Like a desiccated prune I relished the spray falling on my skin. Since my dehydration, I had become fixated on water. *It's flowing fast on either side of me,* I wrote home. *I want to dive in it, drink it, immerse myself in it. I'll never be satiated. I'll never again forget the wonder that is water.* The big paddle wheels grumbling and clunking, we steamed north, past dreamlike shores with golden dunes where the ruined wonders of the ancient world protruded from the sand.

'There's trouble,' whispered Abdul Aziz one morning. 'That policeman...' he inclined his head slightly, indicating a man on the other side of the boat, 'that policeman's Egyptian, and he's been telling everyone you're an Israeli spy. He also insists that I'm Egyptian, not Sudanese, and that I'm feeding you information.' Perhaps stupidly, I wasn't terribly worried by this declaration. I had frequently come across blustering cops and soldiers who boosted their own importance by being officious to foreigners. It wasn't that different from the Kenyan Air Force suggesting Mike and Carol were American spies. I was less concerned about myself than I was about Aziz.

We had been travelling for a couple of days when I suddenly remembered that I'd bought some antihistamine pills in Ethiopia, medication never used. Hoping they would act as a decongestant, I took one. Antihistamine or not, they were certainly hallucinogenic. Someone caught a fish off the side of the boat, and as they reeled it in I saw it looming larger and larger until its bulging fishy eyes were but an inch from my own. Aziz's face came and went, gigantic, and then receding into the distance like an elusive genie. Eventually, in the evening, when everyone bedded down, I fell into a drugged slumber on the deck.

I awoke to find the Aswan High Dam towering above me like a mountain. I whipped out my camera to record this magnificent feat of engineering and the Egyptian cop pounced: 'No photos! No photos!' he screamed and everyone turned to look at the suspicious behaviour of the Israeli spy. I had arrived in Egypt.

Egypt – the Last Lap

Gradually the chanting of the funeral march penetrated my feverish sleep. I opened my eyes and saw four young French people. They were moving as if in a funeral cortège and were holding high a mug of hot lemonade. They proceeded to give me mock funeral rites, intoning and making signs of the Cross. I sat up slowly, still aching. 'Ah, so you are not dead after all,' said Jean-Francois, who had led the procession. I had met him for a couple of minutes when I'd arrived the previous day. Kind and mildly flirtatious, he knew I was burnt out after my long journey up Africa. 'I had a letter from my mother today,' he said. 'In Paris the leaves are falling. Autumn! Soon you will be home.'

In Aswan youth hostel I had slept in a top bunk in the dormitory for 24 hours. I was beginning to feel a little better, but I was still weak. I was about to go out and find some food in the market when Gamil-Yussuf, a hostel employee, came running in brandishing a bit of paper. 'A telegram! A telegram for Miss Jenny Steele! That is you?' 'Yes,' I admitted, puzzled. My parents didn't even know I'd reached Egypt and anyway, in a crisis, they would have contacted the British Embassy in Cairo. I opened the envelope. The telegram had been sent from the telegraph office on Luxor station, but the message was in Arabic. Gamil-Yussuf was hovering. 'Well,' I said, handing it over to him, 'what does it say?' 'It's from someone called Aziz,' he said, and the message is 'I wish you great happiness!'

My first impression of Egypt was of everyone going about in their night clothes. I was used to Muslim women wearing garments that resembled nighties, but the striped cotton trousers worn by many Egyptian men resembled British pyjamas of the 1950s and lent a Peter Pan quality to my surroundings. The fairy tale was enhanced when, in the midst of a pile of market fruit, I spied one solitary bright red apple. I hadn't seen apples anywhere in Africa. I purchased it and bit into its hard juicy flesh; it was like coming home.

For a couple of days I recuperated, intent on making myself strong for the last lap of the journey. I hung out with my French friends and the ever-present Gamil-Yussuf, who tried to impress us by dropping European literary references into everyday conversation: Sartre for the French; Hardy for me. Like every other young man I was to encounter in Egypt, he also wanted to talk about the War. The year before, Anwar Sadat, the president, had set out to reclaim the Sinai Peninsula, occupied by the Israelis in the 1967 War. On October 6th 1973, the Egyptian Third Army had taken Israeli defences in Sinai by surprise. Even though three weeks later the jubilant Egyptian troops had been surrounded by the Israelis, the original success was referred to by everyone as 'Our Glorious Victory.'

Before I left Aswan, Gamil-Yussuf wanted to take me on an outing to the botanical gardens, situated on an island that had once belonged to Kitchener. We went there in a small *felucca*, a traditional sailing boat, and spent an hour or two walking among exotic plants. It should have been a pleasant, peaceful interlude, but my companion treated me as if I were made of porcelain, helping me along the pathways, fussing over my every move. I suspect he was treating me as he would an Arabic girl, had she been permitted to accompany him unchaperoned – or maybe he had been reading too much Jane Austen. As we departed the island, he helped me into the small boat, entreating me to take care, holding my elbow in case I slipped. 'Be careful! Be careful!' he wailed as I shoved him aside and climbed into the boat. 'Leave me alone!' I snapped, icily. He smiled benignly, shaking his head from side to side: 'My little wild flower!' he exclaimed. 'You are my little wild flower!'

Later that afternoon, travelling third class on a slow train to Luxor, I was to encounter the antithesis of Gamil's protective behaviour: five youths stood over me, making lecherous kissing noises and jeering at me in Arabic. I ignored them, but they continued until an angry old man sent them packing. After the gentle hospitality I had experienced from Muslim men throughout Sudan, this incident was a shock. Despite getting off to a poor start, the journey was beautiful. The train creaked and crawled through lush farmland bordering the Nile, past traditional villages with mud dwellings and small mosques. *Feluccas* sliced the sparkling river, graceful as swans. Donkeys picked their way along sandy lanes, their panniers overflowing with crops, while water buffalos squelched through the silt. The backdrop of desert hills left me in no doubt that Egypt was the gift of the Nile.

Arriving in Luxor late at night, I stumbled on two Scottish lads who gladly shouldered my bag and guided me to the youth hostel. 'Is it expensive to get to the Valley of the Kings?' I asked, concerned that the pittance that remained of my budget might be insufficient. 'Och, no,' they said. 'All ye need is a wee bike!' The next day I rented a bicycle from the youth hostel and, after crossing to the west bank of the Nile on the *felucca* used by locals, I cycled five miles through the desert to the site of the tombs. The tarmac road shimmered in the heat as I slogged uphill, overtaken by taxis which had met the ferry used by wealthy tourists. On arrival, I was set upon by small boys who produced fake scarabs and tacky souvenirs from their pockets. They were known for removing bicycle wheels and charging to reinstate them. I had been advised to pre-empt this by paying them upfront to guard my bike.

I had arrived at the Valley of the Kings to find there was no water at the souvenir shop and café, presumably to ensure tourists purchased overpriced fizzy drinks. When popping into the ladies, however, I came across a bucket of water standing in a corner. I had just topped up my water bottle when the door burst open and an Arab appeared, an impressive figure in traditional dress and, to my astonishment, male! 'That's *my* water!' he said, snatching my flask and emptying the contents back into the bucket. 'No it is not,' I protested. 'Half that water was mine. I brought it with me from Luxor.' 'Ok,' he said, reluctantly, narrowing his eyes and fixing me with an angry stare. 'Ok...' He held my flask beneath the waterline in the bucket until it was exactly half full. 'There, this is your water. The rest is my water.' He picked up the bucket and flounced out. What he was doing in the ladies toilets I can't imagine, but our altercation served to remind me that water was a commodity precious beyond all else. *Like Lawrence of Arabia,* I wrote in my diary; *the bit where Omar Sharif shoots Lawrence's guide for daring to use his water.*

It felt strange descending deep into the Pharaohs' tombs and, by the time I had visited a couple, I was sweaty and exhausted from going up and down so many steps. I had marvelled at Tutankhamun's mask at the London exhibition, but nothing had prepared me for the clarity of the pictures in the burial chambers, the colours so bright they might have been recently painted. Despite this, there was no awe, no reverence. I was caught up in a circus with loud tourists who pushed and shoved.

Back then, the Valley of the Queens had yet to be opened up to the public, but I'd been told that if you greased the palm of the custodian he would grant access. Following a rough map someone had sketched for me, I cycled a couple of miles further on, and located the hut where the guardian of the Queens was sheltering from the sun. It was the hottest time of day; sun glanced off the carpet of sand which stretched into the distance. The old man had been dozing when I found him; it was Ramadan, a time when fasting renders everyone listless and irritable. Grumbling, he pocketed my money, shuffled off in the direction of one of the tombs, and unlocked the door. I stepped into the gloomy interior and there before me were paintings of women – the wives and children of the Pharaohs. It was a fusty place, unsullied by tourism. I stood riveted to the spot, staring in disbelief at the beautiful images that had survived the centuries. For several minutes I teetered on the edge of the afterlife, and then the old man reappeared and sent me packing, slamming the door shut behind me.

In Luxor, at crack of dawn, I walked to Karnak, the ruined city of temples. Local people arriving in town from the countryside smiled and greeted me, but I hurried on. I wanted Karnak to myself, before the hordes arrived, and I succeeded. A solitary man on the ticket gate admitted me, and for a full half hour I wandered awestruck among the towering statues, the magnificent temple walls and columns with their intricate hieroglyphics – and then the first tourists arrived shattering the magic.

That evening as I made my way to the station to catch the night express to Cairo, I was invited to break the Ramadan fast with a group of people sitting by the roadside. They had a charcoal brazier and they fed me kebabs and bread and gave me a toke or two on their hookah. I looked at my handsome companions with their large, dark eyes and thought of the painted, almond-shaped gaze of their ancestors, the kings and queens who had stared down on me from the walls of the necropolis. Time in Egypt was strange; the ancients seemed close.

The train was packed with troops. A couple of soldiers sat on the luggage rack, their boots dangling in my face. Uniformed men swaggered and pushed and shouted. A middle-aged woman swiped at them, shrieking reprimands, and then moved, clucking protectively, in my direction. For the rest of the 12-hour journey she was my chaperone. When I got up to go to the toilet, she followed, standing outside the door until I emerged. She meant well and was protecting me as she would her own daughter, but I felt trapped. If it had been the beginning of my travels I would have been more patient, more interested in her behaviour, but I was tired and incapable of the effort required to communicate. It was a raucous night with no sleep. We reached Cairo just before dawn, our arrival heralded by a cockerel crowing in the luggage rack.

Cairo

I had checked in at the youth hostel, only to be whisked away when Aziz and El Sir, my friends from the paddle steamer, came looking for me. Together with Mahgoub, they shared a flat, away from the city centre on the other side of the Nile. It was a simple, middle-class neighbourhood occupied by families and quite a lot of students. There were one or two small shops and vendors selling fruit and vegetables off barrows, but on the whole it was just a friendly little community.

Their apartment was sparsely furnished and they lived simply. They were generous, intelligent young men, and over meals and late into the night we discussed the Middle East and its wars; Marxism versus Islam; the legacy of colonialism. El Sir was the one who instigated most discussion. In studying agriculture he hoped to help his country, Sudan. He also still adhered to the tenets of his Muslim faith.

Religious commitment varied considerably between the three young men and they indulged in endless discussion about the teachings of Islam and how to interpret the Qu'ran. Where El Sir was devout, Aziz was confused and his religious practices had lapsed. Mahgoub merely shrugged: 'I no longer fast,' he said. 'In fact, I'm not even sure I believe Mohammed was a prophet!' They quizzed me about Christianity and, although no longer a believer, I could discuss it up to a point. I was also aware that my presence was pivotal to their religious doubt and constituted a rebellious gesture. In a Muslim world it was inappropriate for me to live with three young men and even more culturally insensitive that I had succumbed to Aziz's attentions. However, they had actively sought me out and invited me to stay. They remained hospitable and caring, treating me with great affection and respect. We joked and laughed and had so much fun.

'We must take Jenny to Khan-el-Khalili,' they announced one evening and I was introduced to the tangled magic of the great souk of Cairo. The Ramadan fast had ended for the day and crowds surged through the alleyways. The night added its mystery: shadows which danced and beckoned; yellow light which spilled in pools across hidden courtyards, then melted away into the dark labyrinth beyond; passageways where vendors offered spices and oils, silk and satin, silver and precious stones. It was a circus, a carnival, a fairy tale. Sometimes, as we pushed our way through the crowds, I glanced upwards. Between gaps in the awnings above, I caught glimpses of a star-studded sky.

We had started the evening in a traditional coffee house with panelled walls and stained mirrors in heavy gilt frames. The table tops were cracked marble, the chairs made of dark brown wood. The clientele engaged in animated conversation, sucked gently on shisha pipes or slapped down domino and backgammon pieces. After sharing a hookah and spiced tea, we went back into the fray, weaving past weightlifters and fire-eaters, until we stumbled on the dervishes. Their whirling wasn't light and dance-like as I had imagined, but heavy and stolid. As the drumming grew louder and they thumped their way into a deeper and deeper trance, they grunted rhythmically, sweating and drooling. Aziz pulled me back against the wall of the narrow alley. I felt nervous, as if I were about to be spun and crushed in their unstoppable fervour.

Later that night, inside a large patchwork tent, we watched bards reciting traditional poems and stories accompanied by music, discordant sounds which whined and twisted, before taking flight in the purity of flutes. At 2am we left the heaving souk behind, walking home across the bridge, over the moonlit Nile. My friends had bought me perfumed oil, prayer beads, and decked me in a garland of jasmine that reminded me of Lamu.

During the day, while my hosts were at the university, I explored the city centre, with its clean streets, luxury hotels, coffee bars and restaurants. Most people, including women, appeared modern and affluent, in stylish western dress, but my solitary forays were far from pleasant. Unlike the Sudanese, Egyptian men wouldn't leave me alone. They would bump into me intentionally so that, in extricating themselves, they could touch me. Suited business men would actually tweak my tits or pinch my bum as they hurried past. Others would block my path, suggesting with innuendo that I might like a coffee. It was wearisome rather than dangerous and eventually inhibited my exploration of Cairo.

One of the problems that beset both me and my hosts was a lack of money. Their student grants from Sudan had failed to arrive, so they had little to live on, let alone pay rent. Moreover, it was incumbent on them in a Muslim society to offer me hospitality and feed me. I picked up the gist of their conversation one evening and insisted I contribute to the household. They were embarrassed; once having offered hospitality, it was unthinkable to retract the gesture.

I, too, had money problems. I needed to set aside the cost of the Channel ferry, otherwise I would be stranded penniless on the continent. I marched into the Cairo office of Thomas Cook, a firm still regarded as the iconic British travel company that had served the nation since the 19th century. 'The price of a ticket from Ostend to Dover?' I enquired. 'Ostend?' said the Egyptian woman behind the counter. 'Where is Ostend?' 'Belgium,' I said. 'I need to go from Belgium to England by boat.' She shrugged. 'I don't know this Belgium.' I tried again. 'Maybe a boat from Calais then? Calais, France.' 'I don't know,' she repeated.' Thomas Cook came crashing off its pedestal. 'Ok,' I said, giving up. 'Where can I get a ticket from Alexandria to Naples?' She smiled. I had entered the realms of possibility. 'Turkish Maritime Lines,' she said.

I set off to find their offices, aware it was the same shipping line I had used to travel to Israel a decade before. I thought of the naïve girl who had been followed by the gendarme to the ticket office in Marseille: before Israel, before India, before Canada and America, before Africa. The clerk at the maritime agency was efficient. 'The boat is *Akdeniz*,' he said, 'departing October 6th.' He could not resist adding, 'The anniversary of Our Glorious Victory.' I smiled. 'The cheapest ticket possible.' He raised his eyebrows. 'Are you sure? Deck Class. No food.' 'Yes, that's it,' I confirmed. 'Deck Class. No food.' Painstakingly he wrote out my receipt: 'El Iskandariya to Napoli,' he muttered, and handed me my ticket home to Europe.

The next few days, strapped for cash, I wandered the streets of our neighbourhood. Sometimes in the evenings I went out with the boys or visited Aziz's cousin and the medical students who shared a nearby house. We rarely went into the city centre, but strolled around the backstreets where, on every corner, there were large earthenware pots of water with dipping cups. I had become obsessed with fresh dates, so much so that my friends teased me about it and bought them for me at every opportunity. Even the man who had a stall at the end of our street knew about it. 'Dates! Dates!' he would shout, every time I passed, sometimes contributing a freebee to my addiction.

Before my departure, I managed two more visits to antiquities. Cairo Museum was a surprise. It was like rummaging in an extraordinary jumble sale of mummies, stray heads and statues, and priceless artefacts from tombs. The flotsam of ancient Egypt lay in disarray, still labelled with yellowing scraps of cardboard, scribed in German, Italian, French, English and Arabic, the handwriting of long-gone archaeologists.

Mahgoub and Aziz took me on a crowded local bus to Giza so I could visit the pyramids and the sphinx. There were only a couple of tourists in the vicinity and two lethargic men offering camel rides. My friends waited while I entered one of the pyramids on my own. The man in charge was slumped sleepily against the wall. 'Ramadan!' he growled. I began to ascend the steps inside and he shouted at me angrily. I waited.

Eventually, grumbling, he led me up and up until we reached a dark, cavernous chamber. I was at the core of one of the seven wonders of the ancient world but, for some reason, I was not overwhelmed. *I prefer the pyramids in Mexico*, I wrote in my diary.

When I emerged and we were returning to the bus stop, a man popped out of a hut and grabbed me. 'Come,' he said. 'You write in my book. Many famous names in my book.' 'But I'm not famous,' I protested. 'You write,' he insisted, giving me a pen. I added my name to the thousands of autographs he had collected. He flipped back several pages, running his finger down the signatures. Finally he stopped triumphantly. 'You know this one?' he enquired, and pointed to where Marianne Faithfull had scrawled her name. It was undoubtedly genuine; a couple of years before she had been there filming Kenneth Anger's film *Lucifer Rising*.

During my stay in Cairo I was seen as Aziz's girlfriend, but he wasn't always easy. Sometimes, as we sat on the banks of the Nile, chatting quietly or gazing into the water, I would feel affectionate towards him. Tall and handsome with dark curly hair, his temperament and appearance were very Arabic. However, at times, his histrionics would make me aloof. He was romantic, emotional, moody and jealous. He would snap his fingers in rage or lapse into a silent sulk. Sometimes he would profess undying love for me and, weeping, declare that it was unrequited – which was true. He wrote poems for me in Arabic, which he then translated and recited. He was funny, kind and loving, but I was run down, worn out, at the end of my journey and the end of my tether.

Aziz's emotional side extended to what he termed Arab politics. He was a firebrand. El Sir and Mahgoub were more grounded. Whereas they would discuss Israel or Middle Eastern politics in an analytical way, Aziz would smoulder, rant, rage and finally erupt into explosive fury. On the fourth anniversary of Nasser's death, 28th September, 1974, he translated President Sadat's speech for me. It began: *Brothers and sisters, revolutions do not take place in laboratories or in test tubes. They rather occur on grounds full of conflicting interests and emotions. Destruction and construction have a great echo and cause much dust...* Aziz grinned.

It was a speech after his own heart.

To further my understanding of Middle Eastern politics, the lads took me to the cinema. The first movie was an Arabic melodrama interspersed with a lot of songs, but this was followed by a propaganda film about Egypt's Glorious Victory. Everyone in the audience shouted and cheered, leapt to their feet and raised their fists. On the way to the cinema I had picked some jasmine and given a sprig each to El Sir, Mahgoub and Aziz. They sat amidst the turmoil, each clutching their delicate white blooms. I could not imagine these gentle Sudanese boys as part of the military, but I had felt the same way a decade before when I had talked to Anmun about the Israeli army. When discussing the futility of war with Aziz, and suggesting soldiers were the pawns of politicians, I also told him about the similarities between Anmun and himself. He was fascinated. 'Tell me more about that Israelite,' he would say. The following year he wrote: *In Sudan I had a chance of being an officer in the army, but I refused, and that was because of you and because of your ideas.*

The day after our outing to the cinema I left for Alexandria. There was a long stilted farewell on Cairo railway station. I loved my hosts dearly and I wanted to throw my arms around each one of them. 'No touching,' hissed Aziz, as if reading my thoughts. 'Not here.' We all shook hands and I squeezed them as tight as I could, hoping to transmit in a few tactile seconds, my affection, appreciation, and sorrow at parting. I boarded the train. '*Ma'a Assalama!*' they shouted. '*Ma'a Assalama*, goodbye!' and as I drew out of the station, Aziz was bold enough to blow me a kiss. *When we got back to the flat,* he wrote me later, *we sat in silence. We were filled with such sadness. Jenny had gone.*

The Top of the Map

Alexandria was an attractive city with colonial architecture, palm-lined streets and old-fashioned hotels on the seafront. There was a traditional coffee house with a panelled interior, where the shisha pipes were stacked along shelves and old men sat reading newspapers. Jacques, the Lebanese proprietor, who spoke French and had hooded eyes and a nose like a hawk, plied me with coffee and sticky cakes on the house. Sitting at one of the creaky old tables I thought of *The Alexandria Quartet*, imagining the door might open and Justine or Balthazar might join me.

I was staying in the youth hostel where there were a lot of European travellers. These were my last few days in Africa. I was burnt out and happy to be in easy company. Late one night, returning with a couple of friends from town, we came across a security guard outside a big warehouse. A jovial character, he invited us to join him. We were smoking a hookah and chatting happily when he pointed to the packing cases stacked from floor to ceiling behind us. 'Guess what's in the boxes,' he said. We had no idea. 'Bullets!' he announced. 'This is a bullet factory.' At about one in the morning, the door burst open and another man appeared. He was something of a clown, grinning, gesticulating wildly and chatting to our host. After about half an hour and a puff or two on the pipe, he handed the security guard an envelope, picked up his bag and departed. 'Postman,' said our host. 'He always comes late at night.'

On my last day in Alexandria I boarded a packed bus and travelled to a wide sandy beach, where I lay in the sun listening to the waves crashing on the shore. *The Mediterranean!* I wrote in my diary. *I've made it. I've reached the top of the map!*

The Fields of Home

Mohmud had lost his spark. It was the same Mohmud who had referred to the paddle steamer as the shame of Sudan. Now we found ourselves fellow passengers on the *Akdeniz*, sailing from Alexandria to Naples. No longer among his countrymen, he was reticent and nervous about arriving in Europe. For the sake of the hospitality I had received in Sudan, I spent a lot of time with him. 'You'll be fine,' I reassured him, 'You'll enjoy Europe.' Secretly, I shared his concern: I anticipated the climate being unbearably cold and the people aloof or hostile. 'Come on,' 'let's learn a bit more English,' I said, chivvying him along,

We had set sail from Alexandria the afternoon before. As I watched the city recede in a heat haze, my heart was breaking: I thought of Chacha and Joseph at Kendu Bay; of the law students in Nairobi; of Richard flying across the parched African landscape. I imagined Haji Shoblo causing ructions in the Lamu market and Australian Jenni driving her truck down the length of Africa. Michael would be in Kenya enjoying sights that I had treasured, and Saad would be in Shendi, ambling along the banks of the Nile. I had brushed with so many lives. Africans, from wayside stalls in Tanzania to the slums of Addis Ababa, had shared their thoughts and dreams with me, had welcomed me into their lives and homes. And then I remembered it was 6th October, the anniversary of Egypt's Glorious Victory, and I knew Aziz would be parading through the streets of Cairo, shouting with jingoistic pride. I looked at my hands resting on the ship's railing. Only the very tips of my fingers bore the remnants of Lamu henna. Africa had nearly faded away.

I was in a bubble, floating between Africa and Europe. An Egyptian woman billowed back and forth across the deck in a long red velvet dress. While the warmth and sunshine lasted, everyone lazed on the deck, a weird assortment of characters whose enforced proximity lent a surreal edge to the voyage. I felt as if I were living in a 1920s postcard. With the coming of the cold, the spell broke. Bundled up in extra clothing, people fluffed themselves up like migrant birds. We were welcomed to Italy by a firework display, Stromboli erupting and belching smoke. Finally we struck land and Naples loomed large: buildings, lights, Europe at last, but I felt nothing. I thought of the muezzins calling the end of the day's fast, of people breaking bread as the sun set. In my diary I wrote: *Tomorrow the tough days begin, the long haul home across the coldlands.*

My first night in Italy was spent in the back of a stationary furniture lorry belonging to Horst and Heino, German truckers bound for Stuttgart. Any negative thoughts about European hospitality had been dashed the moment I met them; they treated me to pizza and wine and provided me with blankets for the night. At dawn, after loading up with furniture, we set off for Germany. Italy was golden, the highway smooth, the truck luxurious. After several hours the road began climbing into the Alps and we passed pretty snowbound villages with small churches.

As night fell, Horst and Heino took it in turns to drive, one of them sleeping on a small upholstered shelf in a cubby hole at the top of the cab. The back of the lorry was packed with furniture. 'You can sleep up here with me,' said Horst. It was a tiny space, but I snuggled up with him and he slept soundly. I dozed intermittently, until dawn broke and I realised we were in Germany. Autumn leaves hung limply in the mist. Inside the cab, the radio was thumping out oompah-humpety-tump music. In Stuttgart the truckers found me a lift with an elderly man in a Mercedes and, after a couple more long rides, I arrived in Ostend. Despite lack of advice from Thomas Cook in Cairo, I'd managed to set aside the right amount of money for a Channel crossing. I sat in a shelter at the docks awaiting the night ferry and surrounded by drunken English lads who'd been to a Belgian beer festival.

We arrived in Folkestone at dawn and I persuaded a lorry driver from Yorkshire to give me a ride to London. The dark, sodden English countryside slipped by, an alien colourless world. I needed silence to come to terms with my homecoming, but the Yorkshireman was garrulous. He deposited me at Vauxhall and I phoned home. 'I'm in London!' I announced. 'Just got in.' There was a yelp of joy and I heard my mother shouting, 'She's back! She's back!' I loved them, I wanted to see them, but I also knew we would find each other difficult; the person who returns is never the same as the one who left.

There was a quotation by Hesse I carried in my diary. Now, on the train home to Dorking, I read it again:

He who travels far will often see things
Far removed from what he believed was Truth.
When he talks about it in the fields of home,
He is often accused of lying
For the obdurate people will not believe

What they do not see and distinctly feel.
Inexperience, I believe,
Will give little credence to my song.

The train rattled out of London, past grim Victorian housing, through toy-town suburbs, until it reached the Surrey countryside with its muddy furrows and wet fields. Nobody on the train spoke. Their clothing was drab. Raindrops slid down the windows like tears.

CHAPTER NINE

THE MOTHER OF WALES

Postscripts

'THAT'S AFRICA GONE,' I said to brother Phil, as I cut my
fingernails. 'No henna left.' 'You can get it here,' he said. I thought
of the Lamu fishermen winding jasmine garlands around my wrists
while the women painted my hands. 'It wouldn't be the same,' I replied.

Back in London, letters arrived daily injecting postscripts of Africa
into my life: *I shall be coming to London*, wrote Richard. *It will be
interesting to see what time has done to us.* Elsir was returning to Sudan
from Cairo... *on the same boat and the same train of hell.* Gebremariam,
an Ethiopian student, wrote: *There is fighting between Eritrean EPLF
and the Ethiopian military.* Haji Shoblo in Lamu used a letter writer:
*You remember when you pressed me to go to hospital? At last I follow
your advice in which I saved my leg.* Aziz professed his great love for me.
At last I found you, found my crazy flower. Then he added: *People here
are asking about the greatest eater of dates!* There were two letters from
Michael signed off *Ich liebe dich.* The letters weren't only from Africa;
they came from Canada, from India, from all over the world. And the
people came, too. It was an extraordinary interlude, when so many
friends from my past turned up in London. It was also embarrassing;
having only just returned from my travels, I had hardly any money, and
was unable to offer guests the hospitality they warranted.

I was living in a flat at Norland Square near Holland Park, an elegant
19th-century building, overlooking gardens with exclusive access for
residents. There were two rooms with high, moulded ceilings, a small
kitchen and bathroom, and a wrought iron balcony overlooking the
street. There was only one bed, but I had a non-stop stream of people,

often stray foreigners, sleeping on the floor. I mixed with the renegades from my old house at Perham Road, film friends from work, and travellers from Africa. Ostensibly I was busy socialising and having fun, but my direction was unclear. Having crawled up the face of Africa and reached my destination, I was left without focus.

I had only just missed Cameron Graham's CBC filming in London, but Cam wasn't the only person willing to employ me at the drop of a hat. George Wightman at Crown Cassette Communications also accommodated my whims and employed me for the third time. The company was no longer an intimate, quirky little concern negotiating video cassette rights on obscure films. VCRs had become big business and Crown Cassette Communications was full of businessmen in suits and striped shirts. My job had become market research rather than film research and I hated it.

It wasn't long before they despatched me on a tour of international organisations to assess their requirements for educational videocassettes, a somewhat vague remit: first stop Geneva; second Vienna. I arrived in Geneva on a Sunday and walked by the lake in the sunshine, where young people with long hair and hippie-style clothes were relaxing on the grass. They were spotless, well-groomed, not a tatter in sight. 'Fake,' I told everyone when I got home. 'With them it's just image, not a way of life.' Everything in Geneva seemed sanitised, not least the gleaming temples to international co-operation emblazoned with acronyms from UNICEF to UNIDO. I visited half a dozen of these, but as I sat inside sparkling, minimalist offices, I kept thinking of the slums of Addis Ababa. It seemed an insult to the Third World to be discussing educational video cassettes when people lacked the basics for survival.

I had telephoned Michael to say I would be visiting Vienna. I could have stayed in a hotel at Crown Cassettes' expense, but I asked to stay with him and he'd agreed. When he failed to meet me at the airport I was puzzled. I took a taxi to his address and was welcomed by his flatmates, none of whom was expecting me. Eventually Michael turned up. 'Sorry, I forgot you were coming,' he said, looking sheepish. 'Around Christmas time, I thought of getting a job in London to be with you,' he told me later, 'but then I met Susanne...' So he had a new girlfriend. Fair enough. I hadn't been loyal to him nor expected him to be so to me. However, I still regarded him as a beloved friend, whereas he had become awkward around me, remaining aloof and refusing to engage. Instead I explored Vienna with his friends. When the time came for me to leave they came to the airport to see me off. Michael came too, but I knew I would never see him again. I put a brave face on it but I was heart-broken at the loss of someone I had considered so special.

Back home, I was in touch with Yorkshire Alan who had been so critical of Richard in Lamu. I stayed in Heckmondwyke with him and his housemate, Dave, a humorous guy who was working as a grave-digger for Kirklees Council. They introduced me to traditional Yorkshire pubs where the patina was nicotine, the décor shabby, and the cloth-capped clientele communicated in a dialect as alien as a foreign language. When I entered a pub alone and asked for a glass of wine, the room fell silent. 'Wine!' exclaimed the barman. 'No wine, but maybe...' He disappeared into the cellar, reappearing with a bottle of port which he dusted off. 'Left over from Christmas,' he explained. 'Owt else.' Down-to-earth Yorkshire with its gruff manners left me refreshed.

In London I continued to feel dissatisfied. For a decade I had been caught up in a world bent on challenging authority. Now there seemed to be cracks in resolution and focus, both personal and political. The 1967 Abortion Act, a hard-won milestone in women's rights, was being threatened by the Abortion Amendment Bill and I joined 40,000 people marching on behalf of the National Abortion Campaign. I was demonstrating for women's right to choose, although I knew that I would never consider an abortion myself. I was also aware of fragmentation and in-fighting within the Women's Movement. Since my initiation in Canada a decade before, I had regarded feminism as an all-encompassing crusade for international women. Now the focus was being challenged by splinter groups: gay, radical socialist, and black. I understood the solidarity inherent in pressure groups, but the factions sometimes created more division than unification. Perhaps my views were too simplistic, but I mourned the passing of that initial spirit which had raised my awareness of women's plight.

In 1975, when Margaret Thatcher won the Conservative Party's leadership campaign, little did I realise that it was the death knell of the decade which had moulded me, an era which had influenced the freedom and attitudes of a generation. She went on to lead the country for a decade, displaying no solidarity with women and behaving like the worst of patriarchs. Her election heralded the beginning of a new jingoistic order, which smashed the unions, focused on privatisation and changed many aspects of British life for the worse. The era which had coined the slogan *love and peace* was truly at an end.

Despite my hectic social life, I was beginning to feel weary of some of its excesses. One weekend compounded this. As I sat at the dinner table with a couple of people who had dropped acid, one of them leapt to his feet and embarked on what he termed an Aztec chant. His hair in dreads, he danced around the table, wild-eyed, and emitting rhythmic grunts. A small part of me revelled in the craziness of the gathering, but the larger part remained objective and I didn't really want to be there.

Yorkshire Alan and Dave mocked me when I suggested I should curb my excesses. 'Ey up, Jen,' said Dave. 'That sounds like penance. Before you know it, you'll be saying ten Hail Marys for every joint, pint and screw!' Strangely, I wasn't worried about sexual excesses. I was promiscuous, but so were most of the people I knew. It hadn't just happened overnight. My generation had run the gauntlet from abstinence and lack of contraception through to sexual liberation; we had been chipping away at sexual taboos for years.

Love-making may have been casual, but more often than not it emerged from a situation that was laid back and mellow. I had few records, but at that time I used to play Dory Previn's *Lady with the Braid.* It summed up a gentle approach that I related to:

Would you care to stay to sunrise

It's completely your decision,
It's just that going home is such a ride…
Would you hang your denim jacket
Near the poster by Picasso,
Do you sleep on the left side or the right?

The song reflected the tenderness of those times. In the years to come that world would disappear. AIDS would arrive like a Biblical plague, viewed by some as a punishment for the licentious. The internet would result in the proliferation of pornography. The mystique and privacy surrounding sex would become laughable in a harsh world where overt sex would pervade everything: television, films, conversation, the social media and even the playground.

One of the reasons I'd never succumbed to LSD was that I'd heard it had adverse effects on fertility, a rumour undoubtedly put about as a deterrent and which was to prove unfounded. I had never doubted that one day I would want children, but neither had I given much thought to my body-clock running out of time. I was taken aback when on a routine visit to the Family Planning Association the doctor said, 'You're 32. Don't you want to have any children?' Even after the consultation I was dismissive. 'He probably said that because he's Indian,' I said. 'People in India have babies very young.' Nonetheless, he had raised the subject and occasionally it would niggle away at my consciousness.

Something else happened around this time which contributed to my sense that the status quo was disintegrating. Phil was in a poor way – run-down, depressed, not coping. I invited him to stay, but my flat, full of visitors sleeping on the floor, was hardly suitable and he soon left. Later I realised I had failed him. He ended up at home in Dorking, where I found him suffering from muscle spasms and in pain. My brother, whom I'd always considered competent and cool, so popular and quick-witted, actually admitted he was a little bit scared. I had never seen him so low and I came away aware of how much I loved and cared about him.

My parents, as ever, took everything in their stride. It never occurred to me until years later, just how much worry Phil and I must have caused them with our rough travelling and unconventional behaviour. On my arrival home from Africa, my initial impression was that Mum and Dad's lives had been reduced to pottering around the house. This could not have been further from the truth; although both in their late 60s, they were extremely active. Mother was teaching two Adult Education art classes a week for the Surrey County Council, each with 20 or more students. It was a job she was to keep until she was 80, when the council suddenly realised that, through a clerical error, her date of birth had been overlooked. Her students sent a petition to the council begging that she be kept on, but it was turned down. Dad, on retiring from his managerial role in the Sun Alliance, had taken on the administration and accounts for Tooting market – a part-time job which he loved and which involved getting to know the stall holders.

After a while I quit Crown Cassettes and did some freelance film research, but the challenge and excitement of the job had died. Many of the people I had spent years with in London were leaving and Phil, now recovered, was off to the USA. In the end, it was the Yorkshire lads who were to change my life. Alan paid a peppercorn rent for a small garret in Biwmares on the Isle of Anglesey, a place he used as a base when scuba-diving in the Menai Strait. 'Could I spend a couple of weeks in your loft?' I asked him. 'I really need to get out of London.' As a result of that visit, I would eventually embark on a country idyll in North Wales.

Môn Mam Cymru

I had never been to Wales before. As I jolted along in the back of a van, squashed between workmen who were speaking Welsh, I was aware I was in a foreign land. I was dropped off in the small town of Biwmares, bleak and stormy, the sea crashing on the shore and inn signs creaking in the wind. Barely able to stand in the gale, I fought my way along wet streets and knocked on the door of the woman who held the key to Alan's loft. She led me out the back and up a narrow staircase to a small whitewashed room. Large, wooden beams supported the ceiling, the floorboards were bare, and there was an ancient settle inscribed with the date 1610. I lit some candles, hung my dirty old sheepskin coat on the hook and lay on the bed listening to the wind howling outside. The musty room felt right.

The next day the storm had abated and I walked a little way out of town to a beach where the ocean was lapping softly on the shore. I stood gazing across the Menai Strait to the mountains of Snowdonia. It was a watercolour sea, pale turquoise streaked periwinkle, washed with light. Cloud shadows scudded across the backdrop of mountains, playing hide-and-seek with a landscape patched lime and rust. As I stood there dreaming, I heard a chuckle right behind me and a voice said, 'You'll drown if you stay there.' I looked down and realised the sea had crept in around my feet. I was standing on a small mound of sand surrounded by water. I turned to see a handsome young man with shoulder-length dark hair grinning at me. There was certainly no question of my drowning; one large step would span the tiny bit of water that encircled me. 'It's so beautiful here,' I said, nodding towards the distant mountains. 'I'll take you somewhere beautiful,' was his cheeky retort.

His name was Steve, and for the next few days he and I and Bozo the dog walked the winding lanes of Anglesey. We explored beaches, drank Southern Comfort, and flew kites. In a deluge we hid in a shelter on Biwmares Pier and, as the rain lashed the decking, his talk was of typhoons and of the smallness of man. 'This space is ours,' he whispered, his arms encircling me. 'We're in the eye of the storm.' In the evenings, back in the loft, we drank wine in the candlelight while he played his guitar and sang. He was as wicked as they come, funny and romantic, one of those rare lovers with whom one can exchange affection completely. I felt as if I were on the road again, passing through, no strings.

I met his friends, drank in the George and Dragon pub, stayed on an extra day or two. When it was time for me to leave, I walked out of town with Steve and the dog, a little way along the road towards Porthaethwy.

He unknotted the thong with a tarnished St Christopher he wore around his neck. 'Take it,' he said. 'Wear it for me.' Then he turned on his heel and departed, his hound trotting in his wake. I started the long hitch homewards to London, but I knew I'd be back; not for Steve, for that would break the rules of the game. I would return to the island, the mountains, the sea and the peace, to Anglesey, Mother of Wales - *Môn mam Cymru.*

The Apple Loft

After a couple of months I was back in Biwmares, living full-time in Alan's loft. I had brought few belongings with me: clothes, a couple of saucepans and plates, and a cylindrical paraffin heater on which I managed to boil water and cook soup and porridge. I had also brought my bike. Life was basic and snug. Once used as an apple loft, the room was small and furnished with nothing but a double bed, a tiny table and the old wooden settle. At the foot of steep stairs which led to the loft, there was a small room with a toilet and cold-water wash basin. 'No shower? No hot water?' people enquired, but after Africa it all seemed more than adequate.

I had met some of Steve's friends on my previous visit. Now I got to know even more of them. Mostly from the Midlands, they had dropped out and sought a rustic lifestyle in North Wales. Although living a quasi-hippie existence, they were not hardcore like the people I had met on the road; instead the ambience was laid back self-discovery. Everyone smoked a lot of weed, played guitars and revelled in their pastoral idyll. They were also creative. My friend Janette, with her long, straight, blonde hair and full hippie skirts, was a budding artist. She was naughtier than the rest and less earnest about her rural lifestyle. Gareth, a bearded, bespectacled nurse, the only Welshman in the group, would sit in the corner of the pub knitting a long scarf patterned with runes. Nick 'Knob-Twiddler', sound engineer for musical endeavours, was also a skilled woodworker and dedicated gardener. There were others who came and went: weavers, potters, musicians, they were a close-knit group to which I quickly became attached.

I travelled around on my old-fashioned postman's bike which I'd bought from a gypsy beneath the Shepherds Bush underpass in London. A dodgy purchase, the vendor had obliterated the post office scarlet with black paint, despite which the PO registration number still showed through. The bike was solid and slow-moving, but I loved it. I spent hours in solitude, exploring beaches, collecting shells, pausing every so often to take in the splendour of the distant mountains on the mainland. I would walk or cycle for miles along the lanes, often ending up at Fedw Fawr, where banks of white pebbles clashed and grated as they were sucked into the receding waves. Sometimes I would visit my friend Sarah in her cosy whitewashed cottage at Traeth Coch. Her house was perched on the edge of a wide expanse of sand, where the tide receded for miles leaving a sheen which reflected the sky; where the seabirds' laments were carried on the wind and shells crunched underfoot. I would stay until I could hear the sea outside the window. 'It's coming in fast,' she'd say. 'Go now or you won't make it.' It was a new experience being at the beck and call of the tide.

Biwmares was a small town, compact, accessible, and in those winter days before the onslaught of tourists I quickly became acquainted with the inhabitants: the shop-keepers on the main street, the landlords of the various pubs and the old man who frequented the 15th century Old Bull's Head, always occupying the same tall wooden seat. I loved the deserted seafront with its small pier and kiosk, soon to be stocked with ice cream and postcards for the summer. There was a green overlooking the sea, where my friends flew kites and, at the end of the main street, a toy-town castle, concentric and neat, with swans gliding on its moat. Ever-present, just across the sea, was the backdrop of mountains. When their slopes glowered in shadow or were washed with sunshine it was reflected in the mood of the people, and when snow fell on those distant peaks during the night, we were aware of it before even rising from our beds, as we awoke chilled to the bone. I loved the solitude of the wet, night-time streets where the wind howled, the pavements glistened, and I could hear the sea.

It was my honeymoon period on Anglesey, when every day brought a fresh discovery: an ancient priory and holy well; a lighthouse; a disused quarry by the sea. One of my favourite destinations was a tiny church perched on a small plateau, part of an ancient hill fort. I would park my bike and scramble up the sides, battling thick undergrowth, until I reached my eyrie in the lee of the church. As I explored the island, I heard whispers of legends and tall tales which only added to the magic: a coach-and-horses which had sunk in quicksand at Traeth Coch; a submerged settlement in the Menai Strait, lost long ago beneath the waves; a village peopled by the descendants of witches, or were they shipwrecked Armada Spaniards? 'Dark people anyway, a bit different, you know.'

I didn't need witches and Spaniards to make the place feel foreign. I was surrounded by the Welsh language: road-signs, books, Welsh-speakers greeting each other on the street. I had landed in a community of diverse and sometimes eccentric individuals. There was Les, a skinny middle-aged man, whose party piece, singing *Nights in White Satin,* was accompanied by provocative writhing. There were a couple of heavy-duty druggies: one an amusing larger-than-life character who managed to survive years of junk, another, pale and sickly, who didn't. The latter stole to feed his habit and, notebook in hand, would go round the George and Dragon pub inviting theft requests. 'Might as well pick up something for you while I'm at it,' he would say. There were two cheeky fresh-faced lads, painters and decorators, who ran away with the circus leaving property half painted, and for a while there were a couple of volatile Turks fleeing conscription. I spent time with elderly people, too: my landlady, Beryl, a lonely, complaining woman, who would trap me in her gloomy pre-war kitchen, and old Charlie whose tiny parlour in nearby Llangoed was crammed with caged song birds.

I began to travel further afield. I went on excursions to the mountains and towns on the mainland, returning across the Menai Bridge past the

Môn Mam Cymru sign: 'Anglesey, mother of Wales,' I was told, 'from the time when Anglesey was the breadbasket of Wales.' By the time spring came and the countryside was overwhelmed by wild flowers, I was totally in love with the place. The few weeks I had seen as a break from London had already turned into months. The island had become home.

After a while I began to undertake scraps of research for a local graphic design company: rough notes gleaned from library books which provided a new insight into my immediate surroundings. Eventually this work expanded and I travelled all over the island collecting information and writing copy for the *Isle of Anglesey Official Guide*. I was used to doing research for film and television programmes, but condensing information into a tiny entry for a gazetteer was a new skill which I found really difficult. I liked selling advertising for the Guide because I made new acquaintances and I also enjoyed meeting the specialists and academics who were contributing articles to the publication: Bedwyr Lewis Jones, Welsh scholar; Richard White, archaeologist. My favourite was Aled Eames, renowned for his work on Welsh maritime history, who divulged his wisdom whilst plying me with excessive quantities of gin and flirtation. The cover of the Guide was to be an oil painting by the celebrated artist Kyffin Williams and I was privileged to meet him at his isolated house on the edge of the Strait. Through contacts made during that time, I went on to compile reports on film for both the Welsh Arts Council and the Welsh Film Board.

When the guide was finished, I embarked on a crazy interlude working at a hotel. It was run by a diminutive Welsh woman called Delyth, who smoked like a chimney, dressed provocatively, and tottered around on exceptionally high heels. A leopard-print woman, she wore a lot of makeup and spoke with a husky fag-ash voice which sounded seductive. My tasks were dictated by daily crises, and I did everything from waitressing and office work to changing bed linen and cleaning. It was a mad-house, with everything done at the last minute or too late. When the VAT returns were due she appeared in the office with large cardboard boxes overflowing with crumpled receipts. 'I'd forgotten these,' she lilted. 'The inspector's due tomorrow. Calculate the tax and enter it here. Urgent, it is!' When it came to bedding she'd say, 'Don't change the sheets unless they look dirty. Nobody will know.'

Sometimes I had to use a heavy electric polisher on the wooden floors and stairs. One morning, I had coated the long staircase with wax, but was yet to buff it. Busy with the hall floor I failed to notice the party of pensioners which had materialised on the landing and begun to descend the stairs. 'Stop!' I shouted. 'Stay there!' but it was too late. I stood rooted to the spot as a nightmare unfolded before me: one by one the old ladies went up on their backsides, slipping and sliding down the stairs like some crazy cartoon. Astonishingly no one was seriously injured and none pressed charges. 'Oh dear, we'd better get a sign,' said Delyth. '*Take care, polishing in progress,* something like that.'

Life at the hotel became even crazier when Delyth fell in love. She and her new lover would hole up for hours in her bedroom, a sizeable boudoir sleek with satin. When a crisis required it, I would pound on the door and she would appear scantily clad, and issue instructions. I admired this tiny firebrand of a woman, her forthright manner, her blatant excesses and her crazy exuberance.

I had bought a secondhand motor-scooter which I rode to work. Sometimes I wore an ankle-length hippie skirt and, on the scooter, I would simply hitch it up, tucking the hem into the waistband. One day, as I drove away from the hotel, I nearly did an Isadora Duncan; the skirt unwound and got caught in the engine. The clogged vehicle ground to a halt leaving me trussed up like a chicken. One of the hotel waiters came to the rescue, savaging my flowing skirt with a pair of scissors and hacking me free.

It was a happy interlude. When I wasn't working, friends introduced me to Snowdonia's snow-covered peaks, where craggy gorges, waterfalls and deep dark lakes were veiled in mist and mystery; where fields in isolated settlements were fenced by slabs of slate, and grazing sheep defied gravity on precipitous slopes. Another year had passed. it was time to search for a new home.

I was lucky to find Bryn Ddol. Someone had told me there might be an unoccupied cottage attached to an old farmhouse, so I buzzed up there on my scooter and sought out the farmer's wife. 'No one's lived here for some time,' Mrs Pritchard said, taking me inside. 'There's no toilet, no bathroom, no hot water.' I took one look at the tiny, old-fashioned dwelling, with its view across the farmyard to the distant mountains. 'I'll take it,' I said, and within a couple of weeks I was living there.

A stone cottage, it had small windows and a bright blue door. In the front, a dirt farmyard sloped down to patchwork pastures. At the back, a field climbed skywards until, from the top, the blue smudge of mountains was visible over the rooftop below. Lining one side of the farmyard was a barn containing an old-fashioned wagon and farm machinery, as well as a mountain of hay, tousled at the edges by cats and scratching hens. At the end of every afternoon a gaggle of geese would appear like clockwork, honking their way homewards down the lane. Inside the cottage was a small sitting room with an open fire place, and a narrow kitchen from which a creaky staircase led to two cramped upper rooms. I could lie in bed and look across the sea to Snowdonia.

Mr Pritchard and his wife were elderly, religious and, with a long-suffering tolerance of their new tenant, polite and friendly. Despite my constant stream of unconventional visitors, the only time Mr Pritchard voiced a complaint was when he caught me planting tomato seedlings on a Sunday. 'Gardening on the Sabbath!' he reprimanded, the sing-song of his Welsh voice rendering him less stern than intended. Clearly the Good Lord upheld Mr Pritchard's objections because, come summer, my plants remained barren whilst his were laden. Occasionally the Pritchards would invite me into their large, traditional kitchen for a cup of tea and a slice of cake, or even the ultimate luxury, tinned peaches and custard.

I loved living in the cottage but facilities were basic. I washed in cold water, standing naked in a large washing up bowl in the kitchen and sluicing myself down from a jug. As for laundry, the kitchen sink could accommodate small items, but when it came to sheets or anything large, I washed them in the garden, filling an old tin bath from the outside tap. This was fine in summer but, come winter, my hands froze and my fingers became raw. The lack of a lavatory was another inconvenience. Initially there was a rickety privy perched on a small promontory at the edge of the field. 'Off to the Tardis, are you?' my friends would mock, but when I had been in residence a month or two, the precarious Tardis was replaced by a portaloo.

One of the contributors to the Anglesey guide had been an antique dealer and furniture restorer. He wanted to open a shop in the market square in Biwmares, a cobbled yard surrounded by several run-down units, only a couple of which were occupied. His plan was to fill the shop with his furniture and I would find crafts to sell alongside the antiques. I was excited by the project and went all over Anglesey and the mainland on my scooter, locating people who produced hand-made knitwear, quilts, ceramics and woodwork. The shop was called *Stolen Dreams* and along the outside wall we stencilled a frieze of silhouetted burglars, tiptoeing along with sacks on their backs.

I arrived at the shop early every morning and remained until late afternoon. However, it didn't take me long to realise that the antique dealer, had got himself an unpaid shopkeeper. I had assumed that sometimes he and I would work there together, but this never happened. He would turn up without warning, dragging furniture in and out of the place. 'I'm taking these,' he would say, removing the smaller antiques I had spent hours dusting and arranging. 'Don't worry. I'll bring something else to replace them.' After each upheaval I had to clean and reorganise the entire shop. The deal was that I would get a cut of sales, but the percentage was a poor reward for the hours I put in. Despite this, I enjoyed my new role, particularly discovering the secrets of the ancient artefacts I was selling: a concealed drawer, a hidden date scratched by someone long-forgotten.

Everyone I knew would pop into the shop for a chat, making

themselves scarce when customers arrived. It was different when the tramp visited – a rheumy, fetid old fellow, with threadbare clothes and a red neckerchief. One day when I saw him hovering outside, I invited him in to share my tea and sandwiches. Unsurprisingly he reappeared the next day. He told me about the age-old routes used by men-of-the-road to cross the island. He slurped his tea, his nose dripped on the floor and eventually he departed, having marked his territory with a lingering whiff of hobo. I was reprimanded by a woman who ran another outlet in the square. 'How do you expect us to get any customers with that smelly old man sitting there?' she growled.

One long day, devoid of customers, I took some wine into the shop and started drinking with friends. On the way home my scooter skidded round a corner and I came off, fracturing the top joint of one of my fingers. I'd had too much to drink and had been travelling the muddy lanes too fast. The scooter was a write-off. In hospital the finger joint was reset crooked and remained so permanently.

I was now stuck out at the farm without any transport. Undeterred, come rain or shine, I hiked to the shop and back daily, about five miles round trip. My route took me along a little-used lane with grass growing up the centre of the road and I began to delight in the minutiae of my surroundings: the hedgerows wet with early morning dew; each new bud and flower; how things changed daily. *Stolen Dreams* was never a great success. The tramp and the wine-drinking were not the norm. I worked really hard, keeping in touch with craftworkers, replenishing stock, enduring the idiosyncratic comings and goings of the antique dealer. The shop limped on until the end of the season and then closed for good. Although I had only earned enough to pay off my small bank loan, it had been a worthwhile experience.

Summer 1977 was hot. Everyone I knew was scattered across the countryside, tucked away in cottages and caravans. None had a telephone. If you wanted to visit someone you walked and if they were out you left a note. That summer I trekked miles, through flower-filled meadows, along leafy lanes and across beaches. There were picnics and parties, music and skinny-dipping. One morning I awoke to the sweet smell of hay. I went downstairs and stood in the doorway overlooking the farmyard. The sun was up, the harvesting underway, the machines throbbing in the field behind the barn. Lads from the village had come to help, and Mrs Pritchard, jug in hand, a basket of bread on her arm, emerged from her front door. 'Breakfast.' she said, 'They'll be working till dusk.' It was a timeworn pattern of sowing and reaping; another summer gone, and I was still on the island.

Rob, a student from Bangor University, had been playing music with some of my friends. I got to know him well and our friendship flowered into a brief relationship. A Jethro Tull fan, he would sit on the hill behind Bryn Ddol serenading me in the sunshine: *Let me bring you love from the field, poppies red, and roses filled with summer rain.* We had some good times.

My injured finger had taken longer to heal than anticipated and, one day, after physiotherapy in Bangor, I had arranged to meet Rob at the house of his friend, Bill Scolding. Rob was late. As I chatted with Bill over a cup of tea, he told me about the monthly magazine he put together with a group of local writers, and about the posters he designed. I found his enthusiasm compelling. A few weeks later Rob asked me to deliver some paper to Bill and, once again, we chatted awhile. Afterwards, I remember stepping out into the pouring rain wearing my bright yellow oilskin mac – and looking up. He was watching me out of the window. He likes me, I thought.

Winter came to the island. Waking each morning with glacial breath, I would scrape a hole in the Jack Frost window ferns and, like a mariner through a spyglass, gaze at the faraway mountains where the snow stretched down to the sea. I began each day by lighting a coal fire in my tiny front room, before working at a table by the window, compiling my reports for the Welsh Film Board and the Welsh Arts Council. Cocooned in my cottage, I listened to the wind or watched snowflakes whirling past the window pane.

Both Bill and Rob went home for Christmas, but on his return Bill

Above left: Steve, Anglesey, September 1975.
Above right: Puffin Island boat trip to celebrate my 34th birthday, March 1977.

Right: selling crafts and antiques at Stolen Dreams, Biwmares, September 1977.
Below left: with brother Phil.
Below right: friends Janette and Rob.

Above: with Bill at Fedw Fawr, Llangoed, Anglesey; Bill's sisters Naomi and Emily at Bryn Ddol, May 1978.
Below: summer days at The Shack, with visiting dogs, Llangoed, 1978.

Below: the Artex Gang, Cornelyn Manor, 1978. *Below right:* our wedding, March 1979.

invited me to a New Year's party at his house. It was a typical students' party, everyone dancing to loud music, or sitting on the floor swigging out of bottles. Later that night I was busy chatting to someone when, to my surprise, Bill took centre-stage with a Mick Jagger impersonation, pouting his lips and gyrating up and down the room to *Brown Sugar*. It seemed out of character, amusing rather than cool, but it turned out to be a party piece which was to manifest itself whenever alcohol dulled his inhibitions. We had a good time that night in all the chaos, dancing, talking and finally squashing into his single bed. We spent the night in an uncomfortable and far-from-sexy encounter, with two of his old school friends sleeping on the floor next to us.

The January days grew colder, the snow on the mountains thicker. Bill and I saw each other a few times and then, one night, Rob was back at Bryn Ddol, knocking on my door. 'Belated happy Christmas,' he said, and handed me a huge soft toy, knitted by his mother. I think it was a bird. I can't quite remember now, but whatever it was, the incongruous creature sat beside me on my bed while I told Rob I had been going out with Bill. 'Oh,' said Rob, surprised. 'I'd better go and see him. He'll be feeling very bad about me!'

The Shack

I had always been a baby-snatcher and Bill, 12 years my junior, was the same age as my African boyfriend, Richard. That's where the similarity ended. Bill had no madcap tendencies but came across as rather sensible. A refreshingly easy and straightforward man, he had soft grey eyes, dark collar-length hair and a beard. His wardrobe consisted of a donkey jacket, desert boots, jeans that were patched and flared, and over his shirt he wore a green waistcoat pinned with badges advocating peace or protest. In other words, he had not really moved on from being a student. He was kind, gregarious and good fun. The sweeter more vulnerable side of his nature was redeemed by a sharp, often sarcastic wit, and sardonic banter.

He had just finished his Post-Graduate Certificate of Education, but his teaching practice at a rough school in Wrexham had furnished him with enough material to write a short story entitled *A Good Day in Hell.* He was lucky to have got through the experience in one piece; the student teacher who followed him was stabbed. He had left Wrexham disillusioned, and far from certain he still wanted to become a teacher.

He began to spend more and more time on the island, travelling by bus from Bangor, and trekking across the fields to visit me at Bryn Ddol. Gradually, I introduced him to my favourite haunts: a ruined castle submerged in vegetation; tiny St Michael's church perched on a promontory high above the sea; stretches of sand adorned with yellow winkles bright as beads. We would make our way home across the frosty fields, light the fire, and slowly thaw, as we awaited the homecoming of the geese which heralded the day's end. During those treasured interludes we were becoming acquainted, gently exploring mutual empathy and affection. Sitting in the firelight, cracking open a bottle or two, we would talk until late, putting the world to rights, discussing our favourite authors and artists and inevitably I would embark on travellers' tales of places far away.

We each had a large number of friends and were soon involved in an even wider circle as we mingled with both sets. There had always been a loose geographical divide between social groups on the island and those who lived on the mainland, particularly people who inhabited remoter parts of the mountains. Now these barriers dissolved as Bill and I travelled between the two, relishing new acquaintances.

By late spring, Bill was so taken with the island that he decided to move there. Friends of ours were about to vacate a shack at a farm just outside Llangoed, so we went to inspect the place. It resembled a run-down scout hut, but it had potential. The exterior was corrugated iron, but inside it was lined with planks, painted cream. The main room was spacious with a tall chapel-like ceiling following the line of the roof, and thin beams spanning its width. On a large wall at one end someone had painted a huge mural of a black horse, backside on. 'I'm not sure I want to spend every day staring at a horse's arse,' said Bill. 'You can easily paint it out,' I shrugged. 'The whole place needs decorating anyway.' There was a bedroom, a tiny kitchen and an outdoor flushing lavatory. In the front of the shack, a cement yard designed for use by cattle, would serve nicely as a patio with a view of the distant mountains. 'Well, what do you think?' I asked. 'It's perfect,' said Bill, and dashed off to make arrangements with the farmer's wife.

He had not been living in the shack long when his mother, Marian, suggested she bring his two youngest sisters, aged nine and 11, to Anglesey for a holiday. 'They're welcome to stay at Bryn Ddol,' I told him. 'That way the little girls can have their own bedroom, and your mother the room at the front, overlooking the sea and the mountains.' 'I'm sure the kids would love staying on the farm,' said Bill. His mother accepted my invitation.

I spent hours getting the cottage ready: washing the sheets by hand in the old tin bathtub outside; cleaning every room from top to bottom; putting a vase of wild flowers on the table; stocking the kitchen with basics. 'Goodness!' exclaimed my friend, Sarah, who turned up in the middle of my preparations. 'It looks like you've polished the fruit as well!' I had one or two children's books which I put in the little girls' bedroom, together with the large stuffed toy knitted for me by Rob's mother. When Marian and the girls were due to arrive, I moved into the shack to make room for them. It was late May. The sun shone and the countryside and farm looked spectacular. 'They'll love it,' Bill said, but he was mistaken. The cottage proved too primitive for his mother and too isolated. One afternoon we persuaded her and the girls to accompany us to our favourite beach. When we arrived I changed into a swimsuit. 'Surely you're not going in the sea,' she exclaimed, 'not at your age!'

Come the summer, I left Bryn Ddol behind and moved in with Bill. We embarked on a period of immense happiness, a seemingly endless interlude of hot summer days. Before breakfast, one of us would go to the barn with a jug and help ourselves from a vat of fresh creamy milk, straight from the cows, a habit that fulfilled all our expectations of country living. We went walks along the beaches and in the mountains. We swam and had picnics and partied. Life was carefree, full of fun, good company and music.

On the farm we were surrounded by a menagerie: a resident rat that scratched and gnawed, disturbing our nights; cows, pigs, goats, cats and numerous dogs. There was also a sneaky ferret with bright red eyes which would flatten itself and squeeze under our front door. This varmint belonged to Gareth, he of the rune-patterned knitting, who inhabited a caravan just across the field from us. 'He's a lovely little fellow,' Gareth kept saying. 'I don't understand why you dislike him so much.' Our friend Angela also appeared from time to time on horseback, her steed side-stepping across the space in our little yard. Finally, we were visited by a ringed carrier pigeon which arrived exhausted from France and lived with us for a month before dropping dead.

Bill was still doing some artwork for the university. Although untrained, his design was competent, his approach thorough, and I began to encourage him to put together a portfolio and look for work further afield. All enquiries were initiated from the public telephone box down the road and we had to store up a mountain of coins before approaching potential clients. His efforts paid off and he got a few commissions. In the meantime, I was busy with research for the Snowdon Mountain Railway. I enjoyed exploring the Gwynedd Archive in Caernarfon and I even got a free train ride to the top of the mountain with the maintenance engineer.

To supplement our income we worked as painters and decorators at nearby Cornelyn, a neglected manor house being renovated as a hotel and activities centre. A labyrinth of rooms and corridors, crumbling plaster and rotten wood, it was to be ready for its first guests within a couple of months. Under the expert eye of an exasperated Welsh builder called Ned, an army of us set about achieving the impossible. It was a mad-house, but we revelled in the chaos and in the camaraderie induced by working under pressure. When the first guests arrived I was asked to show them to their room. 'The paint's still a little tacky,' I said apologetically. I opened the bedroom door to find a plumber's cleavage protruding from the bathroom, where pipes were still being welded. It was pure *Fawlty Towers*.

Once the hotel had limped into operation, Barry, the proprietor, began experimenting with office equipment. 'This fax machine,' he announced, 'is the thing of the future.' Two were installed on different floors so he could demonstrate their magical powers to clients. Bill was invited to create some line drawings to be faxed from one machine to the other; 'Something amusing,' Barry requested. The result was a split picture: Queen Elizabeth I on one side, a bubble containing a question mark coming out of her head, and Sir Walter Raleigh on the other, smoking a large cigar. We all stood around in awe as Bill's picture was fed into one machine and a perfect copy was spat out by the other.

Not long after this, we read of another innovation: 'Just look at this,' said Bill, pointing to an article in the newspaper. 'You'll go into a shop and at the checkout they'll scan each item of shopping with something that looks like a pen; it will read information off a code on the product and record the sale.' When I relayed this information to the tiny supermarket in Llangoed, the prospect of the strange 'pen' caused much amusement.

Autumn arrived, and we harvested blackberries and made rose hip syrup. Snow returned to the mountains and the shack with its thin walls and lack of insulation was like an ice box. We kept two paraffin heaters on the go, wore long johns, and walked about in coats and gloves and woolly hats. Despite the cold we were incredibly happy.

Christmas came and we visited both our families in Surrey. We had known each other more than a year and had come a long way together. 1979 was just around the corner and my life was about to change.

Marriage

I remember the defining moment, the point at which I thought how perfectly Bill and I complemented each other. It was a Sunday afternoon in April, only five months after we had first met. We were sitting on the roots of a large tree, leaning back against the trunk. The branches above us were laden with unseasonal snow and the fields around us were soft and white, banked up into drifts where the wind had blown off the sea. The sun shone and the world glittered. We were making our way back to Bryn Ddol from the British Legion, where everyone in Biwmares drank on Sundays – Gwynedd being the last county to repeal laws which kept Wales dry on the Sabbath. We had been drinking and talking, watching Les writhing around doing his party piece, *Nights in White Satin,* and enjoying the few old Welshmen who were Sunday devotees of the demon drink. Now we were leaning against the tree talking nineteen to the dozen. To me it seemed a moment of perfection, an ideal merging of personalities, how things should be.

Ours was never a mad, passionate all-embracing love affair, the kind where you are blindly obsessed with the person concerned. On the couple of occasions when I'd fallen desperately in love and been swept off my feet, there had always been a tiny part of me that remained rational, aware that the turmoil of love and passion was short-lived. The closeness between Bill and me had crept up gently: a gradual meeting of minds; humour, affection and a lot of fun. It was special. We never ran out of things to say, we delighted in each other's company, and we were both gregarious. We discussed travelling together; with my missionary zeal about seeing the world, such suggestions were the norm and essential to any serious liaison.

We had known each other a year when I came up with an ultimatum. I wanted to stay with Bill for good, but I was aware he was very young and unlikely to want such commitment, particularly one that would inevitably involve having children. I was adamant the discrepancy in our ages should be discussed in a way that was honest and fair to both of us. I also made it clear that if he wasn't serious about the relationship, I would move on. We talked about it for days: the pros and cons, the potential effects of the age-gap, how we felt about each other. I began to realise that so much analysis might ruin everything. 'You need space and time to yourself,' I told Bill. 'I'll go to London, stay with Phil, and do a few weeks' work while you think about what you want from me.'

During my time away, we exchanged long letters daily. Sometimes he phoned me, but there was the usual problem with using a phone box; coins running out mid-discussion did little to clarify the situation. He spent a night or two in Bangor, discussing our relationship with his friends, but ended up the next day with an exceptionally bad hangover and embarrassed he had broached the subject. 'I wouldn't want to go back to that life,' he told me afterwards; his student days were finally over. He continued with his artwork, and numerous friends turned up at the shack to see him. 'Everyone seems to be having babies,' he told me. Others were leaving, moving on.

Brother Phil was now living in a large house in Tufnell Park which he shared with friends we had known for years. I felt relaxed. I visited my parents in Dorking and went long walks in the countryside. They were fond of Bill and they were supportive, but they exerted no pressure on me. In many ways the trial separation seemed unreal: letters crossed; thoughts and emotions expressed in writing could be laboured or misconstrued; attempts at humour seemed flat. In London it was snowing and in the shack Bill was slowly freezing to death. After over a month apart and daily thoughts from Bill on what constituted happiness, he finally wrote and asked me to come back. It was a *carpe diem* letter. He said he missed me, he loved me, and would go along with what I wanted. I returned to Wales.

Back at the shack, everything quickly reverted to normal. We had reached a decision to stay together, but it was a while before we talked about getting married. We were still dithering when we discussed applying for jobs overseas. Bill, with the teaching qualification, had to be the main applicant, but having seen how desperate they were for teachers in Africa, I was pretty certain I'd get work in a school as well. We also realised that unless we were married we might not be posted to the same location. We went for the nuptials.

Marriage in those days was not the great commercial rigmarole it has become today. Around that time we received a postcard from a couple we knew: *Well we've gone and done it. Getting married at Bangor Registry Office... going to the pub for a piss-up straight afterwards. Do come.* In subsequent years those of our friends who actually bothered to get married, continued to do so in just such a casual manner, often with children already in tow.

Having taken religion seriously when I was young, making vows in a church was something I could not entertain. I no longer believed and neither did Bill. To use a pretty church for a fairy-tale wedding would have seemed hypocritical. I had been raised at a time when virginity was all-important and, having taken so long to break down that barrier, a white wedding with all the trimmings would have also seemed a sham. Not only had I been living with Bill for over a year, but my record before that was about as far from virginal purity as one could get. We settled on the registry office in Llangefni. 'Just family?' I said. 'Yes,' said Bill. 'We could have a party in the shack the day after,' I suggested, 'just a low-key sort of thing with a few friends.'

In January 1979 Bill stood in the same old phone box at the end of the lane, ringing his family with the news, but we had underestimated the degree of antipathy which was to follow. I was surprised. I had always got on so well with my boyfriends' parents: Bruce White was the first person who had proposed to me and his mother and I became close friends and wrote to each other for years; Pat Crawley's mother, Judy, had cried when Pat and I broke up. 'Never mind,' I said to Bill. 'We'll win them over in the end.'

Around this time I was offered a few weeks' work in London. We needed the money and I took the job. By the time I arrived back at the shack, there was little more than a month remaining until our wedding day. Mum, Dad and Phil were to attend, but Bill's family, with the exception of his oldest sister, Anne, were staying away. I rushed off to Chester to look for a suitable garment for the big day, but there was nothing I liked. For a moment I hesitated over a white cotton hippie dress, trimmed with broderie anglaise, but it was ankle-length and a bit too much like the virginal trappings I eschewed. I only had one day for

314

shopping and hardly any money. I settled for a cream dress with black splodges, reasonably elegant compared with my normal wardrobe, but it wasn't really what I wanted. Bill was planning to wear a jumper and cord trousers, but at the last minute succumbed to convention and donned his one and only suit. Courtesy of my parents, we ordered champagne for the day itself and for the subsequent party. It was to be such a small, simple wedding and I knew what a disappointment it would be for Mum and Dad.

We were married on 17th March, 1979, the day before my 36th birthday. In the morning, when we were getting ready, I decided a splash of colour might be in order. I pulled out a scarlet beret from a drawer and tried it on for effect. It didn't go with the outfit, but I thought it might be fun; I had always liked berets. 'What do you think?' I asked Bill. 'I don't know,' he shrugged. 'It's up to you.' I sat on the sofa wearing my new dress, black tights, high heels and the red beret. Oh God, perhaps I've ended up looking like a French tart! I thought. To add to the haphazard nature of the event, it began to snow. I'd chosen the dress because it was light and spring-like but I had nothing to wear over it against the cold. My everyday coat was not only brown, but spattered with mud. 'I know what I can wear,' I announced suddenly. 'The cloak!' A couple of years before, someone had given me a short black cloak but I had never worn it; with its red silk lining and fur-trimmed hood, it had always seemed a bit too dressy for Anglesey. I rummaged around in the back of the wardrobe, pulled it out, and started brushing it down. 'This'll do fine,' I said. 'Pity it's black though; a bit funereal.'

We set off for Llangefni in my parents' car: Bill and I, Mum and Dad, Phil clad in jeans, a jumper and a long woolly scarf, and Bill's sister, Anne. We stopped to fill up at a garage in Llanfair PG and took a photo of the full name written above the entrance: Llanfairpwllgwyngyllgogerychwyrndrobwillantysiliogogogoch. 'Well, it's certainly a Welsh wedding!' I said. It was snowing heavily. 'Still six miles to go,' said Dad. 'Not sure we're going to make it.' Eventually we slithered into the registry office car park with half an hour to spare. 'You can get married right away,' said the registrar. 'The people booked-in before you are stuck in the snow.'

We entered a small room dominated by a picture of two swans by the celebrated artist Charles Tunnicliffe, a resident of Anglesey. 'I don't have to obey you,' I told Bill. 'I checked. They say all I have to promise is the love and honour bit.' The ceremony was brief and straightforward. It seemed rather unreal. Crossing the finishing line had become a rather matter-of-fact affair, tinged with belligerence. Bill slipped my late grandmother's wedding ring onto my finger, kissed me gently, and it was done and dusted. We signed the register and came away with a wedding certificate written partially in Welsh.

Back at the shack, the farmer and his wife joined us in their wellies for a glass of champagne. We had decorated the room with a few balloons and, on the table, some flowers sent by Bill's family. My mother, not a proficient baker, had succeeded in making a traditional wedding cake, albeit only one tier. It had the required hard icing and was decorated with a wide pink ribbon and wax flowers. 'Those were on our wedding cake,' she said emotionally. She had kept them safe since 1941. My poor mother! It was her sentimental gesture in the face of the most simple of weddings.

The following morning my parents came round to the farm to say goodbye before the long drive back to Surrey. 'Let's look at the ring,' said Mum, and she held my left hand and smiled at the sight of the wedding ring that had belonged to her own beloved mother. I felt sad as they drove away and a tad guilty that it had not been the festive occasion they would have wished for. In the evening about 25 of our friends gathered in the shack. They were people I had known since I'd first set foot on the island four years before. They came bearing small gifts and a star-shaped, homemade wedding cake.

With our new status more likely to gain approval from would-be employers, we finally began applying for jobs overseas: one in Algeria; another in Nigeria. A few months later, my parents hosted a couple of small gatherings at my childhood home in Dorking, so Bill and I could meet each other's relatives. From there, Bill and I travelled up to London to be interviewed by representatives of the Department of Education for Sokoto State, Nigeria. We were both accepted as teachers. In July we vacated the shack and left behind Anglesey for good. My passport, containing all the stamps from my east African travels, had now been amended. Under Miss Jennifer Anne Steele, there was a hand-written adjustment: *Now Mrs Scolding,* it said, and my Nigerian visa stated *accompanying husband.* By August I was back in Africa once again, and Bill and I had embarked on life in one of the craziest and most difficult countries I had experienced: the Federal Republic of Nigeria.

CHAPTER TEN

DOWN THE RABBIT HOLE

The Paper Chase

BILL AND I FOUGHT OUR WAY along the aisle of the DC10, our progress blocked by Nigerians with grossly oversized hand luggage. People were standing on seats wrestling their goods into overhead lockers, or kneeling in the aisle unpacking bags in an attempt to make them fit. We picked our way through a sea of spilt belongings and settled into our seats. 'Some of those bags are massive,' said Bill. 'The passenger in front of us is pretty big, as well,' I replied, pointing out a seat occupied by a 4ft pink fur-fabric teddy with his seat belt done up. Even once we were airborne, arguments broke out, people shouted, and passengers festooned with gold chains and ostentatious jewellery cruised up and down the aisle. Once the evening meal had been served, everyone calmed down and watched *Jaws 2*. Bill and I dozed intermittently, disturbed by the occasional shark attack.

Lifting the window blind at daybreak I saw we were coming in low over mile upon mile of sand. 'Look,' I said, 'the Sahara!' I was excited for Bill, rather than for myself. I had a missionary zeal about exploring the world and I was handing him a magic key. 'We're nearly there,' I said and we held hands tightly as the aircraft descended, gliding like an egret into the torrid clutches of Nigeria.

Kano airport was small and chaotic. As we awaited our internal flight, I looked around. Everything was familiar, yet slightly different from the Africa I already knew. We bought half-cakes reminiscent of Lamu, and a couple of bottles of Fanta: 'No glasses, sir. Too early for glasses.' It was the costumes that were different. Hausa men wore cylindrical hats with intricate stitching, and flowing robes known as *rigas,* patterned down the front with loops of cord or embroidery. I was familiar with the modest workaday Muslim garb of Sudan and Egypt, but even the simplest Hausa attire lent an exotic air to the wearer.

We boarded the plane. It was the rainy season and from the air the countryside looked unexpectedly lush. A wide brown river meandered through cultivated farmland dotted with compounds containing huts with grass roofs. The plane circled Sokoto town. 'It's small for a state capital,' I said. 'No multi-storey buildings.' We landed at a tiny airport where we were met by a man from the Ministry of Education; little did we realise, that being met off our flight and driven to the Sokoto Guest Inn was nothing short of a miracle.

It was a modern, single-storey hotel, surrounded by a wide sandy space with beds of canna lilies. It had air conditioners, baths, flushing lavatories and one or two televisions which worked erratically. Someone had spent a lot of time doing a Jackson Pollock on the walls, and lighting was softened by disc-shaped lampshades picturing mosques.

We were sitting in the dining room, facing a large mirror on the opposite wall. 'That mirror's tilted at about 30 degrees,' I said. 'It's so crooked, it must be intentional.' 'Look below it,' said Bill, and I saw the pencil line that was the intended alignment of the mirror's base. 'The pelmets are wonky, too,' he said. It dawned on us that none of the walls in the hotel was at right angles. The whole place was cockeyed, an appropriate introduction to two years down the rabbit hole.

We set off to explore the town. Streets were lined with neem trees and stalls selling everything from Nido milk powder and canned margarine, to sunglasses and cassette tapes. Vendors dozed on straw mats in the shade and children sat behind neat piles of fruit, soliciting customers. Hausa hats were displayed on wooden blocks which sprouted from the dust like multi-coloured toadstools. Vultures hunched together on the trees above the butcher's stand.

Rectangular mud houses lined dirt alleys, where open drains and trenches of greeny-brown sludge were blocked with rubbish. Goats picked their way along the sandy lanes and emaciated pye-dogs roamed

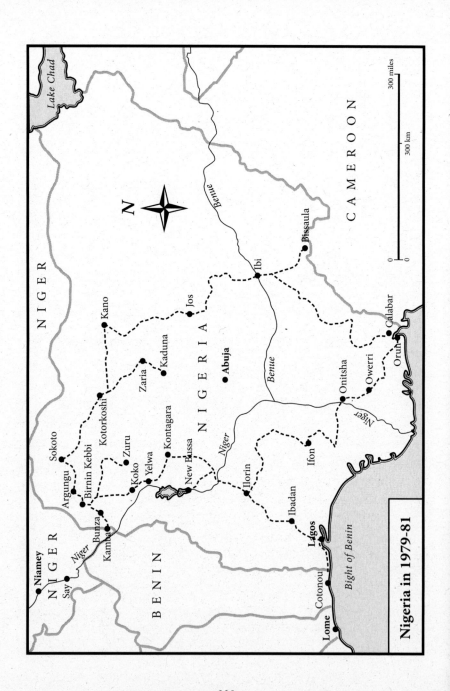

Nigeria in 1979-81

free. Some of the more substantial adobe houses were reminiscent of Sudanese architecture: rectangular and flat-roofed, with decorative horns of mud at each corner and raised motifs above the doors. Down by the river, women and girls were washing clothes as small naked boys plunged into the fast-flowing brown water. A boat hove into sight, heavily laden with passengers and propelled by a man with a single pole. 'It's a large tin bath!' exclaimed Bill. We watched as the galvanised tub tipped and swayed towards us, finally disgorging its passengers safely on the bank.

For over a year, I had been telling Bill about Indian and African markets, but Sokoto's Friday market still took him by surprise. 'It's medieval,' he said, 'like stepping back in time.' Mounds of brightly-coloured spice spilled onto the sand, alongside yams and cassava, green okra and purple onions. Mattress-stitchers sat engulfed by mountains of kapok; blacksmiths, squatting by small charcoal fires, forged ploughshares and knives. Tailors sat cross-legged behind whirring sewing machines, while leather workers sutured camel saddles and scabbards out of crimson hide. Our progress through a labyrinth of alleyways revealed mountains of terracotta pots, giant gourds sliced in half to make calabashes, basins of honeycomb and blocks of solidified molasses. Butchers hacked away at purple and red slabs of flesh which dripped blood onto the sand. Finally, after weaving through tethered donkeys, we found ourselves amidst hundreds of camels, some kneeling, others standing, the grace of their swaying gait lost in gawky inactivity. Most were muzzled, but others bared yellow teeth as we passed, spitting, and rumbling. As we left the market, we were set upon by beggars and lepers whining for alms. Bill's horror at his first experience of real poverty reminded me of the distress I had felt when I arrived in India; that initial shock which gradually fades as unacceptable sights become familiar.

Presidential elections were about to take place and there were polling booths everywhere, each displaying allegiance to a specific political party; no secret ballots. It was the National Party of Nigeria which dominated, with NPN scrawled on walls and children displaying the party symbol, a single finger pointed skywards, and shouting 'NPN! NPN!' In October, 1979, and a few months after our arrival, the Nigerian Second Republic would come into being under the leadership of President Shehu Shagari, a Sokoto man and a Muslim, who would work in conjunction with Vice-President Alex Ekwueme Oko, significantly an Igbo from Anambra State. Their slogan, *One nation, one destiny,* was intended to highlight the nation's diversity and unity. Shagari was of Fulani extraction and, despite his humble background, a court official to the Sokoto Caliphate, whereas Ekwueme, a Fulbright scholar, had studied and worked in the USA and UK. They were to remain in power throughout our two years in Nigeria.

We were excited when we stumbled on the Sokoto dye pits, circular holes dug out of the ground, filled with indigo dye, and covered with conical basketwork lids. Lengths of fabric in various shades of blue were unfurled across the sand to dry. The tradition stretched back centuries to the heyday of the Sokoto Caliphate. One of the most powerful empires in West Africa, when it was annexed by the British in 1903, the sultan was permitted to retain his title and we saw the incumbent shortly after our arrival. Caught up in the crowds outside his palace for the end-of-Ramadan celebrations, we were surrounded by men in ornate robes and marshalled by palace guards, resplendent in green, red and yellow. Confronted by aggressive fast-drumming musicians, who stared at us wide-eyed and pretended to attack us with wooden swords, we eventually fled, pursued by drumming demons and the laughter of the crowd.

Having written letters to tell our families we had arrived, we set off for the post office, only to find they had no scales. We handed three identical letters to the clerk who took the first and balanced it on his hand. 'Ten grams,' he said. He took the second: 'Ten grams.' The third letter, however, resulted in him jerking his hand downwards. 'This one...' He paused, sucking in his breath and making that clicking noise so prevalent in Africa...' This one done bend my fingers. This one heavy.'

'It's exactly the same as the others,' we protested. 'No,' retorted the clerk. 'Too much heavy.' In the end we won the argument and each stamp cost the same 30 kobo.

When we managed to get the television in the hotel lobby working, we were in for further surprises. On the Sokoto channel, programme titles, handwritten on pieces of card, would often appear upside down, before a hand grabbed the card and turned it the right way up. Sokoto Television proved to be something of a circus, which is probably why they were to feature me twice during the following year: once teaching an English lesson and a second time demonstrating my lack of athletic prowess in the staff race at the school sports.

On our first visit to the Ministry of Education we were greeted by Alhaji Nuhu Koko, Director of Education, who introduced us to Mr Dakingari, the chief staff officer. They were effusive in their welcome, expressed their admiration for the British, made jokes about their skin-colour being the result of suntan, and swept us from office to office. Along the way our entourage swelled to eight flapping mandarins, who sailed in our wake, their robes billowing out behind them. It was the only time we saw anyone from the Ministry of Education move at speed.

Mr Dakingari signed our Letter of Offer of Contract and instructed us to regularise our passports at Immigration, two miles away. After a long hot walk, we arrived to find the letter we had been given was invalid. 'It is written by hand,' said the immigration clerk. 'It must be typed.' We returned to the Ministry and waited more than two hours for an acceptable letter and signature. Back at Immigration there was a new demand. 'Where are your qualifications?' asked the clerk. 'Photocopies of education certificates must be attached to this letter.' We produced the originals, but he shrugged. 'No photocopier,' he said. 'Photocopies at the Ministry,' and he sent us packing once more.

'We need to invent a board game called Bureaucracy,' said Bill a couple of days later. 'The winner would be the first person to have all their papers in order.' After three days at the Ministry of Education, we had completed 56 forms, for which our reward had been only two documents. Before being posted to a school we needed numerous personal files and more than 15 documents, each of which required letters of request, completed forms and signatures from officials who went missing for days – 'Not on seat', was the phrase used. We trailed from room to room, where dusty dossiers were piled on desks, stacked in perilous towers on the floor, or scattered randomly. Stray papers lifted in the breeze created by the ceiling fans. *TAKE CARE!* warned a Ministry of Education poster. *You, too, can stay out of trouble by keeping your mouth **shut**. Keep our secrets safe.* Below this admonition was a picture of two fish in a pond, one with its mouth open being caught on a line, the other safe and sound with its mouth closed.

After working in India I was used to Third World red tape, but the bureaucracy at the Nigerian Ministry of Education was so insane, so all-embracing, that the system could barely function. Clerks gave the impression they were busy by shuffling papers back and forth across their desks without actually doing anything. Sometimes we would enter a room to find sleeping typists, dozing clerks, inert messengers. Once we witnessed the unexpected arrival of Mr Dakingari and watched the inanimate staff leap to attention and embark on a brisk display of working hard, only to revert to blatant somnolence the minute he departed.

Other than during our initial welcome, officials at the Ministry of Education were uninterested, discourteous and arrogant. To begin with we felt a mixture of frustration and fascination, but as days went by we became angry and depressed. 'Don't forget they inherited their bureaucracy from the British,' I reminded Bill. Focusing on this justification helped deflate my anger. We both knew that a 10 naira note slipped inside a file would have worked wonders, but we had decided never to bribe; our resolve was put to the test throughout our stay in Nigeria. Alan, a fellow teacher and an old Africa hand, saw our determination as naive. 'It's the system,' he shrugged. 'You'll only make things hard for yourselves.'

After exhausting days at the Ministry of Education, we would spend our evenings in the Sokoto Guest Inn exchanging information with other teachers-in-waiting: make sure you have 10 copies of that one; you can't do anything until you get your Variation Order; Mr So-and-so is never 'on seat' on Tuesdays… We made lists for each other, noting codes, numbers and the problems involved with acquiring each piece of paper. Despite so many hurdles, Bill and I remained optimistic. 'It'll be OK once we've been posted,' we reassured each other. 'We'll be able to get down to work.' In the midst of it all there were moments of peace: *Jenny's immersed in Teach Yourself Hausa*, wrote Bill in his diary. *It's very comfortable sitting here together, working separately and exchanging the occasional word. I think we are going to have a good time in Africa…*

There were several Indian teachers at the Guest Inn. 'Come and sit with us, Mr Bill,' they'd say, waggling their heads from side to side, Indian-fashion. 'Mrs Jenny, Mrs Jenny, come here…' To us they were charming, but their attitude towards Nigerians was arrogant and racist. 'It's so dangerous here,' they said, polishing their cutlery vigorously with napkins, 'so unclean, so unhealthy.' Having witnessed a great deal of squalor in India I could only marvel at their double standards. 'I have a friend who's already been posted,' said one. 'The children he teaches are unintelligent blockheads. That's what we can expect when we're posted. Blockheads!' An Egyptian teacher who gave his cutlery the same precautionary polish, sprayed Bill with perfume in a manner which suggested Bill, too, might be contaminated. 'Here, Mrs Jenny,' he said handing me the atomiser. 'Spray it on your chest!'

We were a motley crew. Viv and Paul from North Wales were kindred spirits, the latter with moustache, earring, and tattoos, resembling a benevolent pirate. Bob, a young guy from Brooklyn, only lasted a week. 'I came here to teach,' he drawled, 'not to go through all this bureaucratic shit.' He distributed his belongings amongst us and departed for the US Embassy in Lagos, taking only a cocktail shaker and an antique secretary-desk lined with mock leopard skin. An Irish couple, Damian and Geraldine, were boiling over with fury and indignation within hours of arriving. David, small and balding, with a great sense of humour, would divulge his gay infidelities to piratical Paul, despite which he was prim. Uneasy when confronted by the sight of bare-breasted Nigerian women, he was also shocked by the surrounding dirt and poverty: 'Fancy building a post office in such a squalid place,' he tutted. Phil and Sue, a pale, lanky couple, with a screaming toddler which wrought havoc in the dining room, devoted their spare time to ornithology, until he was abducted by someone on a motor bike who tried to rob him.

The only black teachers at the Guest Inn were Eddie and Nella from Zimbabwe, who had three children and who had been working in Yorkshire. Kind, honourable and well-educated, they were the antithesis of everything that confronted them in Nigeria. At the Ministry of Education Eddie was treated with even less respect than we were. As the days passed Eddie became more and more depressed. It had been a huge step uprooting his family from England. 'This is the most inefficient country in Africa,' he told us, shaking his head, embarrassed. 'I've never seen anything like it.'

The most enigmatic of the teachers-in-waiting was Alan. In his 40s, his conventional appearance belied his eccentricity. With his bristling moustache, straggly beard and clipped voice he came across as very British and something of an anachronism. On arrival, he had surprised us by enquiring about the local dope and where to exchange Saudi riyals on the black market, while in the same breath, berating us for referring to the British Embassy rather than the British High Commission. He had already spent several years in West Africa. 'I've got a family in Ghana,' he explained. His partner, Barakisu, who had undergone a traditional marriage to a local man, had nonetheless borne Alan a daughter and he consequently treated Barakisu's extended family as his own. 'Once I know where I'm being posted,' he told us, 'I'll be able to smuggle them across the border.' During the years that followed we were to become fond of Alan, a man whom our contemporaries described as having 'gone bush'.

Another friend at the Guest Inn was Fidelis, a 19-year-old Nigerian waiter. Having completed primary school in Benin state and travelled north seeking the free secondary education offered in Sokoto, he'd been dismayed to discover that out-of-state students were not eligible. Struggling to help his widowed mother put his younger brothers through school, he was the first of several bright young men we encountered, helping siblings at the expense of their own education.

Alcohol was unavailable at the Sokoto Guest Inn, but sometimes we visited the Sokoto Hotel, a more upmarket venue which had a bar. One evening, drinking with Alan, we met a Nigerian army officer. Initially he was friendly, but before long he began shouting at the waiters saying he would get them sacked. As he drank more and more whisky, his threat extended to others. 'Foreigners,' he said, toying with the pistol in his belt, 'foreigners who misbehave will be shot!' At the end of the evening, despite our protests, he insisted on accompanying us back to our hotel. No sooner had we set off, than he ordered us to march in time: 'Quick march, one, two, one, two!' He pulled out his pistol and pointed it at our backs. I giggled nervously. We had all had plenty to drink and the situation was so crazy that it seemed quite funny. 'Quiet,' hissed Alan. 'Keep moving and do absolutely everything he says.' When we reached the Sokoto Guest Inn the officer took his leave. 'It was you he was after,' said Alan, nodding in my direction. 'He fancied you.' 'Of course he didn't,' I said. 'I'd have noticed. 'Believe me,' said Alan, 'he did. The whole thing could have turned really ugly.'

The paper chase at the Ministry of Education lasted six weeks. We were to spend the next two years in the small bush town of Birnin Kebbi, two and a half hours from Sokoto. Bill was assigned to Haliru Abdu Teachers' College for boys and I was posted to the Women Teachers' College on the other side of town. We'd been astonished to discover that pupils who did well at primary school went on to Government Secondary Schools, whereas those who failed attended teachers' colleges, to become trainee teachers in primary schools. All secondary education took place in free, state-run boarding schools, attended by pupils from distant towns and villages. In southern Nigeria many schools had been established by missionaries and were of a higher standard than up north, where the focus had been on Qu'ranic schools for boys. An attempt was being made to redress this imbalance by recruiting teachers from overseas – foreigners, even Christians, being more acceptable in the Muslim north than teachers from southern Nigeria.

A couple of weeks before the move, we had paid a brief visit to our schools and been horrified by the smashed windows, broken furniture, filthy classrooms and books half-eaten by termites. By the time we set off for our new life, we were aware that our students and the schools they attended might be challenging, but at least we had escaped the ministerial maze. We were on our way.

Arrival in Birnin Kebbi

At Haliru Abdu Teachers' College – HATC – we were allocated a modern house with a bleak outlook onto semi-desert. Sand and dust had crept under the doors and between the slats in the louvre windows. We crossed the room leaving footprints in the dirt, as an army of lizards, cockroaches and spiders scuttled off into the shadows. 'That's lizard shit,' said Bill, looking at the mattress in the bedroom. 'Termites,' I added, indicating a pile of red dust by the skirting board.

It took a week of sweeping and scrubbing before we were ready to whitewash the walls. We bought brightly-patterned cloth in the market for curtains and cushions, colourful straw mats, and bamboo blinds. Cheap modern furniture was provided and there were ceiling fans which, being dependent on an erratic electricity supply, were often redundant. A modern jerry-built house, our home was like an oven, the interior walls sometimes as hot as radiators. However, we had plenty of space: two bedrooms, a kitchen, a bathroom, a large sitting room and a small veranda. There were two or three rows of similar houses on the school compound, as well as a kitchen block, offices, staff rooms, dormitories and classrooms.

Our day began between 5.30 and 6.00am when, prior to breakfast, we had to fill the bath and every available receptacle with water. The water would go off daily – and sometimes for several days on end – a situation which was linked to lack of power at the pumping station. When there was no water for more than a week, the school water lorry would go into town to fill up, and we would queue with bowls and buckets for our ration – just enough water for drinking, cooking and a jugful to wash with. The *mallam*, an unfriendly, powerful man, would ensure his Muslim flock got served first, Christian students next and foreigners last. Small fights broke out as people tried to get more than their quota.

The National Electric Power Authority, NEPA for short, was a joke; 'Never Expect Power Always,' said the Nigerians grinning. Nearly every letter we were to write home mentioned that the latest generator at the power station had blown up. *It's the sixth*, wrote Bill to his parents, *or is this the seventh? I lose track.* Generators never lasted more than a couple of months. We would watch the latest explosion, purple and blue flashes lighting up the night sky like fireworks, and our hearts would sink, knowing the power would be off for weeks. The weather at its hottest was 45°C in the shade and, with no electricity or fans, we marked our school work sweltering in the heat of paraffin lamps. At night we lay in rivers of sweat, the sheets beneath us like soaked rags.

My school, the Women Teachers' College – or WTC – was on the other side of town. I bought a bike and would cycle to work, as the entire populace fell about laughing at the sight of me; transport equalled status and the fact that I rode a bicycle rendered me only one step up from a peasant on a donkey. When Bill eventually acquired a 'machine', a small motorbike, he was taken aside and told it was unsuitable for the head of the English department.

WTC was older than Haliru Abdu. Mature trees provided shady areas and the surroundings were well cared for. A wide, sandy space with a platform at one end was used for gatherings and nearby, strung between two trees, was the gong used to punctuate lessons and breaks. Most of the staff houses were more substantial than those at Bill's school, one or two of them being old colonial buildings with thick walls, stone floors and wide verandas. There was a traditional compound for the matrons and school labourers – circular adobe huts screened by a tall matting fence – and an old building which housed the school library.

Assembly was at 7am, after which there were classes until the breakfast break at 9.30. By that time the sun was up and my dress, soaked with perspiration, would be clinging to my body. Sometimes I would pop out of school and buy fried spicy bean cakes from a roadside stall. Lessons commenced again at 10.30 and the day's teaching ended at 2.15, when I would pedal home laden with exercise books to mark.

My first assembly took me by surprise. I stood on the platform surrounded by teachers, rows of expectant girls lined up before us. 'No juju!' admonished the vice principal. A strong, stocky Yoruba, she was a force to be reckoned with. 'Is that understood? All juju is forbidden. No juju with the Qu'ran. No juju with the Bible.' The girls shifted and murmured a response. 'Louder,' said the vice principal. 'No juju!' shouted the girls. 'And what happens if we don't sweep?' 'Snakes,' chanted the girls in unison. The vice principal looked severe. 'Yes, snakes. You must sweep every day, or there will be snakes in the compound.' Bill and I had already noticed the frenetic sweeping outside schools, pupils bent double, scratching energetically at the sand with small hand-brooms. It dispersed seeds, prevented grass and scrub from growing, and deprived snakes of their habitat.

I had never taught before and lacked any training, but at the Ministry of Education in Sokoto, they had been perfectly happy with my 10 GCE O-levels. 'And what are you going to teach?' they enquired, as if the decision were entirely mine. 'English,' I replied. It was the obvious choice and my qualifications were to prove more than adequate. I was allocated a full timetable: five classes of 25 girls aged 13 to 22. 'It's remembering their names that's difficult,' I said to Bill. 'Ronke Akinbobola, Abidemi Olajide, Morili Ganiyu... It's OK for you; nearly everyone you teach is called Mohammed.' With lessons to prepare and 125 exercises to mark every time I set an assignment, it was baptism by fire.

I had just started teaching on my first day, when the door opened and there stood the vice principal with a camera crew from Sokoto television. 'This is our new teacher who's just arrived from England,' she told them. 'They've come to film your lesson, Mrs Scolding.' I ditched the grammar exercises I had prepared and switched to the easier option of English conversation. Our friend Fidelis, who visited shortly after, had been impressed. 'I was with the waiters in the hotel reception,' he said, 'and there is my friend on the television. Jenny on the television!'

The WTC students wore colourful school uniform wrappers and matching head scarves, together with white, short-sleeved blouses which bore the school crest. Most of my students were extrovert and robust, but one or two of the younger Muslim girls were more delicate. In their villages they would have been married off to peasant farmers, but education, however rudimentary, would make them eligible brides for wealthy old men, often *alhajis*. Some of the girls were homesick and ran away, only to be brought back by the police and whipped. When the vice principal berated the girls for bad behaviour, they would crawl before her on their hands and knees, wailing and touching her feet in a traditional sign of respect. 'Stop that!' she would snap. 'Get up on your feet at once.'

The college was run along the lines of a British boarding school. There were four houses, each named after famous Nigerians: Crowther, the first African Anglican bishop; Dan Fodio, an Islamic religious teacher and founder of the Sokoto Caliphate; Amina, a Hausa warrior queen; and Balewa, prime minister of the newly-independent Nigeria in 1960. I was the house mistress for Crowther, which involved duties in the evening and at weekends. I had to inspect dormitories, bedding and wash-rooms, and ensure buildings were free of food and rubbish that might attract rats and snakes. I monitored the girls' personal hygiene, checking their hair and fingernails, and distributing soap and sanitary towels. Excessive pilfering necessitated spot checks on the tin termite-proof trunks in which they kept their belongings, and I frequently had to settle disputes. Most of the girls were used to cooking on open fires or small kerosene stoves in their villages, a habit they tried to extend to the dormitories with the consequent risk of fire. Being a house mistress was a never-ending battle, but it was also an opportunity to sit with individuals on their beds while they showed me photographs of their families or had a go at plaiting my hair African-style. Matrons – mature local women – also kept an eye on things.

Bill's school was far more chaotic than mine. As soon as he arrived he was made head of the English department and it didn't take him long to realise why no one else was willing to undertake this role: no text books; absent teachers and students. Even though term had now started, the windows remained broken and the furniture had not been repaired. With ever-encroaching sand and termites it was not surprising that buildings would fall into disrepair over the holidays, but there was no excuse for some of the neglect: 'You wouldn't believe the classroom I was in today,' Bill told me. 'Whoever decorated it left everything pinned to the walls and slapped paint over the top – newspaper cuttings, drawing pins, school notices, timetables. It looked like a giant collage.'

In the mornings, by the time I had cycled over to WTC for an early assembly, Bill was already in the classroom calling out the register: 'Ahmed Mohammed,' 'Present, sir.' 'Abdul Mohammed,' 'Present.' 'Mohammed Abdul, Mohammed Mohammed...' (the boys also gave themselves 'guy names', alternative identities which they carved on the back of their chairs and wrote on exercise books: Andrew Young in Action, Canna Lily Boy, Bob Marley.)

After registration, Bill would attend assembly which kicked off with the oath, 'I pledge Nigeria my country...' followed by the national anthem and the news – all in English and incomprehensible to most of the boys. This was followed by whippings carried out by the school sergeants, men so old they had fought in Burma during the Second World War. When the flogging was over there was self-congratulation among the staff. 'Discipline!' pronounced the principal. 'Discipline! No one can disobey the rules in this school.' 'It's a school spectacle,' Bill told me, 'and it doesn't act as a deterrent. Most of the students steal from the school, even if it's only text books. The thrashing makes the game more exciting; makes them resolve not to get caught.'

The fadama (flood plain) seen from Dukku Hill, just outside Birnin Kebbi, Sokoto State, Nigeria 1979.

Birnin Kebbi, our home from September 1979 – June 1981. **Above left:** *Shehu, our favourite vegetable seller.* **Above right:** *the Friday market.* **Below:** *Ayo and his mechanics.* **Below, right:** *the main road though town.*

Above: *our house on the compound of HATC.*
Right: *with Mr Johnson, our puppy.*
Below: *with Bill and fifth form students.*
Below right: *HATC students on teaching practice.*

Below: *WTC staff photo, 1979; me, Errol and Florence are the last three on the top row.*
In the front row, Sue Rush is second from left, Mrs Fadairo is fourth from left, and the Principal is sixth.

Bill was overloaded with work just as I was, but as head of department his responsibilities were even greater: organising timetables; setting exam papers; allocating classrooms – all in a climate where everyone was playing the grand education game. The Ministry of Education had just opened 26 new schools in Sokoto State, when those already in existence were so understaffed they could barely function. During Bill's first couple of months, the nine English teachers at HATC – responsible for 1,300 students – had dwindled to four. First year boys had virtually no lessons. Straight from the bush and speaking no English, they wandered the school compound until someone collared them to carry water or clean the latrines. 'They must wonder what it's all about,' said Bill. 'As for the fifth years...' He tailed off in exasperation. The fifth years were arrogant, always confident they would pass their final exams despite the standard being unrealistically high. 'Where do we put a full stop?' asked Bill. 'What is the present tense?' Nobody had a clue. In the previous seven years not a single student had passed the national exams.

While the schools were an even greater challenge than we had anticipated, Birnin Kebbi was everything we had hoped for. I loved cycling through town to school early in the morning. The road, a narrow strip of tarmac, was lined by a wide sandy area with neem trees and shack-shops. There was a hairdresser's, run by the wife of our Ghanaian friend Nana, who proudly displayed pictures of African hairstyles painted crudely on the outside wall. Distorted music blasted from a hut where records and cassette tapes were sold. There were stalls selling Fanta, spicy kebabs and bean cakes. Naked children ran after my bike shouting, *'Bature, bature!'* – white person – as I swerved past goats, guinea fowl, chickens and donkeys. I would wave to Ayo and his mechanics who sold petrol, sloshing it out of jerrycans as lighted cigarettes hung from their lips. They mended motorbikes, which were known as 'machines', spreading out the spare parts on the ground. When Bill eventually entrusted his own 'machine' to their care, he had to help them scratch around in the sand, searching for essential nuts and screws that had gone missing.

After passing the mosque and the Emir's palace in the distance, I would pedal past the post office, and then the hospital with its long, covered walkways overhung by trees heavy with fruit bats. Nurses in green uniforms spread bed linen on the bushes to dry, as outpatients queued on the veranda. Another hundred yards, and I would turn left and cycle up the long, sandy driveway to the school.

Further on, beyond the school, the old part of Birnin Kebbi comprised traditional sun-baked dwellings, nestling amidst tortuous sandy alleys lined with matting fences. The houses were built from balls of mud, excavated from large 'borrow holes', a name which acknowledged that the buildings would eventually disintegrate, returning to the land. Residents of the old town travelled on donkeys or, if they were rich, bicycles. Bill and I were therefore astonished one day to stumble on a Cadillac with massive fins, abandoned in a lane, its deflated tyres sunk into the sand. Today Birnin Kebbi is a metropolis and state capital, but in those days it was a small bush town and we pondered who had brought the Cadillac to those remote streets and, indeed, how.

In another part of town, the Union Bank of Nigeria occupied a small stone building with a veranda, where customers chatted to each other during the excessively long time it took to get served. Bill and I were to become friendly with the young men who worked in the bank. They were southerners, who liked a beer and were well-educated, and we socialised with them in our spare time; our banking business was often given priority over other foreigners.

Friday was market day and, after attending the mosque, people would throng the stalls, where sacking and sheets of cloth were suspended on poles as makeshift awnings. Our favourite vendor was Shehu, a smiling, plump man with a shaven head, who would engage Bill in a weekly duel of haggling. Vegetables and spices were laid out on straw mats: chillies in neat piles, pyramids of onions, rows of cassava and lumpy yams. Sometimes schoolchildren would be in charge of stalls, small girls calling out, *'Bature, bature!* You buy. You buy!' Having bought our vegetables and alfalfa, we would approach the butcher's block, where the unrecognisable, bloody lumps of goat, camel and offal were crawling with flies. Despite this, we purchased meat, assuming that if we cooked the hell out of it we would kill the bugs. Kebabs rolled in fiery spices were roasted over charcoal and, at the edge of the market, sorghum, millet and guinea corn were on offer. Sometimes one or two nomadic Fulani women came into town selling a little milk or cheese, but dairy products were not part of the common diet. We bought solid cakes of molasses which we would melt and pour over our morning porridge. Once the basic shopping was done, I loved to linger over brilliantly patterned cloth, amulets, jewellery, and Arabic coins which had come across the Sahara.

On the edge of town the Sokoto River cut through the Fadama, the desert plain, and rising high above that was Dukku Hill, a huge pyramid-shaped mound of reddish sand. Sometimes we would climb to the top and gaze out across the landscape, always aware that the Sahara was close. One day Bill said, 'If anything happens and I die in Nigeria, don't bother to ship my body home. Bury me here, on the top of Dukku Hill.' He said it to express his affection for the place, a tongue-in-cheek statement not rooted in reality. We hadn't anticipated that several people we knew, Nigerians as well as expatriates, would die during our two years in Birnin Kebbi; that we were living in a place that courted danger.

Friends and Foes

'For half an hour,' emphasised Papa John in his Scottish accent, 'for half an hour I was the only *bature* sitting with all them blacks, while the rest of you...' his finger stabbed around the sitting room pointing at each white person in turn – 'all of you, were sat in here. It might not matter to you but this party was for public relations and I spent company money entertaining all these black bastards; and they are bastards every single one of 'em.'

Jean, an elderly Canadian volunteer at Haliru Abdu, had taken us along to a party at Papa John's. A contractor building the new Birnin Kebbi army barracks for a company called Amcord, Papa John was a tiny, wiry, working class Scot who had been brought up on Clydeside and was making a fortune in different parts of Africa. His son, a jockey nicknamed Little John and who had been raised in Rhodesia, was also present. Belligerent, arms folded, his legs apart as if his horse had just escaped from beneath him, Little John was imbued with his father's take on the world. They were the most objectionable duo we were to encounter during our entire stay in Africa.

We had entered the brightly-lit room to find Papa John shouting at everyone – women in particular, his house boys and even his dogs. His chin was covered in stubble and his blotchy face and bulbous nose manifested years of excessive drinking. A few strands of grey hair protruded from a white, cotton, flower-pot-shaped hat. 'Ask any black "Who is next to Allah?" ' said Little John, 'and you know what he'll say – what they'll all say? "The *bature* in the white hat, Papa John!" My Dad and Amcord run this town. We *are* this town. Without us it would die.' 'Aye, son,' said the white god, nodding grandly. 'I have to admit I am the most important man in this state.'

Papa John was surrounded by bored, boozy white people, a few well-heeled Nigerians and a stony-faced couple from Sri Lanka. After a few risqué jokes about gays, Papa John switched his focus to Asians. 'Them Indies and Pakis are bastards,' he said. 'Never met a single one I liked. All those bastards are interested in is money.'

Outside in the darkness the Nigerian District Police Officer discoed with a bulging red-fleshed woman while Little John strutted and clapped and whooped. Under the trees two or three of the house boys were dancing on their own, gracefully unselfconscious, blue cigarette smoke curling up and around coloured light bulbs strung from the branches. The night wore on and women scratched their bare ankles as mosquitos went on the attack. Empty beer bottles cluttered the tables and the houseboys dashed back and forth with trays of full ones. 'This ain't cooled,' bawled Papa John. 'It's warm.' Bill and I slunk off into the shadows and found an Igbo with whom we discussed Biafra.

We had been invited to stay the night and there was no escape. At breakfast Papa John continued in the same vein, but he had become tired of us. 'What are you, some kind of fucking communists?' he asked. 'Naïve, you volunteers.' 'We're not volunteers,' we protested. We're employed by the Ministry of Education.' 'Just you wait and see,' growled Papa John. 'You'll change after living in the arsehole of Africa for a few months. I can help you, you know. I can show you all the right people to meet. The Emir's a friend of mine; Little John here sells him horses. It's up to you.' His voice softened into a patronising purr. 'A piece of advice,' he said. 'Remember, kindness is weakness!' With that he threw his scrambled egg and sausages to the dogs, while beggars stood nearby chanting their call for alms.

After boasting how frequently he beat, tortured and fired his black workers, Papa John despatched us with one more story: 'One of our Amcord workers, a white bloke, was going home to his caravan late at night,' he said 'Lots of our contractors live in caravans, you know. Anyway, he got bitten by a snake, the silly wanker. He was probably stumbling along drunk. Died, he did. I couldn't get his body up to Kano airport for about a month. Only thing I could do was keep him here in my freezer!' Papa John guffawed. 'Kept me beers on top of him, the stupid bloody wanker.' Jean took up the story. 'Papa asked me to fetch a beer from the freezer. I lifted the lid and there was the corpse covered with bottles. I nearly died of fright.'

As we drove away, I thought about racists I had encountered in the past, old colonial types who, despite their disagreeable and paternalistic views, at least displayed a certain well-intentioned altruism and integrity. The majority of the white contractors we were to meet in Nigeria were ruthless mercenaries, often ex-SAS. Out to make a quick buck, they didn't give a toss about the indigenous population. 'These guys are jackals,' I said to Bill, 'the whole damn lot of them.'

We were to get to know Jean well. Posted to Nigeria by the Canadian volunteer service – CUSO – she lived near us on the compound at HATC and we became friends. Slim and elegant, she looked younger than her 69 years. Despite the incredible heat and limited water supply, she always managed to look clean and crisp. A widow, she had found herself condemned to life in an apartment block, playing cards every evening with elderly neighbours. 'I suddenly realised I'd never done anything exciting,' she drawled. 'I decided to escape. Volunteering in Africa seemed like such a worthwhile adventure.' She paused, with a wry chuckle. 'It would've been more useful if they'd shipped out a crate of prosthetic limbs.' After a while we included Jean in our excursions to the bars in town. Coming from her antiseptic safe haven in Canada, it was like dropping her onto another planet. One night when Bill was away I invited her to accompany me to one of these bars. 'What, just you and me?' she enquired, incredulous. 'Of course,' I said. 'Why not?' We had a good evening and from then on she became a little braver.

Our next-door-neighbour on the school compound was a Hausa man, Abubakar Nassarawa. Handsome, with a hawk nose, a pencil-line moustache and thick African hair above a receding hairline, he was a gentle companion who moved happily among the seven children he had sired. Laughter emanated from his home and he was a friendly, kind neighbour. He and Bill shared a love of gardening and in their adjacent plots they would discuss vegetables and plants as they dug away at the infertile desert with their large African hoes. Abubakar was assisted by his children, in particular his six-year-old daughter who would set to work with her baby brother strapped to her back. Bill was helped by boys from the school and one in particular – Mohammed Dandare who came from a farming community and was familiar with the soil. A sweet-natured, handsome boy who was small for his age, he would turn up at the house at weekends and offer his services. 'What do you want to be when you leave school?' asked Bill. 'A farmer, of course,' replied Mohammed. After a while shoots began to appear: paw-paw trees and a teak sapling; aubergines, chillies, tomatoes and cucumbers. However, with the erratic water supply, their survival was precarious and Bill was fighting a losing battle.

Sue Rush, the home economics teacher from my school, and her husband Mike, both from Scotland, also lived nearby. A helpful, genial fellow, Mike had dark hair and a beard. To the African eye he and Bill looked identical and wherever Bill went in town, everyone would shout 'Mr Rush! Mr Rush!' assuming he was Mike. An art teacher, Mike was popular with the students and he always had a project on the go. 'Cement camels!' he said in a eureka moment. 'They'd like that, wouldn't they? Cement camels!' He got his students to paint murals around the school compound and he also introduced woodwork to the curriculum. After teaching the boys to make simple furniture, he arrived one morning to find the classroom doors missing. They had been transformed into tables which were already on sale in the market!

Our home was always full of visitors and we struggled to find time for lesson preparation and marking. Nigerians didn't knock on the door but rather hissed to gain admission. In the evening we would be sitting surrounded by piles of exercise books, when the hissing would begin outside. It would be Aminu, the school's head boy, or some of the students from Bill's debating club, bright articulate lads who in any other education system would have gone far. Sometimes little Mohammed, Bill's garden helper, would pay a visit in his smart weekend clothes, cool striped trousers and his best yellow shirt. Fidelis, the waiter from the Sokoto Guest Inn turned up, having travelled for nearly three hours to see us. Our most frequent visitors, however, would remain friends throughout our two years in Birnin Kebbi: Moses and Garba.

Moses was a lanky Yoruba with a thin moustache, fine features, and an enigmatic startled look. More often than not he wore traditional clothes. He carved large thorns which he glued together into African scenes: people sitting in canoes with their bundles; a woman pounding yam; a street dentist pulling teeth. The whole of African life materialised from his fingers and we bought many of his carvings. He invited us to the small house with a corrugated iron roof where he lived with his wife and baby and he introduced us to his brother Yorubas, the DJs who ran the music shack in town. He would accompany us to their shop to choose music or else to relax and drink Fanta while we listened to distorted 'highlife' blasting down the street.

Garba was local, a Hausa, and far less reticent than Moses, turning up at any time and frequently outstaying his welcome. Tall and broad-chested, he sloped about wearing sandals and western clothes, grinning and at ease. Despite his laid-back appearance he was one of the Waziri's sons – the Waziri being next in pecking order to the Emir. The Waziri's palace, located near Haliru Abdu, was hidden behind a high brick wall, where each brick was painted white and outlined in green. Within this enclosure there was a house of slaves whose antecedents had lost a battle against the Waziri's ancestors two centuries before and who were still paying the price. The Waziri was known to smuggle Benson & Hedges cigarettes into Nigeria, bribing customs officials to let his laden lorries cross the border.

Garba wanted to go back to school, but before doing so he needed to visit 'the brain tree' in Benin, from which he would obtain medicine to help him with his exams. 'Dis tree will give de power,' he said. An excellent mimic who did accurate portrayals of all our white acquaintances, Garba was very concerned about who did or did not have power. Apparently nearly everyone we knew had power – the Amcord contractors, Mike Rush, the Asian vice principal. Bill, however, did not. 'Scolding,' he said – he often used Bill's surname, emphasising the sibilance on the S and letting the unfamiliar word roll slowly round his tongue – 'Scolding, you have no power. Mr Rush, he has power, but you do not.' He paused. 'I discuss dis ting with my friends. They say you walk like a woman!' Garba's general lack of faith in Bill was compounded when Bill told him that man had landed on the moon. He refused to accept this. 'The man who went to the moon, was he a black man or white man?' he queried. 'White,' said Bill, 'an American.' 'When you show me a picture of a black man on the moon,' he said, 'then I will believe you.'

Garba was obsessed with the English football pools and his interest in anyone British focused on which team they supported. Some years prior to our arrival, a contractor had given him four draws and he had won 400 naira. Thereafter he had assumed that 'London people' – his name for anyone British – knew everything there was to know about soccer.

Football players were his heroes and he would mutter their names, his favourite being 'Ke-vin Kee-gan, Ke-vin Kee-gan,' which he whispered like a mantra. He found Bill's lack of interest in soccer incomprehensible. 'I have come for dis ting, dis football fools,' as he called them – there being no letter P in the Hausa language. 'Tell me about Liverpool an' Tott'nam.' When Bill said he had no idea which team was likely to win, Garba would stare at him in disbelief. 'All London people know dis ting,' he would say. The football fool enthusiasts would gather every Saturday in a hut in town where an old lady produced local hooch. They would listen to the football results on the BBC world service, ticking off the mysterious, almost liturgical, names. Later Garba would arrive and recite them to us: 'Tranmere Rovers 2, Wolverhampton Wanderers nil…'

We had a lot of good African friends in Birnin Kebbi. There was Nana, the Ghanaian, whose hairdresser wife fed their baby groundnut stew, so spicy that it nearly blew our heads off. 'How does that baby survive?' asked Bill, struggling to swallow a spoonful. Guy, from Sierra Leone, was a crazy, amusing character, who'd been raised in a village near the diamond mines. 'On the way to school I used to pass the feet of dead miners sticking up out of wet sand,' he told us. 'They'd been buried alive while digging illegally for stones. I did it myself when I was a boy,' he added. 'The company's licence only extended to the edge of the road so at night we would scratch away at the seams beneath the centre. In the morning we'd wash away the gravel in the hope of finding diamonds.'

The people with whom we socialised most were the southern Nigerian bank clerks – Thomas, Pedro, Bello and Sunday. On Saturday nights in the Dukku Hill Bar we would drink a lot of beer together and chat and dance. The bar was in the main room, where the DJ sat twiddling knobs to produce the distorted music that was so popular. We sat outside in a central yard lined by rooms used by prostitutes, girls who sometimes joined us when we danced. If men danced together it was known as 'bone-to-bone'; a man dancing with a woman was 'bone-to-flesh'. The main drawback to the venue was the filthy toilet, a shitty place where the walls were thick with cockroaches – you opened the door and a wave of them would sweep up into the roof away from the intruding light. Of our bank friends, Thomas was the most conventional, a warm, round-faced youth who was to correspond with us long after our return to England. Pedro was a cooler customer, a snappy dresser with spiky hair and shades. Gradually, through knowing the bank lads, our circle of Nigerian friends increased, extending also to Tunde, the bank manager, who entertained us at his home. He would drive us there in his posh car and we would be offered beer and snacks while we watched videos of Granada Television's popular courtroom drama *Crown Court*.

We were acquainted with several Filipinos, but it was the Seguindans, a close-knit family who lived nearby, who were the most friendly and supportive. They had numerous pets and eventually Bill and I relieved them of a puppy and two kittens. At the hospital there was a Filipino dentist who was regarded with suspicion. 'He's a spy,' insisted our Filipino friends. 'He watches us and reports back.' Certainly President Marcos had imposed martial law in the Philippines and closed down the free press, but whether his government's snooping extended as far as Nigeria seemed doubtful. 'Army Dental Corps,' said his compatriots dismissively. 'Extractions on combat duty, that's all he knows.'

We'd kept in touch with the new teachers we'd met on arrival, friends from the days in the Sokoto Guest Inn. Viv and Paul came to stay and one or two others. Of them all, Alan, the man who had worked in Ghana and had African children, became a firm friend. We would visit his extraordinary household at the Government Secondary School in Koko and he would turn up in Birnin Kebbi and hang out for a few days. One December day in 1980 he came pounding up the path brandishing a British newspaper. 'I thought you would want to see this,' he said with some urgency. The headline read: 'John Lennon is dead.'

Other friends and acquaintances turned up from Sokoto, mostly from the College of Education. With no telephones of any kind, let alone reliable transport, we received no advance warning from visitors. They would just appear, together with all the hissing Nigerians, and we accommodated them all as best we could. There was a large woman known as Fizz who would roar up on her motorbike, and Judith who played cassette tapes of English birdsong and church bells on Sundays to make everyone feel at home. There were David and Helen Crabtree, who were generous hosts to us on our visits to Sokoto and who Garba referred to as the 'Craft-trips'.

John, a young VSO guy in the nearby bush village of Bunza, was someone we grew very fond of, as well as his wacky VSO colleague, Verity. John was intrepid, fun and the person in Nigeria with whom we had most in common. He and Bill enjoyed drinking together in local bars and they had already had one or two adventures. Riding through Birnin Kebbi on John's 'machine' in the early hours, they had nearly driven into a body lying in a pool of blood surrounded by broken glass. Thinking the man was dead, they edged closer only to discover he was still breathing. They leapt onto John's motorbike and dashed to the hospital where Bill sought help while John rode on to the police station. It took Bill ten minutes to locate and wake up the watchman and night nurse, both of whom embarked on a litany of complaint: 'Night time, everybody sleepin'. Doctor not on seat.' Having finally persuaded them to accompany him, Bill discovered that starting the ambulance was no easy matter. He lit match after match to illuminate the driver's hands as he tried to join two wires together under the dashboard. Eventually they got the vehicle going and drove to where the body lay. John arrived with two cops who shrugged and said, 'Bottle fight. Injury small, small. Maybe he lose de eye, de ear...' They slung the body into the ambulance, from which it was removed with a similar lack of reverence on arrival at the hospital. John and Bill made their way home. 'I bet they're cursing us for disturbing their sleep,' said Bill.

Sometimes we visited John at his school and once, returning from a long weekend, the packed taxi we were riding screeched to a whiplash halt. A man by the roadside had flagged us down and whispered something to our driver. Suddenly two passengers leapt from the front seat of the car, flung open the rear door, dragged Bill out of his seat, and hauled him off into the bush. I was nervous rather than terrified. I leant forward. 'Where have they taken my husband?' They ignored me. A few minutes later I repeated the question. 'No problem,' was all they said, and the car shot off. A mile or so down the road we came to a police roadblock where our papers were checked and we were waved through. Further on, with the roadblock out of sight, we pulled into the roadside and waited. 'My husband?' I ventured again. It was nearly dark and I was beginning to get worried. Eventually Bill and his abductors emerged, having trekked through the bush. By removing three men from the overloaded vehicle, the driver had got through the roadblock without exceeding the legal number of passengers – his aim to avoid paying a dash rather than adhering to any regulations. Bush taxis, normally Peugeot 504s, were our most common form of transport, and crushing a dozen passengers into a small space was not uncommon, sometimes with the addition of children and babies on laps. 'You ok?' asked Bill as he climbed back into the taxi. 'I was beginning to get a bit worried,' I admitted, 'but yeah…ok.' He didn't seem unduly concerned. 'Nigeria,' he said, shaking his head. 'Nigeria!'

We rarely saw Papa John after that first dreadful encounter, but it was impossible to completely avoid white contractors, all of whom assumed that white people would want to stick together. When we mentioned a remote town or village we planned to visit they would scoff: 'Not worth it, nobody there,' as if the indigenous population did not exist. Very occasionally we would accept one of their persistent invitations to visit their club, where we were offered western food and an abundance of booze. They meant well and were generous, but in no time, having been subjected to their racist, homophobic and sexist attitudes, we would eschew their company again. They were out to shock: tales of dismembered bodies in Indonesia; atrocities perpetrated by the SAS; heists of various kinds. 'Knocked off Peter Sellars' house in 1960!' said one. We were friendly with two of them, Taff and Eddie, who were quieter and less racist, but on the whole we avoided them.

I was surprised to find there were still plenty of missionaries in Nigeria. The Misses Beveridge and Lawson had lived in Birnin Kebbi for decades working as nurses and holding RE classes for the few Christians in the schools. They were the polite elderly ladies one would expect, but we were to meet others who were considerably more eccentric.

On a trip to Yelwa Yauri on the banks of the Niger, we stayed with a jovial Friar Tuck character called Father Peter who ran the Catholic Mission with Brother Clement, a shy Nigerian Dominican. Obese, earthy and beer-swigging, Father Peter wore a dirty T-shirt and a massive pair of shorts. He had written a letter to an American magazine saying how much he missed chocolate, after which parcels of confectionary arrived from all over the world. The mission house was an L-shaped bungalow with a veranda shaded by trees. From the small church a statue of the Virgin gazed out over the bush and behind the mission a village of thatched huts stood in green meadows which sloped down to the river. 'We see hippos occasionally,' said Father Peter, 'Manatees as well, those snub-nosed seal-like creatures which are supposed to look like mermaids.' He guffawed. 'You'd have to be at sea a bloody long time before you thought one of those looked like a woman!'

While we were at the mission, Father Peter drove his pick-up into the bush where he held a service in a village, returning later with his cassock sweat-stained and dusty. Bill and I had already come across the local tribe in a nearby village: muscular women with Mohican hair styles, black leather loin cloths, their naked breasts patterned with raised scars; effete men wearing make-up and leg bracelets. 'I've been visiting these people for 20 years,' Father Peter told us. 'They come to my services and I attend their ceremonies.' We expressed surprise at this reciprocal arrangement. 'Mumbo jumbo with sacrificial cockerels,' said Father Peter dismissively. 'Possessed priests, oracular judgments on village problems...' 'Twenty years!' Bill said to me later. 'It doesn't sound as if the Catholic Church has made much headway.'

A few months later, further south, we were drinking in a typical bar which doubled as a brothel, when an Irish missionary arrived. No sooner was he seated than the barman came running over with a bottle of Guinness, aptly known in Nigeria as 'thickness'. 'Your beer, Father,' said the barman. 'They'll not be charging me,' the priest informed us in his Irish brogue. 'Free beer for the priest, it is!' We chatted awhile and then accepted an invitation to accompany him to a compound inhabited by the Tiv tribe, where he was to spend the night. Bowling along in his rust-heap of a car we skidded through a deluge of tropical rain and squelched along dirt tracks which were fast becoming streams. Thunder rumbled ominously and flashes of lightning picked out lush foliage and crops bowed beneath the rain. We arrived at a small village and entered an enormous circular hut crowned with exceptionally high and pointed thatch. Our host, a Tiv farmer, was an ex-soldier who had fought in Burma and the Congo. His children were sleeping in a tangled heap on a bed in the middle of the room. As the storm raged outside, the missionary outlined which Christian sects had carved up Nigeria and acquired the most converts. He spread a map on the table. 'Catholics here, here, and here,' he said, stabbing at different locations. 'We haven't won these over yet,' he said, shaking his head. 'The Protestants have got 'em: Methodists here, Church of England there.' 'Perhaps it's not as cut and dried as he thinks,' I remarked to Bill later. 'Think of Father Peter!'

In Birnin Kebbi we never knew what extraordinary experience or person the day would bring. Even the gun-toting Nigerian army officer from Sokoto turned up at our local barracks. We glimpsed him once or twice, but luckily he failed to recognise us. However, we did learn of his run-in with a white contractor called John. They had been drinking together and, having drained a glass of whisky, John was set to leave when the CO took umbrage. 'Finish the bottle!' he ordered. The contractor declined. 'Finish it,' growled the CO and whipped out a sub-machine-gun, forcing John to knock back the entire bottle at gun point. Everyone we met, both black and white, considered this army officer insane and dangerous.

Settling in

There was a hiss outside our kitchen. '*Sannu*,' shouted Bill, 'hello.' A student entered with a huge lump of raw meat. 'It is bull, sir,' he said. 'For *sallah*. Ten pounds of meat, sir.' The bloody flesh was slapped down on the table. '*Barka da sallah*,' said the student. '*Na gode*,' we replied, 'thank you.' It was Eid, the end of fasting, and all over the school compound bulls, goats and sheep were being slaughtered. Having seen our neighbour, Abubakar, butchering his lamb, we had gone inside to escape the sight and smell of blood. There was always some kind of festival going on to compensate for the day-to-day nightmare of school life.

When students turned up in his classes, Bill quite enjoyed teaching them, but more often than not, they played hooky. He lacked text books; of 85 distributed the previous term, only 45 had been returned. Books fetched a good price in the market and pupils went to extraordinary lengths to hide their copies from fellow students. When Bill launched a surprise book hunt, one boy led him up a path at the barracks to a small grass-fenced compound where one of the kitchen staff guarded his books. Further textbooks were discovered hidden in a chicken coop.

The tragedy of the education system was compounded by the fact our pupils were student teachers. They were placed on teaching practice at local primary schools, where Bill and I had to assess their progress. Some just about kept their heads above water; others wrote pure gibberish on the blackboard. Questions and answers sometimes proved surreal: 'Who invented the telescope?' 'Peter!' One or two were naturals, their empathy with small children overriding their inadequacies but, on the whole, it was a matter of the blind leading the blind.

I loved touring the primary schools. The shuttered classrooms were full of attentive dusty children with bright eyes and wide smiles. The walls were devoid of pictures or visual stimuli and the teachers were virtually illiterate, but the pupils remained enthusiastic, chanting and clapping and co-operating. I longed to teach them myself; catching them so young I felt I could have made a difference. Outside the primary schools, gnarled old women reclined beneath the trees or gathered round the school well. I enjoyed watching them as they whiled away their time within sight of the latest generation.

Working in the Women Teachers' College I had an easier time than Bill. Despite some inadequacies, my school was organised and functioned reasonably well with 20 or so teachers. Mrs Fadairo, the vice principal, was in her late 40s. A solid woman, she routinely wore western clothing: straight sleeveless shift dresses which were rather too short and revealed her substantial legs and fat knees. Dark-skinned, with a broad flat nose and full lips, she sometimes wore glasses which made her look severe, despite which she was a handsome woman. I found her manner a tad artificial as she ingratiated herself with foreign teachers, but I also admired her. Against all odds, she succeeded in working hard and imposing a strict regime on pupils and staff alike. The principal, the Emir's daughter, who had studied in the USA, rarely graced us with her presence. Quietly spoken, shy, and swathed in yards of cloth and a layered turban, she wore spectacles and was plump and ineffectual.

There were two British teachers besides me: pretty, young Sue Rush, who taught home economics, and Errol, a bearded black history teacher from Nottingham. Sue's curriculum, with its focus on European kitchen appliances, flooring and work surfaces, seemed far removed from anything the girls would experience in their villages. 'In Africa it's important to keep up standards,' Sue said. 'It's so easy to let everything slip.' She and her husband, Mike were kind and hospitable to us, adhering to her mantra and dishing up meals that were impeccably served.

Errol taught history and told the girls about West Africa's ancient kingdoms – Ghana, Mali and Songhay – as well as informing them about the slave trade and the imposition of colonial power. He captured the girls' imagination and respect and they talked to me about his lessons. When he decided to give an extra-curricular lecture to the students, members of staff were invited to attend. I can't remember the exact subject but it touched on Nigeria's colonial past. I wanted to be there, but it was one of those evenings when I felt bogged down with excessive work; when exhaustion got the better of me. I should have gone out of respect for him, particularly as the subject addressed the behaviour of my British antecedents. The next day, Errol said, 'So you didn't come. Not a single foreign teacher attended my lecture.' I think he imagined I had stayed away through lack of interest, whereas, had I attended, I would undoubtedly have agreed with everything he said.

Some members of staff belonged to Nigeria's National Youth Service Corps, or NYSC. Inaugurated in 1973 to reconcile and rebuild the country after the civil war, service in the NYSC was compulsory for all graduates. They were posted to places far from home in order to foster appreciation of other ethnic groups. The NYSC teachers assigned to my school were southern Christians: two young men, and a woman called Florence with whom I became quite friendly. She was petite, funny, and a firebrand. I still have the minutes of a staff meeting where teachers were complaining about being overworked and having to run school clubs on Saturdays. Florence leapt to her feet, tugging at the hair beneath her headscarf. 'For a week,' she shouted, 'for one whole week, my hair stay loose-O! No time for anyting, not even to plait my hair!' Sometimes she was as wise as she was scatty, holding me in check when I smoked too many cigarettes or drank a lot of beer. Apparently her wisdom did not extend to contraception; when she departed at the end of the year she was pregnant from a liaison with one of her NYSC colleagues. One day I lent Florence my heavy sewing machine and I watched with admiration as she carried it on her head to the other side of the school compound. Everyone carried things on their heads, even small items: a single sweet, a pencil, a rubber, a ruler or a book. They would come to class with biros sticking out of their hair like geisha hair sticks.

My girls always said exactly what they thought, a tendency I found refreshing. They referred to me as 'ma' rather than by name. 'You look fat today, ma,' they would say or 'Today too much hot, ma. You sweatin!' They showed no restraint in trying to acquire my belongings. 'Your dress, ma. Very beautiful. You give me this dress.' On the whole they responded well to my teaching and because I had never been trained, I probably fared better than those attempting conventional methods in a challenging environment. The girls left me in no doubt as to the success or otherwise of each lesson. If they didn't like it they would make a clicking noise reflecting disapproval, putting their heads on their desks and closing their eyes. On one occasion a pupil actually escaped through an open window. On the whole, I found I was able to keep their attention, and in the end I taught them quite a lot. Their text books often included unsuitable material, set in England. When this happened I would abandon the prescribed lesson and seek out African texts they could relate to. It didn't take me long to get to know and love my students but, initially, I was a bit too familiar with them; later it proved a struggle to pull back and reinstate discipline.

In the classroom the most unexpected things could cause a disturbance. When a stack of new exercise books arrived wrapped in a single sheet of white paper, I had a stampede on my hands as the girls fought for it. Whenever possible I made teaching an exchange, so that I learned as much as I taught. One lesson I remember concerned baobabs, the thick trees with hollow trunks so prevalent in the bush. I located a passage on the subject and we did a comprehension exercise. Then I invited information from my pupils about the properties of the tree and the lesson took off with a blast. They talked of their villages and a myriad uses for this extraordinary plant: the huge hollow trunks which were used for water storage or as sheds for farm implements and livestock. 'We lock bad people in there,' said one girl. 'It is village prison!' 'And the bark?' I enquired? 'Rope,' they shouted, ''fishing nets, baskets, strings for musical instruments.' 'My grandmother,' said one girl, 'she use it for making cloth.' Soup, soap, fruit, dye, its uses were endless, and in vying with each other to give me the most information, my students spoke a lot of English.

More than anything, the girls loved reciting in front of the class or doing role play. Good actors, they revelled in hamming things up. They enjoyed debates and discussions, smacking their fists down on their desks to drum home a point. To encourage everyone to join in I would give them a controversial subject. 'A man's place is in the kitchen,' I said one day. 'No, ma, no. This is not possible. A man cannot work in the kitchen.' The discussion went on until everyone was on their feet, expressing horror at my suggestion and, more importantly, screaming at me in English. They got so worked up that teachers appeared from neighbouring classrooms to watch. In the annual debate between the girls from my school and Bill's boys, the girls won hands down.

Our students were studying for the West African School Certificate, but within the curriculum there were some weird obsessions, one of which was idioms. Nigerians seemed to think that sprinkling their speech or prose with idioms was a sign of being well-educated and the most bizarre examples cropped up in conversation, usually out of context. My pupils were given long lists of idioms to learn by heart. *To cut one's coat according to one's cloth* or *There's many a slip 'twixt cup and lip* were easy to explain, but for some strange reason their favourite was *Go tell it to the marines*. The prefaces they wrote to written work delighted me: *Now I take up my golden biro* was a favourite, but one of the best I encountered was *Happiness is the pen that jump on this missive, and joy is brain that thought what to write.*

While I was making some progress with my students and teaching in a relatively organised environment, Bill's life was fragmented by frequent visits to Sokoto. As head of the English department, he had endless bureaucratic demands to meet, many of which could only be resolved by completing further paperwork at the Ministry of Education. He would be away three or four days at a time, arriving home physically exhausted from the journey and mentally worn down by the familiar chaos of the Ministry.

Exams at Haliru Abdu were a nightmare: students would register but fail to turn up; others would expect to participate without having registered; teachers entered students for exams in subjects they had never studied. The blustering vice principal, Mr George, would shout at students and teachers alike, adding to the general mayhem. 'Only foreign teachers are to invigilate,' he announced one day. 'Invigilators must be graduates.' It was an insult not lost on the Nigerian staff, many of whom had degrees. Prior to the exams, teachers went through the papers with the boys, hinting at the answers. 'Well, they're *our* boys, aren't they?' Bill was told with a wink. Bill's refusal to help students cheat made him unpopular and they ran after him throwing stones and shouting, 'Go back to your country.' At the end of our second year of teaching, late at night before the national finals, a Filipino teacher sloped up to our doorway, clutching exam papers the principal had removed from the vault at the bank. 'So you can give the boys the questions and answers before the exam,' she told Bill. He sent her away.

Despite Bill's frustration with teaching conditions, some of the drama and intrigue which confronted him daily provided us with endless amusement. Students were regularly issued with soap powder for doing their laundry. A member of staff had been punished for stealing 20 packets of Omo, but the pupils came up with a more subtle plan for making money. In Nigeria most meals included *garri* – dough balls made from cassava flour. The students bulked up some washing powder with *garri* and tried to sell it through the fence to the army wives at the barracks next door. The young go-between was accosted and eventually the older culprits acknowledged the part they had played. The Omo mixed with *garri* was impounded as evidence and labelled: *Awaiting appropriate action from the principal.*

The case of the missing genitals was the strangest of all. The misappropriation took place outside the mosque when a student had felt a hand on his shoulder and simultaneously noticed the absence of his manhood. He reported this to the police who arrested a bystander and charged him with genital theft. The duty master, Bill's friend Shehu Aduack, was summoned from the school. After a doctor had examined the victim and given him 'treatment', the accused was released and charges dropped. All this was reported in the staff duty book alongside mundane events like roll call and sporting activities. Bill, bewildered, discussed the accusation with Shehu. 'I examined the student myself,' he told Bill. 'I did think there might be something amiss, but I didn't know what the boy had looked like beforehand. I was in no position to pass judgement.' 'Perhaps the boy's testes had retracted,' suggested Bill. 'Such things are not unheard of.' Shehu was doubtful. 'Many Nigerians believe that witch doctors go from town to town, robbing men of their genitals,' he said. 'Shaking hands or touching a shoulder in a crowded

Above: drinking with the bank clerks
at Dukku Hill Bar; and dancing bone-
to-flesh with Thomas.
Right: with Alan and family at Zuru.
Below: Canadian volunteer Jean.

Below left: John, our VSO friend at Bunza. *Below right:* with Moses the thorn carver.

*Above left: setting off on our first trip, December 1979. **Above right:** Jack McGory, Niamey, Niger.*
Below: pirogues on the riverbanks, Pont Kennedy , Niamey – our transport downstream to the village of Say.

*Below: travelling in Upper Volta, **(left)** with Austrians on a Trans-Saharan trip, **(right)** in an open truck.*

market place can be enough. It's also an easy way to get rid of anyone unpopular.' We learned that in 1975 more than 20 people in Kano were accused of genital theft and lynched.

One day we heard that a rabid dog had been shot in town. When Mike Rush's dog began to act strangely one vet said it had rabies, but another disagreed. The argument lasted two weeks, at the end of which Mike insisted his dog be put down. 'Please cut off its head and send it to Sokoto for analysis,' Mike urged, but they ignored him. Mike refused to let the matter drop and eventually they chopped off the dog's head and despatched it. 'When do you expect the report?' queried Mike. 'Dis ting take time,' they said. 'Some weeks; maybe one month.' The delay rendered Mike's precaution pointless.

The next drama involved six lorry loads of cement which had gone missing between Lagos and Birnin Kebbi. An aerial search of the route was conducted, but the culprits and the cement were discovered near to home. They were people we knew, Nigerian contractors who had stolen the cement in order to build a new Anglican church for Birnin Kebbi! They had even donated a portion of cement to the Roman Catholic church, where a wall had mysteriously sprung up the previous week. The thieves lost their jobs, but we never discovered whether the clergy concerned saved them from jail, or indeed Hell. If you knew the right people, prison was not that serious. Only the week before, our friend Sonny had been jailed in Niger for running whisky across the border; his friends paid a dash to the guard and he was immediately released.

By the time our first Christmas vacation came round, we were more than ready for a break, but the school holidays were short. 'We might be able to make it as far as Ghana,' I ventured. 'Come part of the way with me,' said Jean who had a car, and we readily agreed.

On the Road Again

When we set off in Jean's beetle for Niger, it was John who drove, with Jean in the passenger seat and Bill and I crammed in the back. Once across the border, we travelled north through desert scenery and adobe villages until we reached Niamey. There were few American Peace Corps volunteers in town so we obtained permission to stay a couple of nights in their hostel and it was there that we met a good-looking young American called Jack who was making his way across Africa. With shortish hair, warm brown eyes and a straightforward manner he was instantly likeable, a smooth type of traveller rather than what we would then have termed a freak. Bill was impressed. 'He's travelled in even more countries than you have,' he teased me.

An ex-French colony, Niger felt different from Nigeria. We gorged ourselves on baguettes, camembert, yoghurt and cheap beer. The centre of Niamey was full of contradictions: luxury hotels towering above shacks; modern roads and bridges clogged with swaying convoys of camels; fashionable French expatriates rubbing shoulders with nomads and dishevelled travellers who had emerged from the desert. The backstreets were similar to Sokoto, wide sandy spaces dominated by Sahel architecture and dirt roads lined with neem trees.

After a day or two, John and Jean departed for the coast and Bill and I decided to travel down the river Niger with American Jack. There were a dozen or so *pirogues* moored by the bank just below Pont Kennedy. People hung about ready to transport goods downriver: bundles of hay, calabashes, chickens and goats. While waiting for a space on a canoe and for the boatman to find further passengers, I fell for the oldest trick in the book. A peddler approached with a tray of oils and perfumes in tiny bottles. He unscrewed the tops so I could sniff them, chatting and making a fuss of me, and while I sat enthralled, his accomplice picked my pocket. By the time the hawker had departed my purse and passport were missing. We found the latter discarded on the ground, but my cash and travellers' cheques, half the amount allocated for our trip, were gone. I was not only furious at my own stupidity, but deeply embarrassed that this should have happened in front of Jack, the globe-trotter, and Bill who until then had supposed I was a seasoned traveller. We were left with hardly any money. 'Shall we go on, or shall we go back?' I asked Bill.

It was the first test of our marriage. 'We'll go on, of course,' he said and I heaved a sigh of relief; I had married the right man.

We boarded a *pirogue* and set off down the Niger with Jack and three or four Africans. The sun glanced off the water, fishermen waved as we passed, and our boatman sang. The river banks were lush with vegetation: palms and fruit trees, long green grass and reed beds. Once the sun had set it turned cold and we snuggled down in our sleeping bags, huddling close in the moonlight.

We had been travelling a while when our boatman nosed up a narrow channel between high reeds. 'Bogart and Hepburn,' whispered Bill. We docked at a settlement where one of our passengers disembarked and a couple of men appeared with paraffin lamps and started unloading goods. High on the river bank we could see the outlines of thatched huts and dancing villagers silhouetted against a large fire. As our canoe slipped away, the throbbing of drums echoed across the water and we were swallowed up by the night.

Shortly after midnight we stopped at the village of Say, where we curled up in our sleeping bags on the river bank. We awoke at dawn to find women bathing and washing clothes at the water's edge; horses decked out in embroidered saddles and harnesses being led to drink; fishermen in small dug-outs floating among the reeds and lilies. The sun rose over the river and the mist dissipated slowly as the day warmed. Say was a large settlement with substantial mud houses surrounded by palms. Piles of large terracotta pots decorated with black and white bands dominated the market. Small children ran after us shouting, '*Fofo! Fofo!*' the Zarma greeting meaning 'Hello!' 'What on earth are we doing in Nigeria when we could be in a beautiful place like this?' asked Bill.

We stayed with a Peace Corps volunteer who was trying to break the stranglehold the Alhaji traders had on the place. 'All they bring in is onions and yams,' he said. 'I'm trying to set up a co-operative so the villagers can get some decent food, more variety.' It was 15 years on from the time I had spent in India with so many Peace Corps friends and sometimes I wondered at the efficacy of the organisation; after all, fish was readily available in Say, as well as goat meat. Bill and I had held a similarly arrogant view when we had first seen our students' school dinners in Birnin Kebbi, but with hindsight their menu was perfectly healthy: a tiny knob of meat, *garri* or yam, and a few green leaves. However well-intentioned the Peace Corps project in Say, it felt to me that western values were being imposed on a community which did not really need them. The big men – Alhajis – would always win out anyway.

Our plan had been to travel downstream into Benin, the neighbouring country, but the boatmen began requesting sums which were way beyond our means. If we had persevered we could probably have negotiated a favourable rate, but we were in a hurry, the Christmas break being the shortest holiday of the school year. Sadly we decided to get a Ford transit bus back to Niamey and from there hitch to the coast. I was desolate when Jack waved us off at the lorry park; I thought we would never see him again.

We hitched a lift to the coast with Daniel, a one-armed Frenchman who drove like a maniac. Sitting beside him was his stunning Malian wife Fanta, her long braids threaded with beads. They were a genial, amusing couple and he was besotted with her. He stopped the car so she could go for a pee in the bush. 'Look at 'er, just look at 'er,' he said. 'She moves like a cat, *comme un chat!*' Daniel proved strangely evasive about where they were travelling and why. '*Ce n'est pas important,*' he said with a Gallic shrug. He was equally cagey about his profession, giving the impression his mission was clandestine. We ascertained that he crisscrossed borders with surprising regularity and he informed us about the easiest, sleepiest border crossings. 'It is useful to know these things,' he said. 'I wonder what he's smuggling?' mused Bill later.

We whizzed through the People's Republic of Benin at breakneck Daniel-pace, catching our first glimpse of a Marxist-Leninist regime. When we stopped at traffic lights kids shouted '*Bonjour camarade,*' through the car window. We passed giant hoardings showing militant farm workers and factory girls marching with red flags. 'You make a phone call in Benin,' said Daniel, and they answer '*Vive la revolution!*'

And you 'ave to reply, 'May the struggle continue!"

We arrived in Lomé, the capital of Togo, in time for Christmas. With its large covered markets and peeling French colonial houses, it was attractive in a seedy, run-down sort of way. There were palm-lined streets and miles of sandy shore where massive breakers rolled in relentlessly, fishermen in giant dug-outs flying landwards on the crest of the waves. 'Christmas on the beach!' I said delighted. 'I'm not so sure,' said Bill. 'There's shit everywhere.' The following day around 7am we were to witness what seemed like half the population of Lomé, squatting, gazing out to sea, and laying their turds of the morning. I thought back to India and my dawn scooter rides to the factory with Walter past all the defecating people. 'That's what happens when people lack proper sanitation,' I said. 'If you haven't any toilets, you go in the countryside or, in this case, on the beach.'

Eventually we found a crap-free stretch and spent four days relaxing on the sand and cavorting in the surf with Jean and various other volunteers who had congregated in the city for Christmas. 'Where's John?' we asked Jean, surprised at his absence. 'He's fallen in love with an African hairdresser,' she said. 'We stopped in a small town for the night. He met the girl in a bar. I waited for him for two days and then gave up.' She laughed. 'I guess I'll have to look for him on the way back!'

Our Christmas Day began at one minute past midnight when a local church blasted us out of our beds with an announcement over a loudspeaker: 'Twenty-four yuletide favourites played on the Hammond organ by Mantovani!' The tunes, with standard West African distortion, were belted out until 3am. Beer and food in Togo was dirt cheap, but we had hardly any money and still had to make it back to Nigeria. After a Christmas dinner of bread and tinned sardines, Bill's stomach started playing up and he took to his bed. Since our arrival in Africa he had suffered frequently from diarrhoea and had become incredibly thin. Much to his embarrassment, this condition had been monitored by a beautiful Filipino girl responsible for analysing stools at Birnin Kebbi hospital. Now, in Togo, Bill needed to sleep and so I set out alone to explore the city – not a bad place but certainly not very festive. I sat by myself in a park and had a beer beneath the palms. A young American guy approached me. 'Happy Christmas,' he said grinning. 'I've got a present for you.' A chat-up line, but what he produced was a rarity, a chocolate bar large enough to make Father Peter's mouth water!

The next day Bill was feeling better. The border with Ghana had been closed because of imminent elections in Togo, so we set off north, hitching rides on trucks bound for Upper Volta (now renamed Burkina Fasso). We passed beautiful villages nestling among palm groves, groups of circular huts with pointy, intricately-woven thatched roofs. It was a land of tropical flowers, lush vegetation and distant blue mountains. We explored markets, spent the night in cheap African hotels, and talked in French to friendly people who asked us about Nigeria. Most of the indigenous population were dark-skinned, blue-black, and I thought of my Togolese friend, Vincent, in Addis Ababa.

The people we encountered talked politics. The sole candidate standing in the election was General Eyadema who had been president of Togo since 1967. Renowned for his great ego, his electioneering involved an entourage of 1000 dancing women who sang his praises. He smiled down on us from posters on hoardings, walls, and shops. Having survived a plane crash, he marketed himself as a super-hero, featuring in a nationally-produced comic book. When Bill and I reached northern Togo, the area from which the president originated, we witnessed a group of his supporters rehearsing political dances and songs for the forthcoming election. 'Away with Imperialism,' they sang. 'Welcome freedom! Vote Eyadama!' Afterwards we spent an enlightening evening with students from this group, drinking beer and talking about politics and life in Togo. Eyadema's despotic rule was to keep the country in a stranglehold for decades.

All national borders were to remain closed until after the election and we were unable to cross into Upper Volta. Amidst the jam of vehicles stranded on the Togo side, we came across a truck which had been converted into a camper for crossing the desert. Inscribed on the side in large letters was AUSTRIA-SAHARA-WESTAFRIKA, with the same legend written beneath in Arabic. The Sahara-crossers were a group of young, left-wing Austrians which included a station master, a midwife and a teacher. We found our new friends stimulating and we talked for hours. 'They're so young and so confident,' I remarked to Bill, when they dropped us off in Upper Volta a couple of days later. However, they were about to be swallowed up by the desert, where they got lost, ran out of fan belts and were stranded so long that they had to ration food and water. They made it home, but the Sahara had put such a strain on their relationships that their co-operative in Austria foundered. *The days with you were some of the most enjoyable of the whole trip,* wrote one of the girls. Perhaps under the circumstances that was not surprising.

The last leg of our journey back to Niamey was rough, 26 hours in an open truck and the most uncomfortable trip of my entire life. A new road was under construction, but only the first layer of corrugated cement had been laid. Deep rigid furrows caused the overloaded vehicle and everyone inside to judder nonstop. There were 20 or so passengers in the lorry – Ghanians, Nigerians and Togolese – but no seats. One or two people sat on their bundles or on small metal trunks, but most people, including ourselves, were flung into a heap of bodies, cooking pots and livestock. When one person shifted, we all shifted, and our trapped limbs seized up. Occasionally we would scale the narrow ridges of wood which supported the interior of the lorry, balancing precariously, our hands clutching desperately at the top of the truck, in order to get a bit of air and to stretch our legs. The only stop en route to Niamey was a hamlet of half a dozen dwellings, one of which served as a bar. The barman tendered the warm African hospitality we had come to expect, providing us with food and letting us sleep the night on a mat on the floor of his house.

We only spent one night in Niamey. Before we knew it we were back at school for the new term, but our glimpse of four West African countries had whetted our appetite for further exploration.

CHAPTER ELEVEN

IN THE STEPS OF EXPLORERS

Summer term

A MAN WITH A BUCKET OF PAINT was sploshing his way up the drive which led to the Women Teachers' College. The stones which lined the route were whitewashed regularly, particularly on special occasions. Painting stones white was a national preoccupation which not only delineated territory but also made the approach to any establishment look neat and official, belying the reality inside. The man ambled along in the heat and as he painted each rock he splattered the whitewash on the surrounding soil, leaving a mottled trail in his wake.

As he was putting the finishing touches to the stones, another man appeared, wobbling along the drive on a bicycle, his back bent beneath a large sack. His dilapidated bike swerved dangerously close to the painted rocks and the vice principal, who had come to inspect the work, was furious. 'Careful for those stones,' she growled. 'It is fresh paint for Speech Day tomorrow!' The cyclist juddered to a halt, took the sack off his back and threw it to the ground whereupon it took on a life of its own, writhing on the pathway. '*Maciji*,' he announced. 'Three! Three snakes for school science exhibition. You want snakes?' The vice principal declined the offer and sent him packing. She knew he was from the nearby village of snake charmers, who were occasionally paid to remove serpents from the school compound. Yet it was never long before teachers would report further sightings. 'I'm sure that snake man comes back at night,' said Bill, 'releases the captured snakes, then charges to remove them again the next day!'

Preparations for the annual Speech Day were intense. Each school house had its own stand and as house mistress I had to provide decorations for ours. 'Use toilet paper,' advised one of the teachers. 'Good for making flowers.' I spent the day with the girls turning pink and white toilet paper into blossoms which were then suspended on strings from bright orange plastic colanders borrowed from the home economics department. Other garlands were strung across the top of the stage, wonkily spelling out 'Crowther House' in what looked like pink roses. 'Beautiful, ma,' sighed the girls who had assisted me. The great day dawned and the Waziri sat on the central stage in his flowing robes, embroidered boots and trousers, surrounded by flowers which were fast disintergrating due to an unseasonal shower the previous night. Speeches were made in splendidly misused English and a brief whirlwind whipped the prizes skywards sending the students in hot pursuit.

We had been in Nigeria a year. Despite the inadequacies of the system, I enjoyed the teaching and I loved my girls: Hassi – naughty, cheeky and little more than a child, who was promised in marriage to an elderly Alhaji; Patricia – a bold southern girl, bright but lazy, inclined to snooze with her head on the desk; Susan – clever, courteous, conventional, the only Jehovah's Witness I encountered in Africa; and beautiful Bosede – serious, affectionate, always responsible, on whom I relied to help me restore order and sort out the library. I had fun with them and because I hammed things up in the classroom they liked me, my antics appealing to their sense of drama. The head girl, however, remained aloof. A bulky young woman, swathed in cloth, she moved like a ship in full sail. Quiet and self-contained, she was revered by her fellow pupils, not because of her senior role, but because she was so fat. 'Isn't she beautiful, ma?' the girls would say. 'So beautiful!' In Africa obesity is often considered attractive.

My extra-curricular duties remained onerous. One of my responsibilities was the school library. I worked for hours trying to put the place in order: discarding books eaten by termites, cleaning, labelling the stacks, putting up pictures. It was a reasonably well-stocked library which included one or two quirky colonial discards, such as *Homemaking 1920*, and a preponderance of English classics, but which was sadly lacking in books with any African content. Bill's school library had only three shelves of books and a full-time librarian who had nothing to do. My school had hundreds of books, but no librarian. I began to feel I might be getting somewhere when some of the students came to me requesting books.

In addition to preparing and marking lessons for five classes of 25 girls, supervising teaching practice, being a house mistress and running the library, I also had to edit the school magazine, run the Red Cross club and arrange film screenings. I wrote off to the International Red Cross for first aid leaflets and posters and while I awaited their arrival I dredged up first aid memories from my girl guide days. My pupils would turn up wearing white overalls and small red crosses pinned to their hair and couldn't wait to leap onto the bed, feigning illness and taking each other's pulses. Editing the school magazine was time-consuming and a waste of time as my amendments were ignored, but films proved popular when they arrived sporadically from the British Council. I put considerable effort into these responsibilities and most evenings I was working until at least 10pm.

The girls' acting skills and role play were not confined to the classroom. Each school house put on annual plays. The standard was excellent, not least because the subject matter was devised by the girls and improvised. One performance depicted the colonial rape of Africa, but cleverly the resources being plundered were bananas. The white men, played by my girls dressed in military fatigues and helmets, demanded bananas from the African king. 'Bananas,' they kept shouting. 'Give us your bananas, all your bananas!' White people walk, talk and sit in a different way to Africans, and to my surprise the girls had got the white man's casual stance down to a T; they sprawled on their chairs, legs splayed or with one leg up, at a right angle to the other, the ankle resting on the opposite knee. The second play was a comedy about a girl who was wearing western clothes and trying to break the news of her pregnancy to her traditionally attired parents. It had everyone rolling in the aisles.

A welcome diversion from everyday school life was a four-day educational trip by coach to Kainji Dam with 60 fifth form girls, supervised by Florence, my Nigerian friend from the National Youth Service Corps; Mr Bajpai, the Indian teacher; and me. After spending their days confined to the school compound, the girls ran amok. No sooner had we driven out of the gates, than any Islamic decorum was dispensed with. 'Out of our way!' they shouted from the coach windows. 'Out of our way! We're the heavy chicks from BK!' They went on to create disturbances in every town we visited, as well as in a game reserve where they jumped from the parked bus and chased a baboon into the bush. As for Kainji Dam, they weren't the slightest bit interested. Built across the river Niger and completed a decade before, the dam was intended to generate power for most of Nigeria, but having experienced power cuts for months on end, I was not convinced of its success. What did interest me, however, was the site itself at New Bussa. The old town of Boosa, which had been inundated when the dam was built, had been familiar to the famous explorers tracing the course of the Niger: Scotsmen Mungo Park and Hugh Clapperton, Cornishman Richard Lander, all of whom had eventually perished in their quests. I gazed into the depths below the dam and thought of these intrepid adventurers and the extraordinary hardships they had encountered on that very spot.

Back in the classroom it wasn't always plain sailing. As the temperature rose, sometimes reaching 40°C in the shade, we sweltered. With frequent power cuts there was no relief from fans, and the students' attention span became shorter and shorter. They made a great show of wiping their brows, fanning themselves with exercise books, and moaning. 'Too much heat, ma. Too hot for studies. We need sleep, ma.' However, there were always some lessons which grabbed their attention and there were a few students in each class who made all my efforts worthwhile and who appeared to learn something.

Occasionally both Bill and I would receive an accolade from a pupil: 'You're the best teacher,' they would say, 'the best we have ever had,' and Bill and I would rush home and relate this phenomenon to each other.

When this happened everything suddenly seemed worthwhile. The whole crazy place with its substandard education, insane bureaucracy and corruption, its floggings and inefficiency, would fade into oblivion before the eager, smiling face of a single boy or girl – a child we had managed to help and who had bothered to thank us.

Towards the end of the school year we heard that one of the old colonial houses at my school was becoming vacant. None of the Nigerian or Asian teachers wanted to live in such old-fashioned accommodation, but we loved the place. With yet another street of jerry-built houses being added to the Haliru Abdu community and everywhere strewn with rubble and rubbish, we jumped at the opportunity of moving elsewhere. Our request for a transfer to the house at WTC was granted and as soon as term finished, we moved our belongings into our new home. 'You'll be able to make it comfortable over the school holidays,' said the vice principal, smiling. In theory we were meant to remain on the school premises during the holidays, but Bill and I had ambitious travel plans for the summer break – our proposed destination, Timbuktu.

Heading for the desert

We were in Niger once again, but before setting off for Timbuktu, we indulged briefly in the luxuries available in Niamey – French food and a swimming pool frequented by bronzed French expatriates. One day we explored *Le Grand Marché* with its Tuareg locks, knives and jewellery, where an old man in the hardware section changed our money on the black market at an excellent rate. We were just congratulating ourselves on the deal, when a gargantuan brown cloud loomed over the city, stacking up higher and higher, eclipsing the sun and the light. 'Where on earth's that appeared from?' I said, and seconds later the sandstorm hit. Choking and coughing, with grit needling our eyes and sand whipping our faces, we dived into a taxi which drove slowly through the murky streets back to our hotel. No sooner had we arrived than we were hit by a deluge. Rain fell all night, the drains backed up, merging with sewers

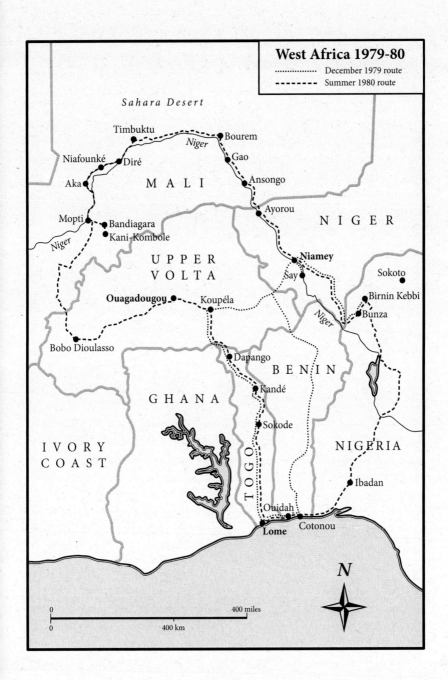

West Africa 1979-80

.... December 1979 route

- - - - - Summer 1980 route

Sahara Desert

Timbuktu
Bourem
Niger
Gao
Niafounké
Diré
Ansongo
Aka
M A L I
Ayorou
N I G E R
Mopti
Bandiagara
Kani-Kombole
Niger
U P P E R
V O L T A
Niamey
Say
Sokoto
Ouagadougou
Koupéla
Birnin Kebbi
Bunza
Niger
Bobo Dioulasso
Dapango
B E N I N
G H A N A
Kandé
Sokode
I V O R Y
C O A S T
T O G O
N I G E R I A
Ibadan
Ouidah
Cotonou
Lome

N

0   400 miles

0   400 km

until we were stifled by the stench.

We were staying at the Domino, a lively lodging house with half a dozen rooms and a bar. Le Patron conducted business from a mattress on the floor, sprawling drunkenly in front of his television set. The bar was illuminated by flashing pin-ball machines and a flickering neon light above the pool table. As the waitresses replenished beers, slopping lethargically from table to table in the outside yard, Beatles songs crackled from an ancient tape recorder. Skeletal cats slunk in and out gleaning scraps, and an aristocratic-looking Tuareg moved among the clientele, hawking leather wallets and swords. 'I wonder what he was doing before this?' said Bill, eyeing up the regal man of the desert. 'Surely it must have been less demeaning than this,' I said.

For a few days we frequented small bars in Niamey where we made friends and acquaintances. Young men from Niger who had studied in France were the most enlightening. Our favourite was Ben. 'We were all subjected to racism in Paris,' he said. 'Sometimes they asked us if back at home we lived in trees, the usual monkey cliché, but most of the time their derogatory comments were more subtle. We were not welcome in France.' Over numerous beers he talked to us about Niger. 'Independence is only superficial,' he told us. 'Our financial commitments to France are enormous. We're rich in minerals, but France takes 50% as if we were still a colony – 50% of the uranium mined, for example.' Educated, outgoing and bright, Ben was determined to change things. 'It won't be easy,' he admitted. 'Religion is almost as big an obstacle as our continuing attachment to France.'

We needed visas for Mali and were directed up a backstreet reeking of piss, to a two-roomed shed which served as the Consulate of Mali. Inside we found ourselves surrounded by herdsmen, some of them mere boys. One youth was standing with his back to the wall being measured by the consul, who was scratching a biro line on the wall above the lad's head. Shepherds squatted in corners or stretched out full length on the floor awaiting their turn. '*Pour les cartes d'identité,*' the consul explained. We waited until everyone had been documented, then watched as they grabbed their staves, whipped a bit of cloth over their heads, drawing the ends across their mouths, and stepped outside. The consul turned to us. '*Alors, Gao?*' he enquired. '*Oui, Gao.*' We were determined to get to Timbuktu, but it wasn't politic to mention our destination at this stage. '*Sept jours*,' he said, stamping our passports. We would have to extend our visas in Timbuktu – assuming we made it that far.

At the Domino one night we met Jonathan and David, VSO lads working in Gongola State, Nigeria. They were also planning to visit Timbuktu, but were flying there on one of the small aircraft that braved the desert. In private we were sarcastic about people who flew. 'They don't see the real Africa,' we would say smugly, even though our own method of travel meant hanging about in lorry parks for hours awaiting a full complement of passengers. One night the VSO boys came running into the hotel. 'There's a bus about to depart for Mali,' they told us. 'We've told the driver to wait for you.' We grabbed our bags and ran to the bus, where we squeezed into a tiny space on a badly-broken seat, our knees wedged painfully against the back of the chair in front. More and more passengers were levered in. The old woman behind us screamed as her legs were crushed. Everyone was shouting and fighting and transistor radios blared. It was dark, agonisingly uncomfortable, and smelly. 'There's no way I'm staying on this bus for two days,' announced Bill suddenly. 'No way!' I was furious. It was the kind of journey I saw as a test of real travelling, and what's more, we had already bought our tickets. Bill ignored my objections and began climbing out of the window, the only possible exit. Reluctantly, I followed. As it turned out, our trip the following day would prove far more interesting than any bus journey.

We had decided to hitchhike from the police post on the outskirts of the city and within a short time we got a ride in a Land Rover with an agricultural statistician working for the UN Food and Agriculture Organisation. He was conducting a survey in the Djerma villages along the banks of the Niger and was using *lycée* students from Niamey to complete his questionnaires. To reach these outposts our vehicle had to ford the river, drive through swamps and traverse rough terrain.

Naked pot-bellied children approached us nervously as we arrived at each settlement, edging closer as their curiosity got the better of them. The word would spread fast and by the time we were ready to leave each village, children would be swarming along the paths towards us. As we travelled north we began to pass through beautiful riverside towns and Tuareg encampments until, mid-afternoon, the FAO driver deposited us at a place called Ayorou.

We were only 200km north of Niamey, but already the countryside had become arid and round grass huts had been replaced by the square-faced adobe buildings of the Sahel. We watched canoes arriving from island villages, women washing clothes in the river, and men carrying water in jerrycans hanging from yokes. Two small boys approached us, reeled off the capital cities and presidents of the world, and enquired whether a third world war was imminent; they had read a newspaper article about the power struggle between the Soviet Union and the USA. These poverty-stricken primary school children knew far more than any teenager in our Nigerian teacher training colleges; our students didn't even know the names of other African countries or where Nigeria was on the map. The little boys asked how old we were and were fascinated by the fact I was older than Bill. One of them, Ali, scratched a quick sum with a stick in the sand and informed us that I was half as much again as Bill in age! He had a horribly twisted leg. 'Rickets?' I whispered to Bill. We told him we were teaching in Nigeria and he clicked his tongue in disapproval. '*On dit que le Nigéria est plein de voleurs!*' he said. We gave the boys some coins and Ali hopped up and down with glee on his crippled leg, while the smart young men hanging around the nearby trucks laughed at him.

We boarded a public transport Hiace and arrived at a check-post early in the evening. Once everyone's baggage had been searched, we had to stay put until morning. We spread our sleeping bags on the dirt road beneath a half-moon and watched the other travellers camped out around the stationary *camions*: some brewed tiny glasses of tea; old men wailed and prayed; lads sprawled across a car bonnet, tapping their feet to music on the radio. Fire-flies darted overhead and we slept badly.

At crack of dawn we set off, following the course of the Niger. The sun glanced off the water and a shadow-show of *pirogues* sliced the silver light. The road deteriorated and we joined the other passengers in pushing the vehicle, or else walking behind as it inched its way across streams and ditches, navigating the rubble of collapsed bridges. The day grew hotter and hotter. Any residue of calm inside the vehicle blistered and erupted into discord. A dock worker from Lagos harassed a young woman who was travelling with her daughter and new-born twins. A little later he began goading a quiet old Hausa man who exploded in wrath, shouting and stabbing the air with his forefinger. Furious passengers joined the fray, shouting above the crying babies and clattering of the vehicle. The man sitting next to us sang quietly to himself, ignoring the ructions. Occasionally we would grind to a halt in the middle of nowhere so someone could disembark. An elderly man headed off with mats and pots stacked upon his head, his figure dark against the glare and sand, walking tall into the empty distance. His fat, sullen wife watched him start off, then heaved herself up from the roadside and plodded after him. Eventually we came upon a broken-down bus. 'It's our Niamey bus,' exclaimed Bill, trying not to look smug, 'the one we escaped from.'

Finally we crossed into Mali, stopping briefly at the beautiful village of Ansongo. We installed ourselves in a café, revived ourselves with river-water-coffee, scoffed a plate of rice, and observed the desert men gliding past in their spotless robes and turbans. 'However do they keep so pristine in all this mud and dust?' I asked Bill. The final leg of the journey was on sand and as the sun set we began to see oval pod houses woven from reeds. Fires burned outside and livestock were tethered for the night. Then suddenly the wind whipped up and we lurched on in the dark, battered by a sandstorm. After more police checks, and a huge punch-up between the aggressive docker and some men sleeping in the road, we limped into Gao, a city of decaying elegance lapped by the Sahara.

We were waiting for the blind man. Every day we listened for the tap-tap-tap of his stick on the stone floor. Gao's fixer, he frequented our hotel, *l'Atlantide*, offering anything you could possibly want – a woman, a man, a camel, an obscure souvenir, transport. What we needed was a lift across the Sahara to Timbuktu, but negotiating without eye contact made it difficult to assess his trustworthiness. Our request wasn't easy; it was the rainy season and vehicles were getting stuck in the desert.

The town was a vast sand-blown waiting room. Those who lingered were hoping to cross the desert or else were waiting for someone to emerge from its wastes intact. People have always been stuck in Gao, from Ibn Battuta, the 14th-century Arab to Heinrich Barth, the 19th-century German, both famous explorers. Long ago, the city's prime location for trans-Saharan trade in salt and gold had rendered it the capital of two empires, but the Gao we saw was rundown and seedy. Elegant French colonial buildings with balconies and arabesque arches had been reduced to chipped stucco, broken shutters, smashed tiles and peeling paint. Away from the large houses, the wide sandy streets were lined with small shuttered shops, their dark interiors smelling of ginger and spices. The silver thread of the Niger was still in evidence, but the rains had only just started and the water was too low for anything but canoes. On the riverbank we found more pods made of woven reeds and matting. Dwellings mostly inhabited by fishermen, they resembled giant woodlice stranded on the shore.

One day as we entered our hotel we saw a grizzled man sprawled on the sofa in the lobby. He raised his head and regarded us out of bleary eyes. 'He looks like Donald Sutherland,' Bill observed. Caked with mud and oil, he wore a sweat-stained rag around his neck. 'I am waiting for my clothes,' he announced. His name was Roget and after a holiday in his native Switzerland, he was returning to the sugar plantation where he worked in Chad. Having set off across the Sahara with petrol, water and spare clothes strapped to his motorbike, he had come across some French lads driving Peugeot 404s and asked them to lighten his load. They agreed to take his baggage and deposit his cans of petrol at designated points en route. Somehow he had arrived in Gao ahead of them. 'This desert can send a man crazy,' said Roget. 'There's a madman out there, you know.' He gestured vaguely into the distance. 'I lost him in the desert. He kept running off into the dunes and I had to drag him back to the main track. He could no longer do something as simple as open a tin can.' Roget shook his head. 'Finally, only a few feet from the road, he decided he was lost and set fire to his only spare tyre to attract attention.' Roget paused. 'Then he disappeared,' he said. 'I lost him.'

The next morning when we arrived for breakfast, Roget had been joined by an equally dishevelled character named Jacques. The French lads' vehicles had run out of fuel, were stuck in dunes about 30km from town, and Jacques had walked in out of the desert to find Roget. When asked about the deranged youth, Jacques shrugged. '*Il a disparu*,' he said. 'Vanished!' echoed Roget, shaking his head in despair. 'The madman has vanished.' We watched as the two men loaded up with jerrycans of petrol to return to the desert on Roget's motorbike and refuel the cars. Roget, sporting old-fashioned goggles, now resembled the Red Baron. By evening they had returned, accompanied by some of the French drivers and later that night three more bedraggled men staggered into the hotel, including Serge, the mentally-disturbed youth; Günther a mild-mannered Bavarian with a plaited beard; and Raoul, a hippy who ran a garage in Ouagadougou. They had walked more than 40km to escape the desert. Over beers we all talked at cross-purposes in French and German and English, while Serge sat glowering, his eyes darting back and forth like a cornered animal.

The French youths were in their early twenties. The lure, apart from adventure, was that cars purchased in France or Algeria could be sold very profitably in West Africa. The drawback was that such vehicles were grossly inappropriate for the desert crossing. The courtyard at the hotel was now transformed into a makeshift garage where the battered, filthy cars were given a makeover to render them fit for sale.

Hotel *l'Atlantide*, Moorish in design and built in 1936, was a sprawling edifice run by a one-armed Arab matriarch. Besides the crazy desert-crossers, an array of eccentric characters thronged its corridors: Arabs, Africans, Tuaregs, small boys and souvenir-sellers. Moving among these disparate groups we were merely scratching the surface of the gossip and intrigue. It was the little boys who were the source of all knowledge; they even seemed to know what was going on far out in the desert. One of them, Idris, took us under his wing, introducing us to the mosque and tomb architecture unique to the West African Sahel – mud edifices where numerous sticks protrude from the earthen body of the structure. These serve as decoration, but also act as permanent 'scaffolding' for when the walls needed replastering with mud.

Once, during our rambles with Idris, we were invited into one of the pod-like huts on the river bank. Our host, a mournful old man, served us sweet tea in tiny glasses and described what the river was like when in full flood. He was 70, he told us, and then proudly introduced us to his pretty 14-year-old wife sitting beside him, a baby on her lap. A younger man, squatting on the dirt floor, brewing tea in a metal jug on charcoal, had a rather beautiful face but was clearly suffering from some kind of disease. We visited the pod a couple of times and so as not to insult their hospitality we tucked some money into the baby's hand. '*Un petit cadeau*,' we said awkwardly, but we were uncomfortable with the etiquette concerned, and depressed at the plight of the teenage mother with her ancient spouse.

Back at the hotel the blind man finally turned up trumps. He had located a 'friend', Yusuf, who had agreed to take us to Timbuktu. We had waited a week. It was our last night at *l'Atlantide* and a film was being screened in the hotel courtyard. A soap opera filmed in Niamey, it attacked corrupt Alhajis and questioned the status of African women. Despite the controversial content, the small boys were beside themselves with excitement, scaling the wall and cheering as the projector chugged along and the flickering images took shape on a screen beneath the starlit desert sky.

We were trussed up in a Land Rover. All the doors were broken, so Yusuf had used lengths of rope to hold the ramshackle vehicle together. Inside, 12 of us were wedged together in sweaty intimacy. I was the only woman. Our fellow-travellers included a strange Arab wearing a brown wig, another in traditional robes and headdress, an obese Alhaji, a self-important soldier and six loud-mouthed youths. The luggage stacked unevenly on the roof threw the Land Rover out of kilter, causing it to sway dangerously. The interior ceiling sagged low, scraping the passengers' heads. A large goatskin bag suspended on the outside of the vehicle contained our only supply of water.

Despite having careered through the palm trees on the outskirts of Gao, screeched around large pools of rainwater, and lurched precariously into the desert, the first leg of our journey went without mishap. After three hours we arrived at Bourem, a small town on the edge of the Niger, where we spent an uncomfortable night in the lorry park.

We set off again at dawn, everyone subdued and barely awake. Gradually sunlight washed the sand beneath a brightening sky and then something magical appeared: rising dream-like from the dunes was a substantial mud fortress. Part of its walls had disintegrated and yet it stood strong, a forgotten sentinel of the Sahara. 'The Foreign Legion!' I whispered to Bill, beside myself with excitement. 'It must have belonged to the Foreign Legion'. 'Beau Geste!' he agreed. I could imagine the French flag flying from the turret, the legionnaires on the march, their red breeches and caps bright against the sand. None of our fellow passengers commented on the fortress or even seemed to notice its presence. An ostrich disturbed by our engine emerged from the ruins, sprinting into the distance, shaking the feathers on its backside. We continued on our way leaving the remnants of colonial power to sink into the shifting sands.

Only Yusuf knew which bit of the vast desiccated landscape constituted a track – or so we thought. We had been travelling about an hour when we came to a roughly-hewn signpost indicating *Tomboucto* one way, and *Algérie* the other. To our astonishment we veered off in the direction of Algeria! 'He's going the wrong way!' I said to Bill. 'He must know what he's doing,' Bill replied doubtfully. 'We're hardly in a position to query his knowledge of the desert.' After a mile or so, it dawned on the other passengers that something was amiss. They began to gesticulate and shout at Yusuf and eventually the soldier managed to convince him that he had missed the turning. Bill and I heaved a sigh of relief as we changed direction and headed west towards Timbuktu.

For a while we traversed plains of flat rock, interspersed with dunes and shallow basins of sand harbouring a fragile fuzz of grass. The occasional stunted thorn tree broke the monotony, a spiky feast for a few errant goats. Once we disturbed a couple of warthogs which thundered off into the desert, creating a wake of dust.

The overburdened Land Rover screamed metal-on-metal as the suspension groaned and squeaked. When we crossed an unexpected ditch at speed, one of the rear tyres exploded like a gunshot and a fountain of rubber shot skywards. We all disembarked and sat on the scorching ground while Yusuf and one of the passengers struggled to change the tyre, the jack sinking again and again into the soft sand. 'As far as I can see, it's the only spare,' commented Bill, who had made a sneaky detour around the vehicle. 'No sign of another.' 'And we're only at the beginning of the journey,' I said.

The sun rose high and the day bore down on us – a searing, caustic, blinding glare. The lads turned on their radios blasting us with a cacophony of Arabic music. Bill took out his camera and the angry soldier pounced. 'I will take you to the police station in Timbuktu,' he threatened. 'I will open this camera and unroll the film to see if you have snapped me!' Our fellow-passengers were becoming unpleasant and irritable, the lads pointing at us and laughing. This sudden antagonism took us by surprise. Perhaps the intense heat had made people edgy or maybe they were taking their cue from the soldier.

Eventually the spare tyre was in place and we set off, lurching at a

Above: Gao, Niger, August 1980 **(left)** with Idris in the fisherman's hut; **(right)** colonial architecture.
Below left: Roget after his trans-Saharan motorbike journey; **(right)** resting on the road to Timbuktu, Mali.

Below left: approaching the outskirts of Timbuktu from across the desert. **Right:** Timbuktu mosque and well.

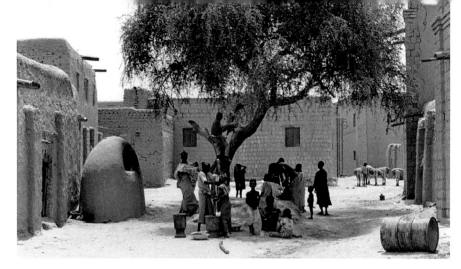

Top: *Timbuktu street life, pounding cassava beside the oven.*
Left: *the house of the trans-Saharan explorer DW Berky .*
Above: *posing with a Tuareg souvenir seller.*
Below left: *a tinned chicken picnic with David and Jonathan.*
Below right: *Général Soumaré finally arrives at Timbuktu.*

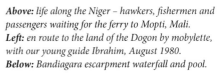

Above: life along the Niger – hawkers, fishermen and passengers waiting for the ferry to Mopti, Mali.
Left: en route to the land of the Dogon by mobylette, with our young guide Ibrahim, August 1980.
Below: Bandiagara escarpment waterfall and pool.

Above: *the thatched granaries of a Dogon village.*
Below: *the animists' dwellings built into the escarpment above Telli village.*

Above and below: *old postcards of Mopti, the impressive mud mosque and the fish market.*

hair-raising pace over deep sand. The elderly Alhaji kept pleading with Yusuf to slow down, but any protest was ignored. The boys in the back were exhilarated by the whole escapade, shrieking every time we went over a bump, deliberately clinging onto my hair and giggling when I tried to stop them. A couple of times we came across a lorry broken down in the desert and the drivers ran at us, begging for food and water. 'I guess we could end up dying out here,' said Bill wryly. 'That applies to our entire life in Nigeria,' I reminded him.

Our scorching desert journey continued and at the turn-off for Bamba, we dropped off the worst of the louts. The day had become hotter than I could bear, and I developed a splitting headache. Eventually we stopped in the spiky shadow of a thorn tree and the Alhaji and the bewigged Arab brewed up refreshing glasses of sweet spiced tea. '*Il va guérir votre mal de tête,*' said the old Alhaji kindly, stroking his brow to emphasise that my pain would be swept away. Within a few minutes of drinking his tea, my headache disappeared.

Towards the evening of the second day we began to pass Tuareg encampments, camels and donkeys at waterholes, dogs and children. We stopped at a well where a young man brought up water to replenish our goatskin sack. Swathed up against the desert, with only his beautiful eyes showing, this Adonis of the desert looked up and held my gaze briefly before reverting to his duties. My heart missed a beat.

As we neared Timbuktu the track was packed harder which enabled Yusuf to drive like the clappers. We were belting across the rutted sand in a cloud of dust, when the Land Rover suddenly tipped to one side, the rope came unknotted and one of the doors swung open. At the same time luggage shot off the roof. Everyone screamed at Yusuf and he screeched to a halt.

It was almost nightfall when we spied, silhouetted against a stormy sky, the low square blocks of buildings on the horizon. Timbuktu! Until that moment the city had been a figment of the imagination. 'From here to Timbuktu…' you would say, denoting a remote unattainable destination. Now we were approaching the fabled city which had lured explorers down the ages to risk life and limb. Our little excursion into the fringes of the desert was nothing compared to theirs, but for me it was a personal pilgrimage. Explorers had always been my heroes; that we were following in the footsteps of some of the most intrepid men in history filled me with awe.

The city of mystery

Visitors to Mali were strictly controlled by the tourist police, *La Société Malienne de Securité et Transit* – SMERT. It was an acronym which was to roll regularly off our tongues, as Mali's Big Brother became the bane of our existence. In Timbuktu there were only two tiny hotels where tourists were permitted to stay. We picked the first we came to, only to discover Jonathan and David, the VSO boys we had met in Niamey, sitting in the lobby. To celebrate our arrival the four of us indulged in a beer or two and the one and only expensive meal we were to eat in Mali, a dish designed for tourists. The hotel, which comprised half a dozen simple rooms and a tiny restaurant, was situated on the edge of town and a regular stream of Arabs, camels and Tuaregs passed our windows as they entered the city from the desert.

The following day we set out to find a cheap restaurant where locals ate, the kind of place we had visited all over West Africa. There was only one. It consisted of a single table in a hovel run by a prune of a man called Baba. '*J'ai travaillé comme chef à Paris*,' he announced unexpectedly. His food bore no resemblance to French cuisine, but in Timbuktu there were few ingredients on sale anyway. The fare he offered was barely edible and, like all food in Timbuktu, was full of sand. 'I can feel the grit in my teeth,' groaned Bill, grinding his way through the meal. Sand was not confined to food. It clogged our hair, eyes, ears, eyelashes and every orifice. The desert coated the entire city rendering us more granular and desiccated by the day.

At the time of our visit, tourism was astonishingly under-exploited. Timbuktu had once boasted Sankore University, the intellectual and spiritual capital of Islam. There had been nearly 200 Koranic Schools, 25,000 students, three giant mosques and vast libraries renowned for scholarship. It had also served as the cross-roads for trade in salt and gold, cattle and grain. Infidels had been barred from the city, thus enhancing the European view that it was an inaccessible enclave, a city of mystery and wonder. Despite its glittering history, we found no information for tourists. '*Où est le musée?*' we kept asking, but were told there was none. The ancient mud mosques were still standing, the signature sticks which supported the architecture protruding from the walls. We climbed to the top of one of these towers, but it revealed no secrets.

The town as we saw it had remained unchanged for centuries. The desert surrounded it like a vast ocean, sand dunes washing up against the buildings. The core harboured a labyrinth of sandy alleyways lined by adobe houses which featured the timeworn portals of the Islamic world, heavy doors studded with large-headed nails and metal discs. Occasionally an alluring beauty would glide past us, a shadow swathed in black with a whisper of veil across her mouth. In places where the streets fanned out into squares, grandmothers baked bread in oval clay ovens while children kicked balls and rolled in the dust.

As we explored the backstreets we stumbled across houses where some of the famous explorers had stayed – Laing, Berky, Barth, Caillié – dwellings which bore plaques erected by foreign governments staking a claim in history. Now the occupants of these houses were ordinary townsfolk whose chickens and children wandered in and out. SMERT had not capitalised on the extraordinary lives of the adventurers who had stayed there. In a way the lack of exploitation was commendable but as I stood in awe in front of the simple dwellings that had housed my heroes, I wondered if they had left anything behind, any tiny tangible trace of their presence.

The celebrated 14th-century world traveller, Moroccan Ibn Battuta, had made it to Timbuktu, as had the equally famous Berber diplomat, Leo Africanus, a century later. These were the people who saw the place in its heyday, a centre of erudition in an empire awash with gold. By the time the 19th-century European explorers arrived on the scene, the city had been reduced to the sandy outpost we were to encounter more than a century later. On arrival, some of these explorers had openly expressed their disappointment, undoubtedly accentuated by the fact they had gone through hell to reach their destination. Attacked by Tuareg tribes, surviving attempted murder, slavery and the physical hardship of the desert, some had travelled disguised as Muslims. Scotsman, Alexander Gordon Laing, the first European to reach Timbuktu, was murdered two days after leaving the city; Frenchman René Caillié made it home alive. Other 19th-century men were to follow: German Heinrich Barth who was more interested in African culture and languages than in commerce; Austro-German Oskar Lenz, a geologist, with Spaniard Cristobal Benitez, and at the beginning of the 20th-century DW Berky who led the first American trans-Saharan expedition. Perhaps SMERT regarded these visitors as mere blips on the temporal landscape, leaving their legends to be obliterated by the sands of time.

Where SMERT had failed, children had taken things into their own hands, and we were followed everywhere by scallywags offering to show us *le mystère de Tombouctou*. One boy took us inside his home where we drank the obligatory three glasses of tea as his mother tried to sell us a camel-skin handbag. It was dark inside the house, which had been constructed to shield the interior from direct sunlight. In our modern hotel room we nearly died of heat, but the simple mud dwellings inhabited by the populace were surprisingly cool. The children were not the only ones who had cashed in on the half-dozen tourists: a few tatty men fawned and whined, offering us swords, knives and pipes. We succumbed to one other home visit, where Bill took a photo of me sitting next to a robed man leaning casually on the sword he had been trying to sell us. Instead we purchased a slim Tuareg pipe which resembled a cigarette holder. Made of horn and striped with ebony and silver, I liked the fact that the inside was stained; it had been used.

Our plan had always been to continue our journey from Timbuktu to Mopti by river. The Niger had been the lifeline of all the villages we had passed since Niamey. Even though we had travelled through desert, the great river had never been that far away. Now, 20km south of Timbuktu, here it was again, curving like a silver scimitar before flowing south. Steamships could only travel when the river was swollen and the rains had come late. We made enquiries at the *Bureau de Navigation* and the *Gendarmerie* where officials shrugged and disseminated rumour: the steamer would arrive the next day; it had been forced to return to Mopti; it was beached on a sand bank. We had booked our boat tickets on arrival but, as in Gao, we were stuck.

Trapped in a maze of torrid alleyways and whipped into retreat by sand blowing off the dunes, we holed up in our hotel. Refreshment offered by SMERT remained beyond our means, but we had discovered Groot, Dutch tinned spam, which became our staple diet. One day in a store, we came across an ancient-looking tin containing chicken, a find which warranted a picnic. Sitting beneath a thorn tree, we opened the huge can to find an entire soft-boned bird inside.

At the end of our week in Timbuktu, excited children thronged the streets, pointing skywards, awaiting the crescent moon which would herald the festival of *Eid al Fitr*. Later that night, drumming lured us to the outskirts where people had gathered to watch tall, elegant, men dancing in the moonlight. Their movements were slow and dreamlike and as they twirled the hems of their robes lifted gracefully. Cloth wound tightly around their heads masked all but eyes, rendering them anonymous and somehow ethereal, like mythological *djinn* who inhabit the unseen world beyond the universe. After a while, as the drums quickened and the dancing became more frenzied, we slipped away, leaving behind a shadow-show lit by the desert moon. The following day the steamer arrived. As we left town and made our way towards the river, people were still celebrating, cocooned in a nest of dunes at the edge of the city.

One of the last great river steamers of Africa, the ship that awaited us had been built in Germany in 1918 and brought overland in sections by donkey and train. Renamed *Le Général Soumaré* in 1960, it honoured Mali's first post-independence chief of army staff. It had three decks and, despite its age, was in far better condition than the paddle steamer I had boarded in Sudan six years before. When *Le Général* arrived at Kabara, port for Timbuktu, we decided to lay claim to our cabin the night before we were due to sail. Having been smug about travelling overland to Timbuktu while Jonathan and David flew, we now found our roles reversed: they were slumming it on the bottom deck, while we opted to travel second class, in a four-berth cabin shared with a young French architect and a local policeman.

At dawn the following day, we leant over the railing on the top deck and watched passengers arriving from town. Trucks screeched to a halt unloading pots and pans, skins and blankets, cooking stoves, vegetables and a herd of goats which was dragged reluctantly up the gangplank and secured in the bow of the ship. The morning became hotter and still more people arrived, dragging and pushing their belongings, hanging on to children, clutching squawking chickens bound by their feet. Amidst shouting, laughter, and argument, wailing children and grumbling elders, everyone slowly settled, sinking down on the bottom deck. Having established their territory with a patchwork of straw mats, they began brewing tea and cooking.

At noon, with engines throbbing and bells clanging, *Le Général* cast off and we drifted slowly upstream. The flood plain on either side was a bare expanse of sand which bordered walled mud villages, each with its pyramidal stick-festooned mosque. In the evening we watched rays of duck-egg blue, yellow and lime-green fan out across the sky as the sun set. And then the moon rode high, sailing on a streak of royal blue.

Eight hours after leaving Timbuktu we docked at Diré in the dark. Steps down to the water's edge were lit by hurricane lamps. Sacks were hauled aboard. Household furniture was dragged precariously up the gangplank. We slipped ashore to buy bread and looked back on the ship looming above us like a Mississippi steamer, lights ablaze, music playing, people thronging the decks. We set sail after midnight with additional passengers, including a cohort of cops. For the next four days we steamed past villagers clad in brilliantly-patterned robes and extravagant head dresses, boys leading donkeys, naked children waving and shouting, and people sauntering along the river bank with giant pots on their heads. As the river widened, fishermen's pod-dwellings clung to the sandbanks midstream and sleek canoes sliced the water, ferrying goods and people.

Jonathan and David, hemmed in by the masses on the bottom deck, were becoming bleary-eyed, but Bill and I, as second-class passengers, had access to all decks. We drank beer in the first-class bar and danced beneath the stars, before descending to the real world far below where we talked with the lads and shared the ubiquitous Groot.

Before arriving at Mopti we docked at the villages of Niafounké and Aka, where children waded into the river carrying bowls of bread and fish upon their heads. A frenzy of splashing, shouting and bargaining ensued as our passengers stocked up with food. Men in ornate robes and shades punted past, observing the mayhem, and hawkers brought their canoes alongside, holding up mats and blankets woven by the Peul people. When we steamed past smaller villages without stopping, people would run to the water's edge to stare and wave. At night, when the upper deck was lit up and music floated across the water, we must have seemed like an elusive dreamboat, a mirage that passed by from time to time, but never stopped.

We reached Mopti at night, and made our way to Bar Mali. A labyrinth of rooms, bars and winding staircases, it was cheap accommodation which doubled as a brothel. After a beer or two, we ascended to the rooftop to sleep, but sounds of the mayhem below assailed us via the stairwell: drunken brawls, women shouting, shrieks of laughter, breaking glass. At 4am, as peace descended, the muezzin took over at the nearby mosque, blasting us into a new day with his wailing. Bar Mali was the star of all cat-houses: copulating couples glimpsed through doorways; drunks lying in the corridors among discarded bottles; the smell of urine pervading every nook and cranny. I loved the place for its craziness, its exuberance and blatant debauchery. The next morning found me queueing with the whores in front of the only two showers available for women. To my astonishment, an elderly white-haired English woman emerged from one of the cubicles. She smiled at me. 'Good morning, my dear,' she said. 'Lovely day isn't it?' and, without pausing, she sailed away up the corridor. 'I just hope I'm like that when I grow old,' I said to Bill.

Situated on the confluence of two rivers, Mopti flooded when the waters rose, reducing the town to a series of islands joined by causeways: '*La Venise de l'Afrique*,' we were told. After breakfast in a bar surrounded by reed beds and floating markets, we set off to explore the bustling town centre, dominated by the Grand Mosque. Based on its celebrated counterpart at nearby Djenné, it was rendered with a mixture of mud and fermented grain husks, giving it a smoother finish that the lumpy mosques we had seen elsewhere. It resembled an elegant cathedral.

After hours of bureaucratic red tape, we managed to extend our visas and depart for the Dogon country, a region of remote villages with a unique culture. SMERT only permitted visits in the company of an authorised guide but, ignoring their restrictions, we headed off with Jonathan and David to Bandiagara, a fly-blown town, gateway to the forbidden area. In the bar of our cheap hotel, we encountered an old man who spoke of the European cities he had visited during the War. '*Pourquoi étions-nous en guerre avec l'Allemagne?*' he enquired. He had been whisked away by the French and seemed at a loss to comprehend the reason for the war or why he had been fighting.

That evening we ate goat's head soup at a shack restaurant. Just as our bowl of steaming broth arrived, the power went off, and we were left with an African version of Nelson's Eye – that childhood party game where you're blindfolded and fish around in a dish for 'eyeballs' of grapes. In this instance, however, if we felt something resembling an eyeball, then we suspected that's exactly what it was. As for other slippery things that squelched between our fingers, they could have been anything. 'I think this may be a piece of brain,' said Bill.

The Land of the Dogon

The next day we rented three mobylettes – one for Bill and me, one for David and Jonathan and a spare for Ibrahim, the cheeky, smiling 13-year-old who had agreed to guide us to the Dogon villages. We were to ride these as far as the Bandiagara escarpment, a cliff 160 km long, where Dogon villages were dotted along the plateau at the top, as well as on the plains below. The route, which wound through mud, boulders, guinea savanna and across rivers, was more appropriate for motorbike scrambling than for our fragile vehicles.

After about 25km we reached Djiguibombo, a traditional village where old men relaxing beneath a tree greeted us warmly. A newly-slaughtered goat hung from the branches, dripping blood and intestines onto the stones beneath. Ibrahim had explained that the most acceptable gifts for village chieftains were aspirins and toothbrushes. Having distributed these to the chief and various people who claimed afflictions, we left our mobylettes in their care and walked another 17km to the edge of the escarpment.

The cliff face we descended was sheer, with great slabs of stone tilted towards the plain far below. Stunted millet plants sprouted from terraces and crevices. Between overhanging rocks we spotted a pond covered in lilies and splashed by a small waterfall. Further down, where rock slabs were wedged like falling dominoes into the cliff-face, we navigated a gulley with lush vegetation overhanging clear pools and streams.

At the foot of the escarpment, we found the village of Kani-Kombole almost deserted. 'Everyone has gone to market,' explained Ibrahim. 'It's about 30km away. There are no roads. They walk along the valley.' A solitary elder appeared. He shook our hands and asked our boy-guide if we had come about a war. Ibrahim translated, explaining that the man was frightened of us; that many years before, white men had abducted villagers and taken them to fight in a war. 'Our men never returned,' he told Ibrahim.

This was the second reference to war in so many days. Until then I had never really given much thought to African involvement in the two World Wars, but I discovered later that in 1912 the French created a permanent black army, and 65,000 men from French colonies in North and West Africa lost their lives in the Great War. Another 190,000 West African troops were to fight for the French in the Second World War, some of them inevitably becoming German prisoners. Like the man in the bar the previous evening, this elderly Dogon had no idea why his people had been taken. His nervous reaction to our arrival was an indication of how few tourists visited the Dogon villages. Having reassured the old man of our peaceful intent, he took us to see the elders' council chamber, an open shelter with carved poles supporting a thatched roof. The low ceiling was designed to prevent violent debates, he told us. He chuckled, demonstrating how anyone leaping to their feet in anger would hit their head on the beams .

The valley which surrounded us was like fairyland: square grain stores with conical thatched roofs rising to points like witches' hats; windows with thick wooden shutters, toy-town hinges and locks; doors carved with strange symbols. Serpentine sandy alleys enclosed higgledy-piggledy gingerbread architecture. As we explored we surprised an old woman bathing in the village pond. Small turtles scuttled down the banks and plopped into the water beside her, yellow butterflies danced overhead, and scarlet and yellow birds settled on the scant foliage. On the outskirts, away from the dwellings, we saw fields of millet and, stretching into the distance, ranks of baobabs marked the route like bloated soldiers. High above us we could see caves and disused cliff-dwellings like halves of broken pots forced into the cliff face. Until four centuries before, these had been occupied by the Tellem, pygmies who had later been usurped by the Dogon. Ibrahim explained how from time to time anthropologists and archaeologists visited these Tellem remnants, climbing up ropes as the ancients had done long before them. We continued along the valley to Telli, the next village. Along the way, amidst small patches of crops, we saw a couple of stuffed baboon skins suspended from poles; perhaps they served as scarecrows or, given the animist influence in the area, they may have had sacred or diabolic intent. Hundreds of feet above us a waterfall spilled over the edge of the escarpment, its spray clouding a nearby pool in mystery.

Telli resembled the previous village, but this time we decided to approach the homes of animists, tall mud dwellings which teetered on boulders and stilts at the foot of the cliff beneath a massive overhanging ledge. To enter the area we needed permission from the chief. Circumventing boulders and piles of stones, we eventually found him sitting cross-legged on a small rise above some stunted trees. He was grunting to himself as he poked about in the rubble, fishing out bird feathers and tying them together. Initially agitated by our presence, he quickly succumbed to the novelty of a yellow toothbrush in a plastic case and waved us on. As we approached the animists' houses, the harsh cries of birds on the ledge above reverberated along the cliff, echoing back and forth like a sorcerer's spell. 'Look up there,' said Ibrahim, pointing to further outcrops high on the cliff face, ledges white with guano. 'That's where they put their dead. The corpses are hauled up there on a rope.' We could see large birds, hunched on their eyrie, awaiting carrion. Vultures wheeled lazily above. 'Sky burials,' I said. 'Like the Parsee Towers of Silence in Bombay. Maybe it's the hygienic way of doing things.' As we descended the rocky path to the plain, the gnarled head of the chief's wife bobbed up from behind a rock. She let out a high-pitched scream and waved her arms in frenzied fury; we had inadvertently edged too close to a sacred mess of dismembered birds.

We set off on our return journey. Having left behind the darker side of the community, the five of us we were light-hearted. It had been a magical interlude and Ibrahim had provided us with a gentle introduction to the area. With people away at market, exploring their villages and dwellings had not felt intrusive and, because SMERT had forbidden the area to tourists, we had seen no other foreigners. Having been together in Timbuktu, on the river trip down the Niger and in Bar Mali, we had bonded. Jonathan, young and handsome, strode along wearing a conical Fulani hat of straw and leather. He was more effete than David, quick-witted and funny with exaggerated expressions and gestures. David was a conventional down-to-earth Scottish lad, dark haired, bearded and good fun but with a shy streak, particularly when it came to relieving himself in the countryside. Bill and I were in our element, enjoying one of the best trips of our stay in Africa. Wearing baggy, embroidered Tuareg trousers I had purchased in Niamey, I was almost dancing along the valley with happiness. As for Ibrahim, he seemed to like us and our banter. We had heard of sacred rites and dramatic masquerades which were part of the local culture, but back then there were no such displays for tourists. Our foray into the world of the Dogon may have been superficial, but for us, our extraordinary day in Shangri-La had been enough.

As we began our steep ascent of the escarpment we were drenched by a sudden shower. The green gulley we had passed on our descent was steaming in the rain, its rocks glistening. Far below us a long line of women were wending their way across the plain with pots on their heads. 'Look,' said Ibrahim, pointing, 'They are returning from market.' Some of them were on their way to the village at the top of the escarpment where we had left our mobylettes. Before we had even reached high ground they had caught up with us and overtaken, gliding easily up the sheer cliff face with pots and calabashes stacked on their heads and babies strapped to their backs.

We slept the night at the village, as guests of the chief's son. His hut was neat and tidy, roofed with twigs and incredibly hot. A thoughtful young man, he switched on the English language Nigerian broadcasts for us on his transistor and provided us with a meal of ground baobab leaves and millet in some kind of a sauce. In return he was happy with more aspirins and toothbrushes. Lying on the floor that night, sweltering in the confines of the hut, I was aware of a juju object dangling just above my head. A large dead bug on a string, it swung back and forth, reminding me of the wedding ring suspended above Pat Crawley's bed in Canada. When we awoke in the morning David found a large scorpion in the folds of his towel. Unperturbed, our host blew on it, muttered a few magic words, and let the vicious-looking creature walk all over his hand. Before we left we went to thank the chief for his hospitality. The door of his hut bore carvings of a nude man and woman with excessively large genitalia.

Torrential rain had fallen overnight, making our return journey difficult. I rode with Jonathan, while Bill set off with David riding pillion. In no time, Bill skidded, hit a rock and swerved, catapulting him and David skywards. Before long we came to the first of the rivers we had to cross. It had swollen but we managed to get the mobylettes to the other bank. Further on, the second river, little more than a stream the previous day, had been transformed into a raging torrent and the bridge had broken. Ibrahim looked dejected. 'We'll have to remain here until the water subsides,' he said, but a man appeared, offering to help us ford the torrent. We were doubtful, especially when we learned that a herdsman's cattle had been swept downstream, but our new acquaintance was persuasive; he would help us wade through the water holding the mobylettes at shoulder height. The men rose to the challenge, while Ibrahim and I waded behind, trying not to get washed away.

Soaked, mud-spattered, cold and exhausted, we mounted the mobylettes once more and bumped and swerved our way back to Bandiagara. We handed in the mobylettes, bade a fond farewell to Ibrahim, and travelled back to Mopti, where the bawdy chaos of Bar Mali seemed warm and welcoming.

A lift with the Chinese

The following day, leaving David and Jonathan behind, Bill and I took a bush taxi to Bobbo Dioulasso and boarded the overnight train to

Ouagadougou, capital of Upper Volta – today's Burkina Faso. There we stumbled on the most luxurious hotel of the entire trip, with a courtyard restaurant, waiter service, a bar, and comfortable bedrooms. But I began to feel ill; my body had reached its limit and I was paying the price with the most terrible flu. I took to my bed and there I should have remained, but time was running short. We were hundreds of miles from Birnin Kebbi and we had to get back in time for the new school year.

The next morning we moved on and, once again, caught up with Jonathan and David. Before long we were installed in the usual crush on top of a truck bound for Lomé, Togo. I felt ill and my sinuses were so blocked I could barely breathe. Reluctantly I tried to blow my nose, a sound so disgusting that the woman beside me was revolted. 'Madame!' she said with a loud clicking noise of disapproval, 'Oh, Madame!'

It was 3.30 in the morning when the lorry dropped us in the autogare at Lomé. At dawn we set off again, hitch-hiking along the coast to Cotonou, capital of Benin, the Marxist-Leninist country we had passed through on our Christmas trip to Togo. Now we discovered that Mathieu Kerekou, President of the People's Revolutionary Party of Benin, was being courted by the Chinese. We were hitch-hiking when a jeep drew up and two Chinese men in Maoist clothes indicated we should climb in. They were unsmiling and apparently unable to speak French or English. We drove along in silence, wondering whether the lift had been offered out of communist duty. Arriving in Cotonou we passed a huge pagoda. The Chinese were certainly in town.

Bill, David and Jonathan were keen to visit the python temple at nearby Ouidah, where sacred snakes represented the voodoo god Dangbe. Despite having a phobia of snakes, I was disappointed to miss out on a voodoo shrine, but it was clearly time to be sensible and stay in bed. My only companion was a large baboon imprisoned in a tiny yard two storeys down. Tethered on a very short chain, the creature was a heart-rending sight. Children kept teasing it and every so often a woman would appear from the kitchen and sling slops at him. Throughout the day I climbed out of bed to peer at the poor creature through the window. The minute Bill returned from the snake temple I begged him to buy bananas, which we tossed out of the window and watched the baboon devour.

After a fond farewell to David and Jonathan, Bill and I stayed on in Cotonou a couple of days. It was a depressing place. We spent a day on the sand bar, where the seascape was marred by the rusting hulks of ships. Our last night in Benin was spent in a clean and regimented truckers' dormitory by the lorry park. At day-break, before our departure, we bought breakfast and coffee from a roadside stall. It was a grey, misty morning. Early-risers, swathed in blankets, greeted us on all sides: 'Bonjour, camarade! Bonjour camarade!' Towering above us, hoardings displayed communist slogans and revolutionary art. Later that morning, just 20 miles down the road, we crossed the border into Nigeria and entered another world.

We were cutting it fine. Before us lay a journey of well over 600 miles, and we had only a few days left until the start of the new school year. After travelling east and through the outskirts of Lagos, we turned north towards Ibadan, a city of rust, where thousands of corrugated iron rooftops stretched into the distance as far as the eye could see – all of them tarnished russet. Tired from our weeks of travelling, Bill and I were nonetheless exuberant. After experiencing the journey of a lifetime, we were returning to life in our newly-acquired house at WTC.

CHAPTER TWELVE

THINGS FALL APART

O UR NEW HOME WAS SET APART AMONGST TREES. What had once been a thatched roof had been replaced with corrugated iron, but otherwise the traditional features remained intact. We loved the place. The substantial stone walls kept the interior cool and, after cleaning, whitewashing, mosquito-proofing and making curtains, we were comfortable. The bedroom and sitting room were quite large, with high ceilings, stone floors, and small diamond-paned windows. The bed had a built-in wooden frame to support the mosquito net, and its legs stood in small tin cans filled with paraffin to deter termites. There was a bathroom, and a small kitchen on two levels with a store room. Tall, wooden double doors led from the sitting room onto a wide veranda at the front of the house, a space large enough to be used as an external room and contained by pillars and a wide balustrade overhung by neem trees. At both sides of the house the veranda tapered into a narrow walkway that continued towards the rear.

There was an abundance of wildlife, some creatures more welcome than others. Huge fruit bats lived in the roof and no sooner had we arrived than Bill found one drowning in the bath. One morning we awoke to find a bat carcass lodged above us on top of the mosquito net, drops of blood oozing through the mesh; it had flown into the ceiling fan during the night and hit the whirring blades.

Occasionally we sighted snakes in the surrounding scrub. After Bill's inept attempt to despatch one with a long piece of pipe, they were dealt with by the school labourers, but we had no reptile identification book and were concerned that some of them were being killed unnecessarily.

We felt obliged to err on the safe side, but after three snakes in so many days it was time to cut the grass and clear the area. Apocryphal or not, I was told that one snakebite victim at my school had been subjected to 15 injections. Perhaps it was true, because not long after I was supervising teaching practice at a primary school where they had just killed a seven-foot snake. 'Thanks to God we kill dis snake,' they told me. 'No serum. Hospital serum done finish!'

We did have a bird book, and Bill delighted in acquainting himself with the exotic West African birdlife: Abyssinian rollers with tail streamers and turquoise breasts, their orange-brown wings streaked electric blue; purple glossy starlings with turquoise wings, chests with a mauve and blue-green sheen, and bright yellow eyes on violet heads; piapiacs or black magpies which shimmered purple; black-and-white pied crows. We spied a solitary stork flying to and fro building a nest, and listened to the homely sound of pigeons and doves cooing and scratching on our rooftop. Every evening, the party of guinea fowl which waddled past the house reminded us of the geese marching homewards to Bryn Ddol farm on Anglesey, when we had first met.

The midsummer rains brought clouds of brown flying bugs which got caught in our hair. Aggressive huntsman spiders sped across the floor and up the walls: their two long front legs poised for the kill. Tropical rain resulted in sudden power cuts which would plunge us into darkness just when the spiders were on the move. A deluge would bring forth other creatures that had lain dormant, the prettiest being tiny scarlet velvety bugs which would emerge from the sand.

There were always lizards, the most common being the rainbow lizard with its indigo body and orange head and tail. Chameleons walked the twigs and stems with slow hesitant steps – three forward, two back, like tightrope walkers – all the time wearing a sardonic grin. Our students regarded these as devils and would set fire to them. Dried chameleons were on sale in all the markets for juju and medicine.

Our veranda was a peaceful oasis in the midst of our crazy school life. Sitting in its shade we could see children sweeping the nearby primary school compound and we overlooked a road where a stream of people and animals made their way towards the old town. The day began with work-parties of convicts followed by bored prison guards. Then came men in robes, trotting by on horseback and holding up large embroidered umbrellas against the sun. Women strode tall and straight-backed beneath the heavy pots on their heads. Donkeys teetered beneath enormous loads and at dusk, herds of goats returning from their grazing would stampede down the hill, blocking the road.

March and April were the hottest months, the temperature regularly rising to over 40°C at midday and dropping by only a few degrees at night. When visiting a friend in Sokoto, Bill had seen a thermometer which registered 45° in the shade. 'Guess what I've discovered,' he announced. 'UN personnel get a hardship bonus for working in Sokoto State!' There was no such allowance for us. It was the itchy season dominated by prickly heat, fungal infections, and sleepless nights in sweat-drenched sheets. With power cuts for days on end and therefore no fans, the discomfort became unbearable.

During the *harmattan* from November to March, when dust was carried on the wind from the Sahara down to the Gulf of Guinea, particles hung thickly in the air for days on end. The trees surrounding our house were barely visible, as if shrouded in fog, and Bill, arriving home on his machine after the short ride home from Haliru Abdu, would be transformed into an old man, his hair, beard and eyebrows white with dust. It was the season of desiccation, when skin became dry and cracked and lungs struggled with the dust. Africans went around in woolly clothes grumbling about the cold, but most of the time, despite the gloom, the temperature was like a hot day in England. In July and August, the rains brought burgeoning foliage, giant leaves forming natural conduits for the torrent of water. The sand surrounding our house became a fuzz of delicate young grass and the neem trees which overhung our veranda became fragrant with tiny white flowers.

Every evening squadrons of mosquitoes droned incessantly and, at sunset, despite the oppressive heat, we would don trainers, socks, and our

Above: our shady house at the Women Teachers' College.
Below: breakfast on the verandah with Johnson and Rat.
Left: on Bill's 'machine'.

Below, left: a visit from Phil, November 1980. *Below, right:* snakes caught near our house.

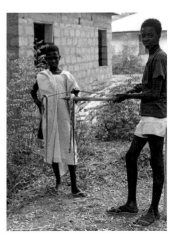

Left and above: Argungu fishing festival, Sokoto State, March 1980. **Below:** *Birnin Kebbi Turf Club.*

Below: *Sallah at Ibi, Gongola State, October 1980.*
Below right: *Jenny at the hippo lake, near Dan Gulbi, Zamfara State, January 1981.*

thickest jeans and shirts. Sitting in a mosquito-coil fug and doused with insect repellent, we would still be dive-bombed and bitten relentlessly. It wasn't surprising. One of the main mosquito research stations for West Africa was located nearby, a site chosen for the diversity of breeds in the area. About once a month school labourers would arrive with pesticide, spraying every nook and cranny in the house with a potion so strong we fled. For two years we lived on a daily dose of Nivaquin, anti-malarial tablets said to have dire side-effects – but luckily we remained free of psychotic episodes, visual impairment, hair loss and symptoms which decades later resulted in the drug being withdrawn.

Housework of any kind was exhausting. Just cooking on the kerosene ring rendered the kitchen unbearably hot, and cleaning the house left us drenched with sweat and tired. The worst chore was doing the laundry by hand. Friday – Muslim prayer day – was when we washed our clothes and sheets, and by the time the locals had finished at the mosque, our laundry was hung out to dry. Eventually we decided to employ someone to do our washing and Aminu arrived on the scene. Having had first-hand experience of the sweaty toil involved, we paid him well over the odds, causing ructions with some of the other teachers who blamed us for wage-inflation.

Friday was also market day when we would stagger home laden with shopping. Apart from meat and vegetables, we would buy canned mackerel, and large tins of Nido milk powder. When the latter was boiled up we added a tiny bit of 'live' yoghurt – initially obtained from the Ministry of Agriculture – and overnight the milk would thicken into creamy yoghurt which we poured over our breakfast porridge. Because everyone sweated profusely they were inclined to smell of whatever food they consumed. 'We stink of yoghurt,' I told Bill one day. 'The teacher next to me at assembly smelt of curry, but I could smell yoghurt. It was me, I know it was.' Sometimes the heat affected tinned goods which had stood on market stalls in the sun for days. The worst of these was tomato purée which would explode as we opened the can, splattering tomato on the ceiling where it solidified like red Artex.

However overburdened we felt by school work, there was always some extraordinary experience to lift our spirits. As one of four teachers selected to attend the Emir's banquet, in celebration of his new role as Chancellor of the University of Calabar, I felt honoured and my expectations were high. The most suitable dress I could drag out to wear was an old hippy dress decorated with embroidery and mirror-work, embellishment I hoped would be in keeping with the ornate Hausa costumes of other guests. The initial panoply was unforgettable, as Emirs arrived on horseback, their heads swathed in lavish turbans, their capes heavy with gold embroidery. The horses' legs were decorated with henna, their harnesses decked with embroidered bunting, coloured leatherwork and bright tassels. As the dignitaries arrived at the palace, servants in livery blew on *kakaki*, thin trumpets three or four metres long and the preserve of the Hausa court, a deep, haunting fanfare redolent of the ancient Songhai Empire and the kings of West Africa. The banquet itself was the antithesis of the exotic. As is so often the case in developing countries, synthetic goods were deemed modern and were therefore status symbols. The food – tiny cold morsels which arrived at half hourly intervals – was served on garish plastic table cloths adorned with rows of ketchup bottles and vases of orange and pink plastic roses. The paucity of food was disappointing, hardly a banquet, but at least fights over meat were avoided; the snatching and grabbing of chicken legs and lumps of goat were common at school staff parties.

School life was also relieved by the horse and camel races at the Birnin Kebbi Turf Club, a relic of colonial times which lacked a single blade of grass. The day before the races, hundreds of men wearing flowing robes, embroidered boots and spurs, rode into town on horses and camels. When VIPs attended the races all the prostitutes in town were forced to sweep the streets in public to atone for their sins. On one occasion when the state governor was expected, I cycled past well over a hundred of these women, sweeping to the rhythm of drums. 'They didn't look very penitent,' I said to Bill later. 'They seemed to be having a whale of a time.' There were four sets of drummers and, wearing their best outfits and grinning from ear to ear, the ladies of the night were dancing enthusiastically as they swept.

Another local event was the extraordinary fishing festival at Argungu, about thirty miles from Birnin Kebbi. We arrived early in order to get a place on the bank amidst the huge crowds which lined the Mata Fada river. Emirs and people of importance sat high on a stand overlooking the water but Bill and I, caught up in the masses, were being controlled by police on horseback. Suddenly cheering broke out as *Sarkin Ruwa*, the King of the River, slid past in his canoe and declared the competition open. The starting gun sounded and tens of thousands of fishermen rose up from behind a distant bank on the opposite shore, a mass of black figures, stripped to the waist, and brandishing traditional hand nets and large gourds. Wave upon wave, they ran towards us down the river bank and jumped into the water. For a couple of goose-bump seconds the stampeding fishermen seemed like thousands of warriors – clichéd images of Africa instilled in us by old movies. *'Zulu!'* whispered Bill.

The fishing frenzy lasted an hour, the allocated time for a winner to catch the largest fish. The river was a blur of spray, of flailing limbs and thrashing bodies, with the occasional glimpse of a silver fish. It was a bare-hand competition where the fishers, mostly working in pairs, had to grab the fish in their fists: giant cat fish, tilapia, or the king of them all, Nile perch. The winning fish weighed 50 kilos and the fisherman who caught it won a number of motor cycles, wristwatches, double beds and a free trip to Mecca.

Historians trace the festival at Argungu back to the 16th century and believe it to be the oldest custom of any of Nigeria's river people. This ancient tradition involved offering libations to the gods for successful fishing, incantations for the protection of fishermen, and, originally, human sacrifice. Bill's students were in no doubt that the winner would not live to see the next festival. 'They give him poison,' they said. 'Dis man will die for the river god. He will never go to Mecca.'

Our only other fishing experience in Nigeria was very different. With our good friends David and Helen Crabtree, with whom we often spent time in Sokoto, we travelled through the bush by Land Rover to a wide expanse of river which boasted hippos. It was an isolated spot with a few small villages scattered about. Nevertheless it had its own *Sarkin Ruwa* who materialised on horseback the minute we reached the river bank. We ventured a little way out in dugouts but the hippos remained specks in the distance. We were accompanied on this expedition by Gordon, a marine biologist whose speciality was West African fish, and who waded into the water collecting specimens in a net. The King of the River and villagers gathered round to see what the white man with the strange thigh-high waders had caught. To Gordon's delight he had trapped a variety of really tiny fish about which his audience was understandably scornful. When he proceeded to put specimens no bigger than a fingernail into a container, the villagers fell about laughing.

A visit from Phil

One day Ali, the school messenger, arrived at our house with Phil in tow. 'Ali, this is my brother,' I explained. 'Same mother, same father?' enquired Ali, the standard question in Africa, where 'brother' is used for any man from a community, or tribe, who commands the same loyalty as a true sibling. 'Yes, same mother same father.' '*Na sani!*' exclaimed Ali. 'I knew it, dis you brudder. Same nose!' 'It's just a *bature* nose,' I protested, a white person's nose. 'No,' said Ali, drawing out his fingers in a Pinocchio gesture. 'Dis nose for you and you brudder.'

We had been anticipating a visit from Phil for some time, but with no landlines and a slow African postal service, we had no idea when he would arrive. He had travelled overland from Europe, through Sudan to east Africa, where he had been taken ill in Nairobi with a large branchial cyst. A German doctor had advised him to return home but, feeling slightly better, Phil had flown to Lagos. When he arrived I was shocked at how thin he had become. I'd looked forward so much to his arrival and was particularly pleased he had turned up in time for teaching practice and could accompany me on assessments to the primary schools. On the first of these he remained uncharacteristically lethargic and uninterested. 'Sorry,' he said afterwards. 'I really don't feel very good.' Despite feeling ill, during the month he was with us he managed to explore Birnin Kebbi: the market, one or two bush bars and chop houses. He attended a couple of my lessons, gave a talk to the students about books and publishing and enjoyed the cut and thrust of a debate between girls from my school and Bill's boys. Garba continued to visit the house regularly, fascinated by yet another *bature*, but profoundly disappointed that Phil, like Bill, knew nothing about football.

We held a party to welcome Phil and to say goodbye to Jean, our friend from Haliru Abdu who was returning to Canada. It was the largest gathering we had hosted during our stay at Birnin Kebbi. It included teachers from both schools, the lads from the bank and various acquaintances from town. The bank boys brought over their speakers and, before long, distorted African music was emanating from our house as if it were a bush bar. We decided not to invite Muslims, assuming they would be unhappy about alcohol being served. Garba never forgave us. 'You had a farty,' he said mournfully, with his Hausa inability to say the letter p. 'You had a farty and you didn't invite me.' We had not included our neighbour, Hussaini, either. It was a *faux pas*. We should have invited the Muslims and left it up to them to decline. It was a good party. People arrived with crates of beer, there was dancing, and we even provided the traditional kola nut, the bitter ceremonial kernel presented to chiefs and guests – although we were uncertain of the ritual involved and I am not sure our Nigerian friends appreciated the gesture.

During the following week or two, Phil became more and more under the weather and even took to his bed for a few days. I began to worry. We had no landlines, no airport, no decent medical care. Eventually I summoned a doctor from the hospital, an Egyptian, who looked Phil over. 'Do you eat spinach?' he enquired. 'Spinach?' said Phil, looking surprised. We did indeed eat the local version of spinach. 'Stop the spinach,' pronounced the doctor. 'Too much spinach is bad.' It was his sole advice and we remained none the wiser regarding Phil's lassitude. My only reassurance lay in the fact that the missionaries, who had moved in next door, had radio communication with mission HQ.

After a while, Phil began to feel a little better. He had intended to return home across the Sahara, but that was now out of the question. Bill and I had been planning a Christmas trip to visit David and Jonathan in Ibi and explore southern Nigeria. We had assumed Phil would accompany us. The three of us set off for Jos in Plateau State, an attractive easy town that had been a government hill station in colonial times. The temperature was cooler and we thought it would be a good place to start our journey. Phil, however, was still feeling wiped out. 'I think I should go home,' he said reluctantly, and so we travelled with him to the airport in Kano.

Booking the tickets was one thing, but boarding the plane was quite another. Even when Kano-to-London seats had been booked and paid for, planes often arrived from Lagos full, additional passengers having bribed to get on. If there were two or three remaining seats these were hijacked by white contractors who approached officials with wads of money tucked into their passports. The airport was packed with passengers shouting and arguing. I watched as one woman dived into the luggage chute with her suitcases, hoping to emerge on the other side of passport control and somewhere near the aircraft. People who made it through then sprinted across the tarmac to the plane, elbowing each other out of the way to gain access to the steps. Phil was in no shape for the battle required to get a boarding pass. 'Right, that's it,' I said to Bill. 'We're going to have to pay a dash.' It was the only time in our entire stay in Nigeria that we decided to bribe someone. We began to look around, trying to suss out where money was changing hands, but at that moment Phil encountered a glamorous blonde who used her looks to chat up and dazzle passport control; he was waved through in her wake with no bribe paid. We waited until the plane took off to ensure he had really gone. 'Thank God,' I said, genuinely relieved. 'He's made it.'

We set off to visit David and Jonathan at the Government Secondary School in Ibi, a small town which was pleasantly green and lush after

Birnin Kebbi. On arrival at the lorry park we were ferried across the river in a dugout, accompanied by several passengers, their chickens, and a goat. We had visited Ibi once before at *Sallah*, when the chief and his retinue, resplendent in turbans and embroidered robes, their horses' legs dyed with henna, had arrived to a fanfare of *kakakai* trumpets. It was the only time in Africa we were to hear the deep unsettling boom of war drums: 'Used only for *Sallah* or in battle,' explained Jonathan. When the *Sallah* procession had ended, we were summoned to the chief's hut, where he and his entourage greeted us before lining up stiffly and requesting we take a photograph.

We enjoyed staying at Ibi. We would progress slowly around town, stopping every few yards while our hosts, with the traditional hand on heart, exchanged drawn-out Hausa greetings. We would visit the chop houses and wade through pounded yam and okra soup – the latter we dubbed 'snot soup' for its glutinous texture – and we would stagger home after drinking Rock beer and *ogogoro* in the bush bars. Once, when ambling along a sandy backstreet, we passed the rubbish dump. 'Graves of British soldiers in there,' said David unexpectedly, and we could see chipped tombstones, the flotsam of lost power, protruding from piles of debris. One day we took a bus into the countryside and stopped at a small settlement where villagers welcomed us with millet beer, which we drank from calabashes beside a mountain of pineapples awaiting shipment.

Time spent in the company of Jonathan and David had always been a relief. They shared our attitude to Africans and, like us, peppered their conversation with dry banter tinged with sarcasm. A visiting Canadian had once asked, 'Why are you all so horrible to each other?' 'It's just English sarcasm,' we explained, 'British humour!' That visit to Ibi in December 1980 would be our last. The following year we were all to depart for England. We lined up on the sofa for a photograph, the four of us together for the last time.

Bill and I planned to spend Christmas in Calabar, and on Christmas Eve we arrived in a city unlike any we had previously seen in Nigeria.

Situated on the south-eastern edge of the Niger Delta, it absorbed the humidity and sluggishness of the multi-veined swamp which surrounded it. On Christmas Day we set off to explore the steamy backstreets of the old city, where two-storey buildings with a patina of flaking paint and mould still boasted wooden verandas. We were seeking out traditional Christmas masquerades, but rather than the procession we had anticipated, we came across small groups wearing distinctive costumes: figures clad in red and yellow raffia, resembling sinister corn dollies; people in black balaclavas, striped knitted tubes topped with pompoms protruding from their heads; dancers covered from head to toe in green grass and leaves. Whereas children's disguises were colourful and jolly, clusters of adult masqueraders wore antique wooden masks, the trappings of tribal secret societies and voodoo. Their ancient, carved faces were terrifying and we cowered before their aggressive approach. Every so often, as if to counteract the witchcraft, we stumbled on Christians clad in white, singing Christmas carols.

In the midst of the waterfront slums, up a winding alley lined with shacks, we finally found a chop house for our Christmas celebration. Pushing aside a dirty curtain, we stepped out of the brilliant sunshine into a gloomy interior. A dozen or so people were relaxing, leaning against the bar or sitting at rough wooden tables. We ordered palm wine and peanuts, declined a Christmas dinner of dog meat, and found a place tucked away at a corner table. A whore, clumsy with alcohol, stomped up and down to music blasting from the radio. As she danced, her wrapper fell away now and then, revealing grey cotton bloomers. 'My students wear big knickers like that,' I said to Bill. 'It's rather modest underwear for a prostitute, though.' There was little conversation, but raucous laughter and giggling filled the room. 'I think everyone's stoned,' said Bill, ordering more palm wine. At that moment the curtain across the door was swept aside and a masquerader entered. A tall, green haystack, he grabbed the woman and they began to dance. Bill and I raised our glasses of palm wine and toasted each other. 'Happy Christmas,' said Bill. 'I wonder where we'll be this time next year.'

Above: with Phil in Kano, December 1980. **Above right:** *Calabar masqueraders, River State, Christmas 1980.*

Above: with Folly and James, Ifon, Ondo State.
Below: *tailor and palm-tapper Samuel, AKA Jimmy-de-Roger-de-Lonesome Cowboy-de-Rock of Gibraltar.*
Right: *too much palm wine and it's only 10.30am.*

Above: with students of Form 4D. *Above right:* saying goodbye to Florence and boyfriend, June 1981.

Above: a last photo with our perennial visitor, Garba Waziri.
Right, top: our Ghanaian friend Nana (on left) outside his wife's hairdressing salon, Birnin Kebbi.
Right, bottom: goodbye to David and Jonathan, Ibi, June 1981.

On Boxing Day we boarded a ferry for Oron, a dilapidated hulk which chugged in and out of small islands, scattering floating seed pods in its wake. The river banks were a tangle of twisted mangrove and impenetrable vegetation, spiked here and there by palm fronds and the occasional flower. We passed thatched huts on stilts in the middle of the river, canoes moored to adjacent jetties. The ferry boat was packed, many of the passengers still wearing white from the previous day's Christian parades. A couple of hawkers were doing a hard sell, taking advantage of the Christmas pilgrims. Their wares included religious tracts and children's colouring books, but their main trade was medicinal. We watched as they pulled antibiotics, syringes, phials of medicine and drugs from their bags. They delivered their medical mantras, shouting above the noise of the engine: 'You listen well well. No dull yourself. De health no be small matter-O.' Random medicines were doled out, purporting to stop heart attacks, clean the blood, cure headaches and increase libido. 'Oh God,' I said to Bill, as we witnessed impoverished peasants handing over their money. 'Are these our European discards they're selling?'

At Oron we took a bush taxi to Owerri, passing through hamlets submerged by tropical vegetation. Outside some homes, often supported on pillars, were Christian tombstones, exhibiting throned effigies of the dead, weathered and occasionally limbless. Tucked away in bushes nearby, we saw animist altars. 'Hedging their bets,' we observed. Groups of children ran past still wearing Christmas costumes and, outside churches, fêtes were in full swing.

When we reached Owerri, the manager of our hotel invited us to his home and gave us a tour of a shrine displaying statues of Igbo gods. In the midst of these deities was a clay figure of Mr H Douglas, District Commissioner during colonial rule. Sitting at his desk and holding a pen, he was surrounded by diabolic-looking gods, some with horns, others with enormous eyes. Later I discovered Mr Douglas had been a despot renowned for flogging Africans.

Although a decade had passed since the end of Nigeria's civil war, our Igbo host remained bitter. In 1967, when northern Muslim Hausas had massacred Christian Igbos in the region, the Igbos fled east to their home territory. Details of these atrocities were not new to us; Garba had furnished us with gruesome tales of those times, sometimes so graphically and with such glee, that we had begged him not to speak of them. As news of the bloodbath spread, Igbos doubted that Nigeria's oppressive regime would allow them to survive. Colonel Ojukwu established the new Igbo Republic of Biafra made up of several Nigerian states with Owerri at its centre. At a local level the conflict may have been about religious and tribal differences, but nationally the focus was on oil fields which lay within the boundaries of the new republic. Using its superior military strength, Nigerian forces reduced Biafran territory and regained the oil fields. Without revenue from oil, Biafra was unable to import food and an estimated one million civilians died of malnutrition. After three years of bitter warfare, Ojukwu fled and Biafra was forced to surrender.

An educated man, our host in Owerri set out to enlighten us regarding the plight of the Igbos. He sat us down in his modern sitting room and produced a pile of photograph albums. 'Have a look at these,' he said and we leafed through page after page of pictures depicting the wounded and the dead. 'The Igbos will be better prepared next time,' he promised. The next day, we boarded a bush taxi for Onitsha and crossed over the river on the famous bridge which separates east and west Nigeria. 'This bridge was blown up during the Biafran War,' announced our driver, without stating his allegiance, or which side of the bridge he came from. We decided to stop at the small town of Ifon. No sooner had we arrived than we were adopted by Samuel, otherwise known by a guy-name of which he was immensely proud. 'I am Jimmy-de-Roger-de-Lonesome-Cowboy-de-Rock-of Gibraltar,' he announced, grinning from ear to ear. Later we discovered that, for the sake of convenience, he frequently omitted the Rock-of-Gibraltar bit. A tailor and palm-wine-tapper by day, at night he worked as a security guard for a German road-building company. Kind and hospitable, he provided us with a bed in a hotel that was closed, got his son to fetch us water, and took us for food in a local bar. Our tour of the village had included the market where, amidst magical juju items, the stalls sold snake skins, bush rats, dried chameleons and dead monkeys. Having seen these, when offered bush meat at the restaurant, we thought it wise to decline.

Ifon was situated on the edge of the great West African sapele forests, the tropical wood famous for its mahogany-like qualities. Early the next day Samuel's lad, James, took us to a saw mill on the outskirts of town, where we were shown the workings by the foreman. Tucked away in a corner I spied a faded photograph of a white woman cutting a ribbon, declaring the mill open. The business had once belonged to a local boy-made-good who had ended up owning half the sapele and numerous other ventures. Later, when we passed the house the big man had owned, we were shown his grave on the front porch, where people still honoured him with flowers.

After that James took us a walk in the countryside, past fields of cassava and patches of pineapple. As we progressed, the bush became thicker, dominated by huge clumps of bamboo and palm. A small shrine stood beside a grove of rubber trees. 'Oro,' said James, referring to the deity and the secret society concerned. Turning off the track we trekked through dense foliage, dark and dappled shade, and into a forest where trees stretched skywards to form a canopy. Descending a steep path towards the river, we emerged into a wide sunlit gorge, where a dark green pool was edged by white sand. Waterfalls tumbled down the rock face into the lake and naked fishermen dived into the cool depths, while a young man barbecued fish on a fire at the water's edge. We stood at peace, serenaded by birdsong, entranced by our surroundings. A boy emerged from the forest and joined us. 'What's your name?' I asked him. 'Folly,' he replied, and I chuckled.

Returning from our walk, we sought out Samuel, ensconced behind his sewing machine. 'This is such a beautiful place,' we said, effusive in our praise. 'The lake, the peace of the forest...' 'Dis forest,' said Samuel. 'I hide in dis forest during de war. Everyone from this village hide in de forest. We are federal troops. We execute Biafran soldiers there.' 'The other side of the divide,' I said to Bill later. 'We've crossed the bridge.'

On the Sunday morning we had been invited to a shack-bar, where our friends had reserved two bottles of palm wine for us, freshly-tapped by Samuel. Up until then we had only experienced the watered-down version offered in southern bars. Samuel's foaming, milky, palm wine was sweet, tasting slightly of coconut. It was like the best milkshake in the world, the nectar of the gods. Encouraged by Samuel we downed a few glasses, relishing every sip. The delicious drink seemed innocuous and we remained unaware of its potency. By late morning when Samuel lined us up for a group photo to celebrate our friendship, we stood slightly askew and pie-eyed.

We left behind Ifon with sorrow. Apart from the vagaries of war, it had epitomised Africa at its best: the kindness of the people; the natural simplicity of the fishermen; the rich agriculture; the beautiful forests. We boarded a bush taxi bearing the incongruous sign, *dont moless me in my office*, and within a couple of days we were back in Birnin Kebbi.

A hospital consultation

Bill and I had not used contraceptives for well over a year and yet I had still failed to conceive. We were in Kaduna to renew my passport and took the opportunity to get checked out by a Nigerian consultant at Ahmadu Bello University Hospital. The consultant was efficient and Anglophile. 'Take a pew,' he said, as we entered his room. After I had been examined, it was Bill's turn and we were despatched to another part of the hospital so Bill could have a sperm count.

The corridor that led to the laboratory was typical of African hospitals. Rows of women sat on the floor with children and babies waiting to be seen. I halted halfway down the passageway and left Bill to hand his paperwork to a lab technician. Rather than taking Bill inside the laboratory, the young man embarked on a consultation in the corridor. 'This is what you must do,' he told Bill. 'You take some soap, get a good lather on your hands and then you start rubbing.' 'Yes, yes, I know,' interrupted Bill. 'You will be surprised to find that this is quite exciting,' insisted the technician. 'Now, let's just go through it once again.' I stood horrified as the technician's clenched hand started to move up and down. He then produced a tiny bottle from his pocket. It was about two inches tall with an opening little bigger than a pin head. 'Put your semen in there,' he said, 'and bring it straight back to this laboratory.' Bill walked the gauntlet of the women in the corridor and joined me. 'Jesus, let's get out of here,' he said'

In the end the lab technicians got what they needed and a month later I received a formal letter: *The sperm count for your husband is normal and he is therefore fit for the purpose of reproduction.* I was apparently fit for conception as well, but I was offered fertility pills to speed things along. I declined; if we were going down that route I would wait until we got home. It wasn't surprising I had failed to conceive: the workload, the overpowering heat, daily anti-malarial drugs, all the rough travelling. Florence, my NYSC colleague whose bump was growing nicely, shook her head. 'Too much Star,' she said, indicating the beer bottles lined up on the table. 'And cigarettes,' she added as an afterthought.

By now we felt at home in West Africa and particularly in Birnin Kebbi. We had numerous friends and acquaintances, both African and expatriate, and we knew what to expect from the education system. It wasn't a question of giving up, but more of lowering our sights and focusing on what little could be achieved. We understood what problems were likely to arise and in some cases were able to pre-empt them. Bill's frequent trips to the Ministry of Education in Sokoto, however, remained unavoidable. Previously, when he had left me alone on the Haliru Abdu compound, I had been surrounded by neighbours, but the old house at WTC was more isolated. During his absence I was slightly nervous at night, particularly at the thought I might encounter a snake. On one occasion when he didn't return for two weeks I began to worry.

With no telephones and no communication whatsoever, I had no idea where he was and whether or not he was safe.

Even after nearly two years in Nigeria, the non-stop dramas never ceased to amaze us. One day Hussaini, our neighbour, came running over to our house. 'The vice principal's kitten has fallen down the well,' he shouted. 'We have sent for Son-of-a-Monkey!' Son-of-a-Monkey's role in life was to rescue objects or creatures lost down wells. Bore holes were deep and the bottom of the shaft lacked oxygen. Anyone who descended that far needed the attributes of a free diver, the capacity to hold his breath for a considerable length of time. Son-of-a-Monkey, a wiry and wizened old man, was lowered into the void on a rope. Word spread fast and several people gathered to gaze down the well. We waited and waited. 'I hope he's ok,' I said, worried. 'Surely he can't hold his breath this long.' After what seemed like an eternity there was a tug on the rope. Everyone heaved and pulled and Son-of-a-Monkey emerged, exhausted, clutching the kitten. Briefly he lay on the ground gasping, then departed in the company of the effusive vice principal. The extraordinary thing was that he had been despatched after a cat in the first place; Nigerians were not known to show undue concern about animals, even pets.

We still had the cats and kittens we had been given by Mr Jimmy when we first arrived, but it was our dog, Johnson, that was to prove controversial. Stupidly, we had failed to realise that Muslims considered dogs unclean; that the only permitted canine duties were hunting, herding or guarding, and that dogs were forbidden to enter the home. Saliva in particular was considered impure and anyone licked by a dog was required to wash seven times. The only acceptably clean part of a dog was the top of its head, a spot inaccessible to its tongue. Despite this, Birnin Kebbi was full of pye-dogs, roaming free, scavenging rubbish, but every so often there would be a cull. Occasionally, against all Qu'ranic teaching, the impurity of dogs was taken as an excuse for abuse, and more than once Johnson came home with a huge gash in his head. Because of this, our sweet-tempered puppy gradually became aggressive, baring his teeth when people approached, although he remained sloppy and friendly with us. One day when we were out, every dog on the school compound was culled – except for Johnson. We could only assume he was spared because he belonged to us. The other problem with keeping a plump, well-fed dog was that he was eyed up by the Filipinos who kept asking if we wanted to sell him for the pot. In other parts of Nigeria we had seen dog meat on the menu, but not in the Islamic north.

Garba was always round at our house. He usually outstayed his welcome, ignoring the possibility we might want privacy or have school work to do, but he provided numerous amusing interludes. One day a Sri Lankan doctor was sitting on our veranda chatting, when Garba suddenly leant forward and interrupted our guest: 'I know you. I am working at your office since two years.' This failed to ring any bells with the doctor but Garba persisted, a huge grin on his face. 'That yellow girl,' he said, using the standard Nigerian description for someone light-skinned. 'That yellow girl, Fulani, slender, she working at your office dat time.' Unflustered the doctor replied, 'This must have been more than five years ago. There have never been any female clerks in the office since I worked there.' 'Oh yes, you know her,' insisted Garba. 'You give her that thing like globe-light.' Garba made a circular motion with both hands. 'Globe-light,' he repeated. 'Have you seen *My Fair Lady*?' interjected the doctor, addressing everyone present. This change of subject threw us all briefly and then, as intended, the conversation shifted. Any further comments from Garba were firmly quashed, but once the doctor had departed, Garba chuckled wickedly. 'He know dis girl,' he said. 'His wife no here. Dis yellow girl, she sleep with him at the house. He give her dis globe-light and he give her 100 Naira. And…there was another girl. Those girls always fightin', so he dismiss 'em!'

A hurried departure

On 18 December, 1980, the day we had seen Phil off at the airport, the Maitatsine Riots, instigated by Islamist militants, had erupted in Kano. Detained by the chaos at the airport, we were oblivious to what was going on in town. The Maitatsine movement was led by Muhammad Marwa, a fanatic, who opposed the Nigerian state and Western culture, regarding himself as a prophet. Best known by his nickname, Maitatsine, meaning *he who damns*, he was renowned for his curse-laden public speeches. His disciples were labourers, who had been displaced by the oil boom, and Islamic students studying in Kano. While we were at the airport, insurgents armed with rifles and bows and arrows began attacking people on their way to the mosque. The army was summoned and cleared the old town by shooting everyone in sight. The Nigerian press put the toll at 4,000; *The Observer* made it twice that. 'Bodies lay in the Central Hotel for days,' Bill's colleague Shehu told him later. 'They had to dig a trench for a mass burial.' Maitatsine died as a result of his injuries that December, but this did nothing to quell the riots, which continued on and off for several years, and – as many believe – morphed into the terrorist attacks waged by Boko Haram 20 years later.

It took two or three months for the unrest to filter down to us in Birnin Kebbi. On arrival at school one morning I was accosted by a Filipino teacher. 'The police have been here,' she said. 'Did you know Mr George, the vice principal at Haliru Abdu, has run away?' She rambled on. 'A man's been jailed, one of those religious fanatics, and the students at Haliru Abdu are organising a protest.' Bill was at home that day, unwell. During the breakfast break I told him the news. 'It sounds like garbled nonsense,' he said, 'you know what rumours are like here.' The next day I found a guard had been put on the gate of my school. 'All visitors are being screened,' I was told. 'The principal is trying to keep all news away from the girls.'

The following morning Bill was better, but when he arrived at school the classrooms were deserted. Outside the staff room there were placards and graffiti: *Al Kaffir Hindu, Al Kaffir Philippinese,* denouncing expatriate staff as infidels. The students were on strike in support of the jailed Islamist ringleaders. Bill sought out the principal. 'I've talked with the commissioner for education,' he said. 'We are not to force the boys into the classrooms. We are to do nothing at all.' Bill returned home.

Later we heard that the principal, vice principal, and all the African staff but one, had fled the Haliru Abdu compound with their families. The only remaining African teacher put on a *riga* so he looked like a Hausa and planned to adopt a Muslim name. One southern teacher hid with his family in the army barracks and our Ghanaian friend, Nana, moved with his wife and children into town. We knew that if the students rioted, expatriates like us would be attacked. Inevitably dear old Garba appeared at our house. 'The army and the police, they know this trouble,' he told us. 'The town is under control.'

This may well have been true, because news from other places was more worrying. In Zuru, boys from the teachers' college invaded the girls' secondary school and terrorised the students. The English principal, an acquaintance of ours, locked herself in her office, pleading with the rioters through the window. Two insurgents were killed, one shot by the police, another run down by a teacher. In Argungu, 15 boys gang-raped a prostitute, and in another government secondary school the southern principal was forced to convert to Islam. In Yabo foreigners' cars were stoned by rioters, and in Sokoto, police detained 37 students for preaching Maitatsine ideology.

It was seven weeks until the end of term, but a directive from the Ministry of Education stipulated that all students – other than seniors sitting national exams – were to be sent home immediately to help with the Green Revolution. The press reported that the Ministry of Rural Development would ensure that the students would work with their parents on farms while studying information about crops and how to assemble farm tools. Only one newspaper revealed the real reason for the students' departure: it would provide a calmer atmosphere for the board of enquiry to investigate religious disturbances.

Packing up at the end of term had always been chaotic: collecting textbooks, cleaning dormitories, distributing journey money so students could travel to their villages; chits and checks, clearance papers, all the usual Nigerian bureaucracy had to be in place. Bill and I were to return to England at the end of the summer term, but during almost two years, in the midst of all the insanity, we had become fond of our students. Now our goodbyes had to be hurried and apologetic. My girls wailed and cried at the thought of my departure and I overheard the ultimate accolade: 'Mrs Scolding, she done pass Mrs Gillespie,' they said, suggesting my teaching had surpassed that of their previous idol. I was brokenhearted to part with them in such haste. I had planned to write personal farewell notes for each girl and to have a small goodbye party for each class. Several of them came to me with photographs of themselves as mementoes. 'Dis for you, ma. You no forget me, ma.' And I never did. They had tried my patience, made me exasperated and angry, but we had had a lot of fun and some of them had even learnt something. They were intelligent, strong, extrovert, funny African women and in a better education system they would have excelled. I was to receive two letters from students after I arrived back in England. *Thanks ma for all your whole hearted teachings*, said the first. *I pray that we may still have a teacher like you.* The second said I was the best teacher the students had ever had. Given the system, that didn't mean much, but I had arrived totally untrained and had given them my all. Perhaps they had realised how much I cared about them and that I had come to love them.

With the majority of boys gone, Bill still had to invigilate national exams. Uncomprehending students sat in classrooms where window panes were cracked, fluorescent lights no longer worked, and broken desks and chairs were strewn across the compound. Over the last six months Bill's school had virtually collapsed. The vice principal had beaten the boys so badly that they had rebelled, refusing to obey teachers or attend classes. Bill was reaching the stage where he could no longer cope. He discovered one Sri Lankan teacher, a bright, dedicated young woman, crying her heart out in her classroom. Many teachers had given up and no longer attended class. Fuelled by religious fanaticism, anti-expatriate sentiment was running high and any pretence of an education system had disappeared. It was certainly time for us to leave.

We had, after all, been lucky to survive thus far. We had witnessed several deaths in Nigeria. A young Filipino teacher at my school had succumbed to cerebral spinal meningitis; she thought she had flu', but was dead within 48 hours. Up until that point we'd had no idea we were living in the African meningitis belt. When having our inoculations in London, nobody had thought to mention that there was a strain of meningitis unique to desert areas and carried by dust. After the death of my colleague, Bill and I had rushed off to Sokoto Hospital and requested a vaccination against CSM. A young lad in shocking pink flares appeared with a phial and injected us with the contents. 'Where you from?' he asked, friendly and smiling. 'We're teaching in Birnin Kebbi,' we replied. 'Teachers!' he exclaimed. 'Perhaps you could get me into school!'

Our friend, John Ebro, had died, as had the principal of Bill's school and his entire family, wiped out in car crashes. Our condolences had been met with shrugs; it was simply the will of Allah. Roadsides in Nigeria were graveyards of twisted metal and burnt-out vehicles, a salutary reminder of this fatalistic approach. Sometimes our crazy journeys in bush taxis had been amusing, but the potential for a terrible accident was ever-present. During one long journey I had noticed our driver nodding off. 'Hey, you!' I shouted, prodding him. 'Wake up! Wake up!' 'No problem, ma,' he said. 'It was a little sleep, small small.'

After nearly two years the repetition of disasters was becoming a bit exhausting. It was 41°C in the shade when the NEPA transformer blew up for the umpteenth time. The lorry bringing the replacement transformer from Lagos overturned. The crane brought to deal with that also met with an accident. Then the pump at the water station lost a roller-bearing and seized up causing the shaft to snap in two. 'Here we go again,' I said wearily. 'I reckon it'll be at least a couple of weeks before we have electricity and water.' 'More than that,' Bill sighed pessimistically. We only had one and a half buckets of sandy water and two inches in the bath. We would have to wait for the water lorry.

In addition to everything else, the ongoing corruption was becoming wearisome. Some situations were so unbelievable that one had to laugh, but the scandal of misspent money in the midst of an impoverished populace was no laughing matter. While we were planning our departure,

Usman, the pharmacist from the hospital, arrived with news of the latest white elephant – an enormous new x-ray machine. Complete with closed-circuit television, it was designed for use in teaching hospitals and was the impulse buy of the commissioner for health on a visit to Belgium. Belgian technicians had been brought over to install the monster which, unsurprisingly, had malfunctioned immediately they left. With non-existent or fluctuating power supplies, any appliance was subject to frequent breakdowns, and spare parts for such sophisticated equipment were unavailable. Staff quickly reverted to using the old x-ray machine. 'That new one,' wailed Usman, 'cost one million naira!' Later on we came across Taff and Eddy the Welsh TCL contractors. 'We had a party in the hospital recently,' said Taff, 'in the operating theatre. Filled the fridge up with beer and used that new X-ray machine as a table!' Whilst amused at the incongruity of it all, we had become tired of the emperor's new clothes. The deception extended from large things down to details that were small but equally ridiculous: illiterate peasants forced to display English language stickers on their carts and bicycles with the boast, *I'm proud to be a farmer.*

Getting out of Nigeria was going to be difficult. The weeks of waiting in Sokoto to be assigned a school in the first place, were now reversed. Numerous signatures were required and it could take a month to obtain just one. 'Not on seat,' was still the standard excuse. We haunted the Leaves & Passages department, the Ministry of Education and the Ministry of Finance. Wherever we went it was the same, 100 or so teachers – Filipinos, Indians, Sri Lankans, the odd Egyptian – pressed up against the office louvre windows, their arms through the slats, waving files and money at the clerks inside. Everyone seemed to be bribing, but even after two years, we still couldn't bring ourselves to do it.

Finally it was all over: papers in order, air tickets purchased. The Principal summoned me to her house where she gave me a Hausa ceremonial fan made of stitched leather and feathers. The note accompanying the gift read: *With best wishes from the Principal, Vice-Principal and the Staff. May all your future endeavours bring greater success than what you have succeeded in the past and present!* We gave our tape recorder to Moses who had arrived with our final collection of carvings. Ali, the school messenger, bought Bill's machine at a reduced rate. Garba requested books about football to be sent from England. The cats were being returned to the Haliru Abdu compound to Mr and Mrs Jimmy, and Johnson the dog was going to live with our good friend Alan in Koko. Taff and Eddy kindly offered to transport us, plus dog, in their van to Alan's house. When everything was loaded up, it was Garba who came to say goodbye. He had been the first person to appear on our doorstep two years before and had visited us almost daily. It was strange to think we would never see him again. 'Goodbye, Scolding,' he said. He never could manage the word Bill. 'Goodbye Scolding,' and then, as an afterthought, 'London people. London people.' We climbed in Taff and Eddy's van and set off for Koko, leaving behind the town which had been our African home.

Alan lived with his ever-expanding extended family at the Government Secondary School in Koko. His partner, Barakisu, who was still married to her husband in Ghana, had finally turned up in Koko with her sister and four children: Margaret, a pretty light-skinned girl sired by Alan; Gifty, the daughter of a Japanese fisherman who had been adopted by Alan; and two smaller children, the progeny of her Muslim husband. Once everyone was safely installed in Koko, the sister had returned to Benin to pick up twin girls who were to skivvy for Alan.

The house was littered with babies asleep on mats, and strewn with clothes, blankets and baskets. Surrounded by this chaos, we sat with Alan drinking beer, while the girls went back and forth bearing bowls of maize and buckets of washing. Outside there was the eternal African rhythm of yam being pounded in a large mortar with the traditional long-handled pestle. Alan, king of the castle, wore the scantiest of loin cloths made from a small curtain and incongruously decorated with tiny flowers. With this Laura Ashley gesture to African fashion, he lounged around the house, usually with his nose in a book, preferably a 19th-century classic. He was an erudite man, fairly silent, whose dry humour made him appear aloof. Once he had downed a few beers, however, he would become more verbose and pompous. We had fun sparring with him, particularly as our politics were further to the left than his.

Sometimes we accompanied Alan to the local hotel, where he was on very good terms with the Madame who, before Barakisu's arrival, had even cooked him Christmas dinner. Nigerian women not only ran the markets, but often had their own small businesses, particularly selling building materials. Alan's Madame was typical of such matriarchs. On one visit we found an impromptu court in session, men sitting round a table with Madame at the head dispensing advice and justice. I had seen the same thing on my school compound, an African way of addressing problems without recourse to official law. It seemed to work well.

Back at Alan's house I played with the children. Margaret and Gifty were happy to be with Alan and he was revelling in his parental role. 'Are you going to take the children to the UK?' I asked. 'Wouldn't your family like to meet them?' 'Not until they can read and write,' said Alan, 'otherwise my sister will think they are savages.' Our dog, Johnson, had already become part of the household and we had no qualms about leaving him behind. Alan's was a good place to end our stay in Nigeria; we were fond of him. We had all come a long way since we first encountered each other in the Sokoto Guest Inn. Our time was over, but he was staying on.

After a week with Alan we set off for home, flying from Kano to Amsterdam, where we spent a few days with our Dutch friend, Marjan. After two years in the African bush we found European luxury overwhelming; the extravagance of goods in the shops seemed unnecessary, surplus to requirements. A week later, back in England and ensconced in Bill's family home in Farnham, our arrival coincided with a royal wedding. While the family crowded round the television watching Prince Charles' marriage to Lady Diana Spencer, we sat in the kitchen drinking tea. After a while Bill's mother stuck her head round the door briefly. 'Do the babies in Africa wear nappies?' she asked.

EPILOGUE

WITHIN A MONTH OF ARRIVING HOME in July 1981, Bill and I both had jobs. I was a researcher on *Pink Floyd: The Wall,* a feature film written by Roger Waters, directed by Alan Parker, and based on the 1979 album. I was working at Pinewood Studios, and initially I was in awe of the place: so many classic films had been made there; so many movie stars had passed through its gates. However, my experience of researching educational films and documentaries had not prepared me for work on an expensive feature film where time equalled big bucks. Whilst Alan Parker was charming and accessible, instantly putting me at ease, I was working for a producer who was abrasive and unsympathetic, spending much of his time ranting down the phone to LA. Although the job was prestigious, I disliked it intensely.

In addition to live action the film included animated scenes by the political cartoonist Gerald Scarfe. One day I bumped into Alan Parker who said, 'You haven't seen the drawings yet? Come and have a look.' He took me into a room where Scarfe's extraordinary sketches covered the walls and where Bob Geldof was also perusing them. At the time I didn't have a clue who Geldof was; it would be another three years, with the forming of Band Aid, that he finally appeared on my radar again.

Bill had intended to get a teaching job but, in the meantime, he was doing temporary work selling advertising space for ECC Publications in Islington. One day an urgent illustration was required and Bill obliged, inadvertently kick-starting his career as a graphic designer. He found himself sharing an office with Harold Mayes, an old-school newspaper man, who taught him everything he needed to know about copy, print and editing. Bill was eventually promoted to editor of *Sinclair User*, a magazine dedicated to the Sinclair Research range of home computers.

Back in the UK, despite a healthier lifestyle, I still failed to get pregnant. In those days IVF was unavailable and I was beginning to worry. I sought help from Wendy Savage, the first female consultant in obstetrics and gynaecology at the London Hospital and controversial for her opinions on childbirth and fertility. However, on the day I received her supportive letter offering me an appointment, I had just taken a pregnancy test which registered positive.

Channel 4 was to be launched in November, 1982, and I was now working on *The Sixties*, a six-part series narrated by James Bolam, and one of the first major documentary series to be aired on television. It was strange to realise that an era that I had lived through, and which still felt like it was only yesterday, could now be regarded as history. I had taken the job before I realised I was pregnant. Big-bellied, I was travelling to film libraries on packed buses, fighting my way onto rush-hour tubes, all the while suffering from the excruciating headaches which were my hormonal response to early pregnancy. I had planned to work up until a month before the birth, but in the end I quit earlier than anticipated.

On arrival in London, Bill and I had rented a dingy basement on the southern edge of Hackney. Having regularly sent money home from Nigeria, however, we had just enough for a down-payment on a newly-refurbished flat in a Victorian house in Evering Road, on the border of Stoke Newington and Clapton. I had lived in London on and off for years – in Earl's Court, Holland Park, Shepherds Bush, West Kensington – but never in such a run-down area or one that was so multicultural. Asian boys played cricket on the streets, the wickets chalked on walls, reminding me of India. Across the road, a Jamaican car mechanic named Milo operated out of a small yard, where car parts spilled onto the pavement and the chatter of his clientele provided a Caribbean soundscape. Our neighbourhood included Africans and Turks, Bangladeshis and Rastafarians, who boldly stamped their identities on their homes. It was like living in a foreign country, and I loved it.

Above: Phil and Dad, Richmond, May 1982. **Above right:** *183 Evering Road, London N16.*
Below: only days to go, in our basement flat, July 1982. **Below right:** *Mum with baby Gwen, August 1982.*

 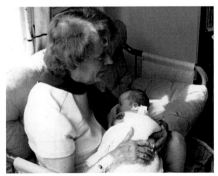

Below: with Gwen on the beach at Lleiniog, Anglesey, Christmas 1983, when I was pregnant with Jake.

Above: newborn baby Jake, March 1984. **Above right:** *our little family is complete, Evering Road, March 1984.* **Below left:** *Gwen at Firestation Nursery, Stoke Newington.*

Above right: *Bill's family, King's Ridge, Frensham, December 1985; mother Marian, brother Martin, Gwen, sister Emily, Jake (in buggy), niece Stella, father Tony and sister Anne.*
Left: *Jake and Gwen in our Morris Traveller.*
Below: *off to Cornwall, March 1986 – Valentine's card from Bill.*

That summer of 1982 the heatwave lasted for weeks. In the final stages of pregnancy, I wilted as I waddled along the streets behind my massive protruding belly. 'Trouble brewing,' warned the milkman. 'Bottles disappearing. They nick 'em off the doorsteps.' 'What for?' I enquired naively. 'Molotov cocktails,' he said. The previous year there had been riots across Britain's major cities, dissent fostered by inner-city deprivation and racial tension; London's Brixton riots were fresh in our minds. Our multi-racial neighbourhood, which included the Nightingale Estate with its boarded-up 1960s tower blocks, was ripe for aggressive dissent, but the milkman's gloomy prognosis failed to come to fruition – in our area at least.

The 28th July 1982 found Bill and me walking across Hackney Downs carrying a suitcase. The baby was ten days overdue and I was on my way to be induced. Having a natural birth was a fairly new concept. 'Not on a conveyor belt' was the catchphrase but, at 39, a home birth was not an option. The Mother's Hospital, a small maternity unit just 15 minutes' walk from home, had seemed an appropriate compromise. It was a peaceful place, with three or four wards housed in single-storey buildings on either side of a walkway surrounded by flower beds. An NHS hospital which operated under the auspices of Barts, it nonetheless retained its connections with the Salvation Army which had established it in the 19th century.

We arrived at the antenatal ward, but after hours of trying in vain to get things going, they sent Bill home. He returned next morning to find there had been no progress whatsoever. Even when they had put me on a drip it was ages before I went into labour and they found it necessary to continue upping the dose. The day seemed endless, paroxysms of violence and pain that went on and on, turning me into a gas-and-air junky. Twenty-four hours after my admission, when our beautiful baby daughter finally entered the world, I was too exhausted to appreciate the wonder of the experience. In the photos Bill took I look like a panda, the pronounced black rings under my eyes reflecting my ordeal.

I awoke the following morning to a steamy hot day and an African nurse in attendance. Exhausted and disorientated, for a moment I thought I was back in Birnin Kebbi. The illusion was shattered when a Salvation Army Officer, a woman in full uniform, stood stiffly mid-ward and embarked on morning prayers. I looked at the women who surrounded me, a typical Hackney mix, including a Rastafarian, a Bangladeshi, a Turk and a Hasidic Jew, and wondered what they made of this plump little Christian soldier. My beautiful baby slept beside me in a transparent oblong bassinet. *Gwendolen Scolding* announced the card clipped to its end. *Birth normal.* Normal, I thought! Normal! Was that violent, unnatural assault on my body really classed as normal? I vowed there and then never to be induced again.

And I wasn't. March 1984 found me back in the hospital, giving birth to a baby boy. Once again I had passed my due date, but this time I had fended them off for three weeks, going into labour naturally two days before their deadline. On arrival at the hospital the midwife examined me. 'Three centimetres already,' she said. 'This baby won't take long.'

A foetal brow presentation is rare. Instead of tucking in its chin and progressing downwards with the crown to the fore, the baby throws its head backwards, presenting the largest flattest part – the brow and sometimes the face – making it impossible to pass through the mother's pelvis. Once the position is diagnosed, it is normal to deliver the baby by Caesarian section. The fact that our baby, Jacob, was a brow presentation went undiagnosed.

Giving birth to Gwen had been a long, violent and painful process. The agony of this birth was different; I didn't realise it, but the baby was stuck and taking a battering. I screamed so much that stray nurses came to see what was going on. Finally, four hours late, they called the registrar who immediately ordered an emergency Caesarian. After the baby was cut out of me and we emerged from the operating theatre, Bill watched horrified as we were wheeled past. 'You both looked as if you'd been in a car crash,' he told me. Our little Jacob, purple from the bashing he'd taken, was despatched to the Intensive Care Unit – the ICU – while I remained on a maternity ward – without a baby.

After a couple of days, Bill and I were told we could visit Jacob in the ICU. A ward orderly pushed me along in a wheelchair. As we approached the unit, however, a nurse emerged. 'Don't take them in there!' she said within ear-shot. 'Baby Scolding's much worse today.' Without explaining anything, he spun the wheelchair around and took us back to the ward. Originally we had been told Jacob needed a day or two's special care to recover from the birth. Now it dawned on us that perhaps his condition was worse than we had realised.

One day, when I was able to walk again, Bill and I were strolling past the ICU when I noticed a sweet pungent smell emanating from inside. 'Dope!' I said to Bill, 'I can smell dope.' 'Don't be ridiculous', he replied, but I insisted. When at last we were allowed to visit, we found our baby boy wired up to drips and tubes and a notice on the basinet which advised minimal handling. It was heartbreaking that he couldn't be cuddled or touched. Eventually, I was able to feed him, and was allocated a room within the ICU, shared with a Rastafarian woman. At visiting time the space was invaded by Rasta men with dreads and all the red, green and yellow trimmings. They were noisy but kind: 'Yuh nuh haffi worry, sistah,' they said. 'Jah guide yuh through de hard times. Jah protect yuh baby.' And then they shut the door and lit up a spliff.

Back on the main ward I began to ask questions. 'What's the prognosis for our baby?' I demanded, but everyone was evasive. After Bill and I became angry, they arranged a meeting with an elderly paediatric consultant, aloof and abrupt. 'Your baby could turn out ok,' he told us, 'or he could be a cabbage. That's all I can tell you. It's a waiting game.' I celebrated my 41st birthday in the hospital. Mum and Dad arrived with little Gwen and they all gave me presents.

Jacob was to be a special child who addressed adversity with gusto, never ever giving up. He would completely change my plans and my life; there would be no return to work. Instead we were embarking on a non-stop cycle of medical commitments. The first of these, Jacob's brain scan, was the worst. Bill was unable to attend, so I drove the children to Queen Elizabeth's Hospital for Sick Children, arriving at reception with Jacob in a sling and Gwen in a buggy. We were sent to a room, where I struggled to entertain the children for well over an hour before anyone turned up. Eventually the door burst open and two brusque men in white coats appeared. Barely addressing me, they wired up Jacob's head and an image of his brain appeared on a monitor. Sitting with their backs to me, blocking the screen, they discussed what they saw and then, without a backward glance, made for the door. Furious, I accosted them. 'Is there any damage?' I asked. 'Your doctor will receive a report,' they snapped. I persisted, and reluctantly they explained that only extreme brain damage would have shown up on the scan, but that they couldn't see any. The 'cabbage' possibility had receded just a little.

Six months after Jacob was born, Gwen started at the nursery up the road. It was a microcosm of how society should be: racially-integrated children playing and learning together, too young to have inherited parental prejudice. A caring stimulating environment, it allowed me to take Jacob to further medical appointments unencumbered by a toddler.

What I missed desperately was the excitement provided by my job. I had always assumed Bill would be happy to job-share – I earned good money as a film researcher, equal to anything he was earning in those early days – but when I mooted the possibility, his reluctance both surprised and hurt me. I let the matter drop and focused on the fact that I'd had an interesting career for 20 years whereas he, so much younger, was just starting out. Rationally I wanted the same opportunity for Bill, but I couldn't help resenting his freedom. He was rubbing shoulders with talented young people from the world of publishing, while I was left at home, literally holding the baby.

I had tried without success to find a nursery that would take Jacob, but back then special needs provision was rare. He was a bright, beautiful baby who, apart from his physical problems, was developing normally, but the fact that he was clever only increased his frustration; he couldn't crawl and his lack of fine-coordination prevented him from playing with age-appropriate toys. Had we known at the time that he would end up as a marine biologist with a Master's degree, how many years of worry and upset it would have saved us!

Despite frustration at not working, I had numerous friends, particularly my Danish neighbour, Pernille, with whom I'd crack open a bottle of wine as we chatted, surrounded by babies knee-deep in chaos. I think fondly of the days I spent meandering through Hackney. I walked miles, pushing the children along in the double buggy, visiting baby and toddler groups, the city farm, playgrounds and parks, and the extraordinary Abney Park Cemetery, full of graves grown over with wild flowers and overlooked by chipped angels. I introduced them to open-air theatre, where they sat riveted despite being so young, and even to the Regent's Park mosque with its massive golden dome.

In 1985 unemployment in the borough was 20% overall, but far higher among black people. Evidence of this was visible every time I stepped out of the door: gangs of young men, black and white, lounged about all day, smoking and looking bored. They had their eye on potential burglary and I was aware they were clocking my comings and goings. One night Bill and I were in bed when I heard someone trying to force entry. Leaping from bed stark naked, Bill shot into the front room where he confronted two guys coming in through the window. The lads took one look at him and fled! Another time a stranger engaged me in conversation at the front door while his partner-in-crime entered the flat at the back. Nothing was stolen; we had so little of value. We weren't nervous. We just took precautions, locking up carefully, even during the day. It didn't sink in for a long time that we were living under siege. After all, we got on really well with people in the neighbourhood and we felt no bitterness towards the miscreants; it was understandable that bored youths without money or jobs might dabble in crime.

I had always loved living in London. I enjoyed the hustle and bustle, the people, the river, the availability of museums and galleries and things to do. In Hackney I revelled in the extraordinary variety of people, the sound of different accents and languages. Bill, on the other hand, always hankered after the countryside. Now he was about to be offered a top job as a publisher for East Midlands Allied Press (EMAP). It would have put him in the management bracket and taken him away from the writing and editing he enjoyed. Despite the fact we would have been very well off, neither of us was tempted.

We began to talk about moving out of London: North Wales and Cornwall were the places we loved. Our next holiday in Cornwall was spent house-hunting and, on the last day, we came across an old coastguard house on the Lizard Peninsula, in the village of Cadgwith, where thatched cottages clustered around a tiny cove and a few fishing boats were drawn up on the pebble beach. There was an old pub, a seasonal shop, another small beach – and that was all.

Sandwiched within a terrace of six, the house looked straight out to sea. The building was solid, its thick stone walls edged with granite quoins. Two backyards, with huge slate slabs underfoot, were lined with sheds and had old-fashioned wells and pumps. The interior of the house was intriguing, with stairs leading off in different directions. It was the only affordable property we had seen with a garden, and it was more than we could possibly have hoped for. There's no doubt we were crazy: we had two small children and insufficient work to last more than three months or so. 'We'll find something,' we both said. 'Something will turn up.' On 21 March 1986 we loaded our old Morris Traveller and departed for Cornwall, preceded by a removal van with our few belongings.

A day or two after our arrival I stood in the cove, my back to the sea and looked up to the top of the hill. I could see the old coastguard station on the skyline, and the house that was to be our family home for decades to come. Inside, waiting to be unpacked, were boxes containing the flotsam of my life: a dog-eared postcard of the 'tin birdie' coming in to land at Eilat, a silver Pakistani ring in the shape of a flower, a Tuareg pipe from Timbuktu and fishbone beads from the Jade Sea. There was an African crib carved by Moses, Ethiopian blue glass rings to keep away the evil eye, and the letters and diaries used to create this book.

This is it, then, I thought. The vagabond girl is finally settling down.